Rewriting the Body

NEUE STUDIEN ZUR
ANGLISTIK
UND
AMERIKANISTIK

Herausgegeben von Willi Erzgräber † und Paul Goetsch

Band 90

PETER LANG

Frankfurt am Main · Berlin · Bern · Bruxelles · New York · Oxford · Wien

Julia Simon

Rewriting the Body
Desire, Gender and Power
in Selected Novels by Angela Carter

PETER LANG
Europäischer Verlag der Wissenschaften

Bibliographic Information published by Die Deutsche Bibliothek
Die Deutsche Bibliothek lists this publication in the Deutsche Nationalbibliografie; detailed bibliographic data is available in the internet at <http://dnb.ddb.de>.

Zugl.: Freiburg (Breisgau), Univ., Diss., 2004

D 25
ISSN 0170-8848
ISBN 3-631-53376-4
US-ISBN 0-8204-7651-X

© Peter Lang GmbH
Europäischer Verlag der Wissenschaften
Frankfurt am Main 2004
All rights reserved.

Printed in Germany 1 2 3 4 5   7

www.peterlang.de

Meinen Eltern

Acknowledgements

The writing of a dissertation is not possible without the financial and intellectual support of numerous people. I would like to take this opportunity to express my gratitude for the generous help and encouragement I received in the last years.

First of all, I would like to thank Prof. Dr. Paul Goetsch for encouraging me to write this dissertation and for offering continuous, helpful support during all parts of the writing. Prof. Goetsch was not only a very thorough reader and astute commentator on drafts of the manuscript, but also an inspiring teacher throughout my studies. I am also grateful to Prof. Dr. Barabara Korte for co-examining my thesis.

Many thanks go to my fellow doctoral students for their encouragement and for reading parts of the manuscript: Nicole Cujai, Haike Frank, Natascha Pesch, Jochen Petzold and, in particular, Ulrike Zimmermann.

I am also grateful to Sheila Gordon-Schröder and Susanne Hägele for being very careful and interested proof-readers of my thesis.

Last but not least, I would especially like to thank my parents for their encouragement and support throughout my studies. This book is dedicated to them.

Contents

IV. Confinement and Metamorphosis: the Body in *The Passion of New Eve*

Abbreviations

BB   Burning your Boats
HV   Heroes and Villains
ID   The Infernal Desire Machines of Dr Hoffman
L   Love
MT   The Magic Toyshop
NC   Nights at the Circus
NS   Nothing Sacred
PE   The Passion of New Eve
SP   Several Perceptions
SD   Shadow Dance
SW   The Sadeian Woman
WC   Wise Children

I. Introduction

Contemporary culture is obsessed with the body. 'High' and 'low' culture, the mass media and academic discourses share this obsession. Sexuality, health, beauty and fitness are major preoccupations in the life of the modern individual. The body is both fetish and subject to rigorous disciplinary technologies like dieting, body-building and surgery. The cult of the body seems to fill the vacuum that has been left by the decline of the 'master narratives' which granted sense and orientation in the past. At the same time science increasingly conquers the body in the age of genetic engineering and artificial reproduction. On the threshold of a paradigmatic change in the history of corporeality, the body seems to make its final, forceful appearance before it vanishes to be resurrected in a new form: as virtual body, as cyborg and genetically reconstructed body.

Theorising the body has become a major project in academia within the last decades. The reconceptualisation of corporeality as a historically and politically inscribed entity has created a new understanding of the relationship between power, sexuality and identity. Particularly within feminist theory, corporeality has become a battleground for different conceptions of subjectivity and resistance. On the one hand, the body has been conceived of as a cultural construct, as a malleable entity which is controlled and produced by 'disciplinary power' in modern society. The body is the surface onto which existing power relations inscribe meaning. The text written on the body points to social structures and hierarchies, and the way they interpellate us as subjects in the patriarchal capitalist societies of the West. On the other hand, the notion of the body as a cultural construct has been criticised for effacing the materiality of the body and foreclosing the notion of an embodied subject as the agent of political resistance. Corporeality represents not just the locus of control but also the site of subjective experience which may contest oppressive power structures. What both these approaches share is the desire to re-write the body, to resist the disciplining of the female body and to envisage a reconfiguration of the boundaries that define the female subject at the turn of the century.

In Carter's novels the image of the body is constructed around the tension between a poststructuralist notion of gender fluidity and a feminist reclaiming of the female body as a source of pleasure and power. The following study will delineate a development in Carter's fiction from the seventies to the nineties. The early seventies mark a change in Carter's writing. Carter's stay in Japan from 1969 to 1972 heightened her socio-political awareness and radicalised her as a feminist. In *Nothing Sacred* Carter comments on her Japanese experience: "In Japan, I learnt what it is to be a woman and became

1

radicalised."[1] In retrospect, she also notes an element of "male impersonation" in her earlier fiction in the sixties.[2] After her stay abroad, her writing grew more allusive and theoretically complex. Carter turned to a highly speculative fiction which fuses an astounding philosophical complexity with a fantastic sense of adventure and a sharp feminist political edge.[3]

Carter wrote four novels between 1972 and her untimely death in 1992: *The Infernal Desire Machines of Dr Hoffman* (1972), *The Passion of New Eve* (1977), *Nights at the Circus* (1984) and *Wise Children* (1991). I have chosen to focus on these 'post-sixties' works because they represent the 'feminist period' in Carter's writing and trace a radical change in her conception of the female body. Between the seventies and the nineties, Carter's fiction moves from the pessimistic negation of a self-determined female corporeality to the assertion of the female body as a powerful site of alterity. The first work she wrote after her return from Japan, *The Infernal Desire Machines of Dr Hoffman*, figures the female body as an absence. It expresses a radical pessimism with regard to the possibility of articulating a female corporeality in a patriarchal society. *The Passion of New Eve* reveals the violent nature of 'myths' of masculinity and femininity and deconstructs fixed gender identities. *Nights at the Circus* continues the 'demythologising project', but, at the same time, transcends the deconstructive approach in the creation of Fevvers who turns the female body into a 'monstrous' site of subversion. A strong female subjectivity is further developed in Carter's last novel *Wise*

---

[1] Carter 1982, 28. See also Carter in Wandor 1983, 72: "Because my female consciousness *was* being forged out of the contradictions of my experience as a traveller, as, indeed, some other aspects of my political consciousness were being forged." In the afterword to her short story collection *Fireworks* she writes: "I was living in Japan; I came back to England in 1972. I found myself in a new country. It was like waking up, it was a rude awakening" (BB 459-460).

[2] Carter wrote five novels in the sixties: *Shadow Dance* (1966), *The Magic Toyshop* (1967), *Several Perceptions* (1968), *Heroes and Villains* (1969) and *Love*, which was published in 1971. In the afterword of the 1987 edition of *Love*, Carter commented on the novel as a "sinister feast of male impersonation" (L 113). In "Notes from the Front Lines" she describes her younger self as "suffering a degree of male colonialisation of the mind", positing a "male point of view as a general one ....". Carter in Wandor 1983, 71. Carter's novels in the sixties are more accessible and closer to realism than her 'post-Japanese' fiction. They merge the realist mode with Gothic, surrealist and expressionist elements.

[3] Carter herself describes her fiction in the seventies as 'speculative': a "writing about ideas ... the fiction of speculation, the fiction of asking 'what if?'. It's a system of continuing enquiry." Carter in Katsavos 1994, 14. Critics have labelled her late work as 'magic realism'. Carter turned against this classification, which she associated with the socio-cultural context of South American societies. Carter in Haffenden 1985, 81.

Children. The stress is also laid upon a subjectively experienced body in this final work.

While this study primarily pursues a feminist approach, a reading of the body in Carter's fiction necessarily draws on a variety of theoretical concepts.[4] Psychoanalysis, deconstruction, Marxism and reader-response theory offer fruitful insights into Carter's writing. While Carter was familiar with most of these approaches, in many cases she anticipated what only later figured prominently in literary criticism. The notion of 'gender as performance' and the deconstructive critique of subjectivity are two cases in point.[5] The multiplicity of philosophical and theoretical intertexts lends a strong allegorical quality to Carter's fiction. However, it should be kept in mind that theoretical complexity is only one aspect of her multifaceted work.[6] Mingling the adventurous and the philosophical, the fantastic and the political, the comic and the melancholic, Carter's fiction is not only erudite but also highly entertaining. It is the unpredictable, the transgressive and the refusal to comply with fixed categories which challenges the reader and constitutes a special pleasure in reading Carter's fiction. In fact, Carter's use

---

[4] Various aspects of corporeality have been analysed from different theoretical perspectives in literary studies in recent years. For a genealogical approach to the history of embodiment see, for instance, Judovitz 2001; for a communicative and semiotic approach to body language in literature see Korte 1997; see Zylinska 2002 for a poststructuralist approach to embodiment in the age of new technologies; for a historical and political analysis of the body in pain see Morris 1991 and Scarry 1985; see Heywood 1996 for a feminist and Olson 2003 for a cultural studies approach to eating disorders in literature. This is just a small selection of the countless recent studies on corporeality in literature.

[5] *The Infernal Desire Machines* (1972) predates the heydays of deconstructive criticism. When deconstruction peaked as a method of literary criticism, Carter's fiction is again ahead of its time, formulating a critique of deconstruction in *Nights at the Circus. The Passion of New Eve* (1977) anticipates Judith Butler's concept of 'gender as performance' in the nineties (cf. II.4). *The Sadeian Woman* (1979) pre-empts the feminist debate on pornography in the eighties (see below note 14). *The Infernal Desire Machines* can be read as a literary illustration of the 'masculine economy of sameness', a concept which Irigaray developed after the publication of the novel (see III.2.2.3). The novel also seems to anticipate Mulvey's feminist psychoanalytic critique of classical narrative cinema (see III.2.2.4).

[6] There remains much more to discover about Carter, as, for instance, her skilful, unconventional use of language (for a narratological analysis see Fludernik 1998; see Lee 1996 for a 'feminist narratology' in Carter); her verbal wit (see Carter in Katsavos 1994 on "playing games with the reader"); her experimenting with genre (see O'Day 1994, Roe 1994, Kaveney 1994, Connor 1996 and Peach 1998). For a historicist reading that situates Carter's novels in the context of Britain's economic and political crisis of the 1970s see Pitchford 2002. A focus on autobiography is provided by Gamble's and Bannock's reading. See Gamble 1997; Bannock 1997.

of allegory does not imply a one-to-one correlation between a surface and a deep structure of meaning. Allegory is multi-layered, complex and ironically self-conscious. It turns the text into an abyss of signification: a *mis-en-abyme* in which one possible interpretation continually hints at another one. Carter's work is characterised by a radical equivocality, the refusal to be pinned down to one meaning. Eluding finality, it celebrates openness, the unexpected, the provocative and the ambiguous.

This ambiguity is reflected in the diversity of critical responses to Carter's work. There has been an amazing output of critical literature on Carter within the last few years. At this point it may suffice to draw attention to two kinds of responses. On the one hand, critics focus on the postmodern and deconstructive elements in Carter's novels. Early critics like Punter and Clark take a sceptical stance towards parody and play in Carter's fiction.[7] Robinson, Jordan, Hutcheon, Müller, Makinen and Wilson foreground the political subversiveness of parody and masquerade.[8] It is one of the concerns of Bristow and Broughton's collection of essays to include "dissenting voices" that question these liberatory readings of Carter's fiction: Palmer criticises Carter for ignoring the problematic aspects of the notion of performativity; Hanson and Britzolakis contend that masquerade and parody deterministically repeat the structures of power in Carter's fiction.[9] On the other hand, recent criticism draws attention to the materialist and politically committed element that coexists with deconstruction, parody and play in Carter's fiction. Four studies on Carter edited in the late nineties turn against a reading that reduces her fiction to postmodern play and pastiche. Analysing the concept of identity in Carter's work, Anja Müller argues that Carter moves towards a "feminist postmodern" which combines the postmodern deconstruction of identity with

---

[7] Punter 1984; Clark 1987; see also Palmer 1987. Reception of Carter reflects her ability to be ahead of her time. While first responses to her work tended to be rather scarce and critical (Mars-Jones 1984; Duncker 1984; Punter 1984), this changed dramatically in the 1990s. Sage's collection of essays that was published in 1994 might be considered as a turning point in this development. Carter's rising popularity in the nineties may not only be due to her untimely death, but also to the fact that her fiction has become more accessible in the context of recent debates in feminism (see note 5). In the seventies and early eighties, by contrast, Carter's writing tended to generate unease and bafflement among readers and critics. See, for instance, Jouve 1994 on her initial reaction to Carter's fiction in the seventies.

[8] Hutcheon and Wilson count Carter among postmodernist writers who "collapse borders" and centralise the marginalised. Hutcheon 1989, 13; Wilson 1989, 104. See also Robinson 1991; Jordan 1990; Müller 1997; Makinen 2000.

[9] See Bristow/Broughton 1997, 14-19. Palmer 1997, 32; Britzolakis 1997, 46 ff.; Hanson 1997, 65-66. For another 'pessimistic' reading of Carter's fiction see Warner 1994, 253.

a politically committed feminism.[10] Aidan Day traces Carter's allegiance to the Enlightenment ideal of rationality.[11] In her analysis of Carter's contribution to the English novel, Peach stresses that Carter's fantasy deals with the social and material reality of women's lives: Carter employs a non-realistic mode to engage with patriarchal culture from a feminist perspective.[12] Sarah Gamble's study also notes that Carter's "metafictional approach is muted by sincere appeals to an extra-textual world in which love is possible, and death is certainty."[13]

The controversial and unorthodox nature of Carter's work is, moreover, reflected in different evaluations of her gender politics. Carter's critique of gynocentric feminism in *The Passion of New Eve* and her feminist study on Sade has made her appear as the *enfant terrible* to parts of the feminist community in the seventies.[14] Referring to Andrea Dworkin's critique of pornography, Kappeler, Duncker and Lewallen accused Carter of reproducing pornographic violence in her fiction.[15] Clark claimed that the depiction of crude patriarchal violence and female victimisation precludes an affirmative feminism.[16] Palmer as well took this view with regard to the early Carter, yet heralded the shift in her later fiction that figures women no longer as puppets of male desire but as self-determined agents.[17] The subversive empowering force of Carter's feminism, by contrast, has been foregrounded by the

---

[10] Müller 1997; see also Michael 1994, 492-3.

[11] Day 1998.

[12] Peach 1998, 160. Peach notes that Carter employs a mode of writing closer to "Gothic, fantasy or the European romance than the English realist novel" and increasingly draws on "pre-novelistic forms" such as the picaresque, fairy stories, folk tales, myth, legend and theatre. Peach 1998, 159,160.

[13] Gamble 1997, 9. Gamble's study of Carter's work focuses on themes like autobiography, camp and subjectivity.

[14] In *The Sadeian Woman* Carter imagines the possibility of putting pornography into the service of women and devises a 'moral pornography' as a critique of the social relations in a society. Carter's linking of Sade's work with a feminist project has raised protest among feminists. *The Sadeian Woman* has been misread as a defence of Sade. In the essay, however, Carter arrives at the conclusion that Sade, for all his revolutionary ideas on emancipation, fails to become a 'moral pornographer' and remains "in complicity with the authority he hates" (SW 132,136). On the debate on pornography see Keenan 2000.

[15] Dworkin 1981, 84; Kappeler 1986, 135; Lewallen 1988, 149; Duncker 1984, 6-7; see also Clark 1987, 151. See Jordan 1992, Keenan 1997 and Makinen 1997/2000 for a defence of Carter against Clark, Kappeler and Duncker's claims.

[16] Clark 1987, 158.

[17] Palmer 1987. Blodgett, Makinen and Schmid perceive a similar progression in Carter's fiction. Blodgett 1994; Makinen 2000; Schmid 1996, 172.

majority of critics in the nineties, for instance, by Michael, Day, Müller, Peach, Gamble and Gasiorek.[18]

Arguing that both a deconstructive questioning of essences and a materialist commitment to feminism are continually present in Carter's work, I would like to trace a progression in the body politics of her fiction which moves from a claustrophobic obsession with sameness towards a radical articulation of alterity. I will begin by giving a brief sketch of theories of the body, focusing in particular on the work of Michel Foucault and Judith Butler in Chapter Two. Chapter Three examines the concept of the body in *The Infernal Desire Machines of Dr Hoffman*. The novel offers a bleak vision of corporeality which either reduces the body to a textual cipher or treats it as 'meat' for consumption. I will investigate cannibalism as metaphor for the elimination of difference in the novel. A Foucauldian analysis foregrounds the entanglement of desire and subjection in the narrative. *The Passion of New Eve* (Chapter Four) traces the construction of the female body within patriarchal discourse and breaks up fixed notions of gender identity through bodily metamorphoses and transgression. Staging the monstrous and grotesque body, *Nights at the Circus* (Chapter Five) marks the emergence of difference in Carter's fiction. This sense of difference prepares for the concept of a lived corporeality that takes shape in Carter's last work. Maternity, death and the comic mode will be at the centre of my analysis in Chapter Six. While Carter keeps to her radical critique of biological essentialism, the ageing body is no longer an allegorical cipher but the site of lived experience in *Wise Children*.

Carter's concept of the body is riven by contradictions and ambiguities. Carter attacks the suppression of the body in Judaeo-Christian Western culture. However, persistently raging against biological determinism, her fiction bespeaks a 'somatophobic' anxiety of being identified with the body. Even though her novels move towards an increased acceptance of corporeality, this contradiction is never fully resolved. Carter, in fact, did not like resolution, which implies stasis, finality, the end of change. Resisting closure, Carter's fiction represents a "continuing enquiry" which never comes to rest in one ideological position. I think it is in Carter's spirit to leave these ambiguities to the reader to make up her own mind, or, as Carter put it, "to construct her own fiction for herself from the elements of my fictions. Reading is just as creative an activity as writing ....".[19]

---

[18] Michael 1994; Day 1998; Müller 1997; Peach 1998; Gamble 1997; Gasiorek 1995. Many of the articles mentioned in the introduction are also included in two collections of essays which have recently been published on Carter. See Easton 2000 and Tucker 1998.

[19] Carter in Wandor 1983, 69.

6

II. Theorising the Body
1. Mind-Body Dualism

The mind-body dualism has been one of the dominant themes of Western philosophy. Platonic philosophy in particular has elaborated on the theme, introducing a cluster of motifs that has permeated Western thinking up to the twentieth century: the body as betrayer of the soul and as impediment to the 'higher aspirations' of the mind. The body denotes the transient in contrast to the permanent. Christian religion took up the Platonic dualism of mind and body, reinforcing the negative construction of the body as appetite. Whereas Plato regards the body as an 'epistemological obstacle', the flesh becomes an agent of sin in Christian thought. Equated with sexuality and animal nature, corporeality has to be tamed and controlled. In sixteenth-century epistemology the body comes to denote human locatedness in time and space. Embodiment impedes objectivity. Dis-embodiment is the prerequisite for grasping the 'real'. Sixteenth-century epistemology thus postulates the "disembodied view from nowhere" as the scientific ideal.[1] Descartes, in fact, believed in the possibility of transcending the epistemological limitations of the body in philosophy. He strictly separated mind and body:

> The human body ... is constituted only by a certain configuration of members, and by other accidents of this sort, while the human mind is not made up of accidents, but is pure substance ....[2]

In Descartes consciousness is elevated above the natural world. Isolated from its environment, the mind becomes "an island unto itself". According to Elizabeth Grosz, the philosophical problem of solipsism can be derived from an extreme Cartesian position: dissociated from its social and natural context, the mind can only be certain about its own existence.[3] Cartesian philosophy introduces the modern conception of nature as a machine, which replaces the pre-modern notion of nature as organism.[4] In the seventeenth century the

---

[1] See Bordo 1982, 75 ff.; Bordo 1993, 3,4.

[2] Descartes 1975, 76,77. However, Descartes still believed mind and body to be connected through the pineal gland. Occasionalists like Arnold Geulincx denied the existence of such a connection and thus radicalised Descartes' notion of the separation of mind and body in the seventeenth century. It is not the mind but divine intervention which is believed to be the source of causation in occasionalism. See Korte 1997, 160-161.

[3] Grosz 1994, 7. Solipsism is a central concern in Carter's work. Carter's feminist critique of male solipsism relates to a critique of bourgeois individualism and the Cartesian notion of subjectivity (cf. III.1.3.2).

[4] The mechanical philosophy of nature was developed by Descartes, Marin Mersenne and Pierre Gassendi in the 1620s and elaborated by Hobbes. It had been prefigured by Bacon's

body is no longer bedevilled as the agent of sin, but constitutes a biologically programmed mechanism. The scientific revolution redefines the body as a machine that requires control and intervention by scientific experts. In the dawning age of capitalist industrialism and colonialism, nature is no longer conceived as an animistic organic unity with an inviolable integrity but as a resource, which can be used and exploited for human ends. From Carolyn Merchant's perspective, colonialist and patriarchal interests are connected with the modern mechanistic concept of nature, which opens up new territories for exploration and exploitation: the earth and the female body.[5]

It is a feminist commonplace that the mind-body opposition has frequently been cast as a gendered opposition, with woman assuming the 'weight' of the body that the male spirit transcends. In such a view woman represents the libidinal, the submission to sexual desire and death.[6] The mind-body opposition is also used to establish a class- and race-coded duality. Racist ideology constructs non-Caucasian races as more libidinal than 'white' races.[7] The sexual drive of the racial other is believed to threaten the 'purity' of the 'white' race through miscenegation. Sexuality is displaced from white men to women to blacks, justifying the subjugation of what is presumed to pose an existential threat to 'whiteness'. Due to her race and gender, the black woman carries twice the burden of associations with the sexual drive and the body. The legacy of slavery further degrades the black female body by turning it into colonial property: in a paradoxical way the black woman is at the same time identified with and dispossessed of her body. A similar rhetoric operates when the mind-body duality is used to express class differences in the old metaphor of the body politic. The state has traditionally been described as a human body with the head representing the sovereign.[8] The 'unruly drives' stand for the lower classes, which require containment and control. In this sense social hierarchies – in terms of gender, race and class – have been projected on the mind-body distinction, with the body assuming the subordinate role of the 'raw material' in need of form and control. The philosophical distinction between mind and body cannot be dissociated from a political rhetoric which buttresses relations of domination and subordination.

---

vision of the scientific conquest of nature as he imagined it in his utopian fragment *Nova Atlantis*. On Bacon, the French mechanists and Hobbes see Merchant 1980, 164-216.

[5] Merchant 1980, 164 ff.; see also Sawicki 1991, 78.

[6] See Schiebinger 1983, 2-3; Bordo 1993, 5.

[7] See Baudrillard on a political economy that eroticises the repressed. Baudrillard 1976, 160. See also Gallop 1988, 20.

[8] The metaphor of the body politic has been used by Plato, Aristotle, Seneca, Macchiavelli, Hobbes etc..

The mind-body dualism is a major theme in Carter's work. *The Sadeian Woman* – Carter's cultural critique of sexuality – particularly attacks Platonic philosophy for laying the groundwork of the anti-sensualism that pervades Judeao-Christian culture. Nevertheless, Carter's work displays an ambivalent attitude towards the body. *The Passion of New Eve* rejects any notion of a female essence and corporeality as compromised by male definitions of femininity. Carter's late work, however, rehabilitates the devalued female body as a source of power and pleasure. The concept of an empowering female sexuality emerges in her final novels, *Nights at the Circus* and *Wise Children*.

The negative construction of the body as 'deceiver', as 'appetite in need of control', is not the only historical representation of the body. In Epicurean ethics bodily pleasures are highly appreciated. According to Spinoza, body and mind are not, as Descartes claimed, two fundamentally different substances but different 'modes' of the single indivisible substance of nature.[9] While the Cartesian subject is lifted above its natural and social context, Spinoza stresses the effect the environment has on the individual.[10] In his radical questioning of Cartesian dualism, Spinoza is an early precursor of contemporary theories that will be recapitulated in the following section.[11] In the eighteenth century, by contrast, Rousseau retains dualism but re-evaluates the terms of the body-mind dichotomy. He contrasts the healthy, natural body with restrictive and corrupted civilisation. In *Emile* he recommends to keep the development of the body unimpaired by civilisatory influences in early education.[12] The natural, healthy body becomes a prerequisite for the development of a healthy personality.

---

[9] Spinoza 1985, Part I, Prop. 13; Part II, Prop. 7. Spinoza's radical monism postulates the identity of nature and god and thus resolves the contrast between religion and science, the soul and the body. See Norris 1991, 24.

[10] He employs the image of geometrical figures which are not static but in process, determined by the shapes of their surrounding figures. Ibid., Part II, Prop. 13, Axiom 2, Corollary 3; Prop. 16.

[11] See II.3; II.4; see also III.2.1 on Spinoza's concept of desire and its influence on Nietzsche and Deleuze/Guattari. See Norris (1991) for Spinoza's influence on poststructuralism.

[12] The notion of the body in Rousseau is, however, ambivalent. On the one hand, *Emile* focuses on the natural development of the child's body. Ideal education is defined *ex negativo* as preventing civilisatory influences from interfering with the child's development. On the other hand, the body is disciplined when physical exercise is regarded as one of the most important elements of early education. See Rousseau 1992, 5 ff.,32. In a Foucauldian analysis this focus on the healthy, adolescent body might be read as an early expression of 'bio-power', which manifests itself in the regulation of individual bodies and populations (see below II.3.1). The adult gaze focuses on the child's body. The healthy

In the twentieth century a major shift has taken place in modern philosophy, which reconceptualised the body as a historical, culturally mediated form. The notion of the body as a political and cultural entity implies a questioning of the nature-culture opposition itself. In the following section I will briefly look at the notion of the body in Marxism, feminism, phenomenology and poststructuralism. I will focus on Michel Foucault and Judith Butler as their approaches are particularly helpful for an understanding of Angela Carter's fiction.

2. The Body in Marxism, Feminism and Phenomenology

Marxism and feminism politicise the body by focusing on class and gender differences as constitutive of the body's experience. Nineteenth-century Marxism defines man and nature as the sensuous products of social processes. Marx historicises the body: the body's experiences are determined by the socio-economic class and the conditions of labour. The notion of static matter that is subject to the transforming force of the spirit is dissolved in Marx's notion of *Praxis*. The body transforms nature through labour and is itself transformed in this process. Marx's concept of human *Praxis* criticises both Hegelian idealism and Feuerbachian materialism, which are based on a rigid dissociation of the mind (active) and body (passive):

> The chief defect of all previous materialism (including Feuerbach's) is that the object, actuality, sensuousness is conceived only in the form of the object or perception (*Anschauung*), but not as sensuous human activity, practice (*Praxis*), not subjectively.[13]

Materiality (the body, labour) does not represent the passive object of transformation but is itself transformative in Marx's notion of active materialism.[14]

In the twentieth century, feminism turns the body into a site of political struggles. At the beginning of the century, first-wave feminists focused on a materialist analysis of culture's 'direct grip' on our bodies. They examined the way in which the female body is disciplined in our daily practices and habits. How much space is a body supposed to occupy? What are the daily rituals in which the female body is involved (make-up, dieting, dressing, corseting etc.)? Today, the materialist feminist criticism of the 'politics of the

---

body is produced through training and the regulation of adolescent sexuality, on which Rousseau gives extensive instructions in the fourth book of *Emile*. See Rousseau 1992, 273 ff..
[13] Marx 1967, 400.
[14] See also Turner 1984, 31; Butler 1993, 250; Johnson 1989, 4-8.

body' deals with issues such as abortion, prostitution, rape, cosmetic surgery, surrogate motherhood and artificial reproduction. Thus, the materialist analysis of the body as it is employed by Marxists and feminists does not investigate the ontological status of the body, nor its representational status. A materialist analysis is concerned with the body as the object of political struggles in a specific historical situation. In *The Sadeian Woman* Carter – who calls herself both a socialist and a feminist – formulates a radical materialist critique of sexuality and comments on the historicity of the body: "Flesh comes to us out of history .... Sexuality is never expressed in vacuum" (SW 11). Sexuality is determined by the power structures and economic dependencies in a given society.

Another strand of feminism that was particularly prevalent in the 1980s does not examine patriarchy's 'direct' control of women's bodies, but formulates a critique of the images of femininity in Western culture. Claiming that there is a materiality to symbols, Carter conjoins both perspectives in her fiction. In fact, the 'politics of the image' and the 'politics of action' are necessarily connected, as representation provides the ideological background for action. In this sense *The Passion of New Eve* presents a materialist analysis of the 'myths'[15] of femininity and derives rape and sexual violence from the representation of gender in Western culture.[16]

Another attack on the mind-body opposition has been launched from the perspective of a very different philosophical tradition. In the twentieth century, existential phenomenology tried to overcome the mind-body dualism through the notion of the lived subjective body (*Leib*), which contrasts with

---

[15] Carter uses the term 'myth' in Barthes' sense as referring to a mode of signification which naturalises the cultural/historical and promotes the interests and values of the dominant class in a society. See Barthes 1984.

[16] In *No Logo* Naomi Klein criticises the exclusive focus on representation and identity politics in the 'political correctness era' of the eighties: attacking patriarchal images of women and the silencing of the racial other in hegemonic cultural representation, the eighties' counter-culture focused on "the representation of women and minorities within the structures of power, not on the economics behind those power structures ....". Feminism restricted itself to a "politics of mirrors and metaphors". Klein 2000, 108,109,121. Carter's fiction attempts to bridge the gap between a materialist and a symbolic feminist politics. It demonstrates that mirrors and metaphors have the power to create a 'material' reality: "... the point is if dreams are real as dreams, then there is a materiality to symbols; there's a materiality to imaginative life and imaginative experience which should be taken quite seriously." Carter in Haffenden 1985, 85. Carter accords a central role to representation in the struggle for equality: "... language is power, life and the instrument of culture, the instrument of domination and liberation." Carter in Wandor 1983, 77.

the Cartesian objective-instrumental body (*Körper*).[17] Merleau-Ponty focuses on the central role of the body in human experience. His *Phénoménologie de la perception* constitutes a critical response to Husserl's early notion of the transcendental subject that reproduces the dualism between mind (transcendental consciousness) and body. In Merleau-Ponty it is not the transcendental subject but the lived body that organises experience. Bound to a particular perspective, human perception is by necessity embodied. As reflection is rooted in perception, even higher mental functions are part of the lived body.[18] The *Phénoménologie de la perception* formulates a critique of Cartesianism, postulating the impossibility of transcending corporeality: mind and body are inextricably intertwined in the phenomenological subject. Referring to Merleau-Ponty, Bernhard Waldenfels stresses the primacy of the 'lived body' (*Leib*) over the body as object (*Körper*). The naturalistic, scientific conception of the body as object is itself a culturally and historically determined notion. As the lived body is necessarily implied in everything we do, perceive and think, the scientific 'objective' perception of the body is also conditioned by lived corporeality.[19]

In phenomenology the body as 'other' is not radically dissociated from the self as it is in Cartesian philosophy. Waldenfels argues that otherness is necessarily part of the self as it is implicated in the experience of lived corporeality. The subjective experience of emotions like sadness and joy presupposes a relation to the other, to the world beyond the self. Waldenfels refers to Merleau-Ponty's concept of 'intercorporéite' which defines a space of differentiation that constitutes the self in relation to the other. A trace of difference always remains present within the self.[20] It is this sense of otherness that forms the basis of an ethics of alterity in postmodern philosophy. The acknowledgement of difference emerges as a central element in the philosophies of Emmanuel Levinas and Luce Irigaray.[21]

---

[17] Phenomenological thinkers like Merleau-Ponty and Helmuth Plessner refer to Husserl's concept of the body as "the point of conversion" ("*Umschlagstelle*") from culture to nature. See Husserl 1989, 299. Locating the body on the borderline between nature and culture, Plessner, for instance, distinguishes between the instrumental 'body-we-have' and the lived 'body-we-are'. Plessner 1970, 41ff., 162. See also VI.2.1.1.

[18] Merleau-Ponty 1945, 81 ff..

[19] Waldenfels 2000, 252 ff.. Waldenfels refers in this context to Kutschmann, *Der Naturwissenschaftler und sein Körper*, Frankfurt,1986.

[20] Ibid., 287. "... der Einzelne ... hat durchaus Eigenes, aber dies Eigene immer in Abhebung vom Fremden." This space of differentiation is reminiscent of Kristeva's concept of the formation of the subject: the subject constitutes itself leaving the m(other) behind and represses this trace of alterity within the self. See II.6.

[21] Levinas 1996; Irigaray 1984. See V.4.2.

Carter's fiction of the seventies neglects lived corporeality in favour of a poststructuralist concept of the body. In fact, Carter's notion of the body as a constructed entity is hardly compatible with the phenomenological concept of corporeality. In her final novel, though, the concept of the lived body begins to emerge. In Carter's late fiction a trace of alterity eludes the dense allegorical structure that governs much of her preceding work. It seems to be no accident that this shift in the representation of the body coincides with Carter's fatal illness and the theme of ageing and mortality in her last novel.[22] As Peter Brooks points out, it is the failure of the body which makes its materiality most dramatically felt.[23] The phenomenological analysis of the lived body focuses on the pathological, defunct body. In most of Carter's fiction, however, the 'lived body' is absent. A phenomenological perspective is at odds with Carter's materialism and historicism: the phenomenological body that organises experience is a conspicuously ahistorical body. Foucault's genealogical project can be read as a critical response to this ahistorical notion of corporeality.

3. Michel Foucault: Discourse, Power and the Body

In Foucault the subject is historically constituted by discourses and institutional practices, which form a complex network of power and knowledge at the heart of modern society. Foucault's investigation into the constitution of the subject concentrates on the body. The body represents the focal point at which power and knowledge intersect to produce the modern subject.

3.1 The Body in *Discipline and Punish* and *The History of Sexuality*

Foucault focuses on the body in *Discipline and Punish* and *The History of Sexuality*. Dealing with specific historical questions – the history of the prison and the history of sexuality – both texts are part of a general analysis of the interrelationship of power, knowledge and subjectivity in modern society. Foucault examines a transitional period which witnesses the emergence of new 'political technologies' that produce and subject the individual in modern society.

Discipline and Punish traces the transformation of penitentiary practices as part of the emergence of the disciplinary society in the eighteenth century.

---

[22] Carter suffered from cancer when she wrote her final novel.
[23] Brooks 1993, 5,7.

Medieval torture was replaced by the prison, the 'panopticon', in which prisoners are isolated and subjected to constant surveillance. Foucault considers the invention of the panopticon as an expression of a new formation of power which does not torture or kill the body (as punishment in the seventeenth century did) but disciplines it, transforming it into a productive body that can be put into the system's service:

> The body is directly involved in a political field; power relations have an immediate hold upon it; they invest it, mark it, train it, torture it, force it to carry out tasks, to perform ceremonies, to emit signs. This political investment of the body is bound up ... with its economic use; it is largely as a force of production that the body is invested with relations of power and domination; but on the other hand, its constitution as labour power is possible only if it is caught up in a system of subjection ... the body becomes a useful force only if it is both a productive and a subjected body.[24]

The function of the prison is to elicit penitence and to reintegrate the individual through work, training and the strict regulation of daily routines. Besides the prison, several other institutions, such as schools, factories and hospitals, are agents of the emerging disciplinary technology. These institutions create an intricate system of surveillance, bureaucratic documentation and normalising sanctions. Constant surveillance produces a self which internalises the gaze and monitors itself for unacceptable behaviour. Normalising sanctions, such as grading in school examinations, have a similar effect and produce a subject which is eager to conform. Bureaucratic documentation subjects the individual to registration and administrative regulations. It produces a database that can be used for statistical and scientific purposes. As a particularly efficient instrument of control, the modern hospital connects these measures, subjecting the patient to administrative control, scientific research and normalisation in therapy.

The disciplinary society develops a highly efficient way of controlling the subject: the subject which internalises the gaze is itself turned into an agent of normalisation who strives to conform to the norm. In addition, scientific research and documentation produce a comprehensive knowledge of the individual that can be categorised and normalised on the basis of this knowledge.

In *The History of Sexuality* Foucault examines how this knowledge has encroached upon the most private, intimate realms of the individual. Foucault traces the emergence of sex as a product of the scientific discourse of sexuality in the nineteenth century. Society has not primarily worked to repress sex (the 'repressive hypothesis'), but intensified it by stimulating an increased production of discourses on sex. As examples Foucault mentions

---

[24] Foucault 1977, 25,26.

the confession in the seventeenth century that elicited the most detailed descriptions of sexual practices, and the proliferation of medical, psychological and juridical discourses on sexuality in the eighteenth and nineteenth century.[25] In an interview given at the University of Paris/Vincennes, Foucault recapitulates the way he proceeded when writing *The History of Sexuality*:

> There were several successive drafts. To start with, sex was taken as a pre-given datum, and sexuality figured as a sort of simultaneously discursive and institutional formation which came to graft itself on to sex, to overlay it and perhaps finally to obscure it. That was the first line of approach. Then ... I came to realise that it wasn't very satisfactory. Then I turned the whole thing upside down .... I said to myself, basically, couldn't it be that sex – which seems to be an instance having its own laws and constraints, on the basis of which the masculine and feminine sexes are defined – be something which on the contrary is produced by the apparatus of sexuality?[26]

Sex is not repressed but produced by the discourse of sexuality. In *The History of Sexuality* Foucault criticises the juridical model which describes power as working in a purely negative, repressive way. This model presupposes a binary opposition between the rulers and the ruled: power is exclusively exerted from the top down. Power represses and silences. The subject and the object of repression are considered to be pre-existent to power. According to Foucault, the concept of juridical power is outdated in modern society, in which power works with various – repressive and *productive* – strategies. Power does not silence, but makes us talk. It produces the discourses that create the very identities of the subject and the object in the juridical model. Constituting the identity of the subject, power is pre-existent to suppression. On this basis Foucault develops the notion of bio-power, which he considers to be *the* characteristic form power takes in modern society. Bio-power aims at enhancing and controlling life. The development of social welfare systems, the politics of health[27] and reproduction, birth control and genocide in modern warfare are expressions of bio-power, which focuses on the life and death of the species. Bio-power operates in two ways: through the disciplining of the individual body and the regulation of populations. The production of sexuality represents the crucial link between these two kinds of body politics. Bio-power works through producing new 'useful' subjects, through inciting desire and establishing

---

[25] Foucault 1990, 17-36.
[26] Foucault 1980, 210.
[27] The obsession with fitness, dieting and health as well as the recent vogue for anti-ageing therapies might be considered as manifestations of bio-power today. See also II.5.

norms and techniques for the observation and control of 'body movements'. It maximises life, renders bodies more useful, powerful and docile.

3.2 A Critique of Foucault's Notion of the Body
3.2.1 Resistance, Ethics and the Body

Foucault's concept of power has been criticised for being politically paralysing. Foucault negates the possibility of adopting a position beyond power from which to analyse and resist its workings:

> Resistance is never in a position of exteriority in relation to power ... there is no single locus of great Refusal, no soul of revolt, source of all rebellions, or pure law of the revolutionary.[28]

There is no 'natural' body which provides the basis for the "great Refusal"; the body is 'always already' implicated within the field of power. Yet from what position is Foucault himself speaking? Does not he himself assume this position beyond the field of power by the very formulation of a theory of power?[29] Foucault is faced with the paradox that any poststructuralist theory is confronted with when he questions the epistemological capacity of the subject and ignores the fact that there has to be a subject to undertake this very questioning. By turning the critical position 'beyond power' into a position of unwitting complicity, Foucault's theory disputes the political efficacy of the 'grand narratives'.[30] In particular, it opposes classical Marxism, which is based on a detached, objective examination of historical processes and employs a juridical analysis of power. However, Foucault does not eliminate the possibility of resistance. Resistance is continually present *within* the field of power.[31] It can be effectively employed in a local, strategic way. Foucault displaces resistance from a macro-political to a micro-political, strategic level.

Foucault does away with the autonomous subject and the 'innocent body' as the site of subversion. Yet at times a mystified notion of power seems to fill the empty slot that the vanishing subject has left behind:

---

[28] Foucault 1990, 95,96.
[29] For the self-defeating force of Foucault's relativism see Habermas 1985, 328 and Waldenfels 1985, 124,125.
[30] Foucault, for instance, argues that sexual liberation in the sixties played into the hands of the existing power structure by inciting discourses on sexuality.
[31] Gilles Deleuze points to the "primacy of resistance" in Foucault's field of power, in which a "multiplicity of force relations" continually enacts the struggle between force and counter-force. Deleuze 1992, 125.

16

The omnipresence of power: ... because it is produced from one moment to the next, at every point, or rather in every relation from one point to another. Power is everywhere; not because it embraces everything but because it comes from everywhere .... Power is not an institution, and not a structure; neither is it a certain strength that we are endowed with; it is a name that one attributes to a complex strategical situation in a particular society.[32]

Foucault has been criticised for displacing agency onto some vague anonymous concept of 'power' which is not located in a socially and institutionally specific way, thus veiling the actual relations of domination and the 'doer behind the deed'.[33] Jürgen Habermas perceives a radical pessimism in Foucault's concept of power that negates the ability of human subjects to change discursive formations through communicative action. Power appears as a 'transcendental-historical' concept that is opposed to a humanist rationality:[34]

Foucault radicalizes Horkheimer and Adorno's critique of instrumental reason to make it a theory of the Eternal Return of power. His proclamation of a cycle of power that is always the same returning in discourse formations that are always new cannot help but extinguish the last spark of utopia and destroy the last traces of Western culture's self-confidence.[35]

Habermas counts Foucault among the neo-Nietzschean "Young Conservatives" who oppose instrumental reason with "a principle accessible solely to evocation, whether this is the will to power or sovereignty, Being itself or the Dionysian power for the poetic."[36] Like differance (Derrida), Being (Heidegger) and the Dionysian power for the poetic (Bataille), power functions as an all-explanatory concept which fills the vacuum that the deconstruction of the subject has left behind. In this sense Habermas considers much of poststructuralist philosophy as another form of a 'philosophy of the origin' that fails in its claim to deconstruct a transcendental centre.[37]

---

[32] Foucault 1990, 93.

[33] Minson 1986, 111; Megill 1985, 250; Hartsock 1990, 165 ff.; Habermas 1985, 323.

[34] In contrast, Habermas does not give up the humanist notion of rationality. His concept of 'communicative reason' is based on the idea that the primary mode of language is not strategic but communicative and aims to reach consensual agreement between the participants in discourse. In Habermas' view speakers are able to restructure their environment in a consensual way through communicative action. Foucault rejects Habermas' notion of a non-strategic use of communication as utopian. See Conway 1999, 60; White 1995, 121. For the debate between Habermas and Foucault see also Ashenden 1999.

[35] Habermas 1991, 52.

[36] Habermas 1996, 53.

[37] Habermas 1985, 213,214.

In fact, Foucault describes power as "non-subjective": power is not something that "one seizes ... and ... holds on to" but is instead exercised "from innumerable points".[38] But, one might wonder, is not effective resistance dependent on the prior identification of the loci of power? Foucault does not solve this problem by displacing resistance from the macro-political to the micro-political level. Even on a local, strategic level it is necessary to identify the agents of power in order to oppose them.[39] Does Foucault's model of power contribute to the paralysing sense of disorientation that Frederic Jameson defines as a dominant feature of postmodernism? In *Postmodernism or the Cultural Logic of Late Capitalism* Jameson describes spatial and social confusion in the age of postmodernism as a consequence of the abolition of (critical) distance:

> ... distance in general (including 'critical distance' in particular) has very precisely been abolished in the new space of postmodernism. We are submerged in its henceforth filled and suffused volumes to the point where our now postmodern bodies are bereft of spatial coordinates and practically (let alone theoretically) incapable of distantiation; .... political interventions ... are all somehow secretly disarmed and reabsorbed by a system of which they themselves might well be considered a part, since they can achieve no distance from it.[40]

The abolition of distance is manifest in Foucault's demolition of the critical viewpoint beyond power and in his scepticism about the possibility of identifying the loci of power. However, from Foucault's perspective this identification of power – with the ruling class, the coloniser or men – is based on a crude simplification of the way in which power works. It plays into the hands of the very power structure it attempts to subvert as it fails to develop apt strategies to resist the minute and subtle operations of power in modern

---

[38] Foucault 1990, 93,94.
[39] Foucault's theory makes a claim for a differentiated analysis of power structures, but refrains from giving concrete guidelines for political action. As he asserted in several interviews: "My books don't tell people what to do". Foucault 1988a, 15. "The role of an intellectual is not to tell others what they have to do." Foucault 1988d, 265. Foucault may be accused of providing a mere formalistic framework in which 'power' and 'resistance' remain semantically empty notions, which may be filled with any arbitrary content.
[40] Jameson 1991, 48,49. Jameson calls for a new "pedagogical political culture" which engages in an "aesthetic of cognitive mapping" to enable us to grasp our position as subjects in the global system of late capitalism and to endow these subjects with the "capacity to act and struggle which is at present neutralized by our spatial and social confusion." Jameson 1991, 54. See also Habermas in "The New Obscurity": "It is by no means only realism when a forthrightly accepted bewilderment increasingly takes the place of attempts at orientation directed toward the future. The situation may be objectively obscure. Obscurity is nonetheless also a function of a society's assessment of its own readiness to take action." Habermas 1991, 51.

society. How to resist a system without an adequate knowledge of the way in which this system works?

Another controversial point, which has been raised by Nancy Fraser and developed by Habermas, concerns the normative foundation of Foucault's critique. As mentioned above (cf. note 34), Foucault does not believe in a non-strategic use of language. He radically questions concepts like 'ethics' and 'truth' as compromised by power. If Foucault precludes questions of normative validity and claims to propositional truth, Habermas and Fraser argue, he cannot answer the question "why fight?".[41] If there are no values which legitimate political action, why oppose power at all? Why fight against the subjection of the body, if there is no body to be liberated? On the one hand, Foucault's rhetoric clearly displays a critical impulse; on the other hand, it rejects a transcendental standpoint of ethico-political judgement. Foucault's critical rhetoric lacks the normative foundations that any critique presupposes. Hence, Fraser accuses his theory of being "normatively confused".[42]

Critics point to Foucault's late work in response to the charge of "crypto-normativity".[43] In *The Use of Pleasure* Foucault introduces the question of ethics and conceives an aesthetic morality on the model of the Greeks. Among the Greeks the organisation of sexual practices was part of an "aesthetics of existence" which aimed at the transformation of the self in the search for a personal ethics.[44] However, as Eagleton argues, the conflation of ethics and aesthetics results in a mere formalistic account of morality in which the "style" and "intensity" of a practice, not the "mode of conduct", counts.[45] Though Foucault introduces the notion of the subject in his late writings, he does not deal with the question of the normative foundation of political resistance. *The Use of Pleasure* conceives an aesthetic ethics that

---

[41] Fraser 1989, 29 (originally published in *Praxis International*, Vol. 1, 1981, 283). Habermas 1985, 333.

[42] Fraser 1989, 17 ff..

[43] Osborne 1999, 45-58. Bennett 1999, 171-185.

[44] Foucault defines the "arts of existence" as "intentional and voluntary actions by which men not only set themselves rules of conduct, but also seek to transform themselves, to change themselves in their singular being, and to make their life into an oeuvre that carries certain aesthetic values and meets certain stylistic criteria". "Personal ethics" means an aesthetic stylisation of life, the elaboration of one's life as a work of art. A central element in this ethics is the exertion of self-governance. In the late Foucault power thus appears in a positive sense as self-discipline which the individual exerts as conscious choice. Foucault 1985, 10,11,22.

[45] Eagleton 1990, 393,394. "What would a stylish rape look like, precisely?" Eagleton provocatively asks.

does not aim at changing the world but at transforming the self in the creation of a *personal* ethics. In fact, in "The Minimalist Self" Foucault gives a rather pessimistic, personal view on the possibility of "changing the world": "... if I refer to my own personal experience I have the feeling knowledge can't do anything for us and that political power may destroy us. All the knowledge in the world can't do anything against that ....".[46] In this context one may again pose the question: "why fight?"

No doubt Foucault's work is driven by a critical impetus. *The History of Sexuality* searches for strategies to "counter the grips of power" that "subject us to that austere monarchy of sex".[47] But there is also a deep strain of political defeatism running through Foucault's texts that calls the possibility of liberation into question. Carter's work displays a similar ambivalence. Critics have read Carter's work either as politically defeatist or as liberatory.[48] Her fiction walks the tightrope between a radical critique of subjectivity and the feminist politics of emancipation. I will argue that Carter's writing expresses a deep distrust towards utopia in Foucault's sense, but is nevertheless driven by an ethical impulse which is committed to the ideal of equality.

3.2.2 Power, Sexuality and the Materiality of the Body

Foucault has been accused of a 'discursive monism' that eliminates the materiality of the body and turns it into a text. Shilling classifies Foucault as a social constructivist: "The body vanishes as a biological entity and becomes infinitely malleable and highly unstable."[49] Foucault anticipates this criticism in *The History of Sexuality* and counters it with the following arguments:

> ... the purpose of the present study is in fact to show how deployments of power are directly connected to the body – to bodies, functions, physiological processes, sensations, and pleasures; far from the body having to be effaced, what is needed is to make it visible through an analysis in which the biological and the historical are not consecutive to one another, as in the evolutionism of the first sociologists, but are bound

---

[46] Instead, Foucault claims to believe in the "transformation of one's self by one's knowledge": "... if I know the truth I will be changed." See Foucault 1988a, 14. Eagleton criticises the focus on the individual in *The Use of Pleasure*. While he attacks the "monadic individualism" in *The Use of Pleasure*, Eagleton himself seems to cling to individualistic concepts when he misses notions of inwardness (emotional intimacy, affection ...) in Foucault's conception of the subject. See Eagleton 1990, 395.

[47] Foucault 1990, 157,159.

[48] See VI.2.5.2.

[49] Shilling 1993, 74.

together in an increasingly complex fashion in accordance with the development of the modern technologies of power that take life as their objective. Hence I do not envisage a "history of mentalities" ... but a "history of bodies" and the manner in which what is most material and vital in them has been invested.[50]

If Foucault does away with the "innocent body" as the site of subversion, this does not necessarily mean that he denies the materiality of this body. In fact, he claims this materiality to be at the very centre of his analysis. The materiality of the body is an effect of the intermingling of the biological and the cultural. The 'natural body' is intricately intertwined with the "technologies of power" that produce this body. While Foucault's genealogy does not deny the existence of a 'natural' body, it does not attempt to extricate this natural body from the technologies of power. Genealogy is not concerned with ontological questions, nor with epistemological ones. Instead of recovering the "truth" about the body, which is "hidden" beneath the layers of a repressive civilisation,[51] it examines how what we perceive as 'natural body' has been historically constituted. Shilling's criticism concerning the malleability of the body seems to simplify Foucault's argument. In fact, a completely unstable, "infinitely malleable" body could never be effectively organised and controlled by society over time. Shilling ignores the "primacy of resistance" in Foucault's concept of power: any force needs a counter-force to produce an effect. The disciplinary society could not exist without the body's resistance. Power and resistance are involved in a perpetual struggle in Foucault's model of power.

Interestingly, whereas Shilling labels Foucault as a social constructivist, other critics accuse him of a hidden essentialism. As Judith Butler states, "at times it appears that for Foucault the body has a materiality that is ontologically distinct from the power relations that take that body as a site of investment"[52]. These very different interpretations of Foucault's position on the body reflect ambiguities in his writings. Foucault seems to adopt the social constructivist point of view when he describes the body as

---

[50] Foucault 1990, 151,152.

[51] In this sense Foucault describes genealogy as dealing not with "depth" (signification behind appearances) but with the "surface" of things. See Foucault, *Nietzsche, Genealogy, History*, 1984.

[52] Butler 1993, 33. In *Gender Trouble* Butler criticises Foucault's idealisation of the hermaphrodite in his introduction to *Herculine Barbin*, particularly his concept of the "natural heterogeneity", of the "happy limbo of non-identity" that the hermaphrodite enjoys before s/he is made subject to legal and medical examinations. She also mentions Foucault's notion of the "bucolic pleasures" in *The History of Sexuality* (Foucault 1990, 31) that draws an idealised image of sexuality before judicial action and medical intervention encroach upon these "pleasures". Butler 1990, 93 ff..

... the inscribed surface of events (traced by language and dissolved by ideas), the locus of a dissociated self (adopting the illusion of a substantial unity), and a volume in perpetual disintegration.[53]

Especially in his earlier work (as *The Order of Things*) the body seems to vanish behind the field of discourse. In his late work Foucault's notion of the body is still radically different from essentialist concepts of corporeality. The notion of sexuality as a product of power starkly contrasts with the body politics of the existentialist Marxists of the sixties (Marcuse, Brown etc.), who tried to liberate the body through taking recourse to the Freudian notion of the "polymorphous perverse drives" (cf. III.2.1). However, Foucault does not seem to be able to do without the concept of the 'polymorphous perverse' body. At the end of *The History of Sexuality* he calls for resistance in a very Marcusian form: "The rallying point for the counterattack against the deployment of sexuality ought not to be sex-desire, but bodies and pleasure."[54] Is what we traditionally call "sex" simply replaced by another name ("bodies and pleasure")? Turner perceives a yearning for the "untrammelled, uncivilised, prediscursive body" in Foucault's writings: "The nostalgia in Foucault's philosophy was the search for the Sexual Body before the social contract."[55] There are indeed passages which support Turner's claim, but there are plenty of others which reveal the search for the pre-social body to be the main target of Foucault's criticism.

Hence, Foucault has been accused of both a "social constructivism" and a "hidden idealism and essentialism". Both critiques find some legitimisation in his work. In a paradoxical way Foucault's concept of power oscillates between materialism, idealism and a poststructuralist constructivism. Still, calling Foucault either a materialist or a constructivist misses crucial elements in his conception of power. The difficulty of labelling Foucault – as structuralist, poststructuralist or materialist[56] – is reflected in the difficulty of pinning him down to a clear position on the body.

Angela Carter's concept of the body in many ways reflects Foucault's approach. As a feminist socialist, Carter focuses on the material conditions of oppression, on the female body as the site of subjection and resistance in a

---

[53] Foucault 1984, 83.
[54] Foucault 1990, 157.
[55] Turner 1992, 54.
[56] Dreyfus/Rabinow see elements of structuralism in Foucault's early work, as well as some poststructuralist affinities. However, like Deleuze they stress that Foucault's work cannot be contained by any of these labels. Bordo considers Foucault as both modern and postmodern, as poststructuralist and descendant of Marx. Megill, in contrast, points to the crucial differences between Marx's historical materialism and Foucault's genealogies. See Dreyfus, Rabinow 1987, 11-24; Megill 1985, 249; Bordo 1993, 38.

patriarchal capitalist society. At the same time, bodies in Carter's novels are highly unstable: bodies melt, fly, explode out of their proper dimension and are magically transformed. Carter's novels oscillate between a materialist analysis of gender and a poststructuralist questioning of bodily boundaries. Yet whereas Foucault's theory tends to ignore the specifically gendered body, Carter focuses on the production of femininity and the disciplining of the female body. Carter's concept of the female body as a cultural construct and her focus on the subversive politics of parody associate her with Judith Butler's theory of gender parody. The following section delineates Butler's approach to the body that draws heavily on Foucault but highlights gender in the analysis of sexuality and the body.

4. Judith Butler: the Body in *Gender Trouble* and *Bodies that Matter*
4.1. Deconstructing the Body

In *Gender Trouble* Judith Butler refers to Foucault's model of power in her deconstruction of the sex-gender dichotomy. According to Butler, the Cartesian mind-body dualism has produced a 'metaphysics of substance' as the dominant concept in Western philosophy. This metaphysics posits the existence of matter prior to signification, of a passive amorphous body which precedes culture and is given meaning and shape through the 'spirit'. Originally conceived by feminists to dispute biological determinism, the sex-gender dichotomy reproduces this concept when it postulates 'sex' as the material origin and basis of 'gender'. Biological sex precedes the cultural concept of gender. Sex and gender correspond to each other: the duality of gender mirrors the duality of sex (male/female). Gender is the cultural inscription of meaning on a given sex. Butler inverts this relationship when she turns sex into an effect of gender: sex is not a natural entity but a product of the cultural conception of gender. Butler's inversion of sex and gender resembles Foucault's inversion of 'sex' and the discursive formation of 'sexuality'.[57] The duality of sex is revealed to be a cultural construction:

... one way the internal stability and binary frame for sex is effectively secured is by casting the duality of sex in a predicursive domain. This production of sex as predicursive ought to be understood as the effect of the apparatus of cultural construction designated by gender.[58]

---

[57] See above II.3.1, note 26.
[58] Butler 1990, 7. Butler further suggests that once we question the predicursive duality of sex, there might as well be a plurality of gender types.

Butler inverts the metaphysics of substance by turning matter into a construction. The notion of sex as the fixed biological basis of gender naturalises and legitimises gender hierarchy. The binary structure of sex is produced by the "heterosexual matrix of desire" – a concept which resembles Monique Wittig's and Adrienne Rich's notion of compulsory heterosexuality. The heterosexual matrix of desire represents a 'norm' which constructs asymmetrical oppositions between the 'feminine' and the 'masculine'. It produces "intelligible identities" by establishing coherence between sex, gender and desire: I have a female body (sex), hence I have a female identity (gender) and desire a man. Intelligible identities are produced through repeated bodily acts which imitate this normative ideal. As in the sociological concept of 'doing gender',[59] gender is not defined as something we 'have' or 'are' but as something we create in our daily interactions: identity is practice. Butler's notion of 'gender as performance' is reminiscent of Goffman's performative theory of identity. Yet whereas Goffman presupposes a self behind the mask, in *Gender Trouble* the performance seems to swallow up the self and its identity. In fact, Butler's deconstruction of the sex-gender dichotomy is part of a wider criticism of the humanist notion of the subject. The humanist notion of the self posits a pre-discursive stable subject which carries different attributes such as 'gender', 'race' and 'class'. The deconstructive approach criticises the notion of the 'juridical subject' which precedes its attributes. In Butler's theory the subject is an effect of its attributes. Gender is not a feature of a pre-existent coherent subject; gender creates and stabilises the subject. It has no material quality, but is constituted through acts which reproduce the heterosexual matrix of desire. Strictly speaking, gender is not an attribute but a process, an activity. In Butler's theory matter evaporates. The subject is dissolved into its attributes which themselves turn into processes and practices.

Butler calls for stirring up gender trouble through incorrectly repeating the "regulatory ideal". Like Foucault, she advocates subversion from within the system. The parodistic repetition of 'intelligible gender identities' exposes the artificiality of gender: "In imitating gender, drag implicitly reveals the imitative structure of gender itself – as well as its contingency."[60] 'Queer politics' puts Butler's theory of gender parody into practice.[61] Primarily practised in the gay scene, it celebrates the performance of transgressive gender identities, such as transvestites, drag and butch/femme identities. Queer politics produces 'gender trouble' by undermining any categorisation

---

[59] West, Zimmermann 1987, 125 ff..
[60] Butler 1990, 137.
[61] For an introduction to 'queer politics' see Hark 1993.

24

of sexuality (female/male, heterosexual/homosexual etc.). It attempts to achieve this in two ways: through 'incorrectly' imitating the norm 'queer politics' reveals the contingency of the norm; as any representation has a performative effect, the incorrect imitation of the regulatory ideal slightly modifies the norm. Through confounding the binarism of sex, 'queer politics' aims to open up more variable cultural configurations of sex and gender.

Butler's theory represents a critical response to French feminist notions of the body. French poststructuralism celebrates the irreducible difference of the female body. Whereas for Butler the female body constitutes the surface of patriarchal inscription, for Irigaray it is a source of authentic female experience. Similarly, Kristeva invests the maternal body with revolutionary potential.[62] Butler, by contrast, turns against the essentialisation and mystification of the female body in theories which idealise maternity and 'female essence' as sources of power.

Angela Carter takes a similar position in most of her writings. In particular, The Passion of New Eve attacks essentialising and mythicising notions of the feminine in gynocentric feminist theories of the seventies as formulated by Hélène Cixous, Mary Daly and Susan Griffin (cf. IV.1.4). Populated by transsexuals, butches and transvestites, Carter's work is ahead of its time in its production of 'gender trouble'. But not only does Carter's fiction pre-empt Butler's notion of 'gender trouble'. Its representation of drag is highly ambivalent. Carter's fiction also suggests a critique of the blind spots of 'gender trouble', which are discussed in the following section.[63]

4.2. Against Disembodiment: Towards a Critique of Butler

Gender Trouble has been criticised on various grounds. The poststructuralist conception of the subject, the vague, ahistorical notion of

---

[62] Kristeva 1980, 133 ff.; Irigaray 1985b, 23 ff..

[63] Müller 1997, Magrs 1997 and Palmer 1997 link Carter's concept of identity to Butler's notion of the performative subject. While Müller and Magrs view the performativity of identity in Butler and Carter as a liberating concept, Palmer criticises Carter (and Butler) for ignoring the limits of 'gender as performance'. Hanson, by contrast, dissociates Carter from Butler's liberating view of performativity. She reads Carter's fiction in a pessimistic way as foreclosing the possibility of social change. See Hanson 1997, 67. I will argue that Carter draws attention to both the subversive potential and the blind spots in the notion of 'gender as performance'. Carter's Marcusian materialism undercuts a utopian vision of gender fluidity in Butler's vein. However, in contrast to Hanson's deterministic reading of Carter, I will contend that Carter's fiction is committed to social change and the ideal of equality. Cf. IV.2.1.2; V.7; VI.2.5.2.

power, the idealisation of sexual minorities and the dissolution of matter are the major points of criticism which I will recapitulate below. On the basis of her latest book *Bodies that Matter*, I will try to reformulate Butler's theory in a way that leaves the materiality of the body intact.

Like Foucault, Butler has been criticised for eliminating the subject as the site of resistance.[64] Butler discards the subject 'woman' as she considers this subject to be the product of the power relations feminism tries to subvert.[65] Pointing to ethnocentric tendencies in feminism, she argues that the category 'woman' in many cases ignores differences in class, race and sexual orientation.[66] The poststructuralist dismissal of the subject, however, seems to be problematic, as it silences those who have only just started to claim subject status, such as the postcolonial subject. As bell hooks puts it:

> Should we not be suspicious of postmodern critiques of the "subject" when they surface at a historical moment when many subjugated people feel themselves coming to voice for the first time?[67]

A politics which dismisses the category 'woman' is strictly speaking not feminist and does not legitimise political measures like 'affirmative action'. It might be argued against Butler that both scepticism towards essentialism and the strategic identification with other women are indispensable for political efficacy in feminism. Spivak's concept of strategic essentialism employs the category of the subject as a strategic, provisional means in the political struggle for equality while remaining conscious of the pitfalls of an essentialist identity politics.[68] In my view 'strategic essentialism' represents a more valid alternative for a feminist politics than the radical dismissal of the subject 'woman' in *Gender Trouble*.

Like Foucault's notion of power, the "heterosexual matrix of desire" is a rather vague concept. How is this "matrix" constituted? Who constitutes it? Again there seems to be no 'doer behind the deed'. However, there is a crucial difference between Butler's and Foucault's theories: whereas Foucault

---

[64] See Nussbaum 1999, 11-12. Nussbaum critically comments on Butler's claim that there is no agent prior to the social forces that produce the self: "Where does this ability [to undertake resistance] come from, if there is no structure in the personality that is not thoroughly power's creation?"

[65] In *The Daughter's Seduction: Feminism and Psychoanalysis* Jane Gallop pursues a similar argument: "For if patriarchal culture is that within which the self originally constitutes itself, it is always already there in each subject as subject." Gallop 1982, 14.

[66] In this sense Wittig provocatively claims that "lesbians are not women" as 'woman' has meaning only in "heterosexual systems of thought". Wittig 1980, 110.

[67] hooks 1990, 28.

[68] Spivak 1996, 214.

historicises the body, Butler's highly abstract and theoretical texts ignore the body's material locatedness in history, practice and culture.[69] Butler's 'body' floats in empty space, strangely dissociated from its historical and institutional contexts. The heterosexual matrix of desire appears as a mystical origin of oppression which is not put into a specific historical context. In its ahistoricity Butler's critique seems to be closer to Derridean deconstruction than to Foucault's genealogical method.

Moreover, Butler's subversive concept of parody relies on an idealised image of sexual minorities. *Gender Trouble* ignores conservative moments in drag performances. Drag shows and cross-dressing may work as safety-valves in the service of a dominant ideology: the dominant culture defuses the disruptive potential of "incoherent identities" by restricting them to specifically demarcated spaces (lesbian/gay festivals etc.). The commercialisation of marginal sexualities puts transgressive sexualities into the service of a system which is dependent on the continuous production of 'shocking' novelties and spectacles. Gay pride has thus become a particularly popular theme in advertising. Naomi Klein traces the way in which companies have adapted their marketing strategies to the postmodern plea for the acknowledgement of sexual and racial diversity. The call for minority representation in the political correctness debate of the eighties has swiftly been accommodated by multi-national corporations, making for "great brand-content and niche-marketing strategies".[70] The blurring of gender boundaries in particular has turned into a popular advertising motif and opened up a new market for products that target both men and women.

> And everyone, it seemed, was toying with the fluidity of gender, from the old-hat story of MAC makeup using drag queen RuPaul as its spokesmodel to tequila ads that inform viewers that the she in the bikini is really a he; from Calvin Klein's colognes that tell us that gender itself is a construct to Sure Ultra Dry deodorant that in turn urges all the gender benders to chill out: "Man? Woman? Does it matter?"[71]

Gender Trouble fails to take account of the recuperative capacity of capitalism, which integrates the subversive and puts it into the service of consumer capitalism. The ambiguously gendered body and transgressive sexualities also seem to be one of the most popular topics in the media, in talk

---

[69] Nussbaum criticises the lack of reference to the "real situation of real women" and the "little room" that the symbolic politics of parody leave for large-scale social change. Nussbaum 1999, 3.
[70] Klein 2000, 112. Klein gives several examples for the "P.C. marketing craze": Diesel commercials depicting two male sailors kissing each other; a television spot by Virgin Cola displaying a gay wedding; racial diversity emerging as a favourite motif in commercials by Benetton and Gap, Michael Jordan featuring in *Nike* adverts etc.. Ibid., 111 ff..
[71] Ibid., 113.

shows and magazines. Our gaping at the 'weirdos', at the other, represents not just a contestation of the norm but also a fascination with spectacle and the 'monstrous', against which we define ourselves. In these contexts the display of gender ambiguity may work to affirm the duality of gender. Claudia Preschl analyses male cross-dressing in the movies and arrives at the conclusion that in most movies (*Some like it hot* represents the classical example) the motif does not question but stabilises the heterosexual structure of gender hierarchy. After a temporary confusion of gender categories, 'true masculinity' is reaffirmed and re-established at the end.[72] To give another example, ethnomethodological studies of transsexuality interpret the stereotypical imitation of gender norms by transsexuals not as a subversive repetition but as a conservative assimilation to the duality of gender. Many transsexuals are eager to describe their anatomy as a 'mistake', which has to be corrected through surgery in order to restore the coherence between sex, gender and desire.[73] Nevertheless, this does not mean that the transgression of gender boundaries may not also have a disruptive potential. In Angela Carter's novels transgressive identities undermine the stability and fixity of gender categorisation. But Carter's fiction also demonstrates that transgressive bodies may be appropriated by the dominant culture and turned into spectacles. Butler's concept has to be contextualised to comprise the different functions that the display of incoherent gender identities can have.

The major point of criticism that has been levelled against Butler's theory concerns the dissolution of the body in a radical constructivist approach. From a phenomenological perspective, Gesa Lindemann points to the absence of a subjectively experienced corporeality in Butler.[74] Duden criticises the concept of the "disembodied woman".[75] According to Lorey, it is problematic that Butler defines the body as a mere effect of a cultural practice of signification: Butler's analysis of drag as parody textualises the body.[76] Considering the central role of the body in the women's movement of the seventies, the dissolution of corporeality seems particularly problematic. Does Butler follow a 'masculine' philosophical tradition, the Cartesian fantasy of the transcendence of materiality and historicity?

Butler herself rejects this criticism. In *Bodies that Matter* she dissociates herself from a radical constructivism:

---

[72] Preschl 1995, 139 ff..
[73] Garfinkel 1967, 128 ff..
[74] Lindemann 1993, 44 ff..
[75] Duden 1993, 31.
[76] Lorey 1993, 16.

The debate between constructivism and essentialism thus misses the point of deconstruction altogether, for the point has never been that "everything is discursively constructed"; that point ... belongs to a kind of ... linguisticism that refuses the constitutive force of exclusion, erasure, violent foreclosure, abjection and its disruptive return within the very terms of discursive legitimacy.[77]

Butler argues that bodies are formed through excluding the abject, the 'other' that does not qualify as "bodies that matter".[78] This exclusion produces materiality which is not an illusion but real – the locus of pain, pleasure and desire. However, the constitutive force of exclusion is not absolute and allows for the "disruptive return of the abject". In this sense Butler's theory is not deterministic; as in Foucault, there is no power without resistance. In *Bodies that Matter* Butler claims that the notion of materiality as an effect of power does not necessarily dissolve this materiality.

What I would propose ... is a return to the notion of matter, not a site or a surface, but a process of materialization that stabilizes over time to produce the effect of boundary, fixity, and surface we call matter.[79]

Materiality is not an origin but an effect which is caught in the act of becoming. *Gender Trouble* employs a rhetoric which likens the body to a fictional, illusory entity.[80] However, on the basis of *Bodies that Matter*, Butler's theory can be reformulated in a way that leaves the body's materiality intact:

Butler calls for a political genealogy and a deconstruction of gender ontology. A *genealogy* of gender ontology inquires into the constitution of the body's boundaries and examines the border that has historically been drawn between the mind and the body, nature and culture. It traces the norms which produce the female and the male subject and analyses the historical process by which normative subjects are formed and "abject beings" excluded.[81] It

---

[77] Butler 1993, 8.
[78] The 'abject' represents the undefinable and transgressive that has been repressed in the formation of an 'intelligible identity'. For Kristeva's definition of abjection see II.6.
[79] Butler 1993, 9.
[80] This is criticised by Hirschauer as Butler's "Irrealisierungsrhetorik" (Hirschauer 1993a, 58). Even though Butler claims that the notion of gender as construction does not imply the illusoriness or artificiality of gender (Butler 1990, 32), her formulations in *Gender Trouble* are frequently ambiguous (the body as "fiction", "copy without an original" etc.).
[81] Butler provides the theoretical framework for a genealogy of gender ontology, but not the genealogical investigation itself. Her text does not examine the historically specific formation of the body in its cultural and social context. *Making Sex* by Thomas Laqueur, in contrast, presents a historicising genealogy of gender difference. Laqueur claims that the notion of sexual difference (the 'two-sex-model') emerges in the eighteenth century as a consequence of complex epistemological, political and social transformations in the

does not claim to be able to distinguish between the natural and the cultural; neither does it state that "everything is discursively constructed". Likewise, a *deconstruction* of gender ontology does not necessarily subsume the body within discourse. A deconstruction of bodily boundaries does not eliminate the border which separates the body from discourse, the ontological from the constructed. It rather shifts this border, plays with it and makes it permeable, allowing for an exchange between abject and normative subjects. In this sense the monstrous body with unstable boundaries represents the ideal of deconstruction. It is opposed to the closed 'fascist' body, which will be analysed below (cf. II.6).

Butler's body politics oscillate between monstrosity and disembodiment as metaphors for the potential chances and dangers inherent in the deconstruction of gender. Disembodiment and monstrosity are central motifs in Carter's fiction. *The Passion of New Eve* deconstructs the gendered body in Butler's sense. Carter has been criticised for dissolving the body and turning sexuality into a text in her novels of the seventies. In her late fiction, though, the excessively physical heroines resist disembodiment and take pleasure from their 'monstrous' corporeality.

Both Foucault and Butler contend that the body is a product of normalising power structures. They do not relate these power structures to the specific economic and cultural context of a society.[82] In what follows, I wish to look at the role of the body in late capitalist culture. This seems particularly relevant as Carter conjoins a Foucauldian perspective with a Marxist critique of commodification in her late work.[83] Referring to Foucault and a (neo)Marxist cultural critique, the following section examines modern consumer society's obsession with the body. Late capitalism both celebrates and represses corporeality and engages in the production of the 'useful' and 'disciplined subject' in Foucault's sense.

Enlightenment. It replaces the 'one-sex-model' that describes woman as a biologically 'inverted' man. See Laqueur 1990, 149 ff..

[82] Foucault mentions specific discursive practices (like the confession) and institutions (like the prison) but does not refer to the economic and cultural context of a society as a whole at a specific historical moment. In fact, he would probably reject an analysis of the body in 'late capitalism' for presupposing a Marxist orientation.

[83] As I will argue in Chapter Five, *Nights at the Circus* connects Foucault's critique of panopticism with a Marxist analysis of commodification (cf. V.4.1).

5. The Body in the Age of Late Capitalism
5.1 Repression and the Cult of the Body in Consumer Culture

The cult of the body is a prominent feature of advanced industrial societies in the West. (Post)modern consumer culture extols the body. The ever-increasing enticements to material enjoyments are characteristic for culture in the stage of 'late capitalism', facing an excess of production on a saturated market. In advertising, the media and the movies the body is omnipresent. Images of the beautiful body celebrate the hedonistic enjoyment of life. After the demise of traditional meaning systems and social structures (religion, the family etc.), the body has become a central reference point in the construction of identity. In particular the adoption of a certain 'lifestyle' represents a crucial element in the creation of the self. Individuals subject themselves to certain "body regimes" as part of their lifestyles:

> The self is no longer seen as a homogeneous, stable core which resides within the individual .... Instead, identities are formed reflexively through the asking of questions and the continual reordering of self-narratives which have at their center a concern with the body.[84]

Just as the self is constructed around a lifestyle, bodies are considered to be malleable. Capitalism fashions the image of the plastic body. As the significance of appearance is tantamount in capitalist consumer society, individuals adopt body maintenance techniques – such as dieting, exercise, cosmetics – to create a more marketable self.

The cult of the body is thus accompanied by a pervasive tendency to discipline the body. Goffman traces the way in which the maintenance of social identity is dependent on controlled face and body work in contemporary society. Failure to keep regularised control of the body in interaction results in embarrassment and poses a threat to social- and self-identity as it questions the person's competent membership in society.[85] Susan Bordo notes contemporary culture's obsession with dieting and hygiene, the spreading of eating disorders such as *anorexia nervosa* and scientific attempts to defy ageing.[86] The slender female body in advertising works as an enticement to bodily pleasure and consumption. Yet, at the same time, the slender body symbolises mastery, the body in control that resists excess. Baudrillard calls dieting, jogging and body-building new forms of "voluntary servitude". Religious practices such as asceticism and fasting have found their

---

[84] Shilling 1993, 181; cf. Giddens 1991.
[85] Goffman 1963, 27,33 ff..
[86] Bordo 1993, 4,5,39. On eating disorders in literature see also Olson 2003.

way into secularised consumer culture in the service of bio-power, aiming at a maximisation of life forces.

> This omnipresent cult of the body is extraordinary. It is the only object on which everyone is made to concentrate, not as a source of pleasure, but as an object of frantic concern, in the obsessive fear of failure or substandard performance, a sign and an anticipation of death, that death to which no one can any longer give a meaning, but which everyone knows has at all times to be prevented.[87]

The desire for the firm, contained body bespeaks a frantic fear of ageing and death. It is the desire for the eternally youthful body which Christopher Lasch identifies as a component of the narcissistic personality.[88] In an era of increasing rationalisation, death disrupts the master narrative of control and scientific progress. In death the body triumphs over the mind, revealing the inevitable failure of attempts to transcend the body and master the flesh. Corporeality denotes mortality. Thus, we wage war on the ageing body through dieting and sports, surgery and cosmetics. The negation of death in Western culture calls forth the repression and disciplining of corporeality.[89]

Adorno and Horkheimer consider the subjugation of nature and the body as a corollary of the rule of instrumental reason in capitalist culture.[90] Referring to Max Weber, twentieth-century Marxist thinkers claim that the accumulation of capital requires the suppression of libidinal drives in the service of production. In the sixties Freudianism and Marxism thus joined forces in the sexual liberation, aiming at the liberation of the body and the revolution of social structures. However, any attempt to derive the disciplining of the body solely from the rise of capitalism seems questionable. As Norbert Elias points out, the repression of the body predates capitalism. Elias traces the development of the "civilised body" – the body which exhibits a high degree of affective control – back to Renaissance court society. Body management and etiquette had a crucial function in the struggle for status in court aristocracy.[91] Foucault as well criticises the 'repressive hypothesis' of the sixties for exaggerating the role repression plays as a form of social control. Power operates at an 'earlier' stage in the very formation of the body that critical theorists try to liberate. Pleasure and power do not

---

[87] Baudrillard 1988, 35.

[88] Lasch 1978, 207 ff..

[89] Death is a taboo in many – if not all – cultures, not just in advanced industrial societies. Yet this taboo is particularly strong in contemporary Western societies, as Ariès has shown in his cultural history of death. Death has been increasingly removed from the public and the private realm and transferred into 'special institutions' (such as the hospital) in modern industrialised societies. See Ariès 1977, 554 ff., 564 ff..

[90] Horkheimer, Adorno 1997, 9 ff..

[91] Elias 1969 I, 89 ff., Elias 1969 II, 369 ff..

cancel each other out as desire is itself an effect of power (cf. III.2). Whereas Foucault stresses the productive mechanisms of power that came to seize the body in modernity, critical theory foregrounds its repressive function.[92]

In modern culture both the repressive and the productive element of power seem to be coexistent. Consumer capitalism is governed by a double-bind situation in which we simultaneously function as producers who have to delay the gratification of desire in the accumulation of capital (the Weberian work ethic), and as consumers who ideally serve the system through indulging in as many pleasures as possible. The contradictory structure of economic life in late capitalism at the same time stimulates and represses bodily pleasures, creating a schizophrenic situation in which the self is torn between two incompatible demands. Thus, body maintenance techniques (slimming, exercise etc.) are a prerequisite for the hedonistic enjoyment of the body:

> Today, it can be ventured, diet and body maintenance are increasingly regarded as vehicles to release the temptations of the flesh. Discipline and hedonism are no longer seen as incompatible, indeed the subjugation of the body through body maintenance routines is presented within consumer culture as a precondition for the achievement of an acceptable appearance and the release of the body's expressive capacity.[93]

Discipline and hedonism both characterise the self's relationship to his/her body. Susan Bordo analyses bulimia as a "characteristic modern personality construction", expressing hunger for unrestrained consumption alongside with the requirement to get back in control and discipline the body (the bulimic's vomiting).[94] The contradictions which fascinate Baudrillard in *America* – the obsession with jogging, dieting, eating and starving (*anorexia*) – reflect these contradictory structures at work in advanced industrial capitalism.[95] It is, in fact, America which *The Passion of New Eve* depicts as the epitome of a late capitalist consumer culture in decline. The novel describes the disintegration of a repressive culture which worships consumption: "Welcome to the country where Mouth is King, the land of comestibles!" (PNE 10).

---

[92] As mentioned above, Foucault does not deny the repressive mechanism that critical theorists see at work in modern society; he incorporates it as *one* element among others in his model of the multiple strategies of power.

[93] Featherstone 1982, 18.

[94] Bordo 1993, 201.

[95] *The Passion of New Eve* is in many ways reminiscent of Baudrillard's *America*. The narrator's voice in the novel seems to echo Baudrillard's travel report, which displays a fascination with America as a postmodern, hyperreal culture. This fascination, however, is ironically undercut in the novel.

5.2 Bodies on Display: the Commodification of the Body

Bodies are increasingly made 'visible' in the twentieth century. In the 1920s the liberation from Victorian constraints on sexuality turned the body into a new market in early consumer culture. The shame about nakedness gives way to the exposure of the body in sunbathing, sports and advertising as well as in a new style of fashion which makes the form of the body visible.[96] The outdoor Californian lifestyle and 'beach culture' emerge in the twenties as an effect of the changing perceptions of the body in early consumer culture.[97] The advent of mass consumption along with new technological developments such as the invention of the motion pictures form the basis of our visually oriented culture, of the dissemination of images of the beautiful body in the movies, television and advertising. Torn out of the protecting darkness of privacy, the body is scrutinised by the public gaze. The omnipresence of the fit, healthy and slender body in advertising establishes a norm against which individuals judge themselves, constantly monitoring themselves for deviations from this norm. The media and capitalist consumer culture thus further develop what Foucault called "panopticism": the subject which is constantly under surveillance internalises the gaze and acts himself/herself as an agent of normalisation. The notion of a malleable self and the dominance of visual images create a culture of panopticism in which individuals constantly attempt to assimilate the self to the normative image.

In particular the female body is increasingly put on display and subjected to the rigorous standards of the body ideal in the twentieth century. The mechanical means of reproduction produce a proliferation of images of the female body. In the media, advertising and pornography female bodies are turned into objects of the gaze. *The Infernal Desire Machines* and *Nights at the Circus* allude to the new scientific-technological formation that subjects the female body to the gaze at the turn of the last century. *The Passion of New Eve* depicts the production of femininity as a marketable commodity in Hollywood in the twentieth century. *Nights at the Circus* and *Wise Children* stage resistance to the process of visualisation and normalisation that controls the female subject in modern society.

---

[96] Featherstone 1982, 22.
[97] See also Fussell on nudism, the sun cult, and the Mediterranean craze in the 1920s. Fussell 1980, 137 ff..

Visualisation and normalisation also define progress in the medical sciences.[98] Ultrasounds, foetal monitors and fetoscopy represent new techniques of medical examination that open a 'window' on the womb.[99] Reproductive technologies represent a new type of body management which maximises life by rendering women's bodies more useful. At the same time, artificial reproduction creates a new market which turns the embryo into a consumer good and the female womb into a service that may be rented by those who can afford it. Eco-feminists criticise the commercialisation of the female womb in surrogate motherhood.[100] Similarly, critical voices fear the exploitation and commodification of the human body when new laws on the transplantation of organs are discussed on an international level.[101]

Hence, advanced capitalism displays a highly ambivalent attitude towards the body. Capitalism extols corporeality: it incites discourses on the body, turns it into a spectacle and commodifies it. The body is constitutive of the self. At the same time, late capitalist culture disciplines the body. The tightening of the bodily boundaries in the beauty ideal and the scientific visualisation of the body represent attempts to master the flesh. The scientific project to decipher the genetic code literally turns the body into a text. Disembodiment – the conquest of nature and the transcendence of the flesh – reaches its climax in the age of genetic engineering, cyber space and poststructuralism: matter melts in the sciences as well as in poststructuralist theory. This melting of matter represents a liberation from the confines of biological determinism (as Butler would argue). Yet at the same time, it relentlessly turns lived corporeality into an object, which is in turn dissolved. Resisting representation and control, death and pain foil these attempt to take control of the flesh. The body's decay disrupts the belief in the possibility of transcending corporeality. Our extremely body-oriented culture is based on the suppression of the body's mortality.

Angela Carter deals with this suppression when she places the abject – the decaying and the monstrous body – at the centre of her novels. In what follows, I will analyse the violence which is at work in the negation of the abject, of death and in the creation of the tightly controlled body.

---

[98] Barbara Duden describes the transition from 'feeling' and 'touch' ("haptische hexis") to 'visualisation' ("optische hexis") as one of the major paradigm shifts in the modern experience of the body. See Duden 1991, 67.

[99] Overall 1987, 44; Sawicki 1991, 84.

[100] See Sawicki 1991, 72; Overall 1987, 113,116 ff.; Raymond 1998.

[101] Treusch-Dieter 1994, 27.

6. Bodily Boundaries and Monstrosity

The young, muscular body in vogue in contemporary culture is the normalised and disciplined body, the body in control and under surveillance. The breakdown of this tightly controlled body is a major source of anxiety in modern society. Turner mentions the "ageing populations" and the "burden of dependency" in advanced industrial societies as well as the emergence of AIDS as sources of 'body panic'.[102] Body panic is the fear of the loss of firm (bodily) boundaries, of death and decay. Bodies have to be tight, contained, healthy and sterile. Barbie represents the ideal postmodern body that resists excess, decay and disease: Barbie is beautiful, hard, smooth and forever young.[103] The firm body keeps internal processes under control and prevents them from erupting through bodily margins. In psychoanalytic terms the fear of losing control expresses anxieties about regression and death: on the one hand, the uncontained body is the defecating and regressive body, which surrenders to infantile impulses and pollutes through its openness (the infant's body); on the other hand, the open, decaying body carries associations of death and old age (the corpse). The open body signifies the dissolution of identity: the womb and the cadaver – the threatening 'outside' that frames the self's existence – encroach upon the self. Klaus Theweleit examines anxieties connected with the dissolution of bodily borders, with bodily orifices and substances like dirt, excrement and blood. His psychoanalytical approach traces these fears back to toilet training, which produces a denial of excremental and other bodily processes and turns them from a source of pleasure into a site of fear and disgust. These early childhood experiences, Theweleit argues, inscribe a law of repression into the body which is reproduced in political repression.[104] Theweleit analyses the political rhetoric in fascist Germany which triggered anxieties about the dissolution of the masculine self by fluids associated with the female and the infantile body. The menace of the 'polluting fluids' was projected onto minority groups and political opponents, who threaten to disintegrate the body politic. The body is a metaphor for the social system, its health symbolised by clearly defined boundaries. Anthropologists and psychoanalytical critics have examined the

---

[102] Turner 1992, 11.
[103] Treusch-Dieter 1994, 25: "Barbie ... nimmt diese "ewige Jugend" vorweg. Sie ist schön, hart, glatt .... Barbie wird nicht von Bakterien zerfressen werden, denn ihre Oberfläche ist dicht. Sie wird nicht ausgeraubt werden, denn sie hat keine Organe. Sie wird nicht mißbraucht werden, denn sie hat keine Öffnung. Sie wird nichts verseuchen, denn sie scheidet nichts aus."
[104] Theweleit 1986, 528,532.

symbolic function of the body as a social system. Mary Douglas describes the role of bodily excreta, of purity and dirt in various cultural rituals:

> The body is a model which can stand for any bounded system. Its boundaries can represent any boundaries which are threatened or precarious .... We cannot possibly interpret rituals concerning excreta, breast milk, saliva and the rest unless we are prepared to see the body as a symbol of society, and to see the powers and dangers credited to social structure reproduced in small on the human body .... The rituals work upon the body politic through the symbolic medium of the body.[105]

With borders representing risks and dangers in social systems, fixed bodily boundaries have to be protected and reaffirmed in rituals involving bodily fluids and the body's orifices that represent major sites of pollution. Any kind of unregulated permeability endangers the stability of the social system. The 'polluting person' symbolically violates norms and taboos through transgression. Simon Watney analyses the way in which homosexuals are constructed as contagious, polluting persons in media representations of AIDS.[106] American right-wing discourses on AIDS have employed the image of the homosexual body that contaminates through its orifices.[107] The body with firm boundaries carries a political message: it is not only the controlled body of the producer-self but also the 'morally correct' body which produces no secretions, no viruses, and engages in safe, heterosexual sex. This rhetoric ignores the existence of the HIV-virus in white middle class heterosexuals in America and conflates the disease with minority groups (homosexuals, blacks, Hispanics). AIDS has thus triggered off a wave of conservatism in the USA that attributes the emergence of the virus to 'moral decadence', which is in turn displaced on minority groups.[108] Thus, the social construction of AIDS fuels the quest for firm bodily margins in a way that is reminiscent of the rhetorical construction of the fascist body that Theweleit describes in *Männerphantasien*.[109]

The 'uncontained' monstrous and transgressive body that violates norms and taboos represents the abject against which "bodies that matter" define themselves. Kristeva refers to Mary Douglas' notions of 'dirt' and 'danger' in her concept of the 'abject'. According to Kristeva, the subject constitutes

---

[105] Douglas 1966, 115,128.
[106] Watney 1987, 38-57.
[107] See also Epstein, Straub 1991, 12 ff..
[108] Ibid..
[109] With the threat of terror turning into a major source of anxiety in American society, a change seems to be taking shape in contemporary political rhetoric: it is not the dissolution of the body's boundaries, but an invisible, insidious threat that is both within and outside of the body that is most feared. Terrorist attacks have been described as an illness, a virus sleeping within the body waiting to break out to strike at the very "heart" of this body.

itself through differentiating itself from the other, which is originally the maternal body. The abject is the undefinable that crosses the boundary between the self and the other that has been repressed in the constitution of the subject:

> It is thus not lack of cleanliness or health that causes abjection but what disturbs identity, system, order. What does not respect borders, positions, rules. The in-between, the ambiguous, the composite.[110]

Abjection threatens the dissolution of the subject by confronting it with the repressed. Transgressive bodies that cross the border between self and other constitute a threat to both the stability of the subject and to the regulations which form normative subjects (such as the heterosexual subject) in society. Monstrosity is a metaphor for the transgression and subversion of established norms and taboos. Thus, Butler's deconstruction of the duality of gender produces the monstrous body. Similarly, Donna Haraway celebrates the monstrous body in her concept of the 'cyborg' which merges the natural and the artificial, the animal and the machine, and creates a new subject that transcends the confines of gender. The cyborg stands for a new feminist politics which does not demonise new technologies, but takes "pleasure in the confusion of boundaries".[111] Like Butler, Haraway advocates a radical deconstruction of identity.

In fact, the notion of the monstrous body as a threat to social hierarchy was developed by Bakhtin in his study of the medieval carnival in the 1930s. In *Rabelais and his World* Bakhtin opposes the classical image of the body as a seamless whole with the grotesque body which was celebrated in medieval carnivals. The grotesque body is bulging, protuberant and incomplete. Its orifices (the mouth, the anus) and its lower regions are emphasised. Bakhtin correlates the classification of 'high' and 'low' parts of the body to social and political hierarchy. Lower body parts revolt in the carnivalesque body. The grotesque body in carnival disrupts the monologic gravity of the official culture. Yet Bakhtin ignores the conservative function the 'monstrous' can have when it is employed to affirm and re-establish the normative.[112] As Paul Goetsch notes in his study on monsters in English literature, the monstrous may also embody a warning of transgression. Goetsch distinguishes two major functions of the monster as a liminal figure in literature. On the one

---

[110] Kristeva 1982, 4. Body fluids such as excreta, blood and pus cause abjection since they are "at the border of my condition of a living being". The corpse represents the utmost of abjection. Kristeva 1982, 3-4.
[111] Haraway 1991, 150.
[112] See also II.4.2 on the subversive and conservative function of transgressive gender identities.

hand, the monster challenges norms and taboos by questioning the boundary between the self and the other, the allowed and the forbidden. On the other hand, it may consolidate the normative structure of a society, policing the boundary between the legitimate and the taboo. It is the first, subversive type of monster that has particularly appealed to gender and postcolonial critics.[113] In fact, contemporary feminist writers and artists appropriate Bakhtin's concept of the subversive, grotesque body and create the 'female grotesque', which employs the monstrous body as a symbol of female transgression.[114] Monique Wittig, Margaret Atwood, Fay Weldon, Jeanette Winterson and Angela Carter rejoice in the production of disobedient bodies, which proliferate beyond their accustomed boundaries.

This study will focus on the breaking up of bodily boundaries in Angela Carter's fiction. Monstrosity carries various associations in Carter's novels. It ironically literalises the process of 'othering', which produces women as monstrous others, as objects of disgust and desire in our culture. Carter's fiction demonstrates how monstrosity can be appropriated by the dominant culture. However, the monstrous body also disrupts the process by which the disciplined female subject is formed. Carter employs the notion of the abject to challenge what has been marginalised and suppressed in the constitution of the white male subject. Carter's fiction turns the violence inherent in the constitution of the male subject back upon this subject itself, as I wish to demonstrate in the following chapters.

---

[113] Goetsch 2002, 18.
[114] On the 'female grotesque' see also Russo 1994.

III. Desire, Appetite and Power: the Body in *The Infernal Desire Machines of Dr Hoffman*

> I would like to make the cultural unconscious apparent.
>
> *Michel Foucault*

The Infernal Desire Machines of Dr Hoffman imagines a liberation of desire that revolts against reason and order. Hoffman's desire machines unleash the imagination and wage war on law and order in the Minister's city. Set in an imaginary South American country, the novel stages a fantastic revolution in a bizarre, sensuos and exotic world which confuses categories. At the same time the narrative portrays an artificial world, which is flat, textualised, made of cardboard, glue and paste: a world which at times loses its three-dimensionality and turns into a film. The narrative describes a journey into the cultural unconscious. But this journey is not constructed on a model of depth. It does not lead into the dark "abyss" of nature, the "down below" (NC 61) of an original libidinal space. The novel depicts the world as a surface, as a screen onto which Hoffman projects the shadow-play of desire. What is the place of the body in this world? One would expect the body to feature prominently in a narrative whose major protagonist is desire. Yet bodies are equally flat, textualised and insubstantial. The narrator and protagonist Desiderio seems to be all voice and disembodied eye, detached from a subjectively experienced body. His physical resilience makes him apt for survival and immune to pain. Female bodies are likewise unreal in the narrative. Women are either elusive, shape-shifting creations, clockwork-driven machines or meat. There is no 'lived body' in the phenomenological sense in the narrative. In *The Infernal Desire Machines* bodies are either absent, insubstantial or objectified: food to be consumed.

The body which is both 'me' and 'other' represents a sign of alterity and death. The narrating voice of the novel swallows the body as sign of alterity. *The Infernal Desire Machines* is a cannibalistic text.

This chapter examines the theme of cannibalism and desire in the novel. Cannibalism appears as the nexus of several interrelated themes. It refers to questions of sexuality and power. As a kind of incorporation, it points to the psychoanalytic concept of melancholia and the theme of identity. Moreover, cannibalism is a form of sacrificial violence which consolidates the social body's boundaries. Desiderio's desire is essentially cannibalistic in the narrative. In Part Two I will analyse desire in this novel as a cultural construct in Foucault's sense. The narrative demystifies desire as primordial libidinal force and questions liberationist theories of sexuality. Referring to feminist film theory, I will particularly examine the role of the peep-show, which produces desire in a violent and misogynist form. In the conclusion I argue that on a textual and metatextual level the narrative negates materiality: the excessive use of intertextuality stifles the materiality of the body; the narrating voice cannibalistically incorporates and assimilates otherness. It is only in Desiderio's final loss of words, in the silence that follows the text that the reader might sense a trace of alterity.

In a parody of the Western literary tradition and its ideological heritage, *The Infernal Desire Machines* alludes to a wide range of literary and philosophical intertexts and merges elements of different genres such as the picaresque, the Gothic, adventure stories, autobiography, pornography, fairy tales, and colonial travel literature. Interweaving a critique of a variety of Western discourses, the novel lends itself to a reading on different levels. In my feminist approach to the text, I particularly focus on the discourse of power and sexuality in Foucault's sense.[1] At the same time I will draw on psychoanalytic concepts in my interpretation. Carter's allusive eclecticism suggests a reading that integrates various theoretical concepts. I will argue that different readings of the highly ambiguous and indeterminate text do not necessarily exclude each other but may be integrated within a Foucauldian approach to the narrative.

1. The Body as Meat: Cannibalism in *The Infernal Desire Machines*
Introduction: Food, Power, Sexuality

> Nobody likes to be reduced to the status of comestible.
> Angela Carter, *Shaking a Leg*

Appetite is an image of power and sexuality in Carter's fiction. Carnivorous animals in "The Tiger's Bride" and "The Company of Wolves" have a distinctive sexual attraction. In *Wise Children* appetite symbolises Saskia's greed for power. Saskia employs food as a weapon in her career as cook, seductress and poisoner. In *Nights at the Circus* Fevvers' appetite indicates her ability to act as subject of desire and to transcend her status as object of the gaze. Like Fevvers, the girl in "The Company of Wolves" turns the cultural stereotype of woman as food for man's sexual appetite on its head

---

[1] Other possible interpretations focus on the text as a critique of the media, capitalism and poststructuralism or read it as a psychoanalytic allegory and postcolonial critique. See 2.2.4.2.

when she "eats" the wolf:[2] "... she knew she was nobody's meat" (BB 219). In contrast, the loss of appetite indicates disempowerment in a psychological, sexual or economic sense in Carter's fiction. In *Several Perceptions* Joseph's rejection of food is an expression of his melancholia and his "limitless capacity for enduring suffering" (SP 80). Food is part of the imagery of abjection that pervades the novel, a reminder of illness, mortality and death: a green apple turns into the image of a liver-sick man, lungs are "rotten as gorgonzola" (SP 77). While women in Carter's late fiction tend to be hearty eaters, many female characters in her early fiction suffer from a lack of appetite and vitality. Annabel's fleshless body prefigures her premature death in *Love*. Annabel – a creation of Carter's 'pre-feminist' phase – embodies a stereotypical image of femininity as death-prone fragility, powerlessness and dependence: unable to nurture herself, she has to be fed by Lee. In *The Magic Toyshop* Aunt Margaret's emaciated body indicates her subjection and economic dependence, while Uncle Philip's voracity epitomises patriarchal exploitation.[3] Aunt Margaret is prevented from eating by a tight necklace which her husband has given her for a wedding present. The omnivorous husband and the anorexic wife function as trope for a certain constellation of power. The most extreme version of this constellation is the cannibalistic scenario in which the other is not only prevented from eating but literally transformed into food. The Marquis in "The Bloody Chamber" regards his wife as meat, viewing her with the "eye of a connoisseur inspecting horseflesh" (BB 115). The Erl-King's sexuality threatens to swallow the young girl in the story "The Erl-King". In *The Sadeian Woman* Carter conceives cannibalism as the most extreme metaphor for exploitation:

> Necrophagy is the exposition of the meatiness of human flesh .... Cannibalism, the most elementary act of exploitation, that of turning the other directly into a comestible; of seeing the other in the most primitive terms of use .... The strong abuse, exploit and meatify the weak, says Sade. They must and will devour their natural prey. The primal condition of man cannot be modified in any way; it is, eat or be eaten. (SW 140)

However, cannibalism is not a simple metaphor for economic and patriarchal exploitation in Carter's novels. In a feminist and a postcolonial critique, it is an image of the appropriation of difference. Carter also employs cannibalism as a complex metaphor in the psychoanalytic sense. Psychoanalytic theory focuses on appetite and its frustration in the early mother-child relation. On the basis of these early experiences, eating becomes the focal point for several contradictory emotions. The desire for incorporation expresses a desire for identification with and destruction of the other. In *Several Perceptions* Joseph

---

[2] See Carter in Haffenden 1985, 83.
[3] See also Sceats 1997, 106; Sceats 2000, 36-38.

dreams of eating Mrs. Boulder, who in turn swallows him. The dream literalises infantile desire for incorporation and fear of maternal engulfment. As the pre-oedipal desire for incorporation becomes a model for identification in later life, cannibalism is bound up with the theme of identity: we literally are what we have eaten.[4] As an image for identification, cannibalistic metaphors also pervade the psychoanalytic discourse on melancholia: the incorporation of a lost object drains the ego of its vitality in melancholic depression.

Cannibalism is a recurring theme in *The Infernal Desire Machines*. The river people plan to serve Desiderio as the main course at his wedding celebration. Cannibalism is the common diet of the tribe on the imaginary African coast. The Sadeian Count is boiled alive by his shadow, who wishes to "taste" himself (ID 162). Cannibalism is also an important element in the centaurs' religion, which considers the eating of the Sacred Horse as the 'Fall' from original 'horsehood'. Finally, on a metatextual level the description of Desiderio's quest on the African coast parodistically functions as a 'cannibalistic' narrative which denies difference to the other.

1.1 Cannibalism and Melancholia: Unity, Loss and Desire
1.1.1 Cannibalism and the Desire for Unity

As Freud points out, the early consumption of food implies the division of the world into "good" and "bad" – that which "is to be either *inside* me or *outside* me".[5] The desire to turn the outside inside, to make the uncanny canny and assimilate the other in an act of incorporation expresses a nostalgia for an original state of unity in which the self feels no separation from the other. The notion of an original unity which is lost in the course of individual and historical development is a central concept in Western cultural history. The Biblical myth of the unity of man and nature before the Fall and the Greek myth of the Platonic hermaphrodite both express a yearning for an unalienated state of wholeness. Hegelian philosophy postulates the concept of an original plenitude which has been lost with the intrusion of consciousness only to be recovered on a higher plane.[6] The 'Golden Age' narrative of

---

[4] Freud 1953j, 29. Freud argues that the ego's character is the residue of regressive identifications. The ego identifies with the sexual object it has to give up.

[5] Freud 1963, 214-15.

[6] "For the latter [self-consciousness], just in that it is a self to itself, and proceeds to act, lifts itself out of the state of *simple immediacy*, and itself sets up a *division into two*. By the act it gives up the ... pure and simple certainty of immediate truth ...." (Hegel 1956, 488). Hegel

various idealistic discourses which derive the split human self from a fall from unity shares certain features with psychoanalytic theories. Not only the Freudian pre-oedipal oral stage but also Kristeva's notion of the semiotic and Lacan's concept of the imaginary imply the notion of an unconscious unity that the child experiences in the pre-verbal phase.[7] Yet whereas the Hegelian narrative of return implies reconciliation and closure, in Freudian psychoanalysis the struggle between ego and id, between the pleasure and the reality principle, represents an insoluble conflict: the self is irrevocably divided. The subject in Freud is a split subject whose desire for unity is necessarily unfulfillable.

Derrida attacks narratives of lost presence, of origins, which have to be recovered on a higher plane. He criticises the Hegelian notion of *Aufhebung* ('sublation') for its denial of difference.[8] Purporting to produce a unity of two terms, 'sublation', he argues, conceals a repressive project which aims at the assertion of the dominant term. It implies no reconciliation of opposites but a cannibalistic incorporation of one term by the other. Cannibalism thus becomes an image for an imperialist discourse which aims at the subsumption of difference. Hence, Hegel has been considered to be the founder of a German idealistic tradition that privileges identity over alterity, sameness over difference[9] and assimilates otherness within an overarching unity.

---

illustrates his concept of consciousness as 'fortunate Fall' in a parable which compares philosophy to the sun moving from East to West: "The history of the world travels from East to West, for Europe is absolutely the end of history, Asia the beginning .... Here rises the outward physical sun, and in the West it sinks down: here consentaneously rises the sun of self-consciousness, which diffuses a nobler brilliance" (Hegel 1956, 103-4). The internalisation of the sun in the course of this movement from East to West symbolises the power of reason and involves the effacement of the sensible. The Hegelian narrative thus implies the sacrifice of the body. Whereas in Rousseau the sacrifice of the sensible is deplored, in Hegel it is justified: the sacrifice of the 'physical sun' leads to a greater, more illuminating 'inner sun', the sun of reason and self-consciousness.

[7] In Lacanian psychoanalysis the imaginary precedes the symbolic stage, the entry into language and subjectivity. In the imaginary the borders between self and other are blurred. Kristeva's notion of the semiotic denotes the pre-verbal unity the child experiences with the maternal body. On the semiotic see also IV.1.4. Kristeva 1984; Kristeva 1980; Lacan 1977, IV.

[8] Derrida 1986, 91. In Hegelian dialectics the term *Aufhebung* denotes a process which simultaneously 'preserves', 'negates' and 'raises' to a higher level: a thesis is negated by an antithesis; through the negation of this first negation, a synthesis is postulated which contains ('preserves') the original thesis in a modified, 'higher' form.

[9] In particular Nietzsche and the post-Nietzschean philosophers like Foucault, Deleuze and Derrida oppose Hegelian dialectics with notions of difference and plurality. See Deleuze 1983, 9; Derrida 1986, 86; Foucault 1990, 92 ff..

The Infernal Desire Machines contains several mock versions of the cannibalistic merging of self and other, revealing the violence inherent in the 'narrative of synthesis'. The regressive fantasy of unity is grotesquely literalised in several acts of incorporation which do not lead to a new sense of unity but to the destruction of the ego. A case in point is Desiderio's experience among the river people. Yearning for an end to his quest, Desiderio almost ends up as the main dish at his wedding feast. His regression into the community of the river people is described as a loss of personality, a process of de-individualisation that he succumbs to when he goes native and becomes Kiku:

> The limited range of feeling and idea they expressed with such a meagre palette of gesture no longer oppressed me; it gave me, instead, that slight feeling of warm claustrophobia I had learned to identify with the notion, 'home'.... Desiderio himself had disappeared because the river people had given him a new name. ... I was called Kiku". (ID 77)

Not only is Desiderio absorbed by the community spirit, which is ruled by tradition and rituals;[10] he also entertains a relationship with both "Mama" and his future child wife Aoi, Mama's granddaughter. Regressing to pre-oedipal incestuous fantasies, Desiderio increasingly surrenders to the semiotic and experiences a merging of self and other:

> ... those nights of autumn passed in elaborate love play with my erotic, giggling toy, every night adorned with different coloured bows, while in the mornings I screwed the toy's grandmother up against the wall. I began to feel like a love slave. (ID 85)

Desire – in the form of incest and paedophilia – overcomes Desiderio. Yet incestuous desire is revenged in due course. The fish – Aoi's toy and symbol of sexuality – is transformed into a knife and the toy lover into a castrator:

> I saw there was no fish's head under the lace but the tip of the blade of one of the very large knives Mama used in the kitchen. The boat swayed with the current and Aoi, half-waking, drowsily clutched the knife to her bosom. With great distinctness, she said, 'Tomorrow. Do it tomorrow.' (ID 91)

Mama and Papa, who want to "adopt" Desiderio, literally plan to absorb him in a cannibalistic wedding feast. The river people episode represents a parody of the Freudian oedipal drama: castration anxiety and the fear of engulfment are grotesquely literalised in the narrative. No idyllic unity but destruction awaits Desiderio.

The Count's unification with his double represents another parodistic version of the regressive desire for unity, which negates difference. At the end of his journey the Count is consumed by his shadow, the black pimp. This

---

[10] See also Sceats 1997, 109.

incorporation is prefigured by the Count's vision of merging with his double that literally negates Lafleur and Desiderio's separate identities:

'I am going to fall into my own arms. They stretch out to me from the bottom of the pit ... I am entirely alone. I and my shadow fill the universe.' Lafleur gasped at that and so did I for I felt myself instantly negated. To my horror, I discovered I immediately grew thinner and less solid. (ID 148)

The Count is not able to take account of a world separate from his ego: "... he had a passionate conviction he was the only significant personage in the world" (ID 123). The refusal of difference is also manifest in the centaurs' attempt to destroy and assimilate the foreign invaders – Desiderio and Albertina – through sacrificial violence (cf. III.1.2.2). The centaurs plan to adjust Desiderio and Albertina's human shape to the horse ideal:

... in his infinite compassion, the Stallion had decided to integrate us with the celestial herd. They would paint us with his picture and then, to make us resemble him even more, they would nail the iron shoes on our feet with red hot nails. After that, they would take us into the forest and give us to the Spirits. That is, the wild horses, who would certainly trample us to death. (ID 190)

The centaurs' rituals violently eliminate difference. To give another example of the elimination of otherness, the description of Desiderio's quest on the African coast parodies a 'cannibalistic' colonial narrative which assimilates difference and turns the other into a mirror of the self. Brian McHale notes that Carter constructs an Africa "wholly derived from European fantasy", populating its coast with "cannibal tribesmen straight out of party jokes, comic-strips, and slapstick comedy"[11]. The aggressive cannibalistic impulse of Desiderio's narrative is projected onto the African tribe. The text presents a parody of the heart-of-darkness theme which employs the wilderness as a projection space of the self. The literary topos of the wilderness as unconscious is explicitly evoked by Albertina, who describes the tribe and the landscape as emanations of Desiderio's and the Count's desire. While the external action of the narrative extends through a vast space and a variety of settings, the internal, psychological space is claustrophobically restricted to the perpetual reflection of the same: the internal landscape of Desiderio's mind. The Africans and the centaurs are not characters in their own right but actors in Desiderio's psychodrama. The quest narrative is metaphorically 'cannibalistic' as it appropriates and assimilates difference.

Whereas *The Infernal Desire Machines* contains several mock versions of the cannibalistic merging of self and other, there is no drive toward synthesis in the narrative's solution. As in Freud's "Civilization and its Discontents",

---

[11] McHale 1987, 55.

there is no reconciliation of the reality principle and the pleasure principle as they are represented by the Minister's and Hoffman's world. The narrative's ending is pervaded by a sense of loss, a lack of closure reflected in Desiderio's spoiling of the climax. By killing Albertina, Desiderio deprives the love plot of its consummation: "If you feel a certain sense of anti-climax, how do you think I felt? ... Those are the dreary ends of the plot. ... I was a traveller who had denied his proper destination" (ID 218,219,220). At the end of his quest Desiderio emerges as a divided self: divided between the world of reason and desire. In *The Infernal Desire Machines* Carter ironically refers to the idealistic quest which looks back to the perfect identification of self and other and reveals it to be a regressive, cannibalistic fantasy. The desire for plenitude and the inability to accept loss are expressions of a refusal to grow up and accept otherness beyond the self. According to Ricarda Schmidt, the novel deals with subject formation in the interaction with the reality principle and the pleasure principle.[12] The ego asserts itself against the id and the super-ego embodied by the Doctor and the Minister, respectively. While the Count's unconscious literally takes over and swallows the self, Desiderio wins the battle with his double Albertina, who tries to kill him in Hoffman's castle. Desiderio rejects Hoffman's libidinous world that merges self and other in sexuality. Yet he also remains sceptical about the Minister's victory at the end of the narrative.

> I might not want the Minister's world but I did not want the Doctor's world either. All at once I was pitched on the horns of a dilemma .... I had been given a casting vote between the barren yet harmonious calm and a fertile yet cacophonous tempest .... Were all the potential masters the world held for me to be revealed as nothing but monsters or charlatans or wraiths? (ID 207,213)

The subject seems to assert itself against the infantile desire for unity and the claims of various father-figures.

The subject, however, which emerges at the end of the narrative is tormented by depression. It is not a 'healthy' subject which has outgrown the cannibalistic desire for unity. The narrative produces the melancholic split subject which has experienced loss and suffering.

---

[12] Schmidt 1989, 57.

1.1.2 The Divided Subject: Melancholia, Mortality and the Loss of Appetite
1.1.2.1 Death, Desire and the Divided Self

Condemned to live in the bleak realm of rational reality, Desiderio is tormented by his desire for the dead Albertina after the Minister's victory:

> ... from beyond the grave, her father has gained a tactical victory over me and forced on me the apprehension of an alternative world in which all the objects are emanations of a single desire. And my desire is, to see Albertina again before I die. (ID 14)

The divided self that suffers from unfulfillable desire is reminiscent of the split subject in Lacan's theory of subject formation. The Lacanian subject is constituted upon a lack, upon a loss of unity in the 'real'[13] which emerges with the entry into the symbolic order. Desire results from this lack and aims at the regaining of the irretrievable lost object in the real. The Lacanian subject finds a substitute for the lost unity in language, which yet never wholly makes up for the lack. The subject pursues the unattainable object of desire through the metonymic chain of signification. The structure of writing and desire are in this sense identical: both are marked by absence and deferral. In *The Infernal Desire Machines* unfulfillable desire forms the narrative's drive: shape-shifting Albertina is the ever-elusive object of desire whose pursuit propels the narrative action. As Desiderio's object of desire always remains just out of reach, the fulfilment of desire is perpetually deferred in his quest.

Lacan discusses the origins of symbolisation and desire with reference to Freud's description of the *fort/da* game, in which the child begins to use symbols to designate the absence of an object (*fort*) and to express the desire for its reappearance (*da*). The emergence of language is bound up with absence and death. Thus Lacan derives desire and symbolisation from "the murder of the thing" in the real: "... the symbol manifests itself first of all as the murder of the thing, and this death constitutes in the subject the eternalisation of desire."[14] Desiderio's experience can be read as an allegory of this process. The death of Albertina effects the "eternalisation of desire", initiating Desiderio into a world in which "all the objects are emanations of a single desire" at the end of the narrative (ID 14). Albertina's death delivers

---

[13] Lacan describes the 'real' as the underside of the imaginary and the symbolic. While in the early years the subject lives in the imaginary and enters the symbolic with the acquisition of language, it has no access to the real. Denoting the ineffable world of experience, the real exists outside of speech and represents what is lacking in the symbolic order. Lacan 1977, ix.

[14] Lacan 1977, 104.

Desiderio to the symbolic. It marks the re-entry into time and instigates the process of writing: "Time exerted great pressure on my blood vessels and my eardrums, so that I suffered from terrible headaches, weakness and nausea" (ID 221). Desiderio re-emerges from the pre-symbolic space of the imaginary into the symbolic order of language and representation. Representation is bound up with temporality, loss and death. Lacan conceives death as "primordial to the birth of symbols" and as that "from which his [the subject's] existence takes on all the meaning it has".[15] In fact, death is the origin and telos of representation in the narrative. While Albertina's death triggers the writing process, Desiderio's death terminates it: "What a fat book to coffin young Desiderio, who was so thin and supple" (ID 221). The narrative itself represents Desiderio's tomb: representation symbolically implies the 'murder of the thing' when it puts a seal on Desiderio's existence. In a paradoxical way the narrative's ending stages the birth and death of the subject in the symbolic.

1.1.2.2 Melancholia and Maternity

The subject constitutes itself through killing the object of desire. Yet the subject is haunted by the loss of the loved object. Mourning the loss of Albertina, Desiderio gives in to apathy and depression. The constitution of the subject resolves into melancholia. Melancholia is, in psychoanalytic terms, another metaphorical form of cannibalism. Freud describes melancholia as an aberrant form of mourning which refuses to break attachment to the lost object: "... the ego wants to incorporate this object into itself, and in accordance with the oral or cannibalistic phase of libidinal development in which it is, it wants to do so by devouring it."[16] Identification with the lost object divides the ego against itself: accusations which were formerly levelled at the loved object are turned back upon the self, which is the reason for the loss of self-esteem and depression in melancholia. Albertina lives on in Desiderio and condemns him to live in a "drab, colourless world" (ID 14). She resembles in this sense Annabel in *Love*, who turns Lee into a melancholic. *Love* gives a metaphorical description of melancholia in the Japanese peasant myth of the fox that enters the body and harangues its host: "... he [Lee] would become a Spartan boy and she the fox under his jacket, eating his heart out" (L 15). Refusing to accept loss, the melancholic desires a merging with the other and a transcending of difference. However,

---

[15] Ibid., 105.
[16] Freud 1953f, 249-50.

Desiderio's melancholic fixation on loss is converted into gain through literary production. Melancholia gives rise to artistic production: Albertina's death turns Desiderio into a war hero and an artist. In *The Gendering of Melancholia* Juliana Schiesari traces a history of male melancholia – from Petrarch to Walter Benjamin – which conceives melancholia as a sign of exceptionality and as the source of artistic creativity.[17] Drawing narcissistic gratification from suffering, the subject is paradoxically empowered by the idealisation of loss. Albertina is the female muse over whose corpse the melancholic literary genius establishes himself and mourns the loss of unity.

In *Black Sun: Depression and Melancholia* Kristeva derives melancholia from an unsuccessful detachment from the mother.[18] The loss of the mother as the primal loved object in infancy is disavowed in patriarchal culture. According to Judith Butler, the mother is barred as object of desire and thus subjected to a 'double disavowal', which founds the heterosexual subject: "I have not loved, I have not lost her".[19] Carter's work reflects this negation of the mother. As Jouve notes, mothers are characteristically absent in most of her novels.[20] At some points, however, the unacknowledged lost mother returns to haunt the male protagonists: Desiderio's mother appears in his dreams at the beginning of Hoffman's revolution. Albertina's apparition as black swan reminds him of an uncanny childhood experience when he heard his mother "grunting like a tiger in the darkness ..."(ID 30) and thought she had changed into a beast. The childhood memory evokes an archaic sense of fear: "fear of the unknown" (ID 30) is, in this context, fear of death and of female sexuality, which are expressed in the image of the black swan. Desiderio's recollection resembles the uncanny childhood experience Morris relates in *Shadow Dance*. Morris remembers hearing his mother's "hoarse breathing ... like a wolf" (SD 146) while she was making love in front of his door. Ghislaine's attractive face – half of which has been mutilated by Honeybuzzard – reflects Morris' ambivalent relation to women that is marked

---

[17] Schiesari 1992, 3 ff.. The connection between literary production and melancholia has been derived from Freud's remark about the "insistent communicativeness" that the melancholic displays. Freud 1953f, 247.

[18] Kristeva 1989, 27-28, 43-44. Kristeva advocates 'matricide', a severing of the attachment to the mother, as a therapeutic strategy against melancholia: "Matricide is our vital necessity, the sine-qua-non condition of our individuation .... The ... violence of the matricidal drive ... entails, when it is hindered, its inversion on the self; the maternal object having been introjected, the depressive or melancholic putting to death of the self is what follows, instead of matricide."

[19] See Butler 1997, 136 ff..

[20] Jouve 1994, 152 ff.. See also VI.1.

by fascination, fear and disgust.[21] In *Love* Buzz' memory of his mother who "had given him many fears about the physicality of women" (L 94) likewise evokes a deep-running anxiety, which makes him inspect Annabel's "perilous interior" to check that there are no "fangs or guillotines inside her to ruin him" (L 94). What these three characters – Desiderio, Morris and Buzz – share is their narcissistic relation to women. Melancholia, in fact, implies the inability to refrain libidinal attachment from the original lost object and to reattach it to another object instead. The unacknowledged incorporated mother returns to haunt the male self as fear of femininity that conflates woman with death. Hence, Albertina's apparition as black swan, Annabel's morbidity in *Love* and Ghislaine's mutilated face in *Shadow Dance* conjoin beauty and horror, femininity and death.

1.1.2.3 The Womb and the Flight from Historicity

In *The Sadeian Woman* Carter attacks narratives of 'lost presence' and original unity from a feminist perspective. These narratives are closely bound up with the idealisation of the mother and the mystification of the mother's uncannily ambivalent womb/tomb. The womb represents the eternal site of unity which merges self and other. The yearning for the womb bespeaks a desire for a flight from historicity. In *The Sadeian Woman* Carter calls for a demystification of the womb and the acceptance of temporality:

> The goddess is dead.
> And with the imaginary construct of the goddess, dies the notion of eternity, whose place on this earth was her womb. If the goddess is dead, there is nowhere for eternity to hide. The last resort of homecoming is denied to us. We are confronted with mortality, as if for the first time. There is no way out of time. We must learn to live in this world, to take it with sufficient seriousness, because it is the only world we will ever know. (SW 110)

Carter's fiction destroys the notion of the eternal, of a refuge from history. Carter relates the negation of difference to the inability to accept mortality. In *The Infernal Desire Machines* the Count's journey is, in fact, a desperate flight from death. The Count flees from the embodiment of his own death drive that simultaneously attracts and repels him: "That man – if man he be – is my retribution .... Hold me or I will run into his arms" (ID 139). In "Thoughts for the Times on War and Death", Freud considers the willingness

---

[21] Ghislaine is the archetypal female seductress in *Shadow Dance*. While one half of her face has been disfigured by Honeybuzzard, the other half remained "fresh and young and smooth and warm as fruit in the sunlight" (SD 153) (see 1.4).

to kill to be closely connected to the negation of the self's mortality.[22] Historicising Freud, Philippe Ariès traces a growing fear and negation of death in modernity. He derives the rise of sadism in the eighteenth and nineteenth century from this negation as a violent return of the repressed.[23] The Count exemplifies this modern Sadeian mentality that is driven by a neurotic fear of mortality. Chased by Thanatos, he appeases anxiety in an ecstatic celebration of destruction. The violent death of the cannibal chief gives a mirror image of the Count's journey of destruction:

> ... the juggernaut rose up on his car and stood there ... the corpse stayed upright .... So it started on a headlong career, crushing wives and eunuchs and those of his tribe who, maddened at the sight, ... flung themselves under the wheels of its chariot with maenad shrieks. ... he [the Count] ... crushed and flattened the world as he passed through it, like an existential version of the cannibal chief's chariot. (ID 164,168)

Ironically, the Count's flight from mortality culminates in his self-destruction. In contrast, Desiderio survives. At the end of his quest Desiderio wistfully accepts alienation as a mode of being in time, acknowledging that the "impossible is, per se, impossible" (ID 221). Like *The Passion of New Eve*, the novel ends with a rebirth into historical time.

Ahistorical, mythic realms are typically violent, destructive spaces in Carter's work: superstition and irrationality rule among the centaurs, the river people (*The Infernal Desire Machines*), the Barbarians (*Heroes and Villains*), Zero's harem, the women in Beulah (*The Passion of New Eve*), and the Shaman's tribe (*Nights at the Circus*). In *The Passion of New Eve* Beulah is a world of terror which cherishes a mythic ahistorical concept of motherhood. In *The Infernal Desire Machines* it is the myth of a loss of difference and individuality in desire which is debunked and revealed to entail a cannibalistic appropriation of otherness. While the rejection of the mythic and the ahistorical is an invariable theme in Carter's novels, her work is marked by a growing optimism with regard to life in history and time. In *Wise Children* the ageing body is turned into a site of vitality and *jouissance*. In *The Passion of New Eve*, Eve leaves myth behind and enters history at the end of the narrative; pregnant Eve embarking on the ocean can be read as a final image of hope in the novel. In contrast, in *The Infernal Desire Machines*

---

[22] Freud 1953g, 296-297.
[23] Ariès 1977, 363 ff., 387 ff.. According to Ariès, this growing fear is related to increasing secularisation and individualisation in modernity. Death is no longer experienced collectively: religion and rituals, which gave meaning to death in the past, decline in modernity. In *The Sadeian Woman* Carter suggests that, given the violent outrageous nature of death in his novels, Sade "must have found it ... hard to reconcile himself to the fact of mortality" (SW 141).

regret and melancholia are the dominant emotions accompanying Desiderio's re-entry into historical time. "And so I identified at last the flavour of my daily bread; it was and would be that of regret" (ID 221). The omnivorous narrating voice of the cannibalistic narrative finally loses its taste for life: "The food I begged from cottagers had no savour of sweetness or rankness" (ID 220). The incorrigible separation of desire from the 'real' condemns Desiderio to "disillusionment in perpetuity" (ID 220). While cannibalism represents the violent attempt to restore unity, melancholia emerges from the failure of this attempt as obsessive fixation on loss.

In *The Infernal Desire Machines* there are no healthy eaters such as Fevvers in *Nights at the Circus*. The choice seems to be between a cannibalistic omnivoracity and the loss of appetite in melancholia.

1.2 Variations of the Totem Meal: the River People and the Centaurs
1.2.1 Masochism and the Repression of the Body

Cannibalistic violence recurs in the myths that the river people and the centaurs believe in. The snake myth and the myth of the Sacred Stallion both deal with a cannibalistic act of incorporation that constitutes culture and religion. In the river people's myth it is the snake that is eaten by the brothers and the father. In the centaurs' religion it is the Sacred Stallion who is slain by the Bridal Mare and the Dark Archer. In the description of the centaurs' cannibalistic feast Carter alludes to the Freudian notion of the totem meal as the origin of culture and religion. In "Totem and Taboo" Freud traces the origin of culture back to the revolt that the sons instigate against the ruling father-male of the primitive horde. After the sons have killed and eaten the father in a cannibalistic feast, feelings of guilt and remorse emerge. To appease these feelings, the sons renounce claims to the father's women. They institute taboos on incest and on the consumption of their totem that is identified with the father and God. The eating of the father/totem is ceremonially repeated in a ritual that commemorates his death. The totem meal is both a celebration of the triumph over the father and an expression of remorse. The incorporation of the father constitutes the guilt complex as the basis of religion. As the eating of the father implies the internalisation of his authority, cannibalism functions as metaphor for identification. It symbolises the desire to destroy the father and to identify with him by appropriating his power and internalising the law. The internalisation of the law constitutes patriarchal society.[24]

In *The Infernal Desire Machines* the centaurs' religion is an explicit parody of the totem meal. After killing the Sacred Stallion, the Dark Archer and the Bridal Mare cook and eat the stallion to conceal their crime. The cannibalistic act represents the origin of guilt and religion: it constitutes the original sin, the fall that the centaurs have to atone for their whole lives. The evolution of civilisation follows from the totem meal. Culture develops as a way of relieving the guilt complex of the centaurs:

> The remainder of the liturgical year was taken up with lengthy and overbearing forgiveness and his many teachings – of the art of singing; of the technique of the smithy; of corn growing, ... and of writing – and all the almost countless ways in which they must conduct their lives in order to atone for their sins. (ID 185)

After the Dark Archer and the Bridal Mare have eaten the Sacred Stallion, desolation comes upon the land. The forty-days period of repentance and the Sacred Stallion's descension parody Lent and the Second Coming. As the centaurs believe themselves to be the degenerated seed of the Dark Archer, they detest the human part of their nature that distinguishes them from the Sacred Stallion. The mind/body dualism, the split nature of human beings, is inverted when it is the animal nature and the abject (horse dung) that is worshipped among the centaurs:[25]

> These hippolators believed their god revealed himself to them in the droppings excreted by the horse part of themselves since this manifested the purest essence of their equine natures, and it was quite as logical an idol as a loaf of bread or a glass of wine, though the centaurs had too much good sense to descend to coprophily. (ID 175)

While the myth is obviously a satire on Christianity, the depiction of the centaurs' self-mortifying religion appears in a broader sense to be a parody of "the Judaeo-Christian heritage of shame, disgust and morality" (SW 11) which castigates the animal part ("horsiness") of human nature. The virtue, cleanliness and discipline of the civilised Houyhnhnms in *Gulliver's Travels* degenerate into a neurotic masochism among the centaurs.[26] By superimpos-

---

[24] Freud 1953c, 141 ff..

[25] Carter ironically inverts the excremental theme in Swift. In *Gulliver's Travels* the Yahoos' defilement is expressed in their obsession with faeces. The adoration of horse dung yet assumes another meaning if the psychoanalytic equation of money and faeces is taken into account.

[26] While Swift's depiction of the Yahoos expresses disgust at the animal nature of human beings, Carter ridicules this very disgust in the portrayal of the self-mortifications of the centaurs. Read as a critique of the repressive masochistic streak of the Christian religion, the satire is turned against the Anglo-Catholic Swift himself, who believed in the fallenness of human nature and would thus make an excellent misanthropist and misogynist centaur.

ing references to the Freudian totem meal on a parody of Christian religion, the narrative points to Freud's notion of the neurotic origins of religion in repression and guilt. In the religious masochism of the centaurs the incorporated father – the "horse-ideal", religion – becomes a gathering-place for the death instinct and rage against the body. As in melancholia, incorporation produces a divided self: one part of this self castigates the other. In an interview with Helen Cagney Watts, Carter calls herself a "Darwinian" and criticises the negation of the animal part of human nature in Christianity:

> I am interested in the division that Judaeo/Christianity has made between animals and humans: no other major religious system has made this great division. One of the scars in our culture, I feel, is that we align ourselves with the angels rather than with the primates ....[27]

The anti-sensualism that defines Judaeo-Christian culture is based on a Platonic idealism that represses the body. In the repression of the body the mind turns against corporeality as the site of alterity within the self. A recurring image of the masochistic disciplining of the body in Carter's work is the tattoo that is violently inscribed on the skin. In *Heroes and Villains* Jewel wears a tattoo of Adam and Eve, which the doctor has imprinted on him. The last supper is inscribed on the body of the leader of the Christian militia in *The Passion of New Eve*. Both novels allude to the violence that a Christian puritanism perpetrates on the body. In *Love* the heart that Annabel inscribes onto Lee's skin becomes a symbol of the obsessive sado-masochism that defines and destroys their relationship. In *The Infernal Desire Machines* it is particularly the female species of the centaurs that is subjected to tattooing as the horses believe women to be "born to suffer" (ID 172). Thus the rape of Albertina is – as Desiderio conjectures – a punishment for her "being female to a degree unprecedented among them" (ID 181). In "People as Pictures" Carter describes Japanese tattooing as a refined form of sado-masochism among the lower classes in Japan. Viewing sadism and masochism as different sides of the same coin, she claims that "a repressive culture can only be maintained by a strong masochistic element among the repressed".[28] The association of femininity with masochism is a reflection of male domination in a patriarchal society. Masochism is not only a crucial element in religion, as Freud claimed; masochism and sadism are the concomitants of a repressive culture in general. Like the Count's sadism, the masochism of the centaurs is the product of an immensely repressed consciousness. Living among the centaurs, Desiderio suspects that he himself may unknowingly be the "instigator of this horror" (ID 180), that "all subjects

---

[27] Carter in Watts 1987, 164.
[28] Carter 1982, 38.

and objects we had encountered in the loose grammar of Nebulous Time were derived from a similar source – my desires ...." (ID 186). The sadism of the Count and the masochistic desires of the centaurs are the repressed underside of Desiderio's detached rationality and the Minister's bourgeois city.

Carter wrote *The Infernal Desire Machines* after her return from Japan, where she was impressed by the strong masochistic streak in Japanese culture. In "A Souvenir of Japan" she reflects on the repression that goes along with the harmonious and utterly disciplined life-style of the Japanese:

> ... repression does not necessarily give birth only to severe beauties. In its programmed interstices, monstrous passions bloom. They torture trees to make them look more like the formal notion of a tree. They paint amazing pictures on their skins with awl and gouge ... They boast the most passionate puppets in the world who mimic love suicides in the most stylised fashion .... (BB 33)

The Infernal Desire Machines gives various illustrations of the "monstrous passions" that the repression of the body produces. Like the centaurs, the puritan mountain dwellers believe in the inherent evil of human nature and passionately castigate the body. The repression of the body among the "malevolent saints" (ID 114) calls forth the sexual violence of the puritans' doubles, the Moroccan acrobats, who gang-rape Desiderio. The landslide that destroys the puritan city stages a violent return of the repressed and asserts the dominance of nature over the human attempt to subject it to the mind.

1.2.2 Cannibalism and Sacrificial Violence

As mentioned above, the snake myth of the river people shares certain similarities with the centaurs' religion. As in the centaurs' mythology, patriarchal civilisation is founded on an act of incorporation. The snake myth describes how the river people acquired the knowledge to make fire. In the myth Sister has transgressed a taboo when she touched a snake that impregnates her. Subsequently, a little snake lives in Sister's belly that periodically pops out to teach her to make fire. In order to appropriate this knowledge from her, the brothers and the father kill Sister and eat the snake:

> ... they picked up their big knives and cut Sister open just like you'd fillet a fish ..... they killed Snake and cut him into little pieces. Then they each ate their piece and ... after that ... they could all make fire .... (ID 90)

The myth is a mock version of the Biblical Fall, the Prometheus myth and the Freudian totem meal. Eating is associated with power, food is knowledge and incorporation an image for identification and the appropriation of power. Snake, the Fire Bringer, symbolises phallic power and knowledge. The

Promethean access to fire is associated with Sister's womb and the power of giving birth. The myth inverts the Biblical Fall: it is not Sister's seduction by the snake/phallus but her loss of the latter which causes her fatal Fall from grace. Sister falls into "castration": the phallus as a symbol of power is literally ripped from her womb and appropriated by the men in a cannibalistic inversion of the act of giving birth.

While in the centaurs' religion patriarchal civilisation is based on parricide (the murder of the stallion), in the snake myth it originates in the sacrifice of the mother, in Sister's death. In "Totem and Taboo" Freud traces the foundation of society back to parricide on a phylogenetic level, even though ontogenetically the primordial lost object is the mother. The snake myth gives an ironic answer to Freud's omission of the mother in "Totem and Taboo". For Luce Irigaray this omission is just one example of the neglect of the maternal in the cultural history of Western civilisation. Irigaray considers matricide as the founding moment of Western philosophy and culture. Our society, she argues, is based on the exploitation of natural fertility and the maternal that is not sufficiently appreciated as the nourishing ground of our being. Irigaray believes sacrifice to be specific to technocratic, patriarchal societies and imagines alternative, utopian communities based on fertility and fecundity.[29]

Sacrificial violence dominates the various patriarchal societies that Desiderio enters on his quest. The snake myth of the river people prefigures the cannibalistic sacrifice that the river people plan to make of Desiderio. In Nao-Kurai's drunken speech the ability to make fire is conflated with the ability to write: "... every one of them could *scribble* away in fire in a twinkling, easy as anything" (ID 90). Through eating Desiderio, the tribe hopes to acquire his literacy. The struggle for power between Caucasians and Non-Caucasians symbolically focuses on the ability to write. The economic power of the white merchants is partly based on the ability to cheat the illiterate Indians. Desiderio as racial hybrid of both white and Indian blood functions as scapegoat (*pharmakos*) and remedy (*pharmakon*)[30] for the

---

[29] Irigaray 1989, 125,132-133; Irigaray 1981b, 81. Irigaray's notion of 'matricide' as the foundation of Western culture concurs with Kristeva's and Butler's concept of the denial of the loss of the mother. Yet while Kristeva pleads for 'matricide' as a therapeutic strategy against melancholia, Irigaray's work aims at uncovering the buried mother in Western culture (see 1.1.2.2, note 18). Kristeva 1989, 27,28. Butler 1997, 136 ff..

[30] I am referring to Derrida's use of the terms *pharmakon/pharmakos* in his reading of Plato's *Phaedrus*. In the *Phaedrus* Socrates condemns writing as *pharmakon* ('poison'). Derrida deconstructs the Platonic privileging of speech over writing and foregrounds the polysemy of the word *pharmakon* which means both 'poison' and 'remedy' in Greek. He describes writing as the scapegoat (*pharmakos*) to be expelled by Plato/Socrates in order to

Indians. He will die as the scapegoat of the privileged race and benefit the river people by endowing them with the ability to write. In "Plato's Pharmacy" Derrida describes the *pharmakos* as "... beneficial in so far as he cures – and for that, venerated and cared for" (Desiderio as literally "the desired") and as "harmful insofar as he incarnates the powers of evil – and for that, feared and treated with caution".[31] This ambivalence is reflected in the mixture of awe and hostility that Nao Kurai displays towards Desiderio. Among the river people and the centaurs Desiderio is the alien intruder who disrupts the homogeneity of isolated, static societies.[32] Desiderio, the bastard and racial hybrid, is a transgressor who travels between the world of reason and the world of desire. The *pharmakon/pharmakos* is ambivalent and transgressive. The displaced alienated subject who lacks a sense of belonging

is pernicious ... because ... it doesn't come from around here. It comes from afar, it is external or alien .... Apprehended as a blend and an impurity, the *pharmakon* acts like an aggressor or a housebreaker, threatening some internal purity and security .... The purity of the inside can then only be restored if the *charges are brought home* against exteriority as supplement ..., a surplus that *ought* never to have come to be added to the untouched plenitude of the inside.[33]

Desiderio is "that dangerous supplement"[34] whose ambivalent identity is located at the same time within and outside of the society. Both Indian and white, he is an "impurity", a "blend" among the river people; sharing the upper part of the body with the centaurs, from the waste down he is alien to them – human and "vile" (ID 190). Desiderio's identity resists the conventional scheme of categorisation of the tribes: its 'hybridity' breaks

---

purify speech. Derrida's notion of the *pharmakos* is related to René Girard's concept of the scapegoat as the innocent victim on whose murder order and community are established. The expulsion of writing in philosophy corresponds to the expulsion of the victim in Girard's theory. Derrida and Girard describe a violent sacrifice as the founding act of philosophy and culture, respectively. Derrida 1981, 61-172; Girard 1972, 410; Plato 1993a, 132.

[31] Derrida 1981, 133.

[32] The isolated, static communities of the centaurs and the river people mirror the isolation of the Minister's city that is cut off from the outside by a wall of barbed wire. As the centaurs are emanations of Desiderio's unconscious, their attempt to close themselves off against the outside might be read as a reflection of Desiderio's narcissistic subjectivity that negates difference.

[33] Derrida 1981, 104,128.

[34] In *Of Grammatology* Derrida analyses Rousseau's notion of writing as "dangerous supplement". Writing, which represents an addition to and a substitute of the spoken word, at the same time makes up for a lack (the missing presence) as it usurps the place of the voice. As 'ersatz' which usurps the centre (the site of full presence), writing is the scapegoat of a violent metaphysics of presence. Derrida 1974, 141,144,145.

down the duality of inside and outside, self and other. It is this very ambivalence which produces Desiderio's capacity for assimilation and ensures the picaresque hero's survival on his quest: his ability to pass for an Indian saves him from the Determination Police.[35] Yet at the same time Desiderio's hybridity mimics and mocks the rigid notion of identity as it is defined by the societies he intrudes into. Mimicry effects a metonymic displacement of identity which is 'part the same, part different'.[36] Undermining their definition of the categories 'horse' and 'human', Desiderio's intrusion throws the centaurs into the deepest confusion:

> We had disrupted their cycle and they were still going through a painful period of readjustment .... We were the first visitors they had ever had ... and when we learned to say their equivalent of 'good morning', their consternation reached a giddy height for there was no sound in their language with which to define a sentient, communicable being who was not mostly horse. (ID 183,184)

The centaurs do not try to solve this problem by readjusting their categories 'horse' and 'human' but by sacrificing and assimilating the intruders' bodies to the horse ideal. Ambivalence turns Desiderio into the sacrificial victim whose assimilation and expulsion affirm the tribe's identity. Similarly, the Indians plan to dispose of the "dangerous supplement" by literally turning exteriority into interiority. The incorporation of the other into the self eliminates ambivalence and restores the integrity of the social body, whose boundaries have been violated. The community strengthens its identity in a ritual which eliminates the transgressor.

> The city's body *proper* thus reconstitutes its unity ... by violently excluding from its territory the representative of an external threat or aggression. That representative represents the otherness of the evil that comes to affect or infect the inside by unpredictably breaking into it.[37]

Yet the purifying effect of the expulsion of otherness implies that the other is already part of the self that defines itself in opposition to it. The scapegoat – as he is defined by René Girard – is chosen from within the community. In *Plato's Pharmacy* Derrida argues that writing as *pharmakos* is 'always

---

[35] Desiderio is the hybrid postcolonial subject that is able to pass as both white and Indian. His ability to pass as white enables him to work as a civil servant in a government office in the city.
[36] Homi Bhabha and Irigaray elaborate on Lacan's conception of mimicry as camouflage. The mimicking of the dominant authority signals assimilation and subordination while making a mockery of this authority: part same, part different, mimicry produces a parodistic copy of the original. Yet in contrast to Irigaray's notion of mimicry, Desiderio's mimicry is not a conscious strategy of subversion even though it has a subversive effect on the communities he enters. See Bhabha 1994, 86 ff.; Irigaray 1985b, 27,36,220.
[37] Derrida 1981, 133.

already' inscribed in speech and thus forms the origin of the speech/writing opposition itself. The sacrifice has the function of negating traces of otherness within the self and of re-establishing the self in strict opposition to an other.

Sacrificial violence is a recurring theme in *The Infernal Desire Machines* and in Carter's fiction as a whole. Albertina's mediating position between Hoffman and the Minister turns her into the ambivalent sacrificial victim on whose death the narrative and the Minister's order are established at the end of the novel. The prostitutes in the House of Anonymity are – half animal, half human – sacrificial victims of the Count's eccentric sadism:

> They were ... inverted mutations, part clockwork, part vegetable, part brute .... The dazed, soft-eyed head of a giraffe swayed on two feet of dappled neck above the furred, golden shoulders of one girl and another had the striped face of a zebra and a cropped stiff, black mane bristling down her spine. But, if some were antlered like stags, others had the branches of trees sprouting out of their bland foreheads .... (ID 132,133)

The narrative literalises the patriarchal construction of woman as ambivalent and transgressive. Woman particularly qualifies as a victim of sacrificial violence in a patriarchal society due to her ambiguous role as mediator between nature and culture. Woman is ambivalent as she is believed to be both within and outside of culture.[38] Fevvers' hybrid body, which also visualises this ambiguous positioning in nature and culture, turns her into the *pharmakos/pharmakon* that Rosencreutz and the Duke attempt to sacrifice in *Nights at the Circus*. The transvestite Tristessa in *The Passion of New Eve* and the disfigured Janus-faced Ghislaine in *Shadow Dance* are further examples of ambivalent scapegoats in Carter's fiction (cf. IV.2.2.3).

To summarise, the cannibalistic sacrifice represents a means of attaining mastery of that which blurs the distinction between inside and outside. The victim is both same and other, identical and different, within and outside of society. The cannibalistic incorporation of the ambivalent serves the policing of boundaries which are drawn around the individual and social body. Like the puritan repression of the body's alterity, it aims at the annihilation of difference. *The Infernal Desire Machines* uncovers the violence at the heart of a rigid notion of the self that constitutes itself through the sacrifice of the other.

---

[38] Ortner 1974, 67 ff..

1.3 The Count: Cannibalism and Sadistic Violence
1.3.1 Cannibalism as Psychoanalytic Metaphor

The cannibalistic nature of desire in the novel is displayed by the samples in the peep-show. The peep-show depicts two portions of ice-cream in the form of female breasts. The image alludes to the Freudian notion of the cannibalistic origins of desire: the breast is "the place where love and hunger meet" (SW 134). In his "Three Essays on the Theory of Sexuality" Freud associates the oral phase of infantile sexuality with an atavistic regression to early stages of phylogenetic development. In the oral phase sexuality is not differentiated from ingestion. The infant's sexuality aims at the cannibalistic incorporation of the breast as the primal object of desire.[39] The Count's double reverts to the infantile fantasy of incorporation when he boils the Count up for a soup.[40] Infantile sexuality being of an autoerotic nature, this regression to early orality entails a narcissistic pleasure in self-destruction: the Count's double literally looks forward to "tasting" himself. In the personification of his shadow, the Count's libidinal aggressive energies turn back upon himself: "'He is my twin. He is my shadow. Such a terrible reversal; I, the hunter, have become my own prey'" (ID 139).

In *The Sadeian Woman* Carter defines sadism as a regression to the 'polymorphous perverse' world of infantile sexuality:

> Juliette, as Theodor Adorno and Max Horkheimer say, embodies 'intellectual pleasure in regression': ... Her will triumphs over the barriers of pain, shame, disgust and morality until her behaviour reverts to the polymorphous perversity of the child, who has not yet learnt the human objections to cruelty because, in a social sense, no child is yet fully human. (SW 148)

Referring to Melanie Klein, Carter gives a psychoanalytical explanation of the excessive hatred that the Sadeian libertines feel towards the world. According to Klein, both love and hate are derived from the child's early relation to the mother. In the oral stage the child discovers the dualism between self and (m)other, experienced as eater and eaten in breast-feeding. The infant develops both desire and hostility toward the mother. On the one hand, the maternal body is the "great, good place, the concretisation of the earthly paradise" (SW 134). On the other hand, envy and greed – the desire to devour and spoil the breast – are early emotions associated with the female breast. When the child discovers the difference between self and (m)other and learns that the breast is not an eternal source of satisfaction, it experiences anxiety

---

[39] Freud 1953a, 198.
[40] See also Sceats 1997, 108 ff.; Sceats 2000, 54.

and aggression against the loved object. It copes with this ambivalence by splitting the breast into a good and a bad breast.

> ... object relations exist from the beginning of life, the first object being the mother's breast which to the child becomes split into a good (gratifying) and bad (frustrating) breast; this splitting results in a severance of love and hate.[41]

The desire to incorporate the breast expresses both a destructive urge to obliterate the bad breast and a yearning for unity with the good breast. The child's fear of being devoured by the mother is a projection of its own desire to incorporate what is external to the self. *The Sadeian Woman* traces Sade's misogyny back to these feelings of impotence, aggression and fear in early childhood.[42] Correspondingly, *The Infernal Desire Machines* reveals an infantile anxiety beneath the Count's violent egocentricity. The Count is modelled on the Marquis de Sade in the novel.[43] His violence recalls the libertines' regressive transgressions in Sade's work. The megalomania of the Count turns into an infantile sense of impotence when he is imprisoned by the sailors:

> For the first twenty-four hours of our incarceration, he screamed all the time on a single, high-pitched note and when the first mate came in with our meagre rations, he cowered away as if he expected the Finn to kick him .... This display of quivering pusillanimity fascinated me .... (ID 145)

The Count experiences the infant's anxiety that the world he endeavours to swallow will turn back upon him and devour him. By acting out this fantasy, his double grotesquely literalises the Kleinian phantasmagoric horror scenario of early childhood.

In Carter's fiction sadism is typically connected with a feeling of impotence and loneliness. The sadistic executioner in Carter's short story "The Executioner's Beautiful Daughter" is "locked in the solitary confinement of his power" (BB 40). Bound to iron rings in the ceiling, the king of the cruel tribe is confined to immobility: "Heir of the barbarous, he is stripped of everything but the idea of an omnipotence which is sufficiently expressed by immobility" (BB 39). The "atrocious loneliness" (BB 138) of the sadistic Marquis in "The Bloody Chamber" resembles the hunter's desperate brutality in "Master", which is psychologically motivated as a desire to "destroy them all in order to feel less lonely ... to penetrate this absence with this annihilating presence" (BB 78). In *The Sadeian Woman* the

---

[41] Klein 1986, 176-177.
[42] Carter 1979, 135.
[43] The Count's journey appears as a violent parody of the Marquis de Sade and his valet's flight from legal persecution for "poisoning" and "sodomy" in France. Carter mentions Sade's flight in *The Sadeian Woman*. See Carter 1979, 30.

libertines' regressive cruelty hides a feeling of impotence that is associated with early childhood:

> The triumph of the will recreates ... the world of early childhood, and that is a world of nightmare, impotence and fear, in which the child fantasises, out of its own powerlessness, an absolute supremacy. (ID 148)

The fantasy of omnipotence turns the other into an extension of the self and leaves the subject in isolation. Like Sade's Juliette, the Count suffers from the "lonely freedom of the libertine": "... a tautological condition that exists only for itself and is without any meaning in the general context of human life" (SW 99). This sense of lack and loneliness, however, suggests a need for recognition and relation to the other. The Count represents the Hegelian master who is dependent on the slave. Interestingly, it is the slave – the Count's Valet – who provides an analysis of the Hegelian interdependence of master and slave:

> Master and slave exist in a necessary tension of a twinned actuality ... his [the Count's] insistence on the authority of his own autonomy made him at once the tyrant and the victim of matter, for he was dependent on the notion that matter was submissive to him. (ID 147,168)

The Count turns the world into food. The assertion of the self is based on the subjection of the other.[44] Yet the master who is dependent on recognition by the slave is himself negated when he deprives the slave of his/her subjectivity. The Count's annihilation is the logical consequence of his negation of the world: "I am my own antithesis .... I unleash negation ...." (ID 35).

1.3.2 Cannibalism as Economic Metaphor

The Count's violence is grounded in his infantile sense of impotence and in his inability to acknowledge an other beside the self: "He was the emperor of inverted megalomaniacs .... his lusts always blinded him completely to anything but his own sensations ...." (ID 123,168). Embodying an extreme version of male solipsism, of the inability to "experience experience as experience",[45] the Count represents an aspect of Desiderio's self. At the beginning of his quest Desiderio appears as sardonic narrator who does not

---

[44] Aidan Day argues that the Count embodies the Cartesian subject that is driven by the desire to become an "absolute self" by uniting with the other. As this other is objectified and lifeless, unification turns into self-annihilation. Day 1998, 95.

[45] The inability to "experience experience as experience" is a recurring motif in Carter's fiction. See, for instance, *Nights at the Circus* (NC 10), *The Sadeian Woman* (SW 51,144), "The Flesh and the Mirror" (BB 69) and "Black Venus" (BB 231).

seem to be affected by the events around him. He shares this disaffection with several other detached male characters in Carter's fiction, who either undergo a change through suffering (Walser, Evelyn) or become victims of their own narcissism (Master, Uncle Philip and Zero). Experience does not change tyrants like Master, Uncle Philip, Zero and the Count, who remain "isolated in [their] invulnerability" (ID 125). In the Count's case this invulnerability is expressed in his inability to feel pain; only when pain is inflicted on him does he acquire a sense of a world existing beyond his solipsistic ego. Thus, he feels liberated when he is boiled by his shadow: "... he began to laugh with joy – pure joy ...'Lafleur! I am in pain! ... he rose up out of the cauldron in an upward surging leap, as of a fully liberated man" (ID 163). However, there is no sense of reciprocity between the world and the Count when the latter is in pain; the subject position immediately collapses into the object position. The voracious eater is transformed into food. The Count's world view does not allow for a mutual reciprocity of self and other. Relations between self and other are necessarily conceived as relations between subject – which inflicts pain – and object – which is subjected to pain. If the self is no master, it is necessarily a slave.

The Sadeian Woman presents a critique of Enlightenment reason and bourgeois individualism. Sade is described as the "last, bleak, disillusioned voice of the Enlightenment" (SW 34). His heroine Juliette incarnates rationality turning against humanity: "... Juliette ... can say, as a hero of Voltaire might: 'I have no light to guide me but my reason'" (SW 35). In the solipsism of the Sadeian Count, Carter exposes the egocentric nature of a perverted form of bourgeois individualism which is based on an eat-or-be eaten version of reality. Like Juliette, the Count has reached the "lonely freedom of the libertine" (SW 99).

> All living creatures are born and die in isolation, says Noirceuil; in the cultivation and practice of egoism and self-interest alone may be found true happiness. Juliette is immediately drawn to this credo of bourgeois individualism. (SW 84)

The Cartesian distinction between subject (eater) and object (eaten) – the philosophical underpinning of bourgeois individualism – is mutated to an "infernal egoism" (ID 124) in the figure of the Count.[46] This infernal egoism

---

[46] Day reads the narrative as a critique of an egocentric individualism based on the Cartesian dualism of self and other. According to Day, Desiderio's attachment to the common good at the end of the narrative endorses a model of reason based on reciprocity. Day seems to ignore that Desiderio is himself attached to the Cartesian dualism of transcendental self and inert other. He does, in fact, participate in the objectification of women on his picaresque journey. I would argue against Day's reading that Desiderio is not

manifests itself in a capitalist theory of sexual pleasure as it is devised by the monk Clement in Sade's *Justine*:

... Clement argues that there is not enough pleasure to go round and he must have it all.... Pleasure may never be shared, or it will be diminished. A shared pleasure is a betrayal of the self, a seeping away of some of the subject's precious egotism .... (SW 142)

In her analysis of Sade, Carter refers to Adorno and Horkheimer's critique of the Enlightenment. Adorno and Horkheimer relate the rise of totalitarianism in the twentieth century to the instrumentalisation of reason in modernity. Kant split the notion of reason into 'practical reason', which deals with ethical and moral questions, and 'speculative reason', which points to the epistemological limits of human reason and refrains from the formulation of transcendental values. By distinguishing 'practical reason' from 'speculative reason', Kant prevented his radical critique of traditional metaphysics from turning back upon itself and opened space for a moral practice which is not derived from formal rationality alone. Sade's radical scepticism, by contrast, employs 'speculative reason' to destroy 'practical reason':

Just as Kant's moral philosophy restricted his enlightened critique, in order to preserve the possibility of reason, so – conversely – unreflective enlightened thinking based on the notion of survival always tends to convert into skepticism .... the work of the Marquis de Sade, like that of Nietzsche, constitutes the intransigent critique of practical reason .... It makes the scientistic the destructive principle.[47]

Juliette embodies this destructive force of a radical scepticism. Her atheist rationality does not only lead her to a rejection of Christian values but furthermore to an apotheosis of vice:

Goodness and benevolence become sin, whereas domination and oppression become virtue .... When all ideologies have been abrogated, she [Juliette] adopts her own morality what Christianity ... always held to be execrable.[48]

The Count's iconoclastic atheism re-enacts the apotheosis of vice that Juliette proclaims in the name of rationality. In the ruins of a Jesuit chapel the Count blatantly exhibits his atheism by urinating on the altar and raping his valet. After having devoured his breakfast with a "blind voracity" (ID 125), he turns Lafleur into food for his sexual appetite. It may seem strange to associate the Count's insatiable appetites with notions of scepticism and rationality. However, the Count's transgressions are "never unpremeditated" (ID 168).

---

radically opposed to the Count's egocentric individuality. The Count rather embodies an exaggerated version of Desiderio's solipsism, an externalisation of Desiderio's psyche. See Day 1998, 94 ff..
[47] Horkheimer, Adorno 1997, 93-94.
[48] Horkheimer, Adorno 1997, 103-104.

Like the libertines' violence in Sade, they are characterised by a "cerebral", "intellectual" quality (ID 167, cf. SW 142). The Count's voracity is not libido running wild against the forces of reason. His violence is grounded in a modern sceptical rationality that serves self-interest and degenerates into cynicism and nihilism.

However, it is not only the Count who embodies Sadeian destructiveness. The totalitarian potential of the Enlightenment, the formalisation of reason, is also evident in the efficiency with which the Minister's Determination Police extinguishes any person whose reality status seems to be dubious. In fact, in their black leather coats and polished boots the officers look "as if they had been recruited wholesale from a Jewish nightmare" (ID 22).[49] The police's violence mirrors the Count's journey of death. The guardians of a positivist rationality exemplify reason overreaching itself and turning into the opposite of reason: "Scientific order, ruthlessly applied, reduces the world to chaos" (SW 115). Both the Count and the Determination Police are the destructive products of the instrumentalisation of reason in modernity. Sadism arises from a perverted rationality that serves an "infernal egoism" and culminates in the cannibalistic objectification of the other. In fact, the Count shares certain features with the Minister, who is the very embodiment of rationality in the narrative: his charismatic appearance, his "iron determination" (ID 124) and his "earth-shaking treads" (ID 169) are reminiscent of the Minister. Both the Count and the Minister suffer from a desperate sense of "self-absorption" (ID 124). In the course of Desiderio's quest the basic opposition between reason and irrationality increasingly breaks down, identities are confused and apparent opponents turn out to be each other's doubles.

1.4 Conclusion

The Body as Meat: Cannibalising the Other

In *The Infernal Desire Machines* cannibalism is an image of aggression and exploitation. Cannibalism epitomises an "omnivorous egocentricity" (SW 32) that 'meatifies' the other. Various sadistic figures are characterised by their perverted appetites in Carter's *oeuvre*. In "The Executioner's Beautiful Daughter" the executioner only eats eggs on the point of turning into chicken. The Duke in "Wolf-Alice" lives on the corpses he desecrates in the village graveyard: "His eyes see only appetite. These eyes open to devour the world in which he sees, nowhere, a reflection of himself" (BB 222). They resemble the eyes of the Erl-King: "There are some eyes can eat you" (BB 187). These

---

[49] See also Peach 1998, 105.

omnivorous gothic figures are joined by several man-eating women in Carter's fiction. Saskia in *Wise Children* is a greedy meat- and man-eater. The female protagonist in "Master" takes revenge on her Master's brutality and becomes a carnivore and killer. The Countess in "The Lady of the House of Love" is a sensitive vampire who feels sorry for her victims but nevertheless eats them with relish. These voracious eaters seem to be modelled on various characters in Sade's work such as Juliette and the cannibal Minski, who embody calculated cruelty and a presumptuous egocentricity. In *The Sadeian Woman* Carter distinguishes between flesh and meat: while "flesh plus skin equals sensuality" (SW 138), meat – as "flesh minus skin" (SW 138) – is "dead, inert, animal and intended for consumption" (SW 137). Cannibalism reveals the "meatiness of human flesh" (SW 140). Sadism represents the 'meatification' of the sexual object: it is not a sensual but an analytical, clinical pleasure which turns living flesh into dead matter. From this perspective, Sade is regarded as a "great puritan" (SW 138) who purges sexuality of the sensual and considers it as a matter of butchery and meat. Sade conceived sexual violence as an image of authoritarianism and political despotism. Cannibalism and sadism are metaphors for the power relations in a society:

> Sexuality, in this estranged form, becomes a denial of a basis of mutuality, of the acknowledgement of equal rights to exist in the world, from which any durable form of human intercourse can spring. (SW 141)

In a patriarchal society female flesh is in perpetual danger of being transformed into meat. This is illustrated in the most drastic way in *Shadow Dance*. After Honeybuzzard has slashed Ghislaine with a knife, the scar divides her face into smooth flesh and monstrous meat:

> There was the healed scar of a great wound down one side of her face. The whole cheek was a mass of corrugated white flesh, like a bowl of blancmange a child has played with and not eaten. Through this devastation ran a deep central trough that went right down her throat under the collar of her coat .... But the other half of the face was fresh and young and smooth and warm as fruit in the sunlight. (SD 152,153; cf. note 21)

The image of the blancmange that has been played with but left unconsumed conceives of Ghislaine's face as a comestible: a piece of meat "red and raw as if, at the slightest exertion, it might open and bleed ...." (SD 2). In *The Infernal Desire Machines* the flagellated prostitute and the samples in the peep-show represent further appalling images of meatified female bodies: "... her back was a ravelled palimpsest of wound upon wound ... this torn and bleeding she was ... the most dramatic revelation of the nature of meat that I have ever seen" (ID 133). The sample "Everyone knows what the Night is for" displays a female body whose breast has been partially segmented to reveal "two surfaces of meat" (ID 45). Cannibalistic metaphors epitomise the objectification and exploitation of the other in its most extreme form in the novel.

Freud and Melanie Klein: Melancholia and Regression

In *The Infernal Desire Machines* Carter draws on several psychoanalytic theories that deal with the body and its relation to food. Cannibalism emerges as a complex metaphor that can be interpreted on different levels in the novel. Freud employs the cannibalistic metaphor in the description of infantile sexuality. While cannibalism symbolises exploitation in an economic and political sense, it is an image for infantile regression and the negation of difference on a psychoanalytic level. The desire to devour the other and the fear of engulfment are derived from the child's early ambivalent relation to the mother, as described by Melanie Klein. The child fears the mother is taking revenge and turning back on the object that wishes to consume her. Images of maternal violence express this anxiety in *The Infernal Desire Machines*. The samples display a nursemaid gobbling up a baby "with every appearance of relish" (ID 107). The man-eating African amazons are projections of Desiderio's and the Count's cannibalistic omnivoracity.

Freud also employs the cannibalistic metaphor in "Mourning and Melancholia" and in "Totem and Taboo". Incorporation in melancholia leads to a division of the ego, which prefigures the topographic distinction between the ego and the super-ego in Freud's later work.[50] "Totem and Taboo" describes the same process on an anthropological level: the incorporation of the dead father constitutes religion as society's superego. In both cases incorporation produces the divided self. In *The Infernal Desire Machines* Desiderio emerges as melancholic divided subject that is haunted by the lost object of desire at the end of the narrative. The centaurs' bodily hybridity is another image of the split self. One part of this self – the horsy part, the incorporated Sacred Stallion – violently turns against the other, human part in masochistic self-mortification.

Hearty Eaters in Carter's Late Fiction

In *The Infernal Desire Machines* eating is an aggressive, violent activity. The novel offers the choice between a cannibalistic voracity and the loss of appetite in depression. In Carter's later work the imagery of appetite, eating and food takes on a more positive meaning. Fevvers, whose appetite indicates

---

[50] The incorporated lost object that berates the self corresponds to the super-ego in Freud's model of the psyche.

vitality and power, represents a humane version of her *femme-fatale* predecessors in Carter's short stories. In *The Bloody Chamber and Other Stories* the wolf as "carnivore incarnate" is not only a threatening but an equally fascinating creature, which may be fatal for grandmothers but quite attractive to their granddaughters (cf. V.6). Eating as transgression of bodily boundaries is an image of metamorphosis in "Wolf-Alice" and in "The Lady of the House of Love". Alice licks off the blood of the wounded vampire-Duke and transforms him into a human being. In "The Lady of the House of Love" the British officer redeems the Countess from her vampire existence by sucking her wound. In "The Tiger's Bride" the beast does not gobble Beauty up but tenderly licks off her skin until she is furred like he is. The sensual licking of skin ("flesh plus skin equals sensuality" [SW 138]) is a recurring image in Carter, which is opposed to the skinning of the sexual object ("flesh minus skin equals meat" [SW 138]) as it is described in "The Erl-King":

> He is the tender butcher who shows me how the price of flesh is love. .... He strips me to my last nakedness ... like a skinned rabbit .... I should like to grow enormously small, so that you could swallow me. (BB 189,190)

In the House of Anonymity the Count's torturing of the prostitute's corroded skin is juxtaposed to the licking and melting of skin in the love scene between Desiderio and Albertina: "... our skins melt and fuse .... I sucked great mouthfuls of the cold water of her breasts ...." (ID 136,137). Metaphors of oral incorporation permeate the discourse of love. In "The Erl-King" this incorporation is a threat to the narrator's autonomy as it will trap her like a bird in a cage (cf. V.4.1). In contrast, *The Passion of New Eve* employs the metaphor of eating in a reciprocal way in the love scene between Tristessa and Eve:

> Eat me. Consume me. .... We sucked at the water bottle of each other's mouth for there was nothing else to drink. Turn and turn about, now docile, now virile .... I licked the water from Tristessa's skin .... I thought we were turning into water and would therefore be able to drink freely. (PE 148,149,153).

While desire is frequently narcissistic in Carter's early fiction, a reciprocal form of desire emerges in her late fiction, as I will argue in the following chapters. This reciprocal desire implies a subject-in-process, a subject which is in dialogue with the other and changes in the course of this dialogue. In *The Infernal Desire Machines* this utopian concept of a mutual sexuality is absent. It is only hinted at in the Count's condemnation of the "death-defying double somersault of love" (ID 124). Instead, the novel features numerous flagellations, mutilations, stabbings, rapes and, finally, the cooked meat of the count. There is not much skin but a lot of meat in the novel. In *The Infernal Desire Machines* the subject remains isolated in his narcissistic egocentricity, which literally swallows the other figures and denies them the right to subjecthood.

2. The Body as Text: Desire in *The Infernal Desire Machines*

> She splits open closed texts and revels
> in what she finds there, blood, scars, perversion.
> *Anny Crunelle-Vanrigh on Angela Carter, 2001*

In *The Infernal Desire Machines* desire is cannibalistic and turns the body into meat. But meat is artificial in the novel, made of plastic, wax and red paint. Meat as "bright and false as the plaster sirloins which hang in toy butcher's shops" (ID 45) is produced and displayed in the peep-show. In *The Infernal Desire Machines* the body and its sexuality are fabricated by Hoffman's machinery. This chapter examines desire as a discursive production in the novel. As the text extensively alludes to liberationist theories of sexuality, I will briefly recapitulate major concepts in these theories before turning to an analysis of desire in the narrative. The discursive production of desire textualises the body. Referring to Foucault, I will argue that both the Minister *and* Hoffman are engaged in a 'disciplining' of desire, which is reflected in their attempts to control time and transcend the materiality of the body.

2.1 Theorising Desire
2.1.1 Desire and Repression: Marcuse, Brown and Reich

Hoffman's revolution of desire is driven by "eroto-energy", which he extracts from the copulations of his 'love slaves'. This release of sexual energy is supposed to trigger the revolution, liberating man from social constraints: "By liberating the unconscious, we shall, of course, liberate man." (ID 208) Hoffman reiterates one of the credos of the sixties: the liberation of sexuality is believed to be a necessary part of the political revolution. As the novel repeatedly alludes to liberationist ideas of the sixties, I will briefly discuss major proponents of these ideas in this section.

In the fifties, Marcuse, Brown and Reich developed Freud's idea that destructiveness may be the product of an excessive repression of instincts. Marcuse (*Eros and Civilization*, 1955) and Brown (*Life Against Death*, 1959) reacted against the privileging of the reality principle over the pleasure principle in neo-Freudian theories of the fifties:

Self-consciousness and reason, which have conquered and shaped the historical world, have done so in the image of repression, internal and external. They have worked as the agents of domination; the liberties they have brought (and these are considerable) grew in the soil of enslavement and have retained the mark of their birth.[51]

In contrast to Freud, Marcuse does not consider civilisation as repressive by necessity; he distinguishes between basic and surplus repression. Whereas the former implies the restraining of instinct necessary for survival, the latter is grounded in social domination and an economy of competition. Industrial societies engender a desire for consumption while requiring a disciplined body in the production process of consumer goods (cf. II.5.1). The body is de-sexualised in the service of labour; sexuality is reduced to the genital procreative function. Social domination is necessitated by the discrepancy between a limited amount of goods and the unlimited production of desire for consumption. However, according to Marcuse, repressive civilisation creates the precondition for the gradual elimination of repression: a society of high productivity radically reduces labour, freeing libidinal energies which were formerly absorbed by work. It enables its members to live a life of self-fulfilment and allows for a return to a polymorphous sexuality and an erotisation of personality. The liberation of desire is based on the unravelling of the Weberian work ethic in advanced consumer society.[52]

In a similar vein, Norman Brown perceives repression as causing "the universal neurosis of mankind". Brown calls for the abolition of repression and envisions a reconciliation of the pleasure and the reality principle in a "Dionysian ego" which affirms instinctual reality. He imagines a "resurrected body" that carries features of the infantile polymorphous perverse body and finds a way "out of human neurosis into that simple health that animals enjoy ....".[53] Hoffman's claim that his world is not an "either/or" but an "and + and world" (ID 206) echoes Brown's critique of the law of contradiction as a repressive concept of rationality. Brown refers to the Freudian notion that

> ... the law of contradiction does not hold in the id .... Instead of the law of contradiction we find the unity of opposites .... Formal logic and the law of contradiction are the rules whereby the mind submits to operate under general conditions of repression. As with the concept of time, Kant's categories of rationality would then turn out to be the categories of repression.[54]

---

[51] Marcuse 1955, 52.
[52] Ibid., 40 ff., 112 ff., 129 ff., 199 ff..
[53] Brown 1959, 9,10,176,311.
[54] Ibid., 320,321.

Referring to the Freudian axiom that "the essence of man consists not, as Descartes maintained, in thinking, but in desiring"[55], Brown reverses the Cartesian privileging of the mind and defines the subject in relation to its sexuality. The Doctor's inverted version of the *cogito ergo sum* – "I desire therefore I exist" (ID 211) – alludes to Brown's dictum.

A similar inversion of the Cartesian mind/body hierarchy can be found in the work of the late Reich. Consciousness and thought grow increasingly irrelevant in the late Reich's conception of life, which focuses exclusively on flows of bioenergy and their obstruction. According to Reich, 'bioenergy' – a concept akin to Freud's libido – exists anterior to matter and constitutes the principle of vitality in the cosmos. The accumulation of bioenergy leads to the formation of desire in the human organism, which is released in orgasm. Reich tried to concentrate bioenergy in his notorious 'orgone box'. Particularly in his early work – *The Invasion of Compulsory Sex-Morality* and *The Sexual Revolution* – he equates sexual liberation with political liberation.[56]

The pseudo-scientific jargon that Hoffman and Mendoza use in *The Infernal Desire Machines* and the notion of libido as a politically liberating form of energy are reminiscent of Reich's notion of orgone energy. In fact, Lorna Sage has identified Hoffman's machinery as the "world's largest orgone box".[57] However, in *The Infernal Desire Machines* the liberation of desire turns into a tyranny of desire. While Brown and the early Marcuse idealise regression to an infantile polymorphous form of desire, the novel literalises Freud's metaphors of the oral (cannibalistic) and anal (sadistic) stage of sexuality and describes regression as a reversion to cannibalistic sadism (cf. III.1.3). David Punter and Ricarda Schmidt consider the text to be an allegory of the failure of the revolutionary hopes of the sixties. Punter reads the novel "as a series of figures for the defeat of the political aspirations of the 1960s, and in particular of the father-figures of liberation, Reich and Marcuse".[58] Whereas Punter seems to regret Desiderio's decision which "brings all the efforts of fantasy to emerge into the world down to dust"[59], Schmidt criticises Punter's nostalgic view of the sexual revolution. According

[55] Ibid., 7,9,175,176.
[56] See Reich, Wilhelm, *Der Einbruch der sexuellen Zwangsmoral*, Köln, 1972, 149 ff., 200; Reich, Wilhelm, *Die sexuelle Revolution*, Frankfurt/Main, 1971, 318 ff.. The English translation was not available. For a summary of Reich's work see also Konitzer 1987 and Raditsa 1987, 17-41. For his development of the 'orgone box' see Sharaf 1983, 276 ff..
[57] Sage 1977, 52; Rosenberg, Clark and Mikkonen read the text as alluding to Reich's ideas. See Rosenberg 1997, 180; Clark 1987, 154; Mikkonen 1997, 169.
[58] Punter 1984, 211.
[59] Ibid., 213.

to Schmidt, Carter does not advocate Hoffman's revolution. The narrative rather demonstrates the rule of desire to be just as sterile and static as the rule of reason.[60] Desire loses the glamour of the marvellous in Hoffman's castle and emerges as a repressive concept at the end of Desiderio's quest. The novel expresses the disillusionment with the sixties' utopian enthusiasm by giving an allegorical illustration of the late Marcuse's concept of 'repressive desublimation'. While in *Eros and Civilization* Marcuse envisaged a non-repressive sublimation of sexuality, he grows more pessimistic in his later work. In *One-Dimensional Man* he observes the contrary development of 'repressive desublimation' in advanced industrial societies. The growing sexualisation of the body at work, in fashion and in advertising serves business interests and defuses the subversive potential of sexuality. The controlled liberation of libidinal energies produces a conformist "happy consciousness" of voluntary subjection.[61] In fact, in *The Infernal Desire Machines* the love slaves have "volunteered" (ID 215) for their enslavement.

> There were no locks or bars anywhere; they could have come and gone as they pleased. Yet, petrified pilgrims, locked parallels, icons of perpetual motion, they knew nothing but the progress of their static journey towards willed, mutual annihilation .... (ID 215)

Desire is mass-produced on the assembly line in the novel. The lovers resemble animals kept in livestock farming for mass consumption:

> 'We feed them hormones intravenously', the Doctor informed me. 'Their plentiful secretions fall through the wire meshes into the trays underneath each tier, or dynamic set, of lovers and are gathered up three times a day by means of large sponges, so that nothing whatsoever is lost. And the energy they release ... rises up through these funnels into the generating chambers overhead.' (ID 214,215)

Hoffman is no Prospero but the 'enterpreneur' who controls and manages the belt production of sexuality.

2.1.2 Desire as Production: Deleuze/Guattari, Foucault and Butler

In the *Symposium* Plato defines desire in a negative way as a void in the subject that requires the acquisition of an object.[62] Many contemporary philosophers and psychoanalysts follow this notion of desire as a lack in the subject. According to Lacan, the repression of oedipal desires constitutes desire as "*manque-à-être*".[63] As unfulfillable lack, desire aims at the recovery

---

[60] Schmidt 1989, 61.
[61] Marcuse 1991, 74 ff..
[62] Plato 1993a, 38-39 (200a-201b).
[63] Lacan 1973, 31. See also 1.1.2.1.

of what has been irretrievably lost. In contrast to Lacan, Kristeva claims that the semiotic pre-oedipal realm is still accessible through the medium of poetic language.[64] Yet even though the poetic is able to disrupt the symbolic, it does not have the power to rearticulate the symbolic terms by which the subject is constituted. A full return to the semiotic remains impossible, effecting the dissolution of the subject in psychosis. Desire appears as a lack which can never be fulfilled.

Spinoza turned against a Platonic negative definition of desire as lack: desire does not primarily aim at the acquisition of an object but at the continuation of desire itself. For Spinoza "the striving by which each thing strives to persevere in its being" is the actual "essence of the thing".[65] Spinoza's *conatus* is in this sense a precursor of the Nietzschean will to power. Desire is not a secondary response to preliminary needs but a primary force. As primary force, desire is ineluctable. Nietzsche's concept of the will is similarly defined by its *"horror vacui"*: *"it needs a goal* – and it will rather will *nothingness* than *not* will".[66] Even in asceticism, the will is not negated, but manifests itself as a 'will to nothingness'. Desire is not grounded in negativity but represents a life-affirming force that is based on plenitude and excess.

In *Anti-Oedipus* Deleuze and Guattari refer to Spinoza's *conatus* and Nietzsche's will to power when they define desire as production. According to Deleuze/Guattari

> ... lack (*manque*) is created, planned, and organized in and through social production .... It is never primary; production is never organized on the basis of a pre-existing need or lack (manque). It is lack that infiltrates itself ... in accordance with ... an already existing organization of production. The deliberate creation of lack as a function of market economy is the art of a dominant class.[67]

Deleuze/Guattary historicise the notion of 'desire as lack' as a product of an economy of scarcity, of social hierarchies and material deprivations. However, they deviate from this materialist approach to desire when they oppose a pre-cultural force of plenitude and excess to the culturally constructed form of desire as lack: desire in its original form is a productive, affirmative force which has to be liberated from repression. Part of this

---

[64] Kristeva 1980, 135 ff..
[65] Spinoza 1985, 499. Describing desire as a primary force, Spinoza argues in a Hobbesian manner: "... we neither strive for, nor will, neither want, nor desire anything because we judge it to be good; on the contrary, we judge something to be good because we strive for it, will it, want, and desire it." Spinoza 1985, 500.
[66] Nietzsche 1967, 97.
[67] Deleuze and Guattari 1983, 28.

repression is the restriction of desire to the oedipal family structure. Investing primal desire with a revolutionary force, Deleuze and Guattari take to a Romantic, emancipatory concept, akin to Brown's and Reich's notion of sexuality. Capitalism emerges as an ambivalent force in their theory. On the one hand, capitalism confines ("reterritorializes") desire by turning all social relations into economic exchange relations, with money acting as a "general equivalent".[68] On the other hand, capitalism frees ("deterritorializes") flows of desires by dissolving traditional codes – such as class, religion and family structures – that define and restrict social relations. According to Deleuze/Guattari, there is a subversive potential in 'deterritorialization' which can be turned against capitalism. 'Deterritorialization' produces the schizophrenic subject which is in the process of becoming other:

> ... the schizo ... plunges further and further into the realm of deterritorialization, reaching the furthest limits of the decomposition of the socius .... The schizophrenic deliberately seeks out the very limit of capitalism: he is its inherent tendency brought to fulfilment .... He scrambles all the codes and is the transmitter of the decoded flows of desire.[69]

The nomadic schizophrenic subject resembles the monstrous body with variable bodily boundaries, which open themselves to change and otherness (cf. II.6).[70] Deleuze/Guattari celebrate the disintegration of the subject under capitalism. They are thus faced with the problem that any poststructuralist theory of an unstable subject is confronted with: how can a disintegrating subject be an effective site of agency and resistance?

Foucault's *History of Sexuality* can be read as a radical refutation of the revolution of desire in the Marcusian and the Deleuzian form.[71] While Deleuze/Guattari adhere to a juridical model of power, in Foucault there is no original revolutionary form of desire, as desire is itself a product of power (cf.

---

[68] Ibid., 226.

[69] Ibid., 35.

[70] Habermeier and Mikkonen refer to Deleuze and Guattari in their reading of *The Infernal Desire Machines*. Mikkonen points to parallels between Hoffman's and Deleuze/Guattari's concept of desire. See Mikkonen 1997, 168. Habermeier reads Desiderio's love for Albertina as "deterritorialised an-oedipal desire" in Deleuze and Guattari's sense. Habermeier 1996, 183 ff.. For a critique of Habermeier see note 89.

[71] Deleuze/Guattari's *Anti-Oedipus* is, however, close to the ideas of the early Foucault, who wrote the preface of the book. In *Madness and Civilization*, Foucault demands to "return, in history, to that zero point in the course of madness at which madness is an undifferentiated experience, a not yet divided experience of division itself". Foucault 1965, ix. Like Deleuze/Guattari, *Madness and Civilization* distinguishes a pre-historical original experience of madness from a discursively constructed form of madness which was first developed in the eighteenth century. This binary model (original versus constructed madness) that the preface to *Madness and Civilization* presupposes has come in for criticism by Foucault himself in *The History of Sexuality* (see II.3).

II.3.1). In fact, the distinction between revolutionary and non-revolutionary desire made in *Anti-Oedipus* is problematic. What is the deterritorialized subversive form of desire, and how can it be distinguished from the reterritorialized paranoiac desire in the service of capitalism?[72] Different strategies of resistance follow from contrasting notions of the primacy of power or desire in Foucault's and Deleuze/Guattari's work, respectively. Whereas Foucault rejects the concept of a "single locus of great Refusal"[73], in *Anti-Oedipus* the deterritorialized flows of desire and the schizophrenic subject are precisely this site of rebellion. Deleuze/Guattari envisage – as Manfred Frank ironically puts it – Dionysos running amok. Frank attacks the idealisation of madness in *Anti-Oedipus*. In the twentieth century the myth of the noble insane, he argues, replaces the myth of the noble savage that was particularly popular in the eighteenth century. Both function as projection space for repressed yearnings in modern, rationalist society.[74]

In *Subjects of Desire* Butler charges Deleuze/Guattari's conception of desire as essentialist thinking. She criticises *Anti-Oedipus* for ignoring Lacan's notion of the cultural construction of desire. Desire is no pre-symbolic force but emerges with the subject's entry into language and culture. In *The Psychic Life of Power* Butler conjoins a psychoanalytic and a Foucauldian perspective, arguing that desire is 'always already' contaminated by power. Analysing the psychic effects of power, she states that we may, paradoxically, desire our own subjection.

> If the unconscious/psyche is defined as resistance, what do we then make of unconscious attachments to subjection, which imply that the unconscious is no more free of normalizing discourse than the subject? What makes us think that the unconscious is any less structured by the power relations that pervade cultural signifiers than is the language of the subject?[75]

Butler defines desire in Spinoza's sense as "desire to persist in one's own being".[76] This desire for existence may work to stabilise relations of domination and subjection. The subject seeks recognition of its own existence in categories, terms, and names (for instance in stereotypical definitions of 'woman' and 'black') that signify existence and subordination at once. These imprisoning social categories are preferred to the denial of social existence.

---

[72] Deleuze/Guattari themselves point to the difficulty of distinguishing these two forms of desire. Deleuze, Guattari 1983, 258.
[73] Foucault 1990, 95,96.
[74] Frank 1984, 419,432. For a discussion of Deleuze/Guattari's *Anti-Oedipus* see also Bogue 1989, 83-107 and Goodchild 1996.
[75] Butler 1997, 88.
[76] Ibid., 28.

Hence, the desire for existence turns back upon the self in the process of subject formation. The subject turning back upon itself – a recurring trope in Hegel, Nietzsche and Freud[77] – produces reflexivity, the separation of the super-ego from the ego. The super-ego controls the adaptation of the self to the ego-ideal ('woman', 'black'), which is also the "common ideal of a family, a class or a nation".[78] Power relations are inscribed into the formation of the psyche. Desire and subjugation are intricately intertwined in the constitution of the subject. The centaurs' practice of tattooing provides an image for the way in which the subject turns back upon itself in the search for social existence. The tattoo indicates the social status of an individual in the centaurs' society. It reflects the power structure of the society: in particular women are subjected to the practice of tattooing: " The females were ritually degraded and reviled. They bore the bloody brunt of the tattooing"(ID 176; cf. 1.2.1). The subject willingly undergoes the painful ritual of social integration. The desire for social existence drives it to the masochistic acceptance of subjugation. Power, desire and subjectivity form a knot which can hardly be disentangled.

Conclusion

The juridical model of power informs Marcuse's, Deleuze/Guattari's and Lacan's concepts of desire. Desire is repressed by civilisation, capitalism and the symbolic, respectively. The liberationists – Marcuse and Deleuze/Guattari – envisage an emancipation of repressed desire. In contrast, in Lacanian psychoanalysis the subject is founded on the unfulfillability of desire, which can only be revoked in the dissolution of subjectivity. The liberation of desire

---

[77] The trope of the subject turning back upon the self recurs several times in *On the Genealogy of Morals*. Nietzsche defines the ascetic ideal not – in Schopenhauer's sense – as negation of the will but as the will to nothingness, the will turning against the body (Nietzsche 1967, 163). In the *Second Essay* Nietzsche defines bad conscience as instincts turning back upon the self (Nietzsche 1967, 85,128). His theory of the formation of conscience as internalisation of aggression has been resumed by Freud in "Civilization and its Discontents" (Freud 1953k, 123). Butler traces the trope of the subject turning back upon the self in Hegel's "The Unhappy Conscience": "The bondsman in Hegel throws off the apparently external 'Lord' only to find himself in an ethical world, subjected to various norms and ideals ... the subject emerges as an unhappy consciousness through the reflexive application of these ethical laws." The self-consciousness of the sceptic produces a "dual structuring of the subject" in which one part of the self berates the other – corporeal – part of the self (Butler 1997, 32,46,52). In fasting and self-mortification the body thus turns against itself (see Hegel 1988, 155). As I have argued above, in *The Infernal Desire Machines* the subject turns back upon itself in the centaurs' masochism and in Desiderio's melancholia (cf. 1.1.2.2; 1.2.1).

[78] Freud 1953d, 81.

is an impossible project that entails the death of the subject. Opposed to these contrasting juridical positions are Foucault's and Butler's view of desire as produced and compromised by power. For Foucault, the liberationist impetus represents a ruse of power that assists the production and proliferation of new areas of control (cf. II.3).

The Infernal Desire Machines presents a very sceptical evaluation of the revolutionary potential of desire. Desire and power are inextricably intermingled in the text. Sadism and masochism blend violence and desire. Anticipating the late Foucault's position, Carter debunks the myth of the revolutionary potential of sexuality. In what follows, I will focus on the role of the peep-show in an analysis of desire as a cultural construction in Foucault's sense. The samples in the peep-show represent the core of the narrative as they reflect the narrative's plot and symbolism in a condensed form. In a reading of the peep-show as proto-cinematic apparatus, the samples are the site at which power, pleasure and knowledge intersect. Referring to Luce Irigaray and Laura Mulvey, I will also look at the place of woman in the cinematographic apparatus of the peep-show. Representing cinema's unconscious, the peep-show gives an exploration of the male imaginary, which is important for an understanding of the novel as a whole.

2.2 The Peep-show: Discourse, Power and Desire
2.2.1 The Samples: the Discursive Production of Desire

In Hoffman's world desire is generated by the stereotyped samples that are displayed in the peep-show. On a metatextual level the slides, models and photographs shape the plot of the novel. They represent basic constituents of the narrative which are derived from a deep structure grammar of the unconscious. Desiderio is subjected to Hoffman's desire machines when he re-enacts the situations he has encountered in the peep-show. Desire is no primordial, affirmative force as Deleuze and Guattari describe it in *Anti-Oedipus*; there is no pre-existing desire that is repressed and disciplined by representation in the narrative. On the contrary, it is representations that produce desire in the peep-show. The discourses that generate desire are violent, pornographic and misogynist. In what follows, I will briefly comment on the voyeuristic, sadistic and necrophilic sexual fantasies that are displayed by the samples.

Depicting Hoffman's castle and the mechanic lovers, the first and the last image in the peepshow anticipate the end of Desiderio's quest.[79] The cyclical order of the images, the way in which the end returns to the beginning, suggests a deterministic structure of narrative. In fact, in the end Desiderio's narrative will return to the old order of the beginning. Similarly, at the outbreak of the war the samples provide the raw material of the narrative to follow. The second sample "The Eternal Vistas of Love" displays a *mis-en-abyme* reflection of eyes. It anticipates the love scene between Albertina and Desiderio on the Indian cemetery where Albertina defines love as eternal regression:

'There is the mirror and the image but there is also the image of the image; two mirrors reflect each other and images may be multiplied without end .... We are two such disseminating mirrors.' In the looking-glass of her eyes I saw reflected my entire being whirl apart and reassemble itself innumerable times. (ID 202)

The mirror metaphor is highly ambiguous in this scene. On the one hand, it can be read as an 'othering' of the self, an intertwining of subject and object in love. The *mis-en-abyme* reflections depict a dialogic construction of identity in the sense of symbolical interactionism: in love the self is (re)constructed in the eyes of the other.[80] On the other hand, the mutual reflections in a model of eternal regression point to a narcissistic 'selfing' of the other: the self reflected in the other is an image of narcissism. Considering the ominous setting of the 'love scene', I would opt for this second, 'narcissistic' reading. The *mis-en-abyme* reflection of eyes takes place in a graveyard in front of the stone Indians, whose sightless gaze prefigures the vacant eyes of the mechanic love slaves. The love that Albertina praises as "progression towards an ultimate state of ecstatic annihilation" (ID 202) does not involve the mutual reconstruction of identity in the eyes of the other but the extinction of individuality and subjectivity. The multiplication of identities and images jeopardises the integrity of the self. The other is reduced to the status of a reflecting screen and deprived of subject status.

---

[79] The anticipation of the climax is a structural element of the narrative. As narrator, Desiderio again and again runs ahead of his story and ruins the suspense. He pre-empts, for instance, the earthquake (ID 107/8), his rape by the Moroccan acrobats (ID 115), Albertina's rape (ID 175) and the final (anti-)climax of the narrative: Hoffman's death and the victory of reason (ID 208).

[80] The lover reflected in the eyes of the other is a recurring motif in Carter. In "A Souvenir of Japan" it represents the lovers' attempt to "possess the essence of each other's otherness" (BB 34) – an attempt which is doomed to failure in the short story. See also IV.2.3.1 for the motif in *The Passion of New Eve*.

As I have argued above, "The Meeting Place of Love and Hunger" alludes to Klein's concept of the breast as the object of love and hate and anticipates the regressive, cannibalistic nature of Desiderio's and the Count's desire (cf. 1.3). Displaying a mutilated female body, "Everyone knows what the night is for" and "Trophy of a hunter in the forests of the night" prefigure Albertina's violent death: sexuality is merged with sadism, violence and death. The image of the female body as a bleeding wound alludes to Western culture's "social fiction" (SW 23) of female castration. *The Sadeian Woman* reveals the misogynist implications of this notion that suggests female disempowerment to be grounded in a biological lack and represents women as 'natural victims':

> Female castration is an imaginary fact that pervades the whole of men's attitude towards woman and our attitude to ourselves, that transforms women from human beings into wounded creatures who were born to bleed. (SW 23)

The phallus in "The Key to the City" points to the phallogocentrism behind this notion. Phallogocentrism dominates Desiderio's narrative perspective and shapes both the Minister's and Hoffman's world in the novel.[81] Anticipating Marie Anne's fate, "Death and the Maiden" finally reveals the necrophilic nature of the male desire for virginal Sleeping Beauties: "She was as white as my last night's anaemic lover .... She lay back in the voluptuous abandonment of sleep ...." (ID 59).[82]

The samples serve as a short-hand description of the violent nature of desire in the narrative. Narcissism, cannibalism, sadism, necrophilia and phallogocentrism shape Desiderio's desire. At the same time they point to discourses which are involved in the production of desire. The peep-show parodies pornographic conventions and imitates the cinematographic apparatus. The samples draw on psychoanalytical concepts, such as female castration and the oral stage, prefiguring the ambivalent role of psychoanalysis in the narrative. Foregrounding the masculine bias in Freud, the novel at the same time cites and undermines psychoanalytic notions which play a crucial role in the (de)construction of desire. Moreover, the peep-show displays mythic notions of femininity as they are produced by phallogocentric

---

[81] Derrida has coined the term portmaneau term 'phallogocentrism'. While logocentrism privileges speech over writing and constructs the center as the word/presence, in phallogocentrism the word/center is identical with the phallus. Phallogocentrism thus points to the masculine bias that structures language, philosophy and culture. See Derrida 1975.

[82] See also Schmidt 1989, 57. Carter also treats the theme of necrophilia in "The Cabinet of Edgar Allan Poe". The story uncovers necrophilic desire beneath the attractions of Poe's virginal childbride, Virginia Clemm. Carter alludes to Poe's famous dictum that the death of a woman is "the most poetical topic in the world" (Poe 1984, 19). Annabel in *Love* is another morbid creation à la Edgar Allan Poe.

discourses: woman appears as meat, prey, wound and fetish, the maternal body as "earthly paradise" (SW 134). As proto-cinematographic apparatus, the peep-show thus anticipates Carter's critique of the 'Hollywood myth of femininity' in *The Passion of New Eve*: "A critique of these symbols is a critique of our lives" (PNE 6).

2.2.2 The Peepshow as Cinematographic Apparatus

The peepshow recalls the optical inventions of the early days of film and photography. "A Young Girl's Most Significant Experience in Lifelike Colours" presents a story in a sequence of pictures which resembles Muybridge's early motion studies and the animated photographs that were designed in Edison's laboratory in the late nineteenth century.[83]

> These new tableaux were .... pictures painted ... on rectangular plates in such a way that the twin eye-pieces of the machine created a stereoscopic effect. These plates were arranged in several layers which slid in and out of one another by means of a system of programmed clockwork which ... gave the impression of stilted movements in the figures. It also allowed sudden transformation scenes. Each picture was lit from behind and glowed with an unnatural brilliance .... (ID 59)

The peep-show bears a striking resemblance to Edison's Kinetoscope, which offered a peep-hole view of motion sequences in exchange for money which had to be dropped into the slot of the viewing device. In fact, Edison's and Lumière's early 'living pictures' were frequently presented by travelling fairgrounds and circuses. Several further references connect the peep-show to the early cinema. The peep-show proprietor and Hoffman repeatedly refer to the optical phenomenon of the "persistence of vision" (ID 107,109,114,186,211) which underlies the illusion of the motion pictures. In Hoffman's study Desiderio discovers a collection of optical toys which work on the principle of the persistence of vision. Mendoza started his research with an investigation of the "neighbourhood fleapits" (ID 102). By offering "the present tense experience of time irrefutably past" (ID 102), cinematography reverses the continuum of time, and hence presents an ideal object for Mendoza's investigations into the nature of time and its subversion. While Hoffman literally conserves his dead wife's body, Mendoza's research aims at a metaphorical conservation of the body in the image. As Mendoza

---

[83] On Edison and the development of early cinema see Pearson 1996, 13-23. As a precursor of cinematography, Muybridge developed the technology of series photography in the 1870s. See Rhode 1976, 369. For Muybridge's study of body movements see Williams 1990, 38 ff.. See also Sadoul 1966 on Lumière.

claims: "Lumière was not the father of the cinema; it was Sergeant Bertrand, the violator of graves" (ID 102). By creating an uncanny double of life, the mechanical means of reproduction raise the dead. The peep-show literally transcends time and space when Mendoza transforms it into a time-machine, which offers trips into the days of early silent comedy. His attempts to defy temporality and death connect Mendoza to Herr M. in *Nights at the Circus*. Herr M. employs various optical toys to "resurrect" dead daughters of paying parents. After he has been revealed a fraud, Herr M. makes a living in the motion-picture business and in pornography.[84]

In *Hard Core* Linda Williams draws a connection between the early development of the cinema and hard-core pornography. She sees both as part of the Foucauldian discourse which focuses on the human body and its sexuality at the turn of the century. Williams interprets the development of the new optical inventions at the end of the nineteenth century as an expansion of what Comolli termed "the field of the visible"[85]. This expansion is part of the modern Western construction of the *scientia sexualis*, the new formation of scientific discourses that Foucault analyses in *The History of Sexuality*.[86] Power, pleasure and the will to knowledge interpenetrate in the *scientia sexualis*. Williams refers to Muybridge's proto-cinematic studies of body movements and claims that the desire to see and know more of the human body underlies the invention of the cinema. The scientific will to knowledge focused on the movements of the female body in particular, thus converging with the voyeuristic pleasure offered by the new medium. Referring to the intermingling of prurience and scientism, Williams further argues that filmic hard-core pornography and its desire to subject the female body to the "principle of maximum visibility"[87] is just another manifestation

---

[84] The peep-show proprietor and Herr M. might have their model in Méliès. Méliès was a professional conjuror who exploited the uncanny quality of the motion picture in his trick films in the late nineteenth century, and – as Rhode critically remarks – "put it on a level with peep–show taste and ... the genteel pornography of his age". Rhode 1976, 36. Certain motifs which appear in the peep-show – like the decapitated floating head – recur several times in Méliès. See Pearson 1996, 18; Rhode 1976, 33 ff.. However, the peep-show proprietor is – like so many characters in Carter – an overdetermined figure, constructed from several intertextual references. Thus, he represents both the vaudeville cinema director and the blind seer, Tiresias, whom Desiderio encounters on his oedipal quest.

[85] Comolli 1980, 122. See also II.5.2. for further examples of the expansion of the field of the visible.

[86] See II.3.1. According to Foucault, several medical, juridical and psychological discourses intersect in the eighteenth century to produce this new discursive formation. Searching for the truth of the body, the *scientia sexualis* produces 'sexuality' and extends power to hitherto private domains.

[87] Williams 1990, 48.

of the *scientia sexualis*: hard core is the answer to the early cinematic questions about the truth of the body.[88]

The peep-show may be said to illustrate William's argument about the common origin of pornography and the cinema in the *scientia sexualis*. As proto-cinematographic apparatus, the peep-show is an important instrument in Hoffman's and Mendoza's scientific research into the nature of sexuality, illusion and time. Mendoza embodies the conjunction of scientism and prurience that Foucault describes as characteristic of the emerging discourse on sexuality. In fact, Mendoza's and Hoffman's research about the nature of time in relation to the sexual act involve some disreputable experiments with the city's prostitutes. Combining pseudo-science and pornography, the samples are also the major instrument in the power struggle with the Minister. Power, voyeuristic pleasure and the scientific will to knowledge intersect in the peep-show. Representing a production machine of desire in Foucault's sense[89], the peep-show does not liberate sexuality from repression but produces it as a site of subjection.

2.2.3 The Peep-Show as Speculum: the Absence of Woman
2.2.3.1 The Cave, the Cinema and the Mirror

Hoffman resembles the magicians in Plato's allegory of the cave, who produce copies, fakes and dissimulating shadows.[90] The apparitions that the Minister pejoratively calls "substantial shadow" (ID 36) are reminiscent of the shadow-reflections that the magicians project onto the back of the cave. In "The Apparatus" Baudry argues that Plato anticipates the cinematographic apparatus in his allegory of the cave. The topography of the cave prefigures the cinematic scenario: the darkness of the movie theatre, the immobility of the spectators, the projection of images with the help of light (the fire) and two screens (the shielding wall and the back of the cave). According to

---

[88] Williams 1990, 34-57.

[89] In contrast, Habermeier identifies Hoffman's desire machines with Deleuze/Guattari's desire machines. She reads the text as the struggle between the oedipal master narrative and "deterritorialised an-oedipal desire", which undermines this narrative. In Deleuze/Guattari "an-oedipal desire" disrupts the oedipal family structure and effects a disintegration of the subject. Habermeier's reading favours this revolutionary form of desire, which she sees embodied in Desiderio's love for Albertina. She does not read Desiderio's desire as ironically undercut and narcissistic. Habermeier 1996, 183 ff..

[90] Peach and Gasiorek suggest that the novel alludes to the competition between the poets (Hoffman) and philosophers (the Minister) in Plato's *Republic*. Peach 1998, 100; Gasiorek 1995, 128.

Baudry, the cinematic apparatus satisfies a desire for regression to an imaginary state in which representation is not distinguished from perception. He associates the cave and the processes of identification created by the cinema with the pleasure principle and the pre-oedipal lack of differentiation between the subject and its environment.[91] The cave is in this sense a metaphorical womb: "a cavernous cell down under the ground".[92] In *The Infernal Desire Machines* the peep-show and the scopophilic pleasures it provides mirror the regressive satisfaction that the cinema offers. Desiderio enters the illusory world of the peep-show through a 'womb' which frames the exhibits to follow: "The dark red and purple crenellations surrounding the vagina acted as a frame for a perfectly round hole through which the viewer glimpsed the moist, luxuriant landscape of the interior" (ID 44). In the peep-show Desiderio regresses into the male imaginary.

In *Speculum of the Other Woman* Irigaray deconstructs Plato's allegory of the cave. In Irigaray's reading the cave represents the feminine, which functions as backdrop in the "theatre of representation":

> The feminine, the maternal are instantly frozen by the "like," the "as if" of that masculine representation dominated by truth, light, resemblance, identity. By some dream of symmetry that itself is never ever unveiled. The maternal, the feminine serve (only) to keep up the reproduction-production of doubles, copies, fakes, while any hint of their material elements, of the womb, is turned into scenery to make the show more realistic. The womb ... is transmuted ... into a circus and a projection screen, a theater of/for fantasies.[93]

Woman serves as a projection screen in the construction of a masculine identity. Carter's use of the mirror metaphor recalls Irigaray's notion of the speculum.[94] The speculum symbolises a masculine economy of sameness which negates difference and turns the other into a reflection of the self. The mirror metaphor is closely aligned with the motif of the eye, the gaze and the theme of visibility. Like the mirror, the eye is an ambivalent motif in Carter's work. As argued above, the reflecting eye is either an image of narcissism or of love as the intertwining of self and other (cf. III.2.2.1). The one-directional gaze, by contrast, controls and objectifies the other.[95] The artificial women in

---

[91] Baudry 1986, 306,313,314.
[92] Plato 1993b, 240.
[93] Irigaray 1985a, 268,265.
[94] *The Infernal Desire Machines* (1972), however, predates the publication of Irigaray's *Speculum de l'autre femme* in 1974.
[95] See also Korte for an analysis of the different meanings of eye behaviour in face-to-face interaction in literature: while the one-directional gaze indicates social domination, intense mutual eye contact connotes sympathy, erotic attraction and love. Korte 1997, 57-62. Korte's semiotic and communicative analysis of body language in literature draws both on

the House of Anonymity and in the peep-show are objects of the male objectifying gaze. In *Speculum* Irigaray criticises the primacy of visibility which privileges the eye in Western philosophy. Her criticism of 'oculocentrism' is related to Heidegger's critique of theoretical-instrumental vision, which has dominated Western thinking since the Renaissance.[96] The equation 'vision=knowledge=control' came to organise Western models of knowledge in the eighteenth and nineteenth century. Heidegger describes the modern gaze that dispassionately defines and categorises phenomena and views every being in a calculative way as an object to be acted upon.[97] David Levin traces this hegemony of vision back to the Cartesian gaze. The Cartesian gaze differentiates subject and object as seer and seen. The Cartesian transcendental subject is identical with the central point in Renaissance perspective at which the image is fully visible and endowed with meaning by the subject.[98] This point corresponds to the omniscient narrative perspective in literature which conceives the narrating subject as both omnipresent and disembodied. The subject is not implicated in the world it perceives and represents both the centre and the origin of meaning. Baudry argues that the moving cinematographic image – which implies an eye "no longer fettered by a body" – creates "the most favorable conditions for the manifestations of the 'transcendental subject'".[99] The peep-show epitomises the process by which the subject turns itself into a disembodied eye which controls the field of vision and views the object as dead, inert matter.

According to Irigaray, however, the eye does not see the 'truth' of the object as other but a mere reflection of itself. Moreover, as part of the body, the eye is ineluctably implicated in the material world it perceives.[100] It is this material world that Plato's prisoner tries to leave behind when he ascends from the cave to gaze at the sun. The floating, disembodied eye of the

---

recent research on body language and on narratological categories. Body language in *The Infernal Desire Machines* is described relatively rarely: the depiction of the exaggerated and stylised gestures of the Count serves comic purposes; the stilted movements of the figures on the beach and in the peep-show point to their unreal, constructed nature (see 2.2.4.2). The relative scarcity of body language in *The Infernal Desire Machines* seems to reflect the absence of a 'lived' corporeality in the non-realist, allegorical mode of Carter's novel. It is an indicator of the way in which bodies are deprived of their 'three-dimensional' character in Carter's novels in the seventies.

[96] Irigaray 1985a, 47 ff.. For Heidegger's influence on Irigaray see Berry 1994, 231 ff., Mortensen 1994, 221 ff., Hodge 1994, 191 ff..

[97] Heidegger 1959, 63; Heidegger 1978, 48 ff.; Heidegger 1962, 88,129.

[98] Levin 1988, 98,102,155 ff.,157,163,165; see also Copjec 1994, 22.

[99] Baudry 1986, 292.

[100] At this point Irigaray seems to be indebted to the phenomenological notion of the embodiment of perception. See Chapter II.2 on Merleau-Ponty.

transcendental subject is an illusion. In *Speculum* Irigaray undermines the visual paradigm in order to retrieve woman's alterity from the darkness of the cave. While Plato employs the figure of the ascent to describe the liberation of man from the womb/body/cave into the 'light of reason', Irigaray's reading inverts this trope, evoking the figure of the descent into darkness to recover woman's alterity ('the other woman') from her entombment in Western philosophy.

In *The Infernal Desire Machines* the proto-cinematic apparatus of the peep-show functions both as a mirror of the narrative action and of Desiderio's unconscious. Desiderio gazes at the externalisation of his desire in the samples. The peep-show metaphorically embodies the principles of 'sameness' and 'visibility' which Irigaray sees as the foundation ground of Western metaphysics: "While in the pupils I could see, reflected in two discs of mirror, my own eyes, very greatly magnified by the lenses of the machine" (ID 45). The female body serves as projection space in the specular economy of male desire. Woman as subject remains invisible.

However, it is not only Hoffman's world of "substantial shadow" which is governed by the 'economy of sameness'. The "obtusely masculine" (ID 15) city of the Minister is equally based on the exclusion of the feminine as alterity. In fact, as Irigaray argues, in Plato's *Republic* both the magicians' and the philosophers' world are ruled by the principle of sameness. The Minister's ideal of symmetry echoes the "dream of symmetry"[101] that lies at the heart of Plato's *Republic*: his attempt to achieve a perfect matching between things and labels in the computer centre – which corresponds to his passion for crossword puzzles – is governed by the principle of identity that Irigaray perceives as the central element in Socratic dialectic:

> ... nothing can be named as "beings" except those same things which all the same men see in the same way in a setup that does not allow them to see other things and which they will designate by the same names, on the basis of the conversation between them. Whichever way you turn these premises, you always come back to sameness.[102]

The Minister's "theory of names and functions" (ID 24) projects the principle of identity onto the social level, envisioning a hierarchical and static organisation of society in which each man owns a certain name which unalterably defines his position in society. The notion of a harmonious – yet strictly hierarchical – social structure recalls Plato's concept of the three classes in the *Republic*. Like Plato's republic, the Minister's ideal state negates change and social mobility. The Minister seems to take the philosophers' stance when he murders "the imagination in the womb" (ID 37)

---

[101] Irigaray 1985a, 265; cf. note 93.
[102] Irigaray 1985a, 263.

and fights against the forging of phenomena by the 'poet' Hoffman. "He believed the criterion of reality was that a thing was determinate and the identity of a thing lay only in the extent to which it resembled itself" (ID 23). Hoffman's mirrors, which produce the uncanny apparitions and undermine the notion of a self-same identity, are destroyed by the Minister.[103]

Femininity is absent in the masculine city of the Minister and a mere projection screen in Hoffman's world. Albertina's shape-shifting body is an emanation of male desire: "a woman as only memory and imagination could devise" (ID 13). Hoffman uses her in order to win Desiderio for his struggle. Like Leilah/Lilith in *The Passion of New Eve*, she is transformed from an emanation of man's desire into a "crisp, antiseptic soldier" (ID 193), but unlike Leilah/Lilith, she is not able to take control of the action. Even at the end – in her attempt to seduce Desiderio – Albertina is not autonomous but acts as a puppet of her father: Albertina is an object of exchange in the sexual economy of men.[104] Whereas Leilah/Lilith manages to break out of the image that man creates for her, Desiderio kills Albertina as soon as she reveals an autonomous self that does not comply with his image of her. He feels threatened by her difference: "... a sense of her difference almost withered me for she was the sole heir to her father's kingdom and that kingdom was the world" (ID 187). It is her claim to subjectivity that kills Albertina at the end of the narrative. The plot of the quest narrative appears as a reflection of Desiderio's fantasies, which are only briefly disrupted by Albertina's final transformation. Is the reader able to step out of the solipsistic mirror that the male narrator's subjectivity provides?

2.2.3.2 The Gender Politics of *The Infernal Desire Machines*

The gender politics of *The Infernal Desire Machines* are much more ambiguous and open to misinterpretation than those of Carter's late novels. This ambiguity is reflected in various contrasting interpretations of the novel's treatment of gender. Clark claims that Carter's novels provide an elaborate analysis of women's self-alienation, but fail to postulate an

---

[103] In the allegory of the cave 'Truth' is pure presence which does not allow for mirrors and reflections. 'Truth' is identical with the 'Idea' embodied by the Sun beyond the cave. The Sun/Idea is beyond re-presentation: "Idea holds nothing outside itself. It neither indicates nor indexes anything other than itself .... Like unto self, unaided by any re-presentation or figuration. Certainty of self-identity, unassisted by any mirror." Ibid., 298.

[104] See also Bronfen 1992, 421.

affirmative feminism.[105] Bronfen notes a disquieting lack of disruption in the novel and claims that woman is not even present as "a blank, a silence or an aporia" in the text.[106] Taking the chauvinistically male point of view at face value, Palmer discards the work as "male impersonation".[107] Punter and Bonca consider *The Infernal Desire Machines* to be Carter's last novel "where sexuality isn't gendered".[108] Particularly Punter's reading of the Count as the last figure in Carter's fiction that "escapes or transcends the gender distinction" is questionable.[109] The Count's "priapric garb" (ID 130), which covers his face and grossly displays his genitalia, turns him into the very incarnation of a phallic sexuality. The Count does not represent ungendered desire but a grotesquely exaggerated version of masculinity. *The Infernal Desire Machines* is far from ignoring the gender distinction. The novel's narrating voice gives a conscious parody of male desire. According to Robinson, the text deliberately assumes a man's subjectivity while it invites the reader to take a position beyond this male narrator's voice by revealing the complicity of his desire with domination.[110] Similarly, Rosenberg argues that "Desiderio's collaged voice is essential to ... the novel's plea for gender equality".[111] In fact, from the very beginning the attention of the reader is drawn to the fact that we are dealing with an unreliable narrator who first purports to "remember everything" (ID 11) only to concede a moment later that he "cannot remember exactly how it began" (ID 15). However, it is not only the credibility of the narrator that is at stake. It is the violent nature of Desiderio's desire that particularly disturbs the reader. Desiderio sleeps with the fifteen-year old Marie Anne, even though he "was perfectly well aware she was asleep" (ID 56). When he learns that his kiss did not wake but kill Sleeping Beauty, the necrophilic nature of his desire is revealed to him: "... for her sleep had been a death" (ID 61). Desiderio's final fight with Albertina carries sexual connotations and appears as a violent parody of the sexual encounter he has been desperately waiting for: "I pummelled her breasts with my fists .... I savaged her throat with my teeth as if I were a tiger and she were the trophy I seized in the forests of the night" (ID 216). When he kills

---

[105] Clark 1987, 158.
[106] Bronfen 1992, 424. See also Pitchford 2002, 129. If woman is not even present as an absence in the text, how is it possible that the reader/critic perceives this absence? Does not Albertina's final transformation constitute an "aporia" which disrupts the narrative perspective and foregrounds woman as a blank in the narrative?
[107] Palmer 1987, 190.
[108] Bonca 1994, 61. See also Manlove 1992, 159.
[109] Punter 1984, 214.
[110] Robinson 1991, 102,105 ff..
[111] Rosenberg 1997, 181. See also Peach 1998, 114.

Albertina, he commits the deed that has been prefigured by the wax model of the stabbed woman: his desire for Albertina finally turns her into the "Trophy of a Hunter in the Forests of the Night" (ID 46). The narrative parodies conceptions of sexuality and gender that conceive of man as hunter/subject and woman as prey/object, precluding the possibility of reciprocity and mutuality.

In addition, the narrative ironically undercuts Desiderio's admiration of Albertina. By fetishising Albertina, Desiderio deprives her of her humanity. When Albertina is forced to work in the fields like the female centaurs, he romantically perceives her as "pagan deity in a pastoral ... naked as a stone" (ID 187) and constructs an idyllic situation which is clearly not as idyllic for the maltreated woman as for himself. The narrative voice is continually undermined by an ironic undercurrent. As Robinson argues, the text "... invites the reader to occupy a position not sanctioned by Desiderio's narrative itself but, rather a position on the outside of the narrative."[112]

Nevertheless, the novel does not offer an alternative position for woman to hold outside of the economy of male desire. There is no female voice in the narrative. Nor is there a subjectively experienced female corporeality. The female body is background and frame to Hoffman's desire machine: the material of which the mirror is made. Woman is at the back of the cave. There is no 'other woman' in the *Infernal Desire Machines of Dr Hoffman*.

2.2.4 The Peep-Show and Cinema's Unconscious: Deconstructing the Male Imaginary
2.2.4.1 Scopophilia, Fetishism and Sadism

The peep-show imitates the cinema as 'production machine' of desire. Due to its power to control and shift the gaze, the cinematic apparatus proves to be an ideal instrument for the production of desire. As Laura Mulvey puts it in "Visual Pleasure and Narrative Cinema": "Cinematic codes create a gaze, a world and an object, thereby producing an illusion cut to the measure of desire."[113] Mulvey's psychoanalytic feminist approach focuses on the scopophilic drive and the construction of sexual difference in conventional narrative cinema. The spectator derives scopophilic pleasure from taking the other (woman) as the object of the gaze. Displayed as sexual object on the screen, woman connotes "*to-be-looked-at-ness*", while man appears as bearer of the look. Whereas conventional close-ups of a female face or a fragmented

---

[112] Robinson 1991, 105.
[113] Mulvey 1975, 430.

body part freeze the flow of action, the male protagonist is associated with narrative action in three dimensional space.

> ... conventional close-ups of legs ... or a (female) face integrate into the narrative a different mode of eroticism: one part of the fragmented body destroys the Renaissance space, the illusion of depth demanded by the narrative; it gives flatness, the quality of a cut-out or icon, rather than verisimilitude, to the screen.[114]

Displaying woman as a one-dimensional icon, *The Infernal Desire Machines* mimics these cinematic codes. The peep-show fragments and fetishises the female body. Albertina appears in close-ups – as a glass woman, a black swan or a gypsy woman – which temporarily freeze the flow of the action and add a sense of unreality to the narrative. Yet in Mulvey's psychoanalytical approach the female image is associated with a more complex problem. Signifying sexual difference, the image of woman evokes castration anxiety, which triggers two compensatory reactions in the male unconscious: voyeurism and fetishistic scopophilia. Voyeurism has a sadistic component: "Pleasure lies in ascertaining guilt ..., asserting control and subjugating the guilty person through punishment or forgiveness".[115] Fetishistic scopophilia produces the cult of the female star: castration anxiety is disavowed by the transformation of the female figure into a fetish, an object of beauty and adoration, which is reassuring rather than threatening. Warding off castration anxiety, sadism and fetishism thus appear as two sides of the same coin.

While sadism and fetishism are implicitly involved in cinema's visual pleasure, they are explicit, constitutive elements of pornographic discourse. In *The Infernal Desire Machines* the peep-show parodies the voyeuristic pleasures offered by pornography and cinematography. The narrative grotesquely represents women as symbolically castrated beings, as 'bearers of the bleeding wound' (cf. 2.2.1). In *The Sadeian Woman* Carter claims that erotic violence in pornography reflects the 'myth' of female castration:

> ... the stabbings of erotic violence reawaken the memory of the social fiction of the female wound, the bleeding scar left by her castration, which is a psychic fiction as deeply at the heart of Western culture as the myth of Oedipus .... (SW 23)

The Infernal Desire Machines mimics pornographic conventions which depict women as victims incarnate. In the narrative woman is the victimised object of rape (Albertina among the centaurs), flagellation (the whipped woman in the House of Anonymity) and sadistic mutilation ("Everyone knows what the night is for"). Albertina literally masquerades as a wounded creature when

---

[114] Ibid., 426.
[115] Ibid., 427. According to Mulvey, Sternberg's movies focus on the fetishisation of woman, while Hitchcock provides examples for both voyeurism and fetishisation. In *Vertigo*, for instance, the look oscillates between voyeurism and fetishistic fascination.

she disguises herself as Lafleur: hiding a purportedly mutilated face, whose nose has been destroyed by "hereditary syphilis" (ID 127), she impersonates the born victim: "This pliant valet was almost extinguished by subservience. His walk was a kind of ambulant cringe. He abased himself obsequiously at all times" (ID 124).

Woman as symbolically castrated creature embodies the threat of castration for man. In fact, Desiderio's lovers – Aoi and Albertina – turn out to be potential castrators, who carry knives in order to kill him. The narrative alludes to castration anxiety and stages the compensatory strategies of fetishisation and sadistic voyeurism. On the one hand, Desiderio idealises the unknown Albertina as "sublime": she is the "golden woman whose flesh seemed composed of ... sunlight" (ID 201,164). On the other hand, Albertina poses as fetishised object of sadistic voyeurism in the peep-show:

> ... the wax figure of the headless body of a mutilated woman lay in a pool of painted blood. She wore only the remains of a pair of black stockings and a ripped suspender belt of shiny black rubber .... (ID 45,46)

In the narrative women are stereotyped to become either castrated victims, castrating monsters or fetishes. The peep-show provides an exploration of the male imaginary and makes explicit what Mulvey describes as cinema's unconscious. It undermines the voyeuristic pleasure traditional cinema and pornography offer by grotesquely literalising the psychological mechanisms behind this pleasure.

2.2.4.2 Desire as Construction

The peep-show dislocates the reader's gaze by foregrounding the violence hidden beneath the "field of the visible"[116]. In addition, the peep-show undermines scopophilic pleasures by exposing the artificiality of the object of the gaze. Highlighting the fabrication process of the displays, the samples reveal what the ideology of the visible masks: craftsmanship and artifice. Sadistic scopophilia is disrupted by the exposure of the working mechanisms of the pornographic displays:

> ... once again I noticed the loving care with which the craftsmen who manufactured her had simulated the growth of underarm hair .... The figures, again exquisitely executed in wax, looked as though they might have been modelled in one piece and, due to a clockwork mechanism hidden in their couch, they rocked continually back and forth. (ID 45,46)

---

[116] Comolli 1980, 122, cf. note 85.

By continually stressing the astounding life-likeness of the samples, the narrative draws attention to their very artificiality:

... although the hairs had been inserted one by one in order to achieve a maximal degree of verisimilitude, the overall effect was one of stunning artifice ... the craftsmen had achieved a disturbing degree of life-likeness .... (ID 44,45)

Like the samples, the prostitutes in the House of Anonymity are objects of the male gaze who are revealed to be man-made constructions. Representing parodies of ideational femaleness – woman as meat, woman as nature ("part vegetable, part brute" ([ID 132]) – they are cardboard constructions driven by clockwork mechanisms:

One leafy girl was grown all over with mistletoe but, where the bark was stripped away from her ribcage, you could see how the internal wheels articulating her went round. (ID 133)

The Infernal Desire Machines demystifies the flesh – which is, in fact, not flesh but plaster, papier mâché and wax – and displays the constructed nature of sexuality. The peep-show plays a major role in this construction. However, artificiality is not restricted to the pornographic world of the peep-show and the brothel. The sense of unreality that pervades the peep-show is transferred to the environment as soon as Desiderio steps onto the pier:

... all these Johnny-come-latelies had the yawning, vacant air of those just awakened from a deep sleep and walked uncertainly, sometimes, for no reason ... halting ... to stare around them with startled, empty eyes .... And, for so great a number of people, they made very little noise, as if they knew they had no existential right to be here. (ID 47)

Reality is turned into a silent film. The narrative breaks down a clear separation between the illusory cinematic world of the peep-show and the 'real' world Desiderio lives in: one, in fact, produces the other. Again and again the text blurs the line between representation and reality. The landscape which is inhabited by the centaurs looks like a painting. Characters are bad actors who from time to time forget their texts:

The sailors would sometimes halt, open-mouthed, in the middle of a shanty, as if they were actors who had suddenly forgotten their lines, and mouth away vacantly for a few seconds .... (ID 144)

In *The Infernal Desire Machines* there is no authentic self which is expressed in speech and action. Characters are two-dimensional caricatures, which act the roles culture assigns to them. Aoi appears as "programmed puppet" (ID 92) ordered by ritual belief and tradition to kill her bridegroom. The pirates are two-dimensional marionettes who resemble "Indonesian shadow puppets", looking like "those strings of paper figures, hand in identical hand, that children cut out of sheets of paper" (ID 150,152). Artificiality also characterises the Count. The pathos and exaggerated self-stylisation that mark the Count's appearance turn his cult of masculinity into a mere performance and impart an ironic and slightly comic touch to his speeches:

> I think what made him so attractive to me was his irony, which withered every word before he spoke it ... he had subjected his personality to a most rigorous discipline of stylization so that, when he struck postures as lurid as those of a bad actor ... still they impelled admiration because of the abstract intensity of their unnaturalism. (ID 123)

The Count and most of the other characters are actors, puppets on strings animated by the infernal will of desire generated by the peep-show.

The peep-show denaturalises vision. By revealing "lapses in continuity" (ID 144), the novel disrupts the persistence of vision and foregrounds what the cinematographic apparatus tries to hide: the process of construction. Desire is neither a natural, authentic force in the narrative, nor is it "ungendered", as Bonca argues.[117] In *The Infernal Desire Machines* the unconscious[118] is a production of the symbolic: an artificial, masculine fabrication of Hoffman's machinery.

If the unconscious is a social construction and the peep-show plays a major role in this construction, who does the constructing? What is the critical impulse of the work? Who is Hoffman? The embodiment of capitalist media society that recuperates and defuses the liberatory potential of desire? According to Peach, Hoffman's illusory world refers to postmodern media society.[119] A reading of the peep-show as cinematographic apparatus would support such an interpretation. Images create desire. Hoffman produces the society of the spectacle. In a Foucauldian reading, Hoffman is the agent of a new discursive formation which produces sexuality as a site of power. Bio-power effects the proliferation of discourses on sexuality, which do not repress but implant perversions and produce the sexed body as object of control. What seems to be a liberation of desire plays into the hands of the power structure. As cinematographic and pornographic apparatus, the peep-show extends the field of the visible and displays the intermingling of science, pleasure and power in Foucault's sense.

The novel's allegorical indeterminateness, however, allows for several other possible readings. Hoffman appears as the poststructuralist answer to the structuralist Minister who believes the city to consist of "a finite set of

---

[117] Bonca 1994, 61; cf. note 108.
[118] I am here using the terms 'unconscious' and 'desire' in an interchangeable way in Lacan's sense. Lacan identifies the unconscious with desire: both emerge with the entry into language and are structured like a language. The novel likewise equates the two terms: Hoffman's revolution of desire liberates the unconscious.
[119] Peach 1998, 101.

objects and a finite set of their combinations" (ID 24). Day considers Hoffman to be the "arch-postmodernist" who seeks to unravel the master narrative of Enlightenment reason.[120] In fact, the lectures the peep-show proprietor gives parody poststructuralist discourse in many ways. The essence of Hoffman's theory being "the fluidity of its structure" (ID 100), it is difficult for Desiderio to comprehend the highly abstract discourse. This "fluidity" is reminiscent of the shifting signifier which is not anchored by a transcendental signified in a poststructuralist text. The Doctor's philosophy is "not so much transcendental as incidental" (ID 99) and rejects any notion of a "hidden unity" (ID 99), as the peep-show proprietor vaguely claims. Mendoza seems to echo Baudrillard's concept of the simulacrum when he postulates the identity of the genuine and the artificial: "Mendoza, however, claimed that if a thing were sufficiently artificial, it became absolutely equivalent to the genuine" (ID 102).

Hoffman is the poststructuralist, the capitalist and the media mogul. In addition, he represents the return of the repressed, the father in a rewriting of the Oedipus myth, a mock-version of Wilhelm Reich and a parody of sixties counterculture, an-oedipal desire, the Surrealist imagination and the pleasure principle in an allegory of subject formation.[121] The multiplicity of meanings which can be projected onto the novel is confusing. The allegorical indeterminateness of The Infernal Desire Machines has led some critics to discard the work as "over-determined" and "blank". Clark considers the novel as a postmodern allegory which lacks a meta-position and is not able to put forth a coherent meaning.[122] Manlove sees "no clear 'theme', no evident social, political or even sexual meaning" in the novel.[123] In an interview with John Haffenden, Carter points to the allegorical complexity of her work: "... I do put everything in a novel to be read – read the way allegory was intended to be read – on as many levels as you can comfortably cope with at the

---

[120] Day 1998, 68.
[121] Mikkonen 1997, 169; Peach 1998, 101; Robinson 1991, 98 ff.; Pitchford 2002, 119; Habermeier 1996, 170; Suleiman 1994, 109; Schmidt 1989, 75. According to Suleiman, Hoffman embodies Surrealist ideas about desire and the imagination. She reads the novel as an allegory of the technological appropriation of Surrealism and liberation philosophy. Suleiman 1994, 109. Furthermore, the narrative might be read as an illustration of Peter Brooks' notion of desire as the driving force of narrative. For Brooks' psychoanalytic model of narrative see also VI.2.5.1. Brooks 1984, 103 ff.. Hoffman's name also alludes to another diabolic master of the fantastic, the German Romantic writer E.T.A Hoffmann. Freud referred to Hoffmann's tales in his essay on the uncanny. See Freud 1953h, 227 ff..
[122] Clark 1987, 155-156.
[123] Manlove 1992, 158.

time".[124] In fact, different interpretations of *The Infernal Desire Machines* do not necessarily exclude each other: a reading of the novel as a critique of sexual liberation is compatible with an interpretation of Hoffman's world as postmodern media society. Hoffman produces the society of the simulacrum which defuses the liberatory potential of sexuality. Both readings can be integrated into a Foucauldian framework which criticises liberatory conceptions of sexuality and regards the media, the cinema and pornography as parts of a new discursive formation that produces sexuality in modernity. Nothwithstanding the multiplicity of meanings that can be projected onto the narrative, I would still argue that there is a fundamental message in the novel. This, however, seems to be a very bleak message: desire and domination are inextricably intermingled. When Desiderio opts for reason, he opts for the lesser of two evils: a repressive masculine concept of rationality which is less overtly violent but likewise compromised by power. The "sexual meaning" of the text is even more depressing as it conceives woman only as an absence.

2.3 Transcending Time and the Body: Memory and Writing

In *The Infernal Desire Machines* the force of fantasies and images eliminate the materiality of the body. Desiderio's desire pursues a figment of the imagination. Love is not a mutual reconstruction of identity but a sterile form of narcissism. Albertina's strangely sterile definition of love as dissemination of reflections is based on sight, not touch, and turns bodies into virtual images.[125] Hoffman's object of desire is the embalmed corpse of his wife. Hoffman attempts to conquer time through preservation: not only does he try to ward off decay by embalming his object of desire; he also keeps Mendoza's brain in formaldehyde and preserves the past in cinematography. Hoffman's attempt to defeat death through conservation implies a negation of the body and its mortality. It reveals the paradoxical nature of his project to pen desire in a cage. Mutability and change are at the heart of Hoffman's theory; this seems to distinguish him from the Minister. The opposition between the Minister and Hoffman, however, breaks down once Hoffman's concept of change is revealed to be a paradoxically static concept. The final sample in the peep-show that displays a man and a woman conducting sexual

---

[124] Carter in Haffenden 1985, 86.
[125] See III.2.2.1: "... two mirrors reflect each other and images may be multiplied without end .... We are two such disseminating mirrors .... Love has certain elements in common with eternal regression, since this exchange of reflections can neither be exhausted nor destroyed ...." (ID 202).

intercourse depicts the "perpetual motion" of desire as deathly monotony and stasis:

> ... they rocked continually back and forth. This coupling had a fated, inevitable quality .... they were so firmly joined together it seemed they must have been formed in this way at the beginning of time and, locked parallel, would go on thus for ever to infinity. They were not so much erotic as pathetic, poor palmers of desire who never budged as much as an inch on their endless pilgrimage. (ID 46)

The sample anticipates the copulating lovers' "static journey towards willed annihilation" in open coffins in Hoffman's castle (ID 214). While the lovers – as Hoffman assures Desiderio – have transcended mortality, they are imprisoned in a death-in-life existence. Hoffman's attempt to transcend mortality through a mass-production of desire turns bodies into machines and stifles the lived experience of corporeality.

Moreover, in *The Infernal Desire Machines* it is the narrative itself which aspires to transcend time. His autobiography is supposed to endow Desiderio with immortal fame. At the same time, though, the text "coffins" Desiderio: "What a fat book to coffin young Desiderio, who was so thin and supple" (ID 221). The symbol implies the "murder of the thing"[126] and freezes experience in representation. Memory petrifies the hero into a statue: "I will stand forever four square in yesterday's time, like a commemorative statue of myself in a public place ... upon a pediment" (ID 14). The statue embodies the ideal of stasis and is thus a manifestation of the Minister's victory.

Memory plays a crucial role in the war between Hoffman and the Minister. Memory as the origin of narrative imposes order and creates identity. By erasing the conventional version of history, Hoffman attempts to destabilise national identity. The destruction of memory and identity is the major theme in Carter's short story "The Scarlet House", which combines various elements that occur in *The Infernal Desire Machines* and *Nights at the Circus*. The Count in "The Scarlet House" is dedicated to the dissolution of form, the erasure of memory and identity. He adores chaos and attempts to destroy the identity of the prisoners he keeps in the scarlet house. The story sheds light on the role of memory in *The Infernal Desire Machines*. While desire is oriented to the future (looking for plenitude in the future to compensate a lack in the present) and destabilises identity, memory turns to the past in the creation of a stable identity. In *The Theory of the Novel* Lukács assigns a crucial role to memory in the construction of meaning and sense. Lukács argues that the evanescence of time is inscribed into the narrative form of the novel. The loss of a transcendent meaning in modernity confronts us with the ineluctability of our mortality. Yet the novel finds consolation for

---

[126] Lacan 1977, 104. Cf. note 14.

this loss in memory which assigns meaning and unity *within* time.[127] Rooted in time, memory nevertheless transcends time by subverting its irreversibility. Memory fights chaos. It is opposed to dreaming which blurs the remembrance of reality.

Bound up with a self-same identity and a definite meaning, memory is the natural enemy of Hoffman and the ally of the Minister. Desiderio implicitly announces the victory of the Minister when he begins his narrative with the self-confident claim to "remember everything perfectly" (ID 11):

> So I must gather together all that confusion of experience and arrange it in order, just as it happened, beginning at the beginning. I must unravel my life as if it were so much knitting and pick out from that tangle the single original thread of my self, the self who was a young man who happened to become a hero and then grew old. (ID 11)

Yet the text suggests that the attempt to conserve time in memory, to order and freeze experience in representation is bound to failure. The mixing of memory and desire indicates the impossibility of finding the "original thread" of the self, a self-same identity and an authentic account of experience: "... perhaps I was right. But now I am too old to know or care. I can no longer tell the difference between memory and dream. They share the same quality of wishful thinking" (ID 197). The Minister's statue begins to crumble at the end of the narrative: "I, an old hero, a crumbling statue in an abandoned square" (ID 221). Finally, Desiderio loses control of his recollections and of the narrative thread when Albertina invades his sleep: "Unbidden, she comes" (ID 221).

If the Minister and Desiderio are not able to transcend time and the body, neither is Hoffman. As the smell of putrefaction in his room indicates, Hoffman's attempt to conserve his object of desire fails like Desiderio's attempt to preserve experience in writing. If Desiderio's autobiography appears as a "coffin", so do the love pens (ID 214, 221). The yearning for immortality implies a denial of change and thus paradoxically equals death. In *The Infernal Desire Machines* the putrefying corpse, the crumbling statue and the failing memory are images which announce the victory of time over matter.

---

[127] Lukács 1994, 110. A crucial intertext of the novel is Proust's *A la recherche du temps perdu*. Like Marcel, Desiderio attempts to reconstruct the past in an objective way and to create meaning through memory and writing. Like Albertine, Albertina plays the role of the dead female muse for the male poet's vocation. While Albertine is literally a prisoner of Marcel's possessive love, Albertina is metaphorically caught in the masculine economy of desire. Both novels point to the instability of identity, which is evident in the discrepancies between narrated and narrating I and in the shape-shifting identity of Albertine/Albertina.

2.4 Conclusion

'The powerhouse of the marvellous': Deconstructing Desire

The Infernal Desire Machines reveals what is hidden beneath the 'field of the visible': the dull stage machinery of desire. The magic transformation of reality loses its glamour when Desiderio reaches the production site of the marvellous in Hoffman's castle:

> My disillusionment was profound. I was not in the domain of the marvellous at all. I had gone far beyond that and at last I had reached the powerhouse of the marvellous, where all its clanking, dull, stage machinery was kept. (ID 201)

The narrative demystifies desire by characterising it not as a primal libidinal force but as a cultural production and an instrument in the struggle for power. The master of revels is not a charismatic Prospero, but a cold scientist – "grey, still and fathomless" (ID 204) and extremely disciplined. Facing the mechanical production of desire, Desiderio doubts Hoffman's liberatory intentions: "I was sure he only wanted power" (ID 209).

The Infernal Desire Machines criticises liberationist theories of desire as formulated by Marcuse, Reich and – in a postmodern version – by Deleuze/Guattari. Instead, the narrative takes a sceptical stance akin to Lacan and Freud's position. In "Civilization and its Discontents" Freud argues that civilisation cannot do without a restraining of instincts. Yet in contrast to Freud's essentialist concept of desire, in *The Infernal Desire Machines* desire is culturally constructed. The novel anticipates the late Foucault's sceptical notion of desire as the production of power.

Aidan Day reads Desiderio's final opting for reason as a rejection of a postmodern philosophy of relativity that he sees embodied in Hoffman. Does the novel, as Day suggests, point to the dangers of a poststructuralist sceptical position which discards Enlightenment notions of truth and reason? Day relates Desiderio's choice to Habermas' notion of communicative reason, which rejects the postmodern deconstruction of Enlightenment rationality and redefines reason in intersubjective terms.[128] Habermas considers enlightened modernity not as a failure but as a project which is yet uncompleted. In fact, in an interview with William Bedford, Carter points out that her reading of Sade did not estrange her from but rather returned her to the Enlightenment notion of reason.

---

[128] Day 1998, 68,102 ff.. On Habermas see also II.3.2.1.

... he's [Sade] performed me one great service, sent me back to the Enlightenment, where I am very happy. They mutter the age of reason is over, but I don't see how it ever began so one might as well start again, now.[129]

Day, however, seems to ignore the novel's critique of the gendering of reason. Nor is Desiderio a reliable narrator, as Day claims (see III.2.2.3.2). Therefore it is questionable if "Carter is in sympathy with him".[130] In *The Infernal Desire Machines* reason is an exclusively masculine concept. It does not correspond to Habermas' notion of intersubjective reason, which is a dialogic concept based on reciprocity and conducive to social change and progress. There is no real communication and exchange in the narrative, which is dominated by Desiderio's solipsistic consciousness. In a deterministic way the ending of the novel returns to the repressive order of the beginning. And, as repression engenders revolt, the seeds of the next eruption seem to have been sown: Albertina's ghost haunts the end of the text.

Set in an imaginary South American country, *The Infernal Desire Machines* formulates a critique of Western culture. The collapse of the city is the product of a repressive culture that splits mind and body in order to subjugate the latter to the former. Puritan idealism (the centaurs), the instrumentalisation of reason (the Minister's Determination police) and the Cartesian notion of the subject (the Count and Desiderio) proclaim the rule of the mind over matter. The narrative stages a violent return of the repressed. Desiderio travels through the unconscious of a masculine, rationalist, white[131] society. Destructive desire and repressive reason are interdependent. The novel, however, does not only illustrate Freud's dictum that excessive repression engenders revolt. It also demonstrates that the unconscious is not structured in a fundamentally different way from the symbolic. The text deconstructs the reason-desire opposition when the Minister and Hoffman are revealed to be doubles. Both cherish static conceptions of reality which preclude the possibility of change. While Hoffman constructs his fantasy world from a limited set of samples, the Minister believes the world to be constituted by a finite number of objects. Both attempt to control desire, even though they proceed in different ways: while the Minister's repression of desire exerts power in a traditional, juridical way, Hoffman exploits the productivity of power when he mass-produces, organises and manages desire.

---

[129] Carter in Bedford 1978, 1.
[130] Day 1998, 79. Cf. note 46.
[131] There is an obvious racist component to the Minister's repressive order, as the description of the postcolonial situation of the city suggests: the colonial past of the city produced a powerful Caucasian bourgeoisie that governs the city and slum dweller of "an extraordinary racial diversity" (ID 68).

Both strategies amount to the same thing: a disciplining of desire in the service of power.

As the product of power, the unconscious is not a site of resistance in *The Infernal Desire Machines*. In the peep-show desire does not liberate but subjects woman. If the unconscious is itself a production of the symbolic, this amounts to an identification of the two concepts in Butler's and Foucault's sense. Does the novel destroy any space of alterity by conflating the symbolic and the imaginary? Is there only power and no sense of difference in the masculine economy of sameness? I cannot give a definite answer to this question as the ending of the text remains ambivalent. Is Albertina's final apparition in Desiderio's sleep again the narcissistic reflection of Desiderio's desire or a disruption through otherness? Has her death left a trace of alterity in the melancholic male subject? At the end Desiderio loses his narrative thread. He closes his eyes. The uncanny apparition heralds a breakdown of the subject, which opens itself to that Other which is death. Is it only in death that the subject experiences a radical sense of alterity?

Death, Difference and the Body

In *The Sadeian Woman* Carter describes "the tragedy of mortality", "that all flesh may be transformed, at any moment, to meat" (SW 140). The body signifies the terror of death. The major themes in the novel – narcissism, masochism, egocentricity and regression – point to a central concern in Carter's work: the acceptance of the body and its mortality.

Desiderio's narcissism and the Count's egocentricity reflect an inability to accept the limits of the self. The self is inflated to fill the universe and swallows the other. The narcissistic denial of otherness masks the fear of death as radical alterity; this fear gives rise to the horror of abjection. In *The Infernal Desire Machines* the abject besieges the Minister's city: decomposing corpses are found along the city wall. A smell of excrement and blood pervades the humid summer in the city. Death invades Desiderio's dreams. Woman is a harbinger of death: the black swan, the mother who devours the child, the castrating amazon. According to Melanie Klein, the fear of engulfment by the maternal body associates femininity with death. In Freudian psychoanalysis, it is castration anxiety which turns woman into a sign of death. The fear of sexual difference is bound up with a deep-running anxiety about death and mortality.

The yearning for a regressive unity is likewise grounded in the inability to accept death and difference. The narrative stages regression on several levels: in Desiderio's incestuous return to the semiotic among the river people; in the Count's cannibalistic death; in the merging of perception and representation in the peep-show and in Hoffman's conflation of the sign and the referent. Hoffman disrupts the order of representation: the sign merges with the referent when horses step off the paintings in the city's art gallery. Claiming that the difference between a symbol and an object is "quantitative, not qualitative" (ID 96), Hoffman strives to restore a pre-symbolic state of unity of sign and referent in the 'real', which eludes time and merges self and other.

In masochism and asceticism the self asserts absolute control over the body. The rigorous repression of the flesh bespeaks a desire for transcendence and immortality. In *The Infernal Desire Machines* the religious masochism of the centaurs violently strives to defeat the body and its materiality. The fear of an invasion by otherness calls for a disciplining of the body and a policing of bodily boundaries. This policing of boundaries does not just concern the individual but also the social body. The river people and the centaurs attempt to destroy and assimilate 'foreign invaders' through sacrificial violence. The Minister builds a wall around the city in order to keep "what was outside, out, and what was inside, in" (ID 12). He does, of course, fail in his attempt to ward off the enemy who "was inside the barricades, and lived in the minds of each of us" (ID 12). Both the Minister and Hoffman cannot fully control time and space. Hoffman loses control of the samples and of the plot of the narrative. At the end of the text the statue – the symbol of the Minister's victory – crumbles. And, as Albertina's final apparition suggests, the enemy continues to live within the city's barricades after the Minister's victory.

The attempt to keep body and self closed, tight and in control prevents the self from engaging in a mutual exchange with the other. To open the self to otherness and change means to open the body to death. Reciprocal desire and love are thus dependent on the acceptance of mortality. In *The Infernal Desire Machines* the subject builds a wall around itself. It is only at the moment of death that it permits difference to invade the self.

The Gendered Subject in 'The Infernal Desire Machines of Dr Hoffman'

In *The Infernal Desire Machines* women are either meat or mirrors. The novel precludes the possibility of a self-determined female corporeality in a patriarchal society. Nor is there a transformation of masculinity in the text. Desiderio gains no insight into his reification of women. Taking the most atrocious violations in his stride, he does not seem to be affected by his experiences. The narrative does not provide the male narrating eye/I with a body: the picaresque hero remains all mind and disembodied eye, his body resilient to pain, an instrument of survival. The transcendental male subject is pure intellect speaking.

Only some minor figures in the novel transcend the binary gender distinction, such as the phallic sharp-shooter Madame Buckskin and the bearded Mdme LaBarbe. They anticipate Fevvers and the world of the circus in *Nights at the Circus*. But in contrast to Fevvers, they do not employ their difference as an instrument of power but are merely poor freaks on display. The hermaphrodite is killed in the narrative. There are no transgressive bodies which offer a utopian potential in the novel. *The Infernal Desire Machines* features an oppressively masculine world. Eliminating woman and the 'lived body', the narrative allows for no alternative subjectivities.

Textualising the Body and the Search for Authenticity

In *The Infernal Desire Machines* desire is 'always already' written – by the samples and, on a metatextual level, by the novel's innumerable literary and theoretical intertexts. Experience is always secondary. The text stifles the body. The novel superimposes one intertext on another and makes the world look like a "daguerreotype" (ID 14). Bodies are "flat", textualised, recycled from other texts. The Count's egocentric desire is not an authentic expression of sexuality but "only a simulation" which he "had always planned ... beforehand" (ID 168). At the same time his desire is a 'reprint' of the deathly sexuality in Sade's work. On a textual and metatextual level desire is always 'second-hand' in the novel. This is, of course, consistent with the Foucauldian approach I have used in this analysis. There is no access to an authentic experience of desire, as desire is mediated through discourses. The textualisation of experience is a typical postmodern feature of the novel, reminiscent of Derrida's dictum that there is no body outside of the text. In his reading of Rousseau, Derrida argues that

> There is nothing outside of the text ... in what one calls the real life of these existences 'of flesh and blood,' beyond and behind ... Rousseau's text, there has never been anything but writing ... the absolute present, Nature, have always already escaped, have never existed ....[132]

In fact, there is no real "flesh and blood" in *The Infernal Desire Machines*: characters are schematic, intertextual ciphers which represent – in Carter's words – "symbols, ideas, passions".[133] Bodies are "paper figures" or meat: constructed and objectified (ID 150). The subjectively experienced 'lived body' is absent in the narrative.

---

[132] Derrida 1974, 158,159.
[133] In the afterword to *Fireworks* (1974) Carter claims to be indebted to the Gothic tradition which exaggerates character and events "to become symbols, ideas, passions" (BB 459). Her schematic characters and her preoccupation with mirrors and doubles also link her work to Borges' writings.

If desire is 'always already' written in the novel, so is interpretation. Carter – like Hoffman and the Count – planned it all beforehand. She creates a Brechtian V-effect when her characters momentarily slip out of their roles to prevent the reader from missing the literary and philosophical intertexts that might be relevant for an understanding of the narrative action. The valet gives an interpretation of his role in the Count's sadistic scenario when he expounds the Hegelian master/slave dialectic. The black cannibal chief points to Rousseau. The Count refers to Freud's notion that a patient who denies something secretly affirms it and to Nietzsche's will that is still affirmative in negation:

> It is not in the least unusual to assert that he who negates a proposition at the same time secretly affirms it – or, at least, affirms something. But, for myself, I deny to the last shred of my altogether memorable being that my magnificent denial means more than a simple "no". (ID 123)

The choice of the Jungian term 'shadow' for the black pimp ensures that the reader does not miss the point about the proliferation of doubles in the novel: Desiderio and Albertina, the Minister and Hoffman, the Count and his shadow, the puritan city dwellers and the Moroccan acrobats represent complementary aspects of the self. The literary critic might feel a sense of belatedness as the task of interpretation is usurped by the author and the characters.

An elaborate use of intertextuality and a strong sense of reflexivity are major characteristics in Carter's novels following *Love*. Nevertheless Carter's work seems to be permeated by the search for authenticity. Several characters suffer from the inability to "experience experience as experience" (BB 69). One of these characters is the narrator in Carter's short story "The Flesh and the Mirror", who suffers from a sense of separateness and alienation. An encounter with a stranger and a mirror precipitates her into knowledge of the "real conditions of living" (BB 70). The story closes with the lines: "The most difficult performance in the world is acting naturally, isn't it? Everything else is artful" (BB 74). In "A Souvenir of Japan" the narrator wonders how far "... a pretence of feeling, maintained with absolute conviction, [becomes] ... authentic ...." (BB 33). The narrator in "The Scarlet House" desperately searches for an authentic memory of her capture: "If only I could remember everything perfectly, just as it happened, then loaded with the ambivalent burden of my past, I should be free" (BB 424). However, she discards one memory for being too literary, and suspects another one of being an episode seen in a movie. Again representation eclipses experience.

In an interview with Kerryn Goldsworthy in the eighties, Carter comments on the strong intertextual character of her work in the seventies and expresses a desire for a style which approximates more closely to authentic experience:

For about ten years, between twenty-nine and thirty-nine, I thought that writing, all fiction, really was about other fiction. That there was no way out, really, of this solipsism; that books were about other books.[134]

Carter further characterises postmodern writing as mannerist prose which is "waiting for some new form, which will approximate more closely to the actual real circumstances of our lives."[135] Mannerist prose conceives literature as being about literature but, Carter argues, "at some point it's got to be about something else".[136]

In Carter's later texts the intertextual element is still strong. However, it is not so overpowering as to stifle the bodily presence of the female protagonists which feature in her final novels, *Nights at the Circus* and *Wise Children*. While *The Infernal Desire Machines* states the primacy of the text/writing over the body/voice, of discourse over desire, the body receives its due in Carter's late novels. Fevvers' body and Dora's voice effectively battle the male literary intertexts which eclipse female experience in *The Infernal Desire Machines*. This shift in Carter's writing is part of her adoption of an affirmative feminist politics which constructs women no longer as screens of projections but as subjects of agency.

---

[134] Carter in Goldsworthy 1985, 5.
[135] Ibid..
[136] Carter in Watts 1987, 175.

IV. Confinement and Metamorphosis: the Body in *The Passion of New Eve*
1. The Subjection of the Body in *The Passion of New Eve*

> Carter's language is all wild sex and mind, with nothing in between.
> Breasts? Good Lord no .... No heart, but nominally. Nor womb,
> except surgically: technology and artifice.
>
> *Nicole Ward Jouve, 1994*

The Infernal Desire Machines of Dr Hoffman breaks down the separation
between the real and its representation, flattens the world and turns reality
into a film. The cinematographic metaphor is resumed in *The Passion of New
Eve*. The novel formulates an explicit critique of the Hollywood myth of
femininity and masculinity. The female body in the mirror and the face on the
screen are central images in the text, parodying the production of gendered
identity in patriarchal Western societies. However, *The Passion of New Eve*
does not present a claustrophobic image of a textual body imprisoned within
representation. The novel also stages the transgressive body that undermines
the making of the subject in Western civilisation: the hybrid and grotesque
body, the transvestite, the transsexual and the corpse. Announcing a
transformation, a crack in the mirror, the novel suggests the possibility of a
new, uncontainable body that reaches beyond the Hollywood script of gender.

The following chapter examines the subjection of the body and its
resistance in the novel. The first part will highlight the ways in which bodies
are shaped through patriarchal representations in the narrative. As in *The
Infernal Desire Machines*, the female bodies in the text are not natural entities
but constructions of cultural stereotypes. The critique of the social and
economic context of these constructions, though, is much more explicit in *The
Passion of New Eve*. The novel also departs from the radical pessimism of its
predecessor, enabling the body to disrupt patriarchal discourses and
stereotypes. The second section analyses the ways in which the body resists
representation in *The Passion of New Eve*; it focuses in particular on the
transgressions and sex-changes in the novel. The mock wedding will be
interpreted as the text's allegorical centrepiece which depicts a carnivalesque
celebration of transgression and a symbolic destruction of the myths of
masculinity and femininity.

1.1 The Mirror and the Screen: the Body as Construction
1.1.1 Leilah: Reflections in the Mirror

The Passion of New Eve resumes several themes that Carter explored in *The Infernal Desire Machines of Dr Hoffman*. Like its predecessor, the novel examines the narcissistic nature of male desire. Like Albertina, Leilah and Tristessa are phantasmagoric creatures of the male imagination. Both women are typically framed: by the cinema screen and the mirror. Leilah's body is constructed in the mirror under the controlling gaze of Evelyn:

> I used to adore to watch her dressing herself in the evenings .... Her beauty was an accession. She arrived at it by conscious effort, she became absorbed in the contemplation of the figure in the mirror but she did not seem to me to apprehend the person in the mirror as, in any degree, herself .... We all three knew, it was another Leilah .... She brought into being a Leilah who lived in the not-world of the mirror and then became her own reflection. (PNE 28)

The mirror scene stages the estrangement that woman experiences from her self in a patriarchal system of representations. Leilah/Lilith who lives in the world beyond the mirror is invisible to Evelyn as she is eclipsed by the projection of his desires. "She was a perfect woman; like the moon, she only gave reflected light" (PNE 34). Again, the female body is not a three-dimensional, corporeal entity but a shining surface, a projection screen for the shadow dance of the male imagination. In the representation of Leilah, the novel reiterates Irigaray's critique of the 'masculine economy of sameness' that figures as a central theme in *The Infernal Desire Machines*: in Western patriarchal societies the female subject is made invisible. The self and other are both 'masculine' constructions, which exclude the feminine as radical difference.[1] Yet Leilah is at the same time invisible to Evelyn as her body is marked by a certain overvisibility. A stripper by profession, Leilah professionally exposes her body to the male gaze. Evelyn, watching her dress in the mirror, notes that "the more clothed she became the more vivid became my memory of her nakedness ... all the paraphernalia that only emphasised the black plush flanks and crimson slit beneath it ...." (PNE 30). Leilah turns herself into "dressed meat" (PNE 31). Doane points to the overvisibility of the black body in a scheme of representations in which black is the marked quality distinguished from the white norm.[2] Leilah's black and female body is doubly marked, constructed as physicality in excess. At the same time, Leilah is dispossessed of her body because it is turned into a commodity in the night clubs of New York. The novel formulates a materialist, feminist and

---

[1] Irigaray 1985a, 49. Cf. III.2.2.3.1.
[2] Doane 1991, 225.

postcolonial critique of gender construction: ironically adopting a male point of view, it traces the commodification of the female body, the elimination of woman's subjectivity and the construction of the racial other as corporeality in excess. Leilah's body is turned into a focal point of a variety of discourses that construct the black woman as the 'low other' on display.

1.1.2 Tristessa: Hollywood and the Gaze

Whereas Leilah poses as the object of the gaze in the mirror, Tristessa does so on the screen. In an interview with John Haffenden, Carter comments on the creation of Tristessa:

> I created this person in order to say something quite specific about the cultural production of femininity ... of femininity as commodity, of Hollywood producing illusions as tangible commodities ....[3]

Tristessa represents a modern version of the *mater dolorosa*, a concept of femininity that, as Ricarda Schmidt points out, contains the "psychosexual potential of a masochism that corresponds to male sadistic pleasure."[4] Being "all soul", she represents the angelic woman, whose disembodiment forms the antithetical counterpart of Leilah's excessive physicality. The disclosure of Tristessa's biological maleness reveals masochistic femininity to be a patriarchal construction. The novel employs the motif of transvestism to make a feminist point by literally revealing man behind the concept of ideal femininity. Tristessa constructs herself as the object of male desire on the cinema screen. As in *The Infernal Desire Machines*, Carter seems to refer to Laura Mulvey's analysis of Hollywood cinema that identifies woman with the image and turns her into an object of sadistic voyeurism and fetishism.[5] In fact, in *The Passion of New Eve*, Evelyn's voyeuristic gaze on Tristessa is characterised both by fetishistic adoration and sadistic pleasure. Romanticism and sadism are merged in Evelyn's fantasy of Tristessa "stark naked, tied, perhaps to a tree in a midnight forest under the wheeling stars" (PNE 7). Zero, who believes Tristessa to have "magicked away" (PNE 104) his reproductive capacity, is obsessed by the sadistic revenge fantasy that enacts the violation and the murder of Tristessa. The narrative literalises the process that Mulvey

---

[3] Carter in Haffenden 1985, 85.
[4] Schmidt 1989, 61. Tristessa St. Ange derives her name from Sade's *Philosophy in the Bedroom*, in which Madame Saint Ange teaches Eugenie sado-masochism. Pitchford 1994, 238.
[5] Mulvey 1975, 425 ff.. See III. 2.2.4.1 for Mulvey's theory. Makinen refers to Mulvey's concept of the fetishistic male gaze in her analysis of the novel. Makinen 1997, 159.

traces in *Visual Pleasure*: Tristessa's image triggers castration anxiety in the male spectator who either reacts with fetishistic adoration or sadistic violence. As incarnations of male anxieties and desires, both Leilah and Tristessa are unreal creatures which are produced by the gaze.

1.1.3 "Passing for a Woman": the Social Construction of Femininity

The construction of femininity is grotesquely parodied in the violent sex-change Evelyn is forced to undergo in the novel. Mother models Eve on the blueprint of an ideal woman drawn from a study of the media. Evelyn's transformation in Beulah represents the crucial turning point in the novel, marking the beginning of a series of humiliations s/he is subjected to. Suckled by Mother, Evelyn is degraded to the position of a child before he is turned into a woman and incorporated in Zero's harem. Mother employs Tristessa's movies and images of motherhood to teach Eve womanhood. Femininity is revealed to be a set of postures, attitudes and actions which are learned by imitation through mediators of the dominant culture, such as Hollywood cinema. After Mother's psycho-surgery turns out to be not entirely successful, producing a mentally male and bodily female being, it is Eve's "savage ... apprenticeship in womanhood" (PNE 107) in Zero's harem which initiates her into femininity. Echoing Beauvoir's claim that one is not born, but becomes a woman, the narrative traces the social construction of femininity:

> The intensive study of feminine manners, as well as my everyday work about the homestead, kept me in a state of permanent exhaustion. I was tense and preoccupied; although I was a woman, I was now also passing for a woman, but, then, many women born spend their whole lives in just such imitations. (PNE 101)[6]

As a prisoner of Zero, Eve has to go through a number of ordeals that are reminiscent of Evelyn's previous treatment of women. Denying her the use of language, Zero reduces Eve to animal level so that s/he sounds like Leilah in New York. Eve's body is ruthlessly examined by Zero and Mother, just as

---

[6] Eve's description of her socialisation as a woman echoes ethnomethodological accounts of gender construction. Ethnomethodology analyses the construction of femininity and masculinity through 'crisis experiments' such as transsexuality, which disrupt everyday assumptions about gender. Eve's preoccupation with 'passing' particularly recalls Garfinkel's study of the male-to-female transsexual Agnes. Just as Agnes, Eve constructs an autobiography and often fails by 'hypercorrection' ("my manner became a little too emphatically feminine" [PNE 101]). The depression after Agnes' sex-change parallels Eve's despair after the forced operation. See Garfinkel 1967, 118 ff.; Hirschauer 1993b; Kessler, McKenna, 1978.

Evelyn scrutinised the "exquisite negative of [Leilah's] sex" (PNE 27) in New York. Zero's examination of Eve's anus represents a parody of the male scientist's investigation into the nature of femininity. The narrative mocks Freudian and Nietzschean concepts of femininity when Zero frantically tries to recover the essence under what he senses to be a veil of dissimulation (which he ironically thinks to be located in woman's anus).[7] The reversal of the roles of perpetrator and victim, of subject and object, reaches its climax when Eve is raped by Zero, forcing him to recognise himself as the "former violator at the moment of [his] ... violation" (PNE 102). The narrative defines 'woman' not as an essence but as an effect of female socialisation and victimisation in a patriarchal society. In *Notes from the Front Line*, Carter calls *The Passion of New Eve* her "one anti-mythic novel": "I conceived it as a feminist tract about the social creation of femininity ....".[8] The novel attacks mythic notions of femininity which are as old as the Biblical Genesis and disseminated in the twentieth century through the media. The title of the novel at the same time refers to the Biblical creation of Eve and to Christ's passion. Eve is not created from Adam's rib but Adam is transformed into Eve and suffers woman's fate in a parody of Christ's suffering.[9] While Leilah represents Eve, the archetypal seductress, Tristessa is modelled on Mary, the asexual, virginal and suffering woman. Carter attacks stereotypical concepts of femininity, which she traces back to the founding texts of Judeo-Christian culture, and reveals the pervasive grip these myths have in the twentieth century due to their commodification in advanced capitalism. In the following I will take a closer look at the genealogy of these stereotypes in modernity. I will particularly investigate the way in which class and gender discourses intersect in the eighteenth century to create Leilah's and Tristessa's ancestors: the bourgeois angel and the pornographic whore.

---

[7] Nietzsche and Freud associate femininity with dissimulation. See Nietzsche 1990, 689; cf. V.3.1 note 22.

[8] Carter 1983, 71. The notion of the cultural construction of femininity may not seem particularly original today, yet it definitely was when the novel was published in 1977. As mentioned before, in *The Passion of New Eve* Carter anticipated the analysis of gender in social and radical constructivism (Judith Butler, 1990; Thomas Laqueur, 1990) and in ethnomethodological approaches (Kessler, McKenna, 1978; Hirschauer 1993b). To fully appreciate the originality of the novel, it has to be located in the historical context of the seventies when gynocentric feminists re-evaluated the feminine as a positive category, but failed to theorise the very formation of this category (see IV.1.4).

[9] "The passion" also refers to the passion Eve develops for Tristessa in the desert. For a closer analysis of the integration of several myths in the text see Schmid 1996, 52 ff.; Keenan 1992, 31 ff..

1.2 Tristessa and Leilah: a Genealogy of the Angel and the Whore

Justine is the holy virgin;
Juliette is the profane whore.
(SW 101)

1.2.1 Suffering incarnate: Justine, Marilyn Monroe and Tristessa

In *The Sadeian Woman* Carter relates the melancholic suffering of the screen heroine in classical Hollywood cinema to Justine's masochism in *La Nouvelle Justine ou les Malheurs de la Vertu* (1797). In Sade's text Justine has to put up with the most atrocious violations, yet desperately clings to her virtue and refuses to fight back. The helpless victim of her torturers' savage desires, Justine herself knows no desire. Priding herself on her frigidity, Justine's morality resides in her inability to act as subject of desire. Her "self-regarding female masochism" incarnates an ideal of femininity that was to become the "prototype of two centuries of women": "... a woman with no place in the world, no status, the core of whose resistance has been eaten away by self-pity" (SW 5). Carter considers Marilyn Monroe's suffering to be a reincarnation of Justine's masochism:

> See how alike they look! Marilyn Monroe, the living image of Justine; both have huge, appealing, eloquent eyes, the open windows of the soul; their dazzling fair skins are of such a delicate texture that they look as if they will bruise at a touch, carrying the exciting stigmata of sexual violence for a long time .... Marilyn/Justine has a childlike candour and trust and there is a faint touch of melancholy about her .... (SW 65)

Justine, Marilyn and Tristessa all share a "visible capacity for suffering" (SW 65) that tends to provoke sadistic violence and thus inflicts further suffering. Like Monroe, Tristessa constructs an autobiography of hardship and pain: solitude and melancholia, the degradation of a prostitute and the death of her child are part of her fictional life-story.[10] While in Carter's late fiction self-invention represents a means of female empowerment, in *The Passion of New Eve* Tristessa willingly creates herself in the role of the victim incarnate.

Justine represents the "patroness of the screen heroine" (SW 60), the model on which Tristessa has been constructed. *The Sadeian Woman* thus traces the origin of the Hollywood myth of femininity back to the eighteenth century. In fact, the ideal of the angelic, asexual woman is located at the crossroads of a new class and gender discourse that emerges with the rise of the middle class in the eighteenth century. Barbara Vinken traces the process in which the bourgeois female subject was constituted as 'asexual being' in eighteenth-century discourse. Associating woman with the flesh and

---

[10] Carter refers to Norman Mailer's biography of Marilyn Monroe in *The Sadeian Woman*. See Carter 1979, 63,64.

112

sexuality, Enlightenment rationality and puritan morality considered this sexuality to be a threat to the rational mind and the social order. Woman could only be accorded the status of an 'autonomous subject' on condition that she is purified of this threatening sexuality. In a paradoxical way woman had to be purged of her 'womanhood'. The product of this endeavour, the chaste angelic woman, was employed as a symbol of the superior morality of the rising middle class that strove to set itself off against 'aristocratic voluptuous decadence'.[11] Yet while the 'ideal woman' is purified of the body and its sexuality, she is at the same time hypersexualised as the unattainable object of desire.[12] The prototype of this hyper-sexualised a-sexual woman is Richardson's Clarissa, whose heroic resistance against the temptations of the flesh culminates in the anorectic negation and destruction of her body. Clarissa has been celebrated as the "love goddess of the puritan middle class of the English eighteenth century, of the bourgeois family, and the mercantile society."[13] The tension between her tantalising sexual allure and the simultaneous denial of this sexuality predestines the angelic, virtuous woman for the role of the rape victim: Clarissa turns into her tragic counterpart, her tortured 'sister' Justine. Sade's *Nouvelle Justine* reveals the grotesque implications of the bourgeois ideal of femininity which equates female virtue with frigidity.

The twentieth century witnesses the climax and turning point in the development of this ideal. On the one hand, the 'Twiggy beauty ideal' and the spreading of *anorexia nervosa* may be considered as the very apex of the negation of the female body: woman asserts her subjectivity through the inexorable control of the body. At the same time, the body returns with a vengeance in the proliferation of medical, psychological and sociological discourses on the body and in the feminist reclaiming of female sexuality in

---

[11] In a lecture series organised by the gender studies department in Freiburg, Vinken mentioned charges of sodomy and incest which were levelled against the aristocratic Marie Antoinette in the French Revolution ("männlich/ weiblich/Pornografie als Politik/Pornografie als Perversion", 16/10/2001). See also Vinken 1997, 8.

[12] According to Vinken, it is the denial of its sexuality that makes the female body desirable: "Erst die Verweigerung und Negierung des Körpers konstituiert ihn als einen dauernd präsenten sexuellen, die Figur Sexualität wird erst durch die Negation erstellt. Die Negierung der Sexualität macht den weiblichen Körper zu einem flimmernden Trugbild, zu einer Fata Morgana, die das Begehren erscheinen läßt." Vinken 1991, 50. Carter traces a similar phenomenon in Hollywood cinema: "In the celluloid brothel of the cinema, where the merchandise may be eyed endlessly but never purchased, the tension between the beauty of women, which is admirable and the denial of the sexuality which is the source of that beauty but is also immoral, reaches a perfect impasse. That is why Saint Justine became the patroness of the screen heroine" (SW 60).

[13] Van Ghent 1953, 50.

the twentieth century. Carter's fiction is part of this paradigm shift. Her critique of the myth of femininity in *The Passion of New Eve* reflects the demise of conceptions of gender and sexuality that dominated the last two centuries. While in Carter's early fiction the female body is dissolved in the masculine fantasies that govern the narratives, her late novels depict women as subjects of desire, who experience *jouissance* through their bodies and their sexuality. In fact, Carter's late heroines, Fevvers and D/Nora, represent inverted mirror images of Richardson's female protagonists: while for Clarissa the negation of the body is a source of pride and autonomy, in *Nights at the Circus* and *Wise Children* an autonomous female subjectivity articulates itself through the assertion of a powerful sexuality (cf. V.; VI.).

1.2.2 The Insatiable Body: Prostitution and Pornography
1.2.2.1 Pornography and the Soulless Body

The obsessiveness with which the angelic woman is stripped of any symptom of desire bespeaks a deep-running anxiety about her sexuality. The frantic attempt to purge woman of the body *ex negativo* creates the concept of the insatiable woman who lurks beneath the disciplined ethereal female creature. While the frigid, disembodied woman constitutes the ideal in the eighteenth century, the woman who is all flesh, a soulless libidinous body, is created as her repressed double. Pornography emerges as a discourse in the eighteenth and nineteenth century which claims to uncover this "naked truth" about woman as 'whore', as insatiable lustful creature. As uncanny double of Victorian morality, pornography reveals the heart of patriarchal society: the idolatry of the phallus and the phantasma of woman's insatiable desire for the latter. *The Infernal Desire Machines* gives a shorthand description of these phallic obsessions: the peep-show displays the phallus as the 'Key to the City'; in 'Everyone Knows What the Night is For' Albertina's ecstasy stages the loss of the self in desire. In *The Passion of New Eve* Leilah represents another incarnation of woman's insatiability which has to be held in check by the male subject:

> Sometimes when I was exhausted and she was not, still riven by her carnal curiosity, she would clamber on top of me in the middle of the night ... and thrust my limp cock inside herself ... I would ... remember the myth of the succubus, the devils in female form who come by night to seduce the saints. Then, to punish her for scaring me so, I would tie her to the iron bed with my belt. (PNE 27)

Leilah's unrestrained sexuality demonstrates her inability to exert mastery, to act as an 'autonomous' subject in control of the body and calls for male domination. As Vinken puts it:

Pornography incessantly demonstrates that woman's sexuality makes it neither possible nor desirable for her to become a subject, thus affirming the power of the male subject in a lustful way .... Pornography is a discourse in which man asserts his subjectivity through the loss of her subjectivity.[14]

Like Desiderio and Albertina in the peep-show, Leilah and Evelyn enact the prototypical pornographic scenario in which man adopts the role of the detached observer, the voyeur with whom the audience is expected to identify, while woman enacts the loss of control and the excess of desire.

Analysing the formation of the pornographic discourse in the eighteenth century, Koschorke argues that Enlightenment morality writings produce "two bodies of woman": the transparent woman as all soul and her pornographic counterpart of the sexualised, libidinous body.[15] Class and race discourses intersect in these two bodies: the white angelic woman demonstrates the 'virtue' and 'discipline' of the colonial culture and is contrasted with the black libidinous body in need of control. Tristessa and Leilah are descendants of these intersecting class, race and gender discourses that legitimate the claim to power by the rising middle class in the eighteenth century.

1.2.2.2 Rehabilitating the Whore

Carter's fiction gives a twist to the pornographic representation of woman as 'whore'. It debunks the myth of the insatiable woman by making the social and economic context of sexuality visible. *The Sadeian Woman* devises the concept of a "moral pornography" which reveals the violent nature of social relations in a capitalist, patriarchal society. In contrast to conventional pornography, a moral pornography does not offer an escapist fantasy but a "critique of the current relation of the sexes" (SW 19*)*. Sexuality is a mirror of political reality. In this sense *The Sadeian Woman* describes the brothel in *Juliette* as a "model of the world, in its cash-sale structure" (SW 83). The prostitute epitomises the subject in a capitalist world ruled by this "cash-sale ideology". The whore is rehabilitated as the more honest double of her hypocritical sister, the bourgeois wife, who equally "fucks by contract":

---

[14] Vinken 1997, 21,155: "Pornographie inszeniert unablässig, daß die Frau durch ihre Geschlechtlichkeit Subjekt weder werden kann noch soll, wodurch sich die Macht des männlichen Subjekts lustvoll bestätigt .... In der Pornographie kontrolliert und beherrscht der Mann phantasmatisch den Kontrollverlust, durch den die Frau ihn als Selbst bedroht und ihm als Subjekt unterliegt. Pornographie ist ein Diskurs, in dem der Mann seine Subjektivität durch den Verlust ihrer Subjektivität bestätigt ...." (my translation).

[15] Koschorke 1997, 66,79,80.

Prostitutes are at least decently paid on the nail and boast fewer illusions about a hireling status that has no veneer of social acceptability .... the girl who sells herself with her eyes open is not a hypocrite and, in a world with a cash-sale ideology, that is a positive, even a heroic virtue. (SW 9,58)

In fact, the bourgeois wife and the prostitute share certain similarities in eighteenth-century fiction. Richardson's Pamela, whose 'virtue' earns her a country estate, represents the double of the pornographic protagonist Fanny Hill, who acquires a fortune through vice (whoring) and is thus able to "buy" herself a husband.[16] Prostitution and marriage likewise enable the female protagonist to rise on the social and economic scale. The pornographic novel tears the mask off the moral surface of bourgeois society and reveals the commodification of human relations in early capitalism. Carter provocatively equates marriage as "legalised prostitution" with prostitution as "a form of group marriage" (SW 59). In the short story "Black Venus", Baudelaire's mistress Jeanne Duval learns that prostitution is a question of numbers: of "being paid by more than one person at a time" (BB 234). Taking this insight to her heart, young Jeanne refuses to be paid by the lovers she has besides Baudelaire, who pays for her living: "It was a question of honour. It was a question of fidelity" (BB 234). Through the naivety of Jeanne's eyes, the story reveals parallels between prostitution and marriage from an economic point of view. However, after she has returned to her native island of Martinique, Jeanne learns to capitalise on her sexuality and uses it as a weapon against the very class that humiliated her:

> Until at last, in extreme old age, ... she will continue to dispense, to the most privileged of the colonial administration, at a not excessive price, the veritable, the authentic, the true Baudelairean syphilis. (BB 243-244)

In Carter's work prostitution is a legitimate weapon and a means of survival for women who profit from a system that commodifies them. In fact, *Nights at the Circus* even goes so far as to idealise Ma Nelson's brothel as a female space of solidarity, which offers its inhabitants not only financial independence but also a certain degree of intellectual autonomy.[17]

Carter employs the metaphor of prostitution in her analysis of the cinema, conceiving Hollywood as an "imaginary brothel" (NS 182) that sells the myth

---

[16] In John Clelands pornographic novel *Fanny Hill or, Memoirs of a Woman of Pleasure* (1749), Fanny Hill makes a fortune through prostitution before she retires in a happy marriage. See Cleland 1996.

[17] The brothel in *Nights at the Circus* shares certain similarities with the convent which provided social autonomy and educational opportunities for women in the middle ages and the Renaissance. The female sisterhood in the convent often served as a refuge from undesired marriage.

of femininity. Carter's materialist criticism of a commodifying economic system and her feminist critique of woman's position within this system converge in her analysis of Hollywood cinema. The mechanical means of reproduction make a highly efficient trading of the myth of femininity possible. Hollywood produces the virtuous, asexual woman who prostitutes herself in a symbolic way when she turns herself into a commodity on the screen. *The Passion of New Eve* thus deconstructs the difference between the angel and the whore: Tristessa sells herself to no less a degree than Leilah. If the cinema is metaphorically conceived as a brothel with the star in the role of the whore, the movie director resembles the profiteering and capitalist pimp in Carter's fiction: Herr M. in *Nights at the Circus* is a producer of pornography and a confidence trickster who capitalises on his customers' dreams and desires. The movie director in Carter's short story "The Merchant of Shadows" also profits from the trading of illusions. Colonel Kearney in *Nights at the Circus* and Ghengis in *Wise Children* represent media moguls and ruthless capitalists in the American vein. All these 'merchants of shadows' are engaged in the production of dreams as "tangible commodities".[18] In fact, while N/Dora retain their self-respect and personal integrity in the nude shows, in Hollywood they are close to losing the latter: in Ghengis' production of the *Midsummer Night's Dream,* the twins feel like "tarts" who prostitute themselves to the "love of Mammon" (WC 142). As a symbol of the capitalist structure of society, 'whoring' is dissociated from sexuality in Carter's fiction: a woman's morality is no longer equated with her sexual practice. Undermining the distinction between the virtuous angel and the vicious whore, *The Passion of New Eve* paves the way for Carter's late fiction in which women turn into self-determined subjects of desire who take pleasure out of their bodies and their sexuality.

1.3 The Body of the City, Death and Abjection
1.3.1 The Open Body: Disease, Decay and Dissolution

In "Notes from the Front Line" Carter considers the emergence of the women's movement as symptom of the demise of a culture based on "Judeo-Christianity, a bit of Greek transcendentalism via the father of lies Plato and all the other bits and pieces."[19] The chaos that rules New York in *The Passion of New Eve* illustrates the unravelling of this culture. Torn between warring factions who struggle for power, New York resembles the besieged city in

---

[18] Carter in Haffenden 1985, 85 (cf. note 3).
[19] Carter in Wandor 1983, 72-3.

The Infernal Desire Machines. Yet while the unconscious that Hoffman liberates is of an exclusively masculine nature, in *The Passion of New Eve* it is the women and the blacks who take revenge on a system that represses them. Anarchy and decay are symptoms of the inner disintegration of the capitalist system that thrives on the suppression of marginalised groups, who now take their revenge. Evelyn, however, mystifies this process and produces a rhetoric which conflates decadence and dissolution with the feminine and the racial other. Change and transformation are captured in the metaphorical language of alchemy: "It was chaos, dissolution, nigredo, night" (PNE 16). The city is a huge decaying body, which is conflated with Leilah's black body. This decaying body is highly infectious: "The sickness of the ghetto and the slow delirious sickness of femininity, its passivity, its narcissism, have infected me because of her" (PNE 37). Evelyn describes Leilah in animal terms as "his bird of prey" (PNE 25), a furred and ambiguous creature, whose bodily boundaries blur:

... a strange, bird-like creature, plumed with furs, not a flying thing, nor a running thing, nor a creeping thing, not flesh nor fowl, some in-between thing, hovering high above the ground .... (PNE 20)

Finally, even animal terms do not seem to be fit for Leilah when Evelyn's racist terminology reduces her to inanimate matter: "... a girl all softly black in colour – nigredo, the stage of darkness, when the material in the vessel has broken down to dead matter. Then the matter putrefies. Dissolution. Leilah" (PNE 14). Evelyn's imagination constructs Leilah's body as the disintegrating, undisciplined body, which gives in to the unrestrained gratification of desire and breaks down to dead, putrefying matter. Leilah regularly "fouls" the bed, when Evelyn, in one of his favourite sadistic rituals, leaves her tied to the bedstead in her room. Leilah's open – decaying and defecating – body is conflated with the filth and excremental wastes that are produced by the disintegrating body of the city.

In *Transgressions* Stallybrass and White trace the way in which the bourgeois fear of the 'other' was articulated through the body of the city, through the separations and interpenetration of the suburb and the slums, the grand houses and the sewer in the nineteenth century.[20] The bourgeois white male subject constitutes itself through excluding the savage, the proletariat, and the prostitute who are equated with filth, bodily wastes and excrement. In New York Evelyn descends into this space of exclusion that constitutes the political unconscious of the bourgeois subject. Evelyn leaves Britain to escape "those vile repositories of the past, sewers of history, that poison the

---

[20] Stallybrass; White 1986, 125.

lives of European cities" (PNE 16). Instead of the "clean, hard, bright city" he expects to find, "a lurid Gothic darkness" (PNE 10) closes over his head in New York. Evelyn is sucked in by the very chaos he tried to flee from. The novel depicts the breakdown of the bourgeois city and the return of the repressed. Performing a striptease in the street, Leilah lures Evelyn into the ghetto. Carter has drawn the seduction scene from *La liberté ou l'amour!* (1927), a work by Robert Desnos, which figures a surrealist exploration of the unconscious.[21] The novel, however, adds a highly ironic note to the scene and turns it into a parody of a macho-male fantasy about seduction. The narrative mocks at the overly excited narrator who produces a whole array of misogynist clichés about his "bird of prey". Evelyn's fascination with Leilah's black body is closely linked to abjection of that body which is marked by difference in race and gender: the "grubby little bud who slumbered all day in her filth" (PNE 28). Relegated to the margins of bourgeois culture, the other returns as the object of disgust and desire. To 'purify' himself of Leilah and the city's sickness Evelyn finally escapes into the desert. In a parody of the classical American frontier narrative, he leaves the suffering Leilah behind and departs on a journey to find "that most elusive of all chimeras, myself" (PNE 38).

1.3.2 Snow White or: 'the Death of a Beautiful Woman'

In *The Passion of New Eve* it is not only Leilah's body which carries connotations of death and decadence. Tristessa, "Our Lady of Dissolution" (PNE 15), presides over the catastrophe of the city on the cinema screen. "Cadaverous" and "sepulchral" (PNE 7,123), Tristessa's morbid beauty turns her into an apparition rather than a human being: "The ... woman who was like nothing so much as her own shadow ... as if the camera had stolen, not the soul, but her body and left behind a presence like an absence" (PNE 122/23). In fact, in the movies Tristessa's preoccupation seems to be dying: "... hadn't Tristessa herself conquered New York in 'Lights of Broadway' before she'd died of, that time, leukemia?" (PNE 10). The motif of the glass coffin, in which Tristessa hides among the waxen Hollywood stars, echoes the fairy tale "Snow White". As in "Snow White", the mirror plays an important role in Tristessa's death-in-life-existence: Tristessa kills her 'real' body and transforms it into her mirror image. The simulacrum of ideal femininity eclipses her corporeality. In contrast to Snow White, though, Tristessa will

---

[21] Desnos 1968; see also Suleiman 1990, 137.

not just be resurrected once, but over and over again in the movies after her real, material death:

> ... I saw her ... frozen in amber of innumerable spools of celluloid from which her being could be extracted and endlessly recycled in a technological eternity, a perpetual resurrection of the spirit. (PNE 119)

In the age of mechanical reproduction the image survives the death of its referent. As her death-in-life existence reserves her a place in the "Hall of Immortals", Tristessa "cheats death" by "pretending to be dead" (PNE 119).

> "Passivity," he said. "Inaction. That time should not act upon me, that I should not die. So I was seduced by the notion of a woman's being, which is negativity. Passivity, the absence of being. To be everything and nothing. To be a pane the sun shines through." (PNE 137)

The fetishised woman on the screen is both lifeless and immortal. Elisabeth Bronfen has examined the theme of the female corpse as it recurs in art and literature in modernity. The decomposition of the corpse, she argues, is symbolically arrested in artistic representation. The contemplation of the female corpse enables the male spectator to experience the death of the other and yet to be reassured in his own existence. Woman's death is turned into an allegory that deals with death as an abstract figure and helps the male artist to come to grips with his own mortality.[22] Bronfen discusses the violence engendered by the move from the literal to the figural, from the real body to the sign, which effaces the subjectivity of the dying woman. The image of the female corpse in the glass coffin thus points to the major theme of the novel: the elimination of female subjectivity, the transformation of life into a mythological artefact. Hollywood petrifies Tristessa into an icon of femininity: "She had no ontological existence, only an iconographic one" (PNE 129). Bronfen also points to the scopophilic pleasures and the fascination that the doubled position of the corpse evokes. Still part of this world, the embalmed corpse is at the same time "nowhere": "What makes the 'pure and simple' resemblance of the cadaver to itself so haunting is that its point of reference is ultimately nothing."[23] The uncanny resemblance of Tristessa's corpse to her image on the screen fascinates and bewilders Eve:

> Her face had in no way changed from the face I remembered .... Her prone frame was a little longer than I remembered but otherwise so like her own reflection on the screen it took my breath away. (PNE 118)

Evelyn's fascination borders on horror. In fact, beneath the image of the beautiful dying woman lurks the terror of abjection that the 'real'

---

[22] Bronfen 1992, 49.
[23] Bronfen 1992, 104.

decomposing corpse evokes. The corpse represents death infecting life. Articulating what has been repressed in the rational subject, the corpse produces an ambivalent reaction that oscillates between fascination and disgust.[24] The closeness of adoration and abjection is illustrated by Evelyn's treatment of the beautiful dying bird he encounters in the desert:

> Bird of Hermes, the bleeding bird of the iconography of the alchemists; now the great, white, beautiful bird turns into putrefying matter .... It had ... angelic, Icarian wings .... How ugly and pathetic the bird is, now that it has been forced to come to terms with ... gravity .... I ... took it in my arms ... but a torrent of red, scavenging ants cascaded from its eyes and wound, they'd been feasting on it, already, before it was quite dead. The sight of the carrion ants brought the bile into my throat. I dropped the bird, gagging. (PNE 44)

The Bird of Hermes both alludes to the Czech's picture of the bleeding white birds and to Leilah, the "strange, bird-like creature" (PNE 20). Evelyn instantly drops Leilah, when she leaves the mythical realm of the black seductress and confronts him with her sickness and her pregnancy.

Both Tristessa's and Leilah's bodies are located on the threshold between horror and fascination. Evelyn's deferential love for the dying Tristessa only masks abjection. In her analysis of Freud's work, Irigaray traces the conflation of woman and death as the 'outside' of the narcissistic economy of sameness:

> In this proliferating desire of the same, death will be the only representative of an outside .... Woman will assume the function of representing death ... and man will be sure as far as possible of achieving mastery, subjugation, by triumphing over the anguish (of death) through intercourse.[25]

Like Ghislaine in *Shadow Dance*, Annabel in *Love* and Albertina in *The Infernal Desire Machines*, Leilah and Tristessa represent death, the abject, against which the male subject defines himself.

1.4. Inverting Patriarchy: Mother, Myth and Technology

After Evelyn has descended into the imaginary, surreal space of the disintegrating body of the city, he flees into the desert only to be incorporated within another monstrous female body: Beulah, the underground city in the

---

[24] Kristeva 1982, 4.
[25] Irigaray, 1985a, 27.

desert, is constructed on the model of a womb.[26] Swallowed by this monstrous body, Evelyn experiences a second birth – as a woman.

Beulah is inhabited by a tribe of military women, who prepare the overthrow of patriarchy.[27] The women are led by Mother, a huge black woman, who assumes the status of a deity in Beulah:

> She was breasted like a sow – she possessed two tiers of nipples, the result ... of a strenuous programme of grafting, so that in theory she could suckle four babies at one time. And how gigantic her limbs were! .... Her skin, wrinkled like a skin of a black olive ... looked as rich as though it might contain within itself the source of a marvellous, dark, revivifying river as if she herself were the only oasis in this desert and her crack the source of all the life-giving water in the world. (PNE 59)

Representing femininity in excess, Mother's monstrous body parodies the traditional image of the maternal body. Constructing Mother as a mock version of the maternal goddesses in various mythologies[28], Carter takes a side-swipe at the feminist appropriation of myth in the seventies. The new 'mythopoeic' feminism celebrated the goddesses in matriarchal myths as symbols of female power. Anne Sexton's *Transformations*, Hélène Cixous's *Laugh of the Medusa* and Mary Daly's *Beyond God the Father* are the major works in that vein.[29] "Mother goddesses are just as silly a notion as father gods", Carter comments on maternal myths in *The Sadeian Woman*.[30] The

---

[26] In her description of Beulah, Carter literalises the grotesque as grotto-esque: the cave. The term 'grotto-esque' etymologically refers to an excavation of Nero's Palace in Rome in the fifteenth century which uncovered a series of fantastical drawings combining vegetation, animal and human body parts. See Russo 1994, 3; Harpham 1982, xvi. The concentric descending spheres of Beulah, which contrast with the ascending spiral staircase in Tristessa's house, lead to Mother's grotesque body. Traditional images that align femininity with the earth conceive of the female body as harbouring a cave, as grotto-esque. Russo points to the closeness of the concept of the cavernous body and the misogynist construction of the hidden inner space as visceral. See Russo 1994, 2. The narrative mocks the mythical image of the cavernous female body, depicting Mother as preoccupied with the "evacuation" of her bowels on the beach (PNE 177).

[27] The city represents a dystopian version of Blake's and Bunyan's Beulah. In *The Pilgrim's Progress* Beulah denotes the land of peace where the marriage between man and woman takes place. In Blake's poem *Milton* it is a metaphor for the subconscious and a utopian place where "contraries are equally true" (Blake 1966, 518). In *The Passion of New Eve* Beulah is turned into a terrifying dystopia, in which contraries are simply inverted.

[28] Keenan mentions Mother's resemblance to the multi-breasted Artemis, to Kali and Jocaste. Keenan 1992, 40. See also Schmid 1996, 139.

[29] Sexton 1971; Cixous 1976; Daly 1973. See also Pitchford 1994, 230; Pitchford 2002, 131; Schmidt 1989, 63. Following Schmidt, several critics point to Mother's satirical function in the novel. See for instance Peach 1998, 113; Day 1998, 115; Makinen 1997, 161. Palmer criticises Carter for creating an "anti-feminist caricature". Palmer 1997, 29.

[30] Carter 1979, 5.

idealisation of woman's reproductive capacity colludes with patriarchy as it confines women to the domestic space:

> If women allow themselves to be consoled for their culturally determined lack of access to the modes of intellectual debate by the invocation of hypothetical great goddesses, they are simply flattering themselves into submission .... All the mythic versions of women, from the myth of the redeeming purity of the virgin to that of the healing, reconciling mother, are consolatory nonsense; and consolatory nonsense seems to me a fair definition of myth anyway .... If a revival of the myths of these cults gives women emotional satisfaction, it does so at the price of obscuring the real conditions of life. This is why they were invented in the first place. (SW 5)

Mother's archetypal female body turns out to be no mystical origin but a masterpiece of plastic surgery: "In Beulah, myth is a made thing, not a found thing" (PNE 56). The narrative ironically rewrites French psychoanalytical theory, which considers the pre-oedipal union with the maternal body to be a primal source of female power. French feminists' theorising of the maternal body refers to Lacan's concept of the imaginary and symbolic stage in child development. According to Lacan, language and subjectivity are based on a repression of the primal libidinal relationship to the maternal. Kristeva challenges Lacan's notion of the unrecoverable repression of the maternal body and reinstates maternity into the economy of language by developing the notion of the semiotic.[31] The semiotic is closely connected to the language of the maternal body, which the child experiences in its preverbal and pre-oedipal unity with the mother: the "rhythms and intonations anterior to the first phoneme, morphemes, lexemes and sentences"[32] – the sounds of the bodily fluids and of the mother's voice. Kristeva invests the semiotic with the continuous power to disrupt the paternal law after the oedipal conflict has initiated the governing of the symbolic (cf. III.2.1.2). Poetic language and psychotic discourse reactivate the heterogeneousness of meaning, the "rhythms and intonations" of the maternal body, the "echolalias" of the infant. Similarly, Cixous assigns disruptive power to the maternal body, from which she derives *écriture feminine*, a subversive, bodily way of writing that expresses woman's unconscious.[33] By associating the maternal body with the instinctual and the anarchic, French feminists are in danger of reproducing the common stereotype of female irrationality and instinctuality. *Écriture feminine* is a language in which hypotactical constructions break down, a sensual language which is opposed to scientific 'masculine' language of the

---

[31] For the notion of the 'semiotic' see also III.1.1.1 note 7.
[32] Kristeva 1980, 133.
[33] Cixous 1976, 250 ff..

mind. In fact, the dissolution of logical syntactic structure in Leilah's speech reduces her to the animal level in Evelyn's eyes:

> Her speech contained more expostulations than sentences for she rarely had the patience or the energy to put together subject, verb, object and extension in an ordered and logical fashion, so sometimes she sounded more like a demented bird than a woman, warbling arias of invocation or demand. (PNE 18,19)

It is only a small step from calling a way of speaking "closer to the body" to degrading it on an animal level, from 'psychotic discourse' to dementia.

In *The Passion of New Eve* the recovery of the maternal body from its repression in the symbolic confronts Evelyn with a monstrous conglomerate of the mythic stereotypes of woman. Parodying male castration anxiety and the fear of engulfment, the novel mocks psychoanalytical concepts through their grotesque literalisation.[34] Evelyn sleeps with his mother and is subsequently castrated. Mother plans to impregnate Eve with his own sperm in order to repopulate the world with the progeny of "New Eves". The juxtaposition of Mother's sacral cults and her modern high-tech equipment has a highly comic effect. Carter, who planned the passage as a piece of black comedy[35], follows a narrative strategy which degrades the mythic and the holy by juxtaposing it with the modern and the profane: Evelyn's symbolic castration takes place in front of a group of women who resemble a movie audience. It is, in fact, only consistent that Evelyn's violent transformation into the Hollywood ideal of femininity is turned into a media event. After the ritual sacrifice of Evelyn's maleness, Mother sportily tosses his genitals to Sophia *alias* Lilith, who keeps them in a miniature portable refrigerator.

The grotesque mix of myth and technology in Beulah alludes to the development of new reproductive technologies, which called forth both hopes and fears among feminists in the seventies. Shulamith Firestone advocated the feminist appropriation of the artificial means of reproduction in the seventies.[36] Other feminists, by contrast, feared that reproductive technologies could enable men to dispense of women in the reproduction process.[37] Banishing men from Beulah, Mother appropriates reproductive technologies and turns them into an instrument for the destruction of masculinity. Mother

---

[34] The literalisation of psychoanalytic concepts is reminiscent of the river people episode in *The Infernal Desire Machines,* which likewise stages incest (Desiderio sleeping with "Mama"), castration anxiety (Aoi's knife) and engulfment (the cannibalistic wedding feast) in a grotesque, literal way. Cf. III.1.1.1.
[35] Carter in Haffenden 1985, 86.
[36] Firestone 1970, 219 ff.; see also Pitchford 1994, 239 and Pitchford 2002, 137.
[37] Catherine MacKinnon, Andrea Dworkin, Janice Raymond, Robyn Rowland and Gena Corea criticise the development of reproductive technologies. See, for instance, Corea 1985; Rowland 1992; Raymond 1998.

does not eliminate but inverts patriarchal violence. Her definition of femininity complies with the patriarchal definition of woman as 'mother' or sexual object: looking like a "*Playboy* center fold" (PNE 75) after Mother's surgery, Eve is instantly raped by Zero and taken into his harem. Mother partakes in the violent shaping of the female body when she reconstructs herself: "She was her own mythological artefact; she had reconstructed her flesh painfully, with knives and with needles into a transcendental form ...." (PNE 60). In Beulah, where "philosophy has dominion over the rocks" (PNE 47), Mother joins in the Judeo-Christian tradition which subjugates and re-forms the body in the name of the spirit. The triumph of science over nature in Beulah represents the inverted mirror image of the ruling of the body in Zero's primitivistic community. Both Zero and Mother create dystopian solipsistic systems, which negate the complexity of reality in the name of violent monomaniac mythologies.

The Beulah episode mocks the attempt to reclaim the female body as a site of power without changing the inscriptions that patriarchy has marked on this body. Carter's critique of myth aligns her with poststructuralist feminists such as Judith Butler, Donna Haraway, Gayatri C. Spivak and Rita Felski, who reject essentialising concepts of femininity as they were formulated by feminists in the seventies. Considering empathy, caring and creativity as expressions of women's superior morality, many seventies' feminists reproduce patriarchal stereotypes about the nature of femininity and celebrate the very qualities which have been used to legitimise the restriction of women to the domestic space. Identifying femininity with maternity, women who reject heterosexuality and motherhood are excluded from the definition of the female subject. In fact, any essentialist fixed definition of the female subject marginalises women who do not conform to this definition due to differences in class, race or sexual orientation. Poststructuralist feminists thus call for an open definition of the female subject which remains readjustable in the course of political action. The plea for provisional identities strives to liberate woman from her containment in myth. In fact, Eve will not be contained by mother's project and, like Frankenstein's monster, escapes her master: "Mother tried to take history into her own hands but it was too slippery for her to hold" (PNE 173). Denying history, myth is an inadequate political weapon in a changing world. At the end of her "career" Mother suffers a nervous breakdown and sings herself into oblivion at the beach.

2. Sex Changes: Metamorphosis of the Body in *The Passion of New Eve*

The representation of woman as suffering angel, insatiable whore or monstrous castratrix seems to convey a claustrophobic image of the female body caught within patriarchal representation. Does the novel reiterate the bleak message that *The Infernal Desire Machines* has left the reader with, negating the possibility of a self-determined female identity? Is Carter offering an apocalyptic scenario in which identity is deterministically fixed by hegemonic representations? The following chapter examines the ways in which the body disrupts representation in *The Passion of New Eve*. Focusing on the multiple meanings of the gender transgressions in the novel, I will argue that the transvestite, the transsexual and the hermaphrodite are highly ambiguous figures that may be read as images of subversion or as symbolic embodiments of narcissism and stasis.

2.1 Subversive Bodies I: the Transvestite
2.1.1 Tristessa, Gilda and the *Femme Fatale*

The Passion of New Eve is populated by bodies that radically question the boundaries that constitute identity. Tristessa transgresses gender boundaries when s/he assumes a female identity. Positing a fluidity between gender roles, Tristessa's transvestism undermines Zero's sexist ideology that regards woman as composed "of a different soul substance from man, a more primitive, animal stuff ...." (PNE 87). Transvestism dissociates gender identity from the biological body whose nakedness has traditionally been conceived as a metaphor for ontological essence. Destabilising fixed gender distinctions, the transvestite threatens sexual hierarchy and undermines the concept of a stable unified male subject which defines itself in opposition to the other. As Butler argues, drag exposes the performative nature of gender: femininity is revealed to be a fabrication in the service of gender hierarchy and male supremacy (cf. II.4.1). This fabrication has been naturalised to such an extent that Tristessa herself has come to believe in the natural basis of her femininity. The unveiling of her genitals confronts her with the repressed male part of her personality and thus produces abjection:

> His wailing echoed round the gallery of glass as his body arched as if he were attempting to hide herself within himself, to swallow the cock within her thighs .... I saw how much the heraldic regalia of his sex appalled him. (PNE 128)

The confusion of pronouns points to the 'gender trouble' Tristessa causes. In an interview with Helen Cagney Watts, Carter explained that she was inspired by the film *Gilda* (1946) when she created the figure of the male transvestite:

[The] male mythology of women is neatly illustrated by the publicity for the film Gilda, featuring Rita Hayworth, which was "There was never a woman like Gilda." Well, no, of course not! Only a man could dream up a woman like that, and as far as Tristessa is concerned, only a man could be that perfect woman. [38]

The violent disrobing of Tristessa may be read as a parody of the 'striptease' Gilda performs in the movie that features the taming of the *femme fatale*. The scene in which Gilda only removes a glove and a diamond necklace represents the climax and turning point in the film. After the striptease Gilda is progressively revealed to be a good 'decent' woman, who was only hiding in the guise of the *femme fatale*:

... the narrative itself takes the form of a striptease, peeling away the layers of Gilda's disguises in order to reveal the "good" woman underneath, the one who will "go home" with Johnny. [39]

In *The Passion of New Eve* the "good woman underneath" is nothing but a figment of the male imagination. The narrative, which reveals man as the essence of femininity, parodies the structure of the classical Hollywood movie in which woman functions as a screen onto which male fears and desires are projected. Tristessa's beauty, moreover, recalls the fascination that another famous Hollywood *femme fatale,* Greta Garbo, exerted on the audience. The contrast Evelyn draws between Tristessa as the "lyrical abstraction of femininity" and the new strong women with "bulging pectorals" ("Body, all body, to hell with the soul." [PNE 7]) ironically echoes Barthes' distinction between Garbo and Hepburn. In a language that is reminiscent of Evelyn's fetishistic adoration, Barthes describes Garbo as the lyrical essence of femininity:

Garbo's face represents this fragile moment when the cinema is about to draw an existential form from an essential beauty, when the archetype leans towards the fascination of mortal faces, when the clarity of the flesh as essence yields its place to a lyricism of Woman. [40]

---

[38] Carter in Watts 1987, 165. The novel provides several parallels to *Gilda* and could be read as an ironic commentary on the movie. Whereas impotent Johnny succeeds in domesticating Gilda, Zero obviously fails. The scene in which Ballen stages his own death at a masquerade party to escape from legal punishment provides a striking parallel to the mock wedding in which Tristessa pretends to be dead in order to escape from Zero's violence.

[39] Doane 1991, 107.

[40] Barthes 1982, 83-84.

Hepburn's face is, by contrast, more individualised and 'real' than Garbo's abstract beauty: "As a language, Garbo's singularity was of the order of the concept, that of Audrey Hepburn is of the order of the substance. The face of Garbo is an Idea, that of Hepburn an Event."[41] Like the Hollywood *femme fatale*, Tristessa is both lacking in 'substance' and 'individuality', her beauty at the same time fascinating and threatening.

The *femme fatale* is a stock figure in Hollywood cinema. Her popularity dates back to the end of the nineteenth century when she emerged as a prominent motif in Decadence, Symbolism and *Art Nouveau*. The ubiquity of the motif is an indication of male anxieties about changes in the understanding of sexual difference and the emergence of the emancipated New Woman in the late nineteenth century. In psychoanalytic terms the figure of the *femme fatale* articulates the fear of losing control, of the fading of subjectivity and the submission to uncontrollable drives. Psychoanalytical theory aligns these fears with castration anxiety.[42] In traditional Hollywood narration these anxieties are at the same time articulated through the figure of the *femme fatale* as they are conquered when the latter is identified as evil, punished or murdered.[43] Posing a threat to male control and identity, the *femme fatale* represents a scapegoat figure in Girard's sense: her punishment reinstates the rules of gender hierarchy that have been violated by her transgression. In fact, the star cult surrounding the Hollywood *femme fatale* is reminiscent of the sacredness of the sacrificial object in ritual. The worshipping and the sacrifice of the scapegoat correspond to the fetishising and the sadistic punishment of the female protagonist.[44]

In *The Passion of New Eve* Tristessa turns into a *femme fatale* when she appropriates the agency of the male gaze. Turning the gaze on the audience, Tristessa undermines the conventional constellation of male spectator and female spectacle. Consequently, Zero feels attacked in his masculinity: "Tristessa's eyes, eyes of a stag about to be gralloched, had fixed directly upon his and held them .... With visionary certainty he'd known the cause of his sterility" (PNE 104). Tristessa's face on the screen poses a threat to masculine identity. Zero senses that there is something 'wrong' with her gender identity. Thus his ritual dance in the bar mimes the rape and murder of

---

[41] Ibid., 84.
[42] Doane 1991, 1 ff.; Mulvey 1994, 427.
[43] Gilda, for instance, is several times imprisoned by her husband-to-be. In Hitchcock's *Vertigo* Judy/Madeleine is punished by Scottie, the policeman and detective, who epitomises the law and exposes her guilt.
[44] The sacrificial object is both sacred and dangerous, has to be worshipped and killed. For René Girard's theory see III.1.2.2. For the ambivalence of the sacrificial object in ritual see also Kristeva (1980) and Mary Douglas (1966).

Tristessa, the "dyke" whose gaze stepped out of the cinematic frame and turned the spectator into an object of vision.

2.1.2 Transvestism and Narcissism: 'the Rule of the One'

Tristessa represents a highly ambivalent figure in the narrative. On the one hand, s/he transgresses gender boundaries in a subversive way. Her travesty enacts a parodistic repetition of gender stereotypes in Butler's sense. On the other hand, Tristessa's attempt to turn himself into his object of desire is a potent image of male auto-eroticism. Tristessa assumes both the subject- and the object-position when s/he turns 'his' male gaze on 'her' female appearance in the mirror: "He made himself the shrine of his own desires, had made of himself the only woman he could have loved" (PNE 128,129). Mother rejects her for a sex-change operation both because s/he is too much of a woman "for the good of the sex" and because she detects an "ineradicable quality of his maleness" (PNE 173). Lilith does not see a subversive potential in her travesty either:

> Abandoned on this great continent like a star in space, an atomized fragmented existence, his cock stuck in his asshole so that he himself formed the uroborus, the perfect circle, the vicious circle, the dead end. (PNE 173)

Self-love fosters the isolation of a creature with no rapport to other human beings. Tristessa becomes a symbol of the "Rule of the One"[45], the solipsistic repetition of the same. Different interpretations of Tristessa's transvestism as either subversive or narcissistic[46] reflect contrasting positions in feminist theory on the political potential of transgressive sexualities. Against the liberatory notion of drag, critics have stressed the way in which cross-dressing may be complicit with the ruling power-structure: the transvestite's over-compliance with female gender roles creates the very stereotype of the

---

[45] Irigaray 1985a, 25; Irigaray 1985b, 74,86 ff..

[46] Whereas Müller and Keenan highlight the subversive potential of Tristessa's transvestism, Makinen and Palmer read Tristessa as a "male appropriation of femininity" (Makinen 1997, 158). Palmer even calls Carter's representation of Tristessa "distinctly anti-feminist". Palmer misses the irony of the representation when she identifies the implied author with Eve/lyn's narrative voice that expresses admiration for Tristessa's performance of femininity: "How could a real woman ever have been so much a woman as you?" (PNE 129). She claims that the narrative degrades 'real' biological women as inferior by appreciating Tristessa's performance of femininity. Gamble points to the ambivalent nature of drag in the novel. See Palmer 1997, 30; Keenan 1992, 44; Müller 1997, 34; Gamble 1997, 126.

patriarchal notion of woman.[47] Transvestism is criticised for uncritically appropriating and buttressing sex-role stereotypes. In fact, cross-dressing may produce parodistic identities which degrade women. Far from being subversive, Tristessa might be considered to be the very epitome of female subjugation.

2.1.3 The Transvestite in Carter's Later Fiction

The motif of the Hollywood transvestite is elaborated in one of Carter's later short stories "The Merchant of Shadows". In the story a young cinema student interviews a former Hollywood star, the widow of the famous movie director Heinrich von Mannheim. He meets the ageing star and her butch sister in a glass palace reminiscent of Tristessa's house in the desert. Only after he has left, does the student realise that the widow interviewed was in fact Mannheim in drag, while 'her' alleged sister was the star in butch disguise. As his wife hated the movies, at a certain point in her career Mannheim took over her part. The couple created a "masterpiece of subterfuge" (BB 375) that produced Mannheim's greatest hit and released his wife from the detested movies: "... having made her, he then *became* her, became a better she than she herself had ever been ...." (BB 375). The story echoes several motifs that occur in *The Passion of New Eve*: the necrophilic appearance of the "Spirit of the Cinema" (BB 365); the star's desire to achieve immortality in the eye of the beholder; Mannheim incarnating the ideal woman in a more successful way than his wife. Yet while in *The Passion of New Eve* Tristessa is herself the deluded victim of the Hollywood myth, the drag couple in "The Merchant of Shadows" employ masquerade in a conscious, ironic way. Mannheim rids himself of his unloved masculinity, while his wife is liberated from her unwanted masochistic femininity. Creating a private freedom from gender roles, the couple cheats the audience and profits from the illusion they create. In the end it is neither Mannheim, nor his wife but the student who suffers a "ghastly sense of incipient humiliation" (BB 371). Whereas in Carter's early novels characters are victimised by the representations that enfold them, in her late fiction they increasingly take control and exploit these representations to their own

---

[47] See Epstein, Straub 1991, 5 ff.; Tyler 1991, 40; Williamson 1986, 47-54. See also II.4.2 for different evaluations of the politics of drag. In her later work *Bodies that Matter*, Butler herself points to the fact that "drag may well be used in the service of both the denaturalization and reidealization of hyperbolic heterosexual gender norms". Butler 1993, 125.

advantage: Narcissus' death in the pool is not real but a trick in "The Merchant of Shadows".[48] However, this does not mean that Carter endorses the emancipatory notion of drag in her late work. It is, in fact, only a personal, private freedom that Mannheim and his wife create, while they continue to propagate the myth of femininity on the screen.

In her late fiction Carter explicitly expresses scepticism about the politics of drag. Her short story "In Pantoland" (1991) deals with a carnivalesque pantomime world of drag and gender parody in some 'golden age' "before television" (BB 389).[49] Inhabited by the most famous figures of the British pantomime tradition, such as Widow Twankey and the Principal Boy from 'Aladdin', Dick Whittington and Mother Goose, pantoland represents the "carnival of the unacknowledged and the fiesta of the repressed" (BB 383). Widow Twankey's attempt to restore the pantomime to its original condition, however, fails and the celebration comes to an abrupt end: in a Brechtian manner the reader is reminded of the fictional character of the feast when a hook hauls Widow Twankey from the stage and deposits her back amongst the "dead stars":

> Things don't change because a girl puts on trousers or a chap slips on a frock, you know. Masters were Masters again the day after Saturnalia ended; after the holiday from gender, it was back to the old grind .... (BB 389)

The story depicts a world in which gender is variable as a fairy tale, as an illusory, short-lived escape that does not change the gender relations in a society. Carnival is not a radical counter-culture but relocated to specific culturally demarcated sites within the official culture, such as festivals, pantomime performances and drag shows (cf. II.4.2). In "In Pantoland" subversion is confined to the world of the stage and illusion. In the light of Carter's sceptical view of the subversive potential of drag, a radical emancipatory reading of the figure of Tristessa may be questioned. In fact, at the end of her trip Eve tears up the picture of Tristessa, which suggests that she does not place hope in the transvestite on her future journey. Tristessa's death demonstrates the fate the archetypal woman is destined to suffer: "To

---

[48] Whereas Zero (and Tristessa's glass house) suffer Narcissus' fate when drowning in the pool (see 2.2.2), the couple fakes Mannheim's death in the pool of the garden before Mannheim adopts his wife's identity. It is the student's script of the interview which ends up in the pool at the end of the story.

[49] Expressing nostalgia for the British pantomime tradition in a time "before television", the story seems to allude to the subjecting power of television and the mass media that appropriate the subversive and produce a conformist consciousness. Echoing Adorno and Horkheimer's essay "The Culture Industry", Carter resumes this critique in *Wise Children*. See VI.2.4.4.2.

be the *object* of desire is to be defined in the passive case. To exist in the passive case is to die in the passive case – that is, to be killed" (SW 76,77).

Tristessa's transvestism exposes the arbitrariness of the relation between sex and gender. Yet at the same time it epitomises a signifying system in which representations are monologically produced by one gender.

2.1.4 Transgressive Bodies in Postmodernity

The transvestite is only one example of the various transgressive creatures that populate Carter's novels: the werewolves and the human felines in *The Bloody Chamber;* the winged Fevvers and the monstrous women in the "abyss" in *Nights at the Circus*; the artifical prostitutes in *The Infernal Desire Machines* and the grotesque female automaton composed of fruit and machine parts in the short story "Alice in Prague or the Curious Room". Garber reads cross dressing as an index of "category crisis" in a wide sense, a "failure of definitional distinction" that undermines dichotomies and indicates cultural change. This category crisis may concern class and race and be displaced onto the category of gender in literature.[50] Blurring the boundary between male and female, animal and human, between the human and the machine, Carter's various monstrous creations may be read as symptoms of a postmodern crisis with regard to the definition of 'nature' and 'humanity'. The ubiquity of these transgressive creatures in her fiction indicates a redefinition of culture and identity in postmodernity that erodes traditional binary distinctions that have shaped our understanding of the world in modernity: body and mind, self and other, black and white, male and female, nature and culture, the real and the artificial. It would be beyond the scope of this work to analyse the historical and cultural context of these re-definitions: the advent of reproductive technologies and genetic engineering; multiculturalism and feminism; postcolonialism, globalisation and the decline of the nation state. The destabilisation of these binaries bears both risks and chances. The erosion of the boundary between the natural and the artificial may provide the most obvious example for the dangers that go along with this paradigm shift: in genetic engineering the human triumph over nature threatens to turn against humanity. Following Adorno's critique of Enlightenment reason, *The Sadeian Woman* points to the danger of reason overreaching itself and turning "into

---

[50] Garber 1992, 16. To illustrate her point, Garber refers to David Henry Hwang's *M. Butterfly*. In the play a French diplomat falls in love with a Chinese transvestite, who turns out to be a spy. According to Garber, the motif of transvestism indicates a category crisis in the Orient-Occident distinction, which is the main focus of the play.

the very opposite of reason" (SW 115, cf. III.1.3.2). This destructive tendency may be considered to be inherent in a binary logic that places one term on top of the other.[51] In *The Infernal Desire Machines* the fate of the Count and his double demonstrate the way in which the hierarchical organisation of binary oppositions tends to collapse, with one term consuming the other before it turns to self-destruction: celebrating sadism, egotism and destruction, the Count finally falls victim to his double who boils him up for a soup. The blurring of boundaries in postmodernity may be perceived as an indicator of this destabilising, destructive tendency inherent in the hierarchical organisation of social categories. This view expresses a radical *Kulturpessimismus* which defines postmodernity in a negative, apocalyptic way as the demise of the modern world and its major ordering principles. Donna Haraway, by contrast, adopts an optimistic view of this paradigm shift and pleads for a joyful relishing of the blurring of boundaries: instead of lamenting the decline of traditional definitions, we should take responsibility for their de- and reconstruction. Haraway employs the cyborg as a symbol for the chances that lie in a redefinition of a postmodern, hybrid identity that fuses self and other, the artificial and the natural in a "post-gender-world".[52] Particularly in her late fiction, Carter seems to share this optimism. The deconstruction of fixed gender identity in *The Passion of New Eve* represents a move towards this de-essentialised concept of identity as provisional, open entity. It culminates in the gender confusion of the drag wedding that Zero forces upon Tristessa and Eve.

2.2 The Mock Wedding: Violence and Transgression

The mock wedding enacts a carnivalesque celebration of transgression and a savage outburst of sado-masochistic violence. The wedding scene epitomises what the novel does as a whole: it plays with masks and identities, and presents a grotesque mockery of myth. In what follows, I will first refer to Bakhtin and Butler in a reading that highlights the subversive, liberatory aspect of the scene. Exposing the constructed nature of gender, the drag wedding rejoices in the destruction of the Hollywood myth of femininity. However, in the face of the brutal violence that Zero perpetrates on Tristessa, it seems questionable if the scene should be read in a purely celebratory way. I will take Sade's *Juliette* as a reference point in a reading which stresses the

---

[51] See note 57 and Chapter III.1.3. for the destructive dynamics of this binary logic as it is displayed in the master-slave relation.
[52] Haraway 1991, 35.

destructive force of Zero's transgressions. I will argue that the shattering of Tristessa's glass house symbolises the self-destruction of the 'phallogocentric' economy of sameness in which man and woman enact the Hegelian scenario of domination and submission.[53]

2.2.1 Bakhtin and Butler: Drag and the Carnivalesque

The discovery of Tristessa's maleness destroys the aura the cinematic cult has created around her. Debasing the untouchable cinema star, Zero's violence stages a degrading of myth in Bakhtin's sense: the carnivalesque bonfire of the rolls of films symbolically burns the Hollywood dream. Tristessa who tried "to go beyond the boundaries of the flesh" (PNE 110) is violently dragged down into the bodily sphere. The highly stylised construction of Tristessa's house, the glass sculptures and wax figures embody her desire to transcend the body and its mortality. The destruction of the house symbolises the failure of her project. Reminiscent of the destruction in New York, the shattered Hollywood mausoleum becomes a metaphor for America and the failure of the American dream:

... this city [New York], built to a specification that precluded the notion of the Old Adam, had hence become uniquely vulnerable to that which the streamlined spires conspired to ignore, for the darkness had lain, unacknowledged within the builders. (PNE 16)

America ignored that "Old Adam's happiness is necessarily dysfunctional" (PNE 16). The Dionysian takes its revenge on the Apollonian dream. Zero is the "Old Adam" who has been banished from the city of reason into the desert and now returns for his revenge. Preferring animal sounds to human speech, he reduces Tristessa's lyrics to an "asthmatic rumble" (PNE 116). Zero represents the body out of control and the shattering of language.

Debunking the myth of the ideal woman as 'suffering incarnate', the discovery of Tristessa's maleness triggers an explosion of laughter: Zero guffaws; his harem bursts out laughing; "Mother laughed until her fat, black

---

[53] The wedding scene has received only little attention from critics. In a 'subversive' reading Müller and Johnson argue that the scene triggers a crisis in the binary world-view of the characters and "topples the limits of gender". Müller 1997, 35; Johnson 1997, 175. Gamble also mentions the performative nature of gender in the scene. Gamble 1997, 125. The ambivalence and allegorical complexity of the scene has gone unnoticed in critical literature.

sides shook" (PNE 136).[54] Tristessa's transgression of gender boundaries exposes the arbitrariness of the rules that assign feminine or masculine roles to us and renders absurd Zero's mythology in which women have animal roles. Giving license to subvert these rules, the revelation of Tristessa's biological sex calls forth the grotesque masquerading and the dizzying multiplication of identities in the scene. When they put on Tristessa's clothes and make-up in a random grotesque way, the harem enacts a parody of the myth of woman. Zero performs a parody of masculinity: "He draped himself in a bearskin rug, pulled the bear mask down over his head roaring away" (PNE 135). The wedding is a double drag, in which Eve masquerades as a man and Tristessa as a woman: "... both were the bride, both the groom in this ceremony" (PNE 135). Eve, who was once a man, wears the 'unremovable mask' of a woman, onto which another mask of a man is now placed. Identities are further multiplied by the mirrors in which Eve sees the *mis-en-abyme* reflections of Zero watching him.

> I saw him step back and I saw his reflection in the mirror step back and the reflection of that reflection in another mirror stepped back; an entire audience composed of Zero applauded the transformation that an endless sequence of reflections showed me was a double drag .... I had become my old self again in the inverted world of the mirrors. (PNE 132)

This scene represents an ironic inversion of the mirror scene in which Leilah watches herself dressing in the mirror under Evelyn's gaze. Eve experiences 'himself' as other to 'herself' when he looks into the mirror, just as Leilah was alienated from her body in the mirror. After Eve "mimicked" being a woman in Zero's harem, she now "mimics" being a man (PNE 101,132). Gender is revealed to be masquerade in Butler's sense:

> In imitating gender, drag implicitly reveals ... its contingency. Indeed, part of the pleasure, the giddiness of the performance is in the recognition of a radical contingency in the relation between sex and gender ....[55]

The wedding scene presents a parody of the formation of gender identity in Western culture. Mocking the notion of the individual as self-determined and unique, identity is uncannily turned into a product of role-playing. At the same time masquerade has a comic, liberating effect, revealing the norms that regulate our identities to be constructions, masks we can play with. The self is

---

[54] Bakhtin notes the liberating and regenerative element of laughter in his analysis of medieval folk humour. The comic degrades the serious, the "prevailing concept of the world" with all its hierarchical implications: "The principle of laughter and the carnival spirit ... destroys this limited seriousness and all pretence of an extratemporal meaning and unconditional value of necessity." Bakhtin 1984, 49.
[55] Butler 1990, 137,138.

turned into a malleable entity, open to re-construction and self-invention. The radical de- and reconstruction of the self is illustrated by the dis- and re-memberment of the Immortals:

> ... they put the figures together haphazardly, so Ramon Navarro's head was perched on Jean Harlow's torso and had one arm from John Barrymore Junior, the other from Marilyn Monroe and legs from yet other donors – all assembled in haste, so they looked like picture-puzzles. (PNE 134)

Dismemberment dismantles the idols and myths that shape our identities. At the same time, the image of reconstruction reiterates what Tristessa's transgression has demonstrated: the possibility to invent identity, the freedom to create the self.

2.2.2 Sadism and Destruction

The marriage between Tristessa and Eve is modelled on an incestual drag wedding that Noirceuil and Juliette stage in Sade's *Juliette*. Dressed as a man, Juliette marries her seven-year-old daughter in the novel. Masquerading as a woman, Noirceuil weds his son, before he adopts the role of the bridegroom to get married to his daughter. Anticipating Butler's notion of 'gender trouble', *The Sadeian Woman* reads the passage as a "demonstration of the relative mutability of gender" (SW 98). However, as Carter points out, the Sadeian text does not suggest an anarchy of the sexes in a radically subversive way. It is no accident that Noirceuil omits certain elaborations in the scene that would "truly suggest an anarchy of the sexes" (SW 99): Noirceuil does not stage a drag wedding in which he plays the bride and Juliette the bridegroom as this constellation would grant Juliette a position of dominance over him. Instead, the ceremony closes with the slaughter of the children. Through infanticide Juliette 'unsexes' herself. The annihilation of Juliette's "residual 'femaleness'" (SW 98) does not imply a subversion of gender hierarchy but indicates her identification with the aggressor: "Juliette lives in a country where the hangman rules .... Juliette survives and prospers in this country because she has identified all her interests with those of the hangman" (SW 99).

In a similar way, it might be argued that the drag wedding in *The Passion of New Eve* does not radically challenge gender hierarchy, as an emancipatory reading in Butler's vein would suggest. Like Noirceuil, Zero is in control of the performance: the proliferation of identities assumes the illusory quality of a stage play that is directed by Zero and wreaks death and destruction on its protagonists. The mock wedding seems less a celebration of liberation than a savage outburst of unrestrained aggression. Zero and his women torture

Tristessa, kill her deaf-mute butler and force anal intercourse on Eve.[56] Finally, though, Zero himself is turned into the victim of his feast of destruction: overwhelmed by the centrifugal forces of the rotating mechanism, Tristessa's glass palace is shattered and drowns in the pool. Tristessa's house – the hall of mirrors and the Hollywood mausoleum – epitomises the economy of sameness that produces femininity as a reflection of male desire. Zero's violence enacts an allegoric illustration of the self-annihilating logic of this economy. In fact, Tristessa has been waiting for Zero who is part of this economy. Representing complementary myths of femininity and masculinity, Zero and Tristessa are in complicity with each other:

> While Zero ingeniously tortured you in your gallery of glass, you must have been in absolute complicity with him. You must have thought that Zero, with his guns and knives and whips and attendant chorus of cringing slaves, was a man worth the gift of that female appearance which was your symbolic autobiography. (PNE 129)

Tristessa and Zero enact the Hegelian scenario of domination and submission. The narrative reveals the sado-masochism that lies at the basis of definitions of gender that are constructed around binary oppositions 'active' and 'passive', 'subject' and 'object'. While Tristessa's self-negating masochism represents the complementary counterpart of Zero's megalomaniac sadism, Zero's inflated self is also based on the submission of his harem. Like the Count, Zero represents the master who is dependent on the slave: "Their obedience ruled him. They loved Zero for his air of authority but only their submission had created that. By himself he would have been nothing" (PNE 99,100).[57] Zero's wooden leg symbolises his sterility, his disability to "print out any new Zeroes" (PNE 92). Compensating for his actual impotence, Zero stages a fantasy of omnipotence when he dis- and re-members the waxen bodies of the Hollywood stars. The final image which juxtaposes his bearskin and his wooden leg in the pool exposes him to be indeed the "nullity" with

---

[56] Again, Carter's fiction relates sadism to regression: while Zero tortures Tristessa, the girls urinate on the floor, smear excrement on the walls and pelt each other with Tristessa's food. As mentioned in the Chapter Three, in *The Sadeian Woman* Carter reads Juliette's transgressions as a reversion to the "polymorphous perversity of the child" (SW 148). The Count's violence in *The Infernal Desire Machines* also carries regressive features. See III.1.3.1.

[57] The master-slave dialectics that defines the Count's relation to his Valet in *The Infernal Desire Machines* is related to gender hierarchy in *The Passion of New Eve*. In a psychological approach Jessica Benjamin analyses gender relations in term of the Hegelian dialectics of destruction. For Benjamin's theory see VI.1.1.

which his name equates him.[58] Dependent on the recognition of the other, the master is annihilated through the negation of the slave. While *The Infernal Desire Machines* presents a claustrophobic image of the narcissistic economy of sameness, *The Passion of New Eve* goes one step further and, referring to Hegel and Sade, anticipates the very demise of this economy. In fact, Irigaray's concept can be integrated within the Hegelian dialectics of destruction: as the male subject is dependent on woman as a mirror of his self, the negation of woman as subject entails the destruction of male identity. The fate of Tristessa's house thus mirrors the disintegration of the phallic city which Evelyn experiences on his arrival in America. Suffering Narcissus' fate, the ruins of the house and Zero's dismembered body finally float as grotesque debris in the pool:

> As Tristessa ... gazed at the drowning pool, small items of furnishings now floated to the surface of the ... water – a bearskin rug ... a severed limb or two of an Immortal, limbs dismemberment rendered permanently anonymous .... Arms and legs that might have belonged to anyone. A golden torso bobbed up and floated .... Who could tell who she had been. .... The strangest item of all the grotesque debris swam up through the refuse; it was Zero's wooden leg. (PNE 142)

Dismemberment beyond recognition drowns the Immortals in anonymity. Touching on the medieval *vanitas* motif, the scene figures the death of those who tried to reach immortality by freezing themselves into mythological icons. Death appears as a leveller which renders the corpse anonymous, thus foiling Tristessa's attempt to reach eternity. Tristessa's house and Zero drown in their reflections. Again, mirrors turn out to be fatal in the novel: "The face leaks into the looking-glass like water into sand" (PNE 103).

2.2.3 Sacrificial Violence

The wedding scene ironically inverts the traditional structure of the Hollywood *femme fatale* narrative, in which the male protagonist either kills or tames the *femme fatale*. As mentioned above, Tristessa represents the ambiguous, the sacrificial victim that has to atone for the appropriation of the male gaze (cf. IV.2.1.1). The consummation of the marriage is conceived as a ritual sacrifice in which Tristessa's glass coffin functions as the marriage bed: "The glass bed was cold, hard and exposed as the mountain top on which Abraham presented Isaac with his knife" (PNE 137). The drag wedding – as

---

[58] The bearskin and the wooden leg are images of the masquerade of masculinity that hides a lack. They might be read as ironic answer to notions of femininity as masking castration. For Nietzsche, Freud and Lacan's concept of femininity as masquerade see V.3.1 note 22.

Zero plans it – temporarily plays with gender identity in order to re-establish and consolidate the strict gender regime that has been undermined by Tristessa's gaze: by killing Tristessa, Zero hopes to regain his masculinity. In his camp in the desert Zero habitually performed the sacrificial murder of Tristessa, followed by the apotheosis of his self. Ironically, the desecration of Tristessa's house does not culminate in the sacrifice of Tristessa and in Zero's apotheosis, but turns Zero into the sacrificial object and leads to Tristessa's apotheosis in the desert:

> The sun ... illuminated him [Tristessa] from behind; for a moment, he seemed to me surrounded in the oblong glory of light which emanated from divine figures – an aureole or vessica, celestial limelight .... (PNE 146,147)

The narrative enacts another ironic reversal when it is not Zero but Tristessa who rediscovers his virility after Zero's death:

> Tristessa passed his long hands over his face as if he were rubbing his eyes and looked down with a blank face at his own maleness as if he had never seen it before. He seemed numbed by the rediscovery of his virility .... (PNE 141)

Tristessa, not Zero, will become the New Adam who impregnates Eve in the desert. Renewal is achieved through the sacrifice of the Old Adam. Zero's 'death by water' prefigures the drowning of Evelyn's genitals in the sea. The narrative sounds the death knell of masculinity and femininity incarnate.

Both *The Infernal Desire Machines* and *The Passion of New Eve* depict dystopian worlds that are based on sacrificial violence. In *The Infernal Desire Machines* 'order' is restored through the murder of Albertina. *The Passion of New Eve* inverts the sacrificial structure that founds the social order on the death of woman. Instead, the novel does away with the 'Old Adam' and suggests the dawning of a new, hybrid order to emerge from the grave of the old gender stereotypes. A crucial intertext for this reversal is to be found in discourses that lament the decline of civilisation at the turn of the nineteenth century. In the age of the first major women's movement and nascent - socialism, this 'decline' was believed to be a consequence of democratisation and 'feminisation' in the modern age. For T. S. Eliot, Nietzsche, Spengler, Pound, D. H. Lawrence and Nathanael West the feminised man is a symptom of the degeneracy of modern civilisation. Zero, who models himself on Nietzsche, represents a mock version of the fisher king in *The Waste Land*.[59] He is the "king of a rainy country, powerful, yet impotent" (PNE 102), the

---

[59] In the depiction of Eve/lyn's journey through the desert Carter refers to a wasteland tradition in English literature that owes much of its imagery to medieval romance. Eve/lyn travels through inhospitable regions and encounters various monstrous and mad creatures. Eve/lyn's quest is an allegorical journey through the desolated space of his mind. For the wasteland tradition in English literature see Goetsch 2002, 157 ff..

last representative of patriarchy in the decline of Western culture. However, in *The Passion of New Eve* renewal is not achieved through a 'masculinisation' of power, through a re-empowerment of the patriarchal fisher king and a return to fixed gender roles. It is the blurring of gender roles symbolised by the union of the transvestite and the transsexual which represents a fertile oasis in the waste land of the desert. The fisher king is replaced by Tiresias.

2.3. Subversive Bodies II: the Transsexual, the Hermaphrodite and the Body in Process

2.3.1 The Transsexual and the Hermaphrodite: the Love Scene in *The Passion of New Eve*

Eve(lyn) involuntarily transgresses gender boundaries when he is transformed into Eve. Whereas the figure of the transvestite dissociates gender identity from sex, the transsexual undermines the notion of sex as a stable category. Evelyn's bodily transformation and his experience as a woman reform him. This reformation is apparent in the contrast between the experiencing Evelyn and the narrating Eve, who, in retrospect, ironically looks back on her former self.[60] Having learned to cope with the absence of mother, at the end of the narrative Eve suggests discarding all the symbols "until the times have created a fresh iconography" (PNE 174). When she melts the amber in the cave, she symbolically liberates Tristessa from her confinement in "innumerable spools of celluloid" (PNE 119). Freeing the body from its imprisonment in mythology, Eve releases the feather of the hybrid archaeopteryx: "... bird and lizard at once .... A miraculous, seminal, intermediate being whose nature I grasped in the desert" (PNE 185). The archaeopteryx is reminiscent of the union of Eve and Tristessa in the desert:

> In the heart of that gigantic metaphor for sterility ... we peopled this immemorial loneliness with all we had been, or might be, or had dreamed of being, or had thought we were – every modulation of the selves we now projected upon each other's flesh, selves – aspects of being, ideas – that seemed, during our embraces, to be the very essence of

---

[60] Alison Lee argues that the subversive potential of the narrative lies in the disjuncture of narrative perspective. Through the shifting voice and look of the narrator the novel provides a feminist narratology, multiplying the possibility for gender configurations beyond maleness and femaleness. When Eve/lyn for the first time looks at his/her new body in the mirror before s/he has been subjected to Mother's mental conditioning, different narrative perspectives are superimposed on one another: the narrator Eve looks at 'mentally male' Evelyn looking at the new female Eve in the mirror. Lee 1996, 238 ff..

our selves ... as if ... we had made the great Platonic hermaphrodite together, the whole and perfect being .... (PNE 148)

"We are Tiresias" (PNE 146), Eve enthusiastically exclaims in the desert. Is the utopian vision of the novel the hybrid, androgynous body beyond masculinity and femininity? Critics have interpreted this crucial passage in varied ways. Jordan, Schmid, Müller and Day give a celebratory reading of the scene and identify it as *the* visionary moment which envisages a new iconography.[61] According to Suleiman, the "eerily beautiful scene" succeeds in giving textual embodiment to the desire "of going beyond old dichotomies".[62] Johnson considers the hermaphrodite to be the new symbol that Carter creates: "... the relocation of the chimerical, the hermaphrodite, within the realms of possibility, as a source of origin and a site for pleasure, is written in the bodies of these two characters."[63] Yet other critics like Rubenstein, Gamble and Punter regard the passage as ironic and claim that Carter reduces the figures to "pastiches of bisexuality"[64]. Reading Tristessa as a static character, incapable of development, Gamble calls Eve and Tristessa "would-be-lovers" who "never quite succeed in establishing a mutually reciprocal romantic relationship".[65] According to Rubenstein

> ... the figures of hermaphrodites and transsexuals ... serve to critique the concept of androgyny .... Carter's grotesque phantasmagoria demonstrate that gender, even when ostensibly "bisected," cannot be dissolved or reduced (alchemically or otherwise) to the state of genderlessness.[66]

In fact, the Platonic hermaphrodite might be considered as another rigid, mythic concept that the novel attacks. "The desert would mummify us in the iconic and devastating beauty of our embrace, I nothing but a bracelet of bright hair around his bones" (PNE 151). Again, the narrative imagines an iconic beauty that transcends time and death. Is this "mummification" just another form of imprisonment, reminiscent of the amber and the celluloid that preserves Tristessa's face in the movies? The conventional *Liebestod* motif seems rather anachronistic with regard to this utterly unconventional, postmodern couple. Does it impart an ironic touch to the scene that the object of Eve's passion is the "demented beautiful" (PNE 151), a mad old man? The ironic tone of the novel makes it hard to believe that any image is employed in an unambiguous, affirmative way. The scene might as well be read as an

---

[61] Jordan 1990, 36; Schmid 1996, 151; Müller 1997, 36; Day 1998, 121.
[62] Suleiman 1990, 139,140.
[63] Johnson 1994, 47,48. See also Curti 1998, 126.
[64] Punter 1984, 221.
[65] Gamble 1997, 127.
[66] Rubenstein 1993, 115,116.

illustration of the narcissism of two characters who see their selves mirrored in each other's faces: "I did not close my eyes for I saw in his face how beautiful I was" (PNE 151).[67] Eve's desire for Tristessa arises from the narcissistic contemplation of her own body in the desert:

> I looked down at my slow limbs ... and I thought, how delicious I look! I look like a gingerbread woman. ... I saw myself. I delighted me. I reached out my hand and touched my own foot in a sudden ecstasy of narcissistic gratification at its delicacy and littleness .... (PNE 146)

Does Tristessa break through his narcissistic self-absorption or is it once again the mirror of his self that he loves?

The concept of androgyny was widely discussed in feminist thought of the seventies as a way of escaping the narrow confines of traditional gender distinctions. Carolyn G. Heilbrun puts forth the ideal of androgyny in *Toward a Recognition of Androgyny*:

> I believe that our future salvation lies in a movement away from sexual polarization and the prison of gender toward a world in which individual roles and the modes of personal behavior can be freely chosen. This ideal is ... androgyny ... – a condition under which the characteristics of the sexes ... are not rigidly assigned. Androgyny seeks to liberate the individual from the confines of the appropriate.[68]

Seventies feminists refer to modernist women writers who postulate the utopian potential of androgyny. Virginia Woolf's and Djuna Barnes' visions of transvestism and androgyny imagine a self that is able to combine the best of both genders. Woolf's Orlando and Robin Vote in *Nightwood* are figures that embody this vision: freely shifting between a male and female existence, Orlando "combined in one the strength of a man and a woman's grace"[69].

French feminists, by contrast, oppose the Anglo-American concept of androgyny which suppresses woman's alterity, her absolute difference from what is produced as 'feminine' and 'masculine' in patriarchal language. Ricarda Schmidt also points to the weaknesses of the concept of androgyny, especially to the fact that it defines 'masculine' and 'feminine' in terms of the old stereotypes.

> The so-called masculine traits – for example, rationality, objectivity, autonomy – are precisely those historically based on the suppression of woman's body, desire and difference. On the other side, the so-called feminine, or nurturing traits ... are ... the virtues of the oppressed. Furthermore, it is never specified what kind of "rationality" or "objectivity" would be produced in combination with feminine-identified nurturance and

---

[67] This ambivalence is reminiscent of the ambiguous love scene on the Indian cemetery in *The Infernal Desire Machines*. See III.2.2.1.
[68] Heilbrun 1973, IX,X.
[69] Woolf 1928, 138.

emotional responsiveness. So the ideal of androgyny only repeats the suppression of woman's sexual difference.[70]

Even the visionary moment of Tristessa's and Eve's union equates the object role with the feminine and contrasts it with the subject role of the masculine, which still carries connotations of Evelyn's sadistic streak:

> ... when you lay below me ... I beat down upon you mercilessly, with atavistic relish, but the glass woman I saw beneath me smashed under my passion and the splinters scattered and recomposed into a man who overwhelmed me. (PNE 149)

Schmidt argues that the passage confirms gender stereotypes, depicting love as a struggle in which man is the conqueror and woman the conquered.[71] I would argue against this interpretation that the text does not strictly assign the masculine quality to the biological male and the feminine quality to the biological female. Instead, it imagines an equality which is based on the free interchangeability of the subject- and the object-role irrespective of the biological sex of the partners.[72] The love scene is reminiscent of the concept of a reciprocal desire that Carter envisages in *The Sadeian Woman*. Each of the lovers is both 'passive object' and 'active subject': "Such a partner acts on us as we act on it; both partners are changed by the exchange and, if submission is mutual, then aggression is mutual" (SW 146). In this sense the scene does not simply present the debunking of another mythic concept. Nor is it completely free of the ironic moments that pervade the novel. The love scene represents a de-essentialised image of sexual pleasure, which only refers to gender stereotypes to confound them. Carter resembles the *bricoleur* who rearranges the fragments of an old language in new ways.[73] The novel does not simply discard old gender definitions but also creates a new set of images which do not freeze identities but leave space for the transformation of "what we had been", "what we might be" or "what we thought we were" (PNE 148). The symbolism of alchemy figures the body not as a fixed entity but as a process that resists the inscription of fixed meaning. The union of Tristessa and Eve creates an ambiguous, hybrid body in the act of becoming, reminiscent of the Bakhtinian grotesque body which merges self and other.[74]

---

[70] Dallery 1989, 65.

[71] Schmidt 1989, 66.

[72] See also Day 1998, 121,124.

[73] In *The Savage Mind* Lévi-Strauss describes mythical thought in '"primitive" societies as "bricolage": new systems of meaning are created from the recombination of elements which are taken from old myths. The poststructuralist theorist has been compared to the bricoleur: s/he works with a limited inventory of existing concepts taken from older, universal systems of thought and recombines them in new ways. Lévi-Strauss 1966, 17.

[74] For an analysis of different forms of the grotesque in the novel see Johnson 1994, 43-48.

A mutual concept of desire emerges in the novel that contrasts with the narcissistic nature of desire in *The Infernal Desire Machines*. Is the hermaphrodite the new, alternative myth the novel creates?

The hermaphrodite is a recurring motif in Carter's fiction. In *The Infernal Desire Machines* Albertina appears as a crippled hermaphrodite in a wheelchair before she is killed by Desiderio. In "Reflections" the hermaphrodite represents the origin of gender difference in a timeless realm beyond history.[75] Here, as well, s/he is crippled, rendered immobile by myth and finally left dying by the narrator, who escapes back into time and history. In the short story "Overture and Incidental Music" the hermaphrodite represents the object of everybody's desire, though he himself knows no desire. The herm's inability to desire indicates his impotence and lack of agency. While Carter's fiction undermines binary oppositions like 'male' and 'female', it also rejects the idealisation of a synthesising unity that reconciles and sublates these differences, thus putting an end to sexual conflict. Carter claims: "... I do think that sexual conflict is what-makes-the-world-go-round, is what produces the tensions that any society needs to continue forward ....".[76] Her work pleads for the acceptance of difference and conflict. The Platonic vision of eternal unity denotes a dead-end street: the end of tension and stasis. In the love scene, however, the motif of the hermaphrodite is employed in a different way: as an image for a fleeting moment of unity which does not destroy but retains tension and conflict. In *The Passion of New Eve* the hermaphrodite is not an alternative myth nor a fixed ideal to be striven for but an image for the recombination of gender attributes which the narrative strategically employs to undermine the myth of femininity and masculinity. As Day argues, the hermaphrodite has "a metaphoric status" in the narrative which "goes right into mythic territory" in order to make an "anti-mythic" point.[77] While the novel rejects the merging of differences, it cautiously suggests a dissociation of sex and gender and an interchangeability of gender roles in the love scene in the desert. For a brief moment, *jouissance*

---

[75] In "Reflections" the narrator is thrust into a fantastic world which is the inverted mirror image of reality. In between these two worlds he encounters the hermaphrodite, who knits the real world and its negative mirror image together. Although the "synthesis in person" (BB 95), the hermaphrodite is nevertheless powerless: "'She can,' said Anna, 'go both ways, although she cannot move at all. So her power is an exact equivalent of her impotence, since both are absolute" (BB 87). When the narrator smashes the mirror through which he entered the alternative world, the hermaphrodite rapidly ages and dies.
[76] Carter in Sage 1977, 55. My interpretation of the motif differs from Warner's and Müller's reading of the motif of the hermaphrodite as the embodiment of the utopian "dream of synthesis" in Carter's work. See Warner 1994, 251; Müller 1997, 33.
[77] Day 1998, 124. See also Gasiorek 1995, 135.

enters the text. Yet this utopian moment is only short-lived. The children's militia shoot Tristessa for "lechery".

2.3.2 The Children's Militia and the Body in History

The children's militia join America's project of the denial of the body by adhering to a Christian puritanism which castigates the flesh. Just like Mother and Tristessa, the children privilege the mind over the body. The militia's masochism is reminiscent of the centaurs' self-flagellations in *The Infernal Desire Machines*. Both novels employ the tattoo as a symbol of the painful subjugation of the body (cf. III.1.2.1). Yet in *The Passion of New Eve* the tattoo is distorted by the growing adolescent body of the militia's leader:

> It had been perpetrated upon him before he had finished growing and the features of the disciples would subtly distort with the years, acquire the elongations of El Greco so his skin would soon mock the picture upon it .... (PNE 160)

In *The Passion of New Eve* the body resists signification. The attempt to fix the body within myth – a stable signifying system that freezes history – fails in the novel. The narrative depicts the 'body in process' that will not be contained by static systems of signification. Eve's symbolic rebirth in the cave at the sea leaves him with three symbols: the mirror which does not reflect anymore, the picture of Tristessa, and the feather of the archaeopteryx frozen in amber. The destruction of the photograph, the cracking of the mirror and the melting of the amber indicate a liberation of the body from representations that fix it in one place. However, what will follow this liberation remains uncertain. Pushing Eve into history and politics, the novel pleads for the acceptance of change and transformation.

While *The Passion of New Eve* deconstructs the female body that is marked by patriarchal inscriptions, it does not attempt to give that body a definite new form which distinguishes it from the male body. The empty space in the cave illustrates how Mother/Woman has been deconstructed out of the narrative. Carter is cautious about the naming of the female subject, which might fix that subject in just another mythology. Eve adopts an agnostic attitude towards the miracle of sexual difference:

> Masculine and feminine are correlatives which involve one another. I am sure of that – the quality and the negation are locked in necessity. But what the nature of masculine and the nature of the feminine might be, whether they involve male and female ... that I do not know. Though I have been both man and woman, still I do not know the answers to these questions. (PNE 150)

Eve – the postmodern Tiresias – expresses uncertainty and bewilderment about the issue of sexual difference. Against the background of the bleak scenario of the civil war, the novel ends on an image of hope and renewal: pregnant Eve embarks on the ocean. Eve's transformed mind and her pregnant body leave hope for something better than the violence that Lilith perpetrates on California. Images of death and darkness, however, undercut the hopeful note on which the novel ends. Mother has turned into a senile old hag – the fatal ferryman, whom Evelyn pays with the Czech's alchemical gold. Pregnant Eve embarks in Mother's coffin. The final scene of the novel juxtaposes death and birth as uncertain images of hope and fear about the future of New Eve.

3. Conclusion
Transcending Narcissism and Melancholia

The narcissistic economy of sameness, a recurring theme in Carter's work, is conveyed through various metaphors in her novels: the cannibalistic appropriation of otherness, the incestual love of the same, the motif of the mirror and the double. The structure of mirroring permeates *The Passion of New Eve*. Tristessa epitomises the "Rule of the Same". Eve is constructed on Tristessa's model: "twinned by their synthetic life", both are transformed into their former objects of desire. When Eve finally encounters Tristessa, she thus meets her own double: "I went towards you as towards my own face in a magnetic mirror .... the abyss on which you opened was that of my self, Tristessa." (PNE 110). Eve/lyn's lack of self is also reflected in Leilah ("... she had mimicked ... the fatal lack in me ...." [PNE 34]) and in the landscape's symbolic topography: the endless space of the desert symbolises America's desolation and Evelyn's inner void. When Zero rapes Eve, he as well turns into a reflection of Eve's former self: "I felt myself to be, not myself, but he ...." (PNE 102). Eve/lyn is fenced in by a hall of mirrors that throw back an endless proliferation of images of his self. On his quest s/he encounters various societies that reflect his solipsism. Like Desiderio, Evelyn travels through the landscape of his mind. The novel's characters are organised in a pattern of correspondences and contrasts that turns each figure into the mirror image of another. While Mother is Zero's twin figure of destruction, Tristessa represents the masochistic counterpart of his sadistic masculinity. Both Mother and Tristessa embody stereotypical concepts of femininity which are not located outside of but within the economy of sameness. As in *The Infernal Desire Machines,* sameness structures the narrative, which again and again points to the way in which patriarchal culture reduces woman to a male fantasy. Yet *The Passion of New Eve* goes further than its predecessor novel when it displays the self-destruction of this culture which annihilates difference. The novel turns chaos into a productive 'gender disorder' from which a New Eve, a self-determined female identity, might emerge.

The Passion of New Eve is structured around a downward movement. The novel stages a carnivalesque reversal of hierarchy when it puts the male subject into the female object position. Eve(lyn)'s picaresque journey consists of a series of degradations and humiliations. In New York, in Beulah and in the cave, s/he descends into imaginary spaces and confronts what has been repressed in the formation of the male subject. The alchemical symbolism of the novel reflects this downward movement. Matter is buried in the ground to achieve a magical transformation.[78] The cave episode epitomises Eve's transformation: Eve descends into the repressed space in which he expects to find Mother and learns that myths about the feminine and the masculine are "extraordinary lies designed to make us unfree"[79]. In contrast to Desiderio, who remains caught in the world of his imagination, Eve(lyn) is immersed in a space of otherness.

In Carter's fiction a change begins to take shape with *The Passion of New Eve*. The novel offers a much more optimistic outlook than its predecessor. A comparison of the endings of the two texts may illustrate this point. *The Infernal Desire Machines* closes with the melancholic subject waiting for death and mourning the inevitable loss of an alternative world. Albertina's final apparition heralds Desiderio's death: "I close my eyes. Unbidden she comes" (ID 220). Like Albertina, Tristessa appears in a liminal state between waking and dreaming as a harbinger of death: "He himself often comes to me in the night, serene in his marvellous plumage of white hair, with the fatal red hole in his breast ...." (PNE 191). *The Passion of New Eve* ironically rewrites the motif of the dead beloved as muse. It is not the male melancholic subject writing in remembrance of the lost beloved, but the female (transsexual) commemorating the death of the male (transvestite). The apparition, however, vanishes, Eve opens her eyes and embarks on a new beginning: "We start from our conclusions" (PNE 191). *The Passion of New Eve* does not remain stuck in the melancholic obsession with the past. While Desiderio's narrative

---

[78] See Schmid, Day and Johnson for a closer analysis of the alchemical symbolism in the novel. Alchemical thought postulates the existence of a primordial substance which can be transformed into gold by adding certain qualities and burying it in the earth. This primordial substance is symbolised by the hermaphrodite. See Schmid 1996, 54; Day 1998, 108,109; Johnson 1997, 168-170. *The Passion of New Eve* makes use of the alchemical symbolism in a highly ironic way. The novel employs alchemical symbols to describe Eve/lyn's transformation while mocking the belief in a primary wholeness and unity.

[79] Carter 1983, 71.

is haunted by loss, Eve finally looks forward to the future. The endings of the two novels are inverted mirror images of each other: sharing the motif of the closing of the eyes, the invasion of the present by the past, and the dream of the beloved, one closes with death, the other with birth.

In *The Passion of New Eve* the narrating subject has overcome melancholia. The ending of the text looks to the future as a wide, open mysterious space of uncertainty, awaiting the birth of the new: the unforeseeable that transcends the preordained scripts of the Hollywood narratives of gender. The blank space of the sea epitomises the silence that precedes the emergence of another language reaching beyond the narrow confines of old gender definitions.

Remaking the Female Body

The Passion of New Eve inquires into the making of the subject in Western civilisation. The novel represents an attack on the mirror and the screen as symbols of the containment of the body within representations. Carter deconstructs the female body as it has been conceived in patriarchal representation. Leilah turns out to be not an insatiable prostitute but a guerilla fighter engaged by Mother. Nevertheless, the novel does not attempt to retrieve the 'real' woman beneath the stereotype. Lilith is another stereotype, another creation of male fantasy: the castrating amazon, who reproduces Mother's violence.[80] In *The Passion of New Eve* there is no female essence that can be recovered from repression. Femininity is 'always already' contaminated by its function within a patriarchal system of signification. Does Carter equate the liberation of the female body with the obliteration of that body? Palmer criticises *The Passion of New Eve* for its failure to imagine a positive female subjectivity.[81] As in *The Infernal Desire Machines*, there seems to be no 'lived' female body in the novel. Jouve notes the absence of the subjective experience of pain in the novel:

> The – bloodlessness? – with which a ghastly series of Doomsday horrors were being narrated fazed me .... Whether the pain is hers [Eve's] or someone else's, s/he does keep

---

[80] For different readings of Lilith see Palmer and Pitchford. Palmer argues that Carter inadvertently slips into an "essentialist position" in her portrayal of Lilith as Leilah's "authentic feminist self" (Palmer 1997, 29). Pitchford reads Lilith as embodying a "positive feminist strategy" which chooses "down-to-earth action" over myth (Pitchford 2002, 141). Lilith's guerilla strategy is indeed more efficient than her Mother's mythic project. I still opt for a critical reading of the figure who takes her name from a 'masculine', Biblical myth that is born of the fear of femininity. Lilith is reminiscent of Sade's Juliette, whom Carter criticises for reproducing the violence of her male torturers (Carter 1979, 99).
[81] Palmer 1987, 179 ff..

a near-psychopathic inability to feel it .... Unreality is the name of the game. Bloodless was the right word. No blood flowed from any wounding instrument – not the bungling abortionist's needle when Evelyn's girlfriend Leilah gets messed up, nor the emasculating knife that descends upon Evelyn.[82]

Even though there is the most hideous violence, there seems to be no authentic experience of suffering in the novel. Is the body in pain eclipsed by the allegorical force of Carter's writing? A subjectively experienced body would run counter to the novel's satirical thrust, which requires the distancing of the reader from the satirised illusion. Whether this ironic stance of the narrator makes pain invisible or whether it makes it all the more terrifying is arguable. In fact, I would maintain that the indifferent narrative voice is itself the object of the satire. This satire is most obvious in Evelyn's reaction to Leilah's haemorrhage after her abortion: "I was full of guilt and horror yet, since the easiest way out of my own pain at having caused her so much pain was to cease to feel for her altogether, by the next day, of course, I had done so" (PNE 35). As in *The Infernal Desire Machines*, Carter ironically adopts the male perspective which she undermines by foregrounding the violence implicit in this perspective.

Punter criticises Carter for transforming reality into a text, into a world "where the symbols and signboards are our total environment, behind them lying nothing but vacuity".[83] Is Carter producing a Baudrillardian scenario in which the text eclipses the body? Punter writes:

> For nothing here is accidental: the least curve of a thigh, the faintest hint of proffered pleasure, on the cinema screen ... constitute the geometry of the social formation and can be read as such. Therefore each and every action, and especially each manifestation of sexuality, becomes instantaneously inserted into a code, becomes a fragment of text to be read. The endpoint of this self-consciousness, of this ceaseless plotting of event onto the structure of language, is the pronunciation of sex as impossible ....[84]

Punter's critique bespeaks a desire for the 'pure body', for a sexuality unimpaired by the society in which it takes place. Carter's work radically rejects the notion of sex as a natural force independent of the power relations and the economic context of a society (cf. III.2). Punter's analysis of the novel, though, seems questionable, particularly when he refers to "the lifeless mating of Eve and Tristessa" as illustration of the "impossibility of sex" in Carter's fiction.[85] The love scene employs an old language that is bound up

---

[82] Jouve 1994, 142.
[83] Punter 1984, 220.
[84] Ibid., 220,221.
[85] Ibid.. While I do not agree with this reading of *The Passion of New Eve*, in *The Infernal Desire Machines* sexuality seems to be indeed impossible: adoring and fetishising Albertina

with gender stereotypes and creates this language anew as expression of a de-essentialised *and* embodied pleasure. Even though language exerts a powerful command over the body in the novel, *The Passion of New Eve* does not eliminate the body's resistance against this language. In the metamorphoses that occur in the text bodies slip through the network of the representations that try to imprison them: Leilah turns out to be Lilith, macho-Evelyn is transformed into Eve, Tristessa falls in love with a woman. The body outgrows the tattoo and finds fulfilment in the embrace of the undefined and ambivalent other.

However, even if there is a body beyond the text in *The Passion of New Eve*, it is not a tightly defined body. It is a body in process whose boundaries are open, dissociated from biological origins and the restrictions which essentialist models impose on it. The body that the novel releases from confinement is negatively defined: it negates the boundaries that traditionally constitute the female subject. The novel ends, heralding the birth of New Eve, the offspring of the union of the transsexual and the transvestite: "But I myself will soon produce a tribute to evolution" (PNE 186). New Eve is not yet born in *The Passion of New Eve*. She will be in *Nights at the Circus*. The monstrous body that defies boundaries takes the stage in *Nights at the Circus*. *The Passion of New Eve* deconstructs patriarchal notions of femininity and creates the basis for the construction of the 'New Woman' in *Nights at the Circus*. After the novel has done away with old symbols, *Nights at the Circus* creates a "fresh iconography" in the carnivalesque world of the circus.

---

from a distance, Desiderio wonders at the end of his quest "whether the fleshly possession of Albertina would not be the greatest disillusionment of it all" (ID 201).

V. Alterity, Femininity and the Monstrous Body in *Nights at the Circus*
Introduction

Nights at the Circus marks a radical change in the development of Carter's fiction. Seven years had passed since the publication of *The Passion of New Eve*. Not only did Carter work on *The Sadeian Woman* and *The Bloody Chamber* in this time. She also 'hatched' the female subject whose advent was anticipated at the end of *The Passion of New Eve*. A powerful female subjectivity asserts itself in *Nights at the Circus*. The female body comes alive as the site of this gendered subjectivity. Like its predecessor, the novel mocks patriarchal representations of the feminine. Yet the female body assumes a different role in the narrative. Whereas in *The Passion of New Eve* the male and the female are merged into the hermaphrodite, *Nights at the Circus* turns the female body into a powerful site of subversion.

This chapter traces the emergence of a 'monstrous' female corporeality in Carter's fiction. Fevvers' winged body both parodies patriarchal myths of femininity and creates a new powerful symbol that inverts these myths. In what follows, I will analyse the subversive potential of the monstrous and grotesque bodies in the novel. The panopticon episode will be interpreted as a miniature model of the narration as a whole: it stages the containment of the body through the gaze and the subsequent subversion of this gaze. An examination of the narrative structure of the text foregrounds analogies between the monstrous bodies in the narrative and the de-centered textual structure of the novel. A radical sense of difference emerges in *Nights at the Circus*, which disrupts the sameness that governs Carter's preceding fiction.

1. Fevvers' Body
1.1 The English Angel: Myth in the Mode of Irony

Fevvers' body carries several mythological associations in the novel: a bird woman designed "on the grand scale", Fevvers has been hatched like Helen of Troy and during puberty sprouted a tremendous pair of wings. She poses as Cupid and 'Winged Victory' in Ma Nelson's brothel, and as 'Angel of Death' in the museum of woman monsters. Her winged body invokes various patriarchal stereotypes of female difference: woman as ethereal being, the 'Angel in the House', woman signifying death, the "Virgin Whore" (NC 55), the holy "goddess" and the "atrocious hole" (NC 77).[1] Yet deviating from

---

[1] Christian Rosencreutz addresses Fevvers as "his goddess ... aspiring upwards" (NC 77) and expresses terror at "the atrocious hole ... that sucks everything dreadfully down, down,

the conventional versions of these stereotypes, the narrative both inscribes and subverts myth in Fevvers' body. Playing childish pranks on the customers, Cupid behaves in a slightly different way than might be expected of the conventional symbol of love: "Sometimes, out of childish fun, [she] sprung her toy arrows amongst them, hitting, in play, sometimes an ear, sometimes a buttock, sometimes a ballock" (NC 38). Nor does Fevvers correspond precisely to the Winged Victory she represents after she has turned fourteen: unlike the original, Fevvers possesses arms besides her wings. This enables her to flee *and* to fight back at the various male aggressors that attempt to capture her in the narrative.[2] Ma Nelson further "perfects" the statue with her sword, a phallic token of masculine power. Fevvers presents the body in excess.[3] This excess signifies power and agency: the sight of the large woman with too many appendages intimidates the customers and leads to the brothel's decline.

Moreover, Fevvers is not the ethereal selfless creature we usually associate with the Victorian 'Angel in the House'.[4] A literalised mock version of this myth, she looks like an "albatross fed to excess" (NC 15) and farts and belches uninhibitedly. She literally flies, even though flying does not come easy to her, but is a product of strenuous exercise, as Walser notes, when he watches her performance:

> First impression: physical ungainliness. Such a lump it seems! But soon, quite soon, an acquired grace asserts itself, probably the result of strenuous exercise. My, how her body strains .... The packed theatre could enjoy the spectacle, as in slow motion, of every tense muscle straining in her Rubenesque form .... (NC 16,17)

Fevvers' ability to fly derives from hard exercise and intense study, in which she and her foster mother Lizzie engage. As Russo puts it: Fevvers reveals

---

down where Terror rules ...." (NC 77). Rosencreutz drives the conventional patriarchal representation of women as symbols of transcendence or animality to an extreme.

[2] Ma Nelson, mother figure and leader of the brothel, glosses over this discrepancy by propagating Fevvers as the "perfection of, the original of, the very model for that statue which, in its broken and incomplete state ... has been mutilated by history" (NC 37). Ma Nelson's rearrangement of myth and history is symptomatic for the novel's treatment of myth as a whole: the narrative does not just deconstruct but re-appropriates myth by creating a powerful female subjectivity. The confusion of the original and the copy, the authentic and the inauthentic, destroys the authority of the mythological and points to a central theme of the narrative: the distinction between fact and fiction, the real and the artificial. While *The Infernal Desire Machines* and *The Passion of New Eve* reveal the real to be a construction, an epistemological uncertainty runs through *Nights at the Circus* which is not resolved but consciously exploited by Fevvers: "Is she fact or is she fiction?"

[3] See also Russo 1994, 168.

[4] See also Blodgett 1994, 52; Booker 1991, 230.

"what angels and circus stars normally conceal": labour.[5] *Nights at the Circus* resumes the de-mythologising project begun in *The Infernal Desire Machines* and *The Passion of New Eve* and reveals the divine, the mythic, to be a product of hard work and training in the confidence trick. In the violent hierarchy of the circus, the novel uncovers the crude material conditions of this 'work'. In *Notes From the Front Line* Carter writes:

> I believe that all myths are products of the human mind and reflect only aspects of material human practice. I'm in the demythologizing business. I'm interested in myths ... just because they *are* extraordinary lies designed to make people unfree.[6]

Fevvers parodies the notion of femininity that is embodied by Tristessa in *The Passion of New Eve*. Like Tristessa, she is a star, an angel – in the literal sense – and functions as a fetish object on the stage. Yet, whereas Tristessa embodies the closedness of a system of patriarchal representations, Fevvers represents the very disruption of this system. Not only does she cause the decline of the brothel; she also puts an end to Madame Schreck's museum of horror. Fevvers' presence, moreover, wrecks Colonel Kearney's colonial project ("Tuskers to Siberia"): the outlaws hijack the train because of Fevvers in order to make her plead with the British Queen for their rehabilitation.

By embodying ironic versions of male myths of the feminine, Fevvers' body functions as a reminder of the threat these myths pose for women. The bird woman is constantly in danger of being trapped in male narratives that extinguish her "unique and indivisible me-ness" (NC 280) in order to fix her in a static role, in which she either becomes a toy or an *"elixum vitae"* (NC 83) for the male appropriator:

> Fevvers felt that ... sensation when mages, wizards, impresarios came to take away her singularity as though it were their own invention, as though they believed she depended on their imaginations in order to be herself. She felt herself turning, willy nilly, from a woman into an idea. (NC 289)

Fevvers is in danger of turning into Tristessa, a frozen icon of femininity. Mythologising literally turns out to be fatal for her in Rosencreutz' ritual. Similarly, the Duke plans to divest her of her subjectivity and turn her into a mere object of pleasure: "a bird in a gilded cage". Fevvers, a picaresque female hero, again and again manages to evade this danger, either through her presence of mind, her sword – or her wings.

---

[5] Russo, 1994, 177.
[6] Carter in Wandor 1983, 71.

1.2 Utopia – or: Wings as a Symbol of Liberation

It is Fevvers' wings which place her in danger of being trapped as a 'rara avis'. Yet it is also her wings which enable her to escape confinement. Fevvers' winged body is both a symbol of the confinement of women in patriarchal representations and a powerful image of liberation and transformation. When Fevvers' wings break forth, Ma Nelson, a committed suffragist, is delighted: "Oh, my little one, I think you must be the pure child of the century that just now is waiting in the wings, the New Age in which no women will be bound to the ground" (NC 25). Fevvers' wings symbolise the enthusiasm and hopefulness that marked the early women's movement at the turn of the century. Fevvers anticipates the twentieth century with visionary optimism:

> And once the old world has turned on its axle, so that the new dawn can dawn, then, ah then! all the women will have wings the same as I .... The dolls' house doors will open, the brothels will spill forth their prisoners, the cages, gilded or otherwise, all over the world, in every land, will let forth their inmates singing together the dawn chorus of the new, the transformed – (NC 285)

Fevvers' vision remains incomplete. Her unbound enthusiasm is undercut by Lizzie's scepticism, who sees "storms ahead" in the twentieth century: "'It's going to be more complicated than that,' interpolated Lizzie. '... You improve your analysis, girl, and then we'll discuss it'" (NC 286). In fact, Fevvers' enthusiastic heralding of the new century is undercut by the reader's knowledge of the terrible violence this century will bring.

Paulina Palmer notes a celebratory, affirmative tone in *Nights at the Circus* that distinguishes the novel from Carter's earlier texts.[7] The narrative contains utopian moments which are characteristically absent in Carter's earlier fiction. However, these utopian moments are frequently undercut and questioned in the narrative, as the example above illustrates. In the wilderness of Siberia several utopian concepts are discussed and tested with regard to their viability: the all-female utopia, Fevvers' concept of free womanhood, the Shaman's primitivism and Walser's going native etc..[8] Like the desert in *The Passion of New Eve*, the wilderness is a site of social experimentation. The concept of the prisoners' all-female utopia, however, starkly contrasts with the dystopian scientific Beulah, and the Shaman's irrationality is quite

---

[7] Palmer 1987,179 ff..

[8] *Nights at the Circus* resembles the 'novel of ideas' in the last episode, with characters mainly standing for different philosophical and political concepts (the capitalist Colonel Kearney, the Marxist Lizzie, the Shaman's primitivism, Fevvers' feminism, the idealistic convict who falls prey to Kearney's capitalism etc.).

sympathetic in contrast to Zero's violent primitivism. In *Nights at the Circus* Angela Carter seems to be more optimistic about utopia than she was in her earlier texts. The taming of the wild Blakean tigers on the roof by Mignon's music "that was at the same time a taming and ..., yet left them free" (NC 275) represents a powerful utopian image that lacks its counterpart in Carter's preceding novels. Mignon and the Princess stay in the wilderness to make "music that sealed the pact of tranquillity between humankind and their wild brethren, their wild sistren ... not the music of the spheres but of blood, of flesh, of sinew, of the heart" (NC 275). Carter's utopia is not located in heaven but on earth, it sympathises with the animals, not the angels. The unity of music and the flesh represents a synthesis of the human and the animal, the spirit and the body, which undoes hierarchical relationships and envisages an ideal of freedom and equality. Yet the narrative blurs this vision when it renders the same scene from the Shaman's perspective. For the Shaman's tribe Mignon's music is nothing but the "cacophony of uninvited gods" (NC 268):

> This music had no charms for them, nor did it soothe their savage breasts at all, at all; they scarcely recognized the Schubert lied as music for it had little in common with the scales and modes of the music they themselves ... made .... (NC 268)

Caliban's sensibility towards Prospero's music is just another myth Carter does away with. Music is not ahistorical and divine but the product of a culturally coded aesthetics in a particular society. Western European music is not necessarily an adequate means of uniting human beings beyond cultural barriers.[9]

Nights at the Circus combines utopian enthusiasm with rational analysis and scepticism. When the lesbian insurgents escape from the panopticon in order to found an all-female-utopia (taking with them a supply of sperm from the escaped convict), it is again Lizzie who exposes the naivety of their enterprise: "What'll they do with the boy babies? Feed 'em to the polar bears? To the *female* polar bears?" (NC 240,241). The novel combines the fantastic and the analytic, the utopian and the sceptical. The dialogic relationship between Fevvers, the utopian enthusiast, and Lizzie, the sceptic materialist, embodies Carter's concept of feminist politics as a utopian liberatory project that is based on materialist and rational analysis.[10]

---

[9] For an analysis of the role of music and singing in the novel see Booker 1991, 235 ff.. Booker relates the female prisoners' singing to Cixous and Kristeva's concept of the song as a "feminine form of communication".

[10] For Müller, Lizzie represents the older, materialist generation of feminists, while Fevvers embodies the utopian possibilities of deconstruction. Müller 1998, 6; see also Michael

The prime utopian symbol in *Nights at the Circus* is Fevvers' winged body: "I only knew my body was the abode of limitless freedom" (NC 41). Fevvers represents – as Ricarda Schmidt suggests – Eve's child.[11] She is Eve's "tribute" to evolution: the 'New Woman'. By transcending the symbolic role she is supposed to play in male-centered narratives (the angel in the house), Fevvers creates a new symbol of excess, which spills over beyond its original meaning. Carter is debasing myths, grounding angels, only to let them fly again. However, this act of re-symbolising does not imply the creation of a 'counter-myth'. Fevvers is too alive and human to be frozen into a fixed mythic form. A persistent sense of uncertainty concerning the bird woman's ontological status runs through the novel. Particularly in the first part of the narrative, language reflects this uncertainty. Metaphors are heaped onto each other in the attempt to grasp the phenomenon 'Fevvers': Fevvers is the Cockney Venus, Helen of the High Wire (NC 7), the English Angel (NC 8), a dray mare (NC 12), the Iron Maiden, a condor, an albatross (NC 15), a winged barmaid (NC 16), an Iowa Cornfield (NC 18), a hump-backed horse (NC 19) etc.. This metaphorical language reflects Walser's obsessive attempt to solve the miracle of femininity, to uncover Fevvers as a hoax and reveal the truth of her body beneath masquerade. The journalist Walser tries to fix the elusive phenomenon 'Fevvers' within writing. Yet the endless proliferation of vehicles that try to match the tenor illustrates how the 'essence' of Fevvers remains beyond the journalist's grasp. Walser fills up his notebook and his hand gets limp. The accumulation of metaphors creates an interminable chain of signifiers in the attempt to produce a definite meaning. Reminiscent of Lacan's concept of language (cf. III.1.1.2.1), the text literally traces the emergence of desire from this endless deferral of signification: unable to solve the enigma of femininity, Walser falls in love with Fevvers.

To summarise, Fevvers' body carries several meanings. Through its parodistic quality it both inscribes and subverts patriarchal myths of femininity. At the same time, it creates a new powerful symbol of femininity which is open, elusive and resists appropriation. Carter employs a double perspective which oscillates between deconstruction and construction of femininity. *Nights at the Circus* combines the deconstructive impulse with an affirmative identity politics that recreates the subject 'woman'.

1994, 492. Gasiorek describes Carter's narrative mode as a "double-voiced style" that moves between fantasy and analysis, allegory and rationalism. Gasiorek 1995, 135,136.
[11] Schmidt 1989, 67.

2. The Grotesque Body

In *Rabelais and his World* Bakhtin defines the grotesque body in medieval culture as a body in excess, which 'outgrows' its self and transgresses its limits. The grotesque body breaks down the boundary between the self and the world, "swallows the world and is itself swallowed by the world"[12]. This blending with objects, animals and human bodies illustrates transformation: the death of the old and the birth of the new. Bakhtin opposes the medieval grotesque to the modern, Post-Romantic grotesque. The positive, regenerative aspect of the grotesque body is lost in modernity, with the satirical function taking over. Excessiveness and exaggeration are left as the modes of the grotesque. In *Nights at the Circus* the monstrous bodies both display the regenerative and sombre aspects of the grotesque.[13] In what follows, I will look at the different meanings projected onto the grotesque body in the novel.

2.1 Transformation and Regeneration

Nights at the Circus is populated by hybrid bodies that break down the boundary between self and other in Bakhtin's sense: Fevvers' winged body transgresses the boundaries between human and animal, between the real and the artificial; Sleeping Beauty and Mignon straddle the boundary between life and death; Ma Nelson, a female-to-male transvestite, and the hermaphrodite Albert/Albertina confuse gender distinctions. In contrast to *The Passion of New Eve,* the hermaphrodite plays a minor role in *Nights at the Circus*: Albert/Albertina is just another freak whose monstrous body is less subversive than Fevvers' extravagantly female body. In the circus the apes blur the boundary between human and animal, behaving in a more intelligent and civilised way than their human keepers. The scene which juxtaposes the strong man's brutish orgasm with the apes' classroom performance is just one instance of role reversal in *Nights at the Circus* that unmasks human animality. As mentioned above, the novel also figures the body in excess. While Fevvers' excessive physicality parodies the notion of woman as body,

---

[12] Bakhtin 1984, 26,317.

[13] Surprisingly, Carter did not read Bakhtin until after the publication of *Nights at the Circus* (see Carter in Sage 1992, 187). Several critics such as Müller, Turner, Palmer, Russo, Booker and Peach point to carnivalesque elements in the novel. See Müller 1998, 127-128; Turner 1987, 46 ff.; Palmer 1987, 198; Palmer 1997, 28; Russo 1994; Booker 1991, 227; Peach 1998, 141.

it also creates a carnivalesque image of female power. Fevvers' table manners and her gargantuan appetite carry Rabelaisian connotations:

> She gorged, she stuffed herself, she spilled gravy on herself, she sucked up peas from the knife; she had a gullet to match her size and table manners of the Elizabethan variety ... at last her enormous appetite was satisfied ... she belched .... (NC 22)

The essential principle of the grotesque is the immersion in the lower bodily stratum: "... the lowering of all that is high, spiritual, ideal, abstract ... to the sphere of the earth and body ....".[14] This debasement involves a highlighting of physical functions as well as of specific body parts in Rabelais. Swallowing, devouring, urinating, giving birth etc. are typical processes of the body in transformation. The gaping mouth – the entrance into the lower bodily stratum – is the central image of the grotesque body:[15]

> Fevvers yawned with prodigious energy, opening up a crimson maw the size of that of a basking shark, taking in enough air to lift a Montgolfier, and then she stretched herself ... until it seemed she intended to fill up ... all the room with her bulk. ... Walser ... scrambled to his feet, suddenly panicking. (NC 52)

Images of devouring abound to describe the sexual attraction between Fevvers and Walser: "Walser ... felt the hungry eyes upon him and it seemed to him her teeth closed on his flesh with the most voluptuous lack of harm" (NC 204). In Bakhtin swallowing is an image of transformation. This image applies to Walser as well: in *Nights at the Circus* Walser is the object of transformation with Fevvers acting as the catalyst. The structures of Walser's and Eve(lyn)'s picaresque journeys participate in the same carnivalesque downward-movement that reverses roles and reforms the subject by putting it into the object-position. Walser experiences several debasements when he joins the circus to follow Fevvers. He first loses his profession as a journalist, his privilege of distinguishing between fact and fiction. Walser is 'uncrowned' from his position as the purveyor of truth and facts and becomes a clown who is beaten and abused.[16] He experiences several stages of degradation, which reflect the humiliations the women in the museum of woman monsters suffer. As "Human Chicken" Walser becomes food, now literally in danger of being swallowed by Buffo the Clown. This fate is reminiscent both of Fevvers' bird status and of the Wiltshire Wonder, the claustrophobic midget who was served in birthday cakes. The frequent beatings that Walser is subjected to relate him to Mignon, the child-woman,

---

[14] Bakhtin 1984, 19.
[15] Ibid., 325.
[16] Bakhtin describes the carnivalesque tradition of the uncrowning of the king who is degraded onto the position of a clown. "Debasement and interment are reflected in carnival uncrownings, related to blows and abuse." Bakhtin 1984, 370.

who is habitually thrashed by her husband. After the train wreck Walser appears as "Sleeping Beauty" to the lesbian escaped convicts, who wake him with a kiss. In contrast to Sleeping Beauty, though, he does wake up. The old Walser has died in the wreck. The new Walser is born with a kiss, uttering that "universal word": Mama! (NC 222):

> Like the landscape, he was perfectly blank .... He is a sentient being, still, but no longer a rational one; indeed now he is all sensibility, without a grain of sense .... He still cries: cock-a-doodle-doo! (NC 222,236)

Walser loses his scepticism and learns to believe without seeing. The degradations that he undergoes enact a Bakhtinian reversal of hierarchy. Again, Carter stages a deconstruction of the male subject. Having been immersed in the "gulf of otherness", the transformed Walser is the apt partner for the "new twentieth century woman". Fevvers' grotesque body and Walser's reformation both illustrate the subversive and regenerative power of the Bahtinian grotesque.

2.2 The Clowns: Violence and Stasis

Madness regenerates Walser who gains a different view of the world and learns to "experience experience *as* experience" (NC 10). In contrast, Buffo is destroyed by madness. Wearing a bladder as a wig, Buffo stores his brain in "the organ which conventionally stores piss" (NC 116). Wearing his insides on his outside, he represents the Bakhtinian transfer from bottom to top, from inside out. In the grotesque dance of the buffoons the clowns stage a fantastic mixture of infantile regression, unrestrained sexuality and bestial violence. The carnivalesque transgressions verge on Sadeian violence. The "clown's funeral" celebrates the barbaric body that refuses to be disciplined: Buffo's corpse will not fit into the coffin, and bursts through its lid in a tumultuous carnivalesque resurrection. Yet Buffo is not a comic figure but a tragic one. Turner associates the clowns with the modern grotesque, in which the grotesque body is part of a terrifying world, alien to humankind:[17] "Laughter was cut down to cold humour, irony, sarcasm."[18] The mask that hides "nothing" is a prominent theme in Bahktin's concept of the modern grotesque: "The Romantic mask loses almost entirely its regenerating and renewing element and acquires a sombre hue. A terrible vacuum, a nothingness lurks behind it."[19] Buffo echoes these words: "Take away my

---

[17] Turner 1987, 49.
[18] Bakhtin 1984, 38.
[19] Ibid., 40.

make-up and underneath is merely not-Buffo. An absence. A vacancy" (NC 122). Behind Buffo's mask lurks the horror of the void: the comic is eclipsed by the uncanny.

As mentioned above, Bakhtin attributed a subversive, liberatory potential to the medieval grotesque body that inverts hierarchies, disturbs boundaries and merges self and other. Yet, as critics have argued, in the medieval world the grotesque was firmly established in the marginal spaces of the official culture, offering only temporary release from the regulations and hierarchies of this culture. The grotesque even had a didactic function and pointed to the superiority of the serious and religious.[20] Similarly, in *Nights at the Circus* the monstrous bodies are not inherently subversive. Both the clowns and the women monsters represent the marginalised which has been excluded and banished into the 'lower' (the abyss) and the 'comic' spaces (the circus) of society. The clowns' restriction to the marginal spaces of the official culture defuses their disruptive potential. The clowns are, in fact, the very embodiment of stasis in the novel:

... the beauty of clowning is 'nothing ever changes' .... the baboushka back at home could go on reddening and blackening the charcoal even if the clowns detonated the entire city and nothing would really change. Nothing. The exploded buildings would float up into the air insubstantial as bubbles, and gently waft to earth again on exactly the same places where they had stood before .... Things would always be as they had always been .... (NC 117,151,152).

The clowns are outside of history, unable to effect change in the reality of poverty-stricken Russia. As representatives of the Post-Romantic grotesque, they embody the limits of carnival, its function as a safety-valve in the service of the dominant culture. The modern grotesque throws a dark shadow on the exuberant tone of the narrative and undercuts its utopian overtones.

3. 'To Repeat With a Difference': Masquerade, Parody and the Spectacle
3.1 "The freedom behind the mask": Masquerade as Subversion

Fevvers is a calculating businesswoman, who capitalises on her bodily extravagance. Fevvers' displaying herself as a spectacle in the circus is highly ambivalent. Posing as the object of the gaze, she assumes the traditionally female role. Yet, literally making a spectacle of herself, Fevvers parodies the role woman is supposed to play: her size, her artifice, her "Elizabethan" table manners (NC 22) and the "kitschness" of her act produce spectacle in excess. By financially exploiting this occasion for her own good, she turns the tables

---

[20] Kröll 1994, 11 ff..

on the economics of exploitation which commodifies women's bodies. Fevvers adapts herself to the capitalist system in order to finance Lizzie's Marxist struggle against this system. Living in first-class hotels and dating "fucking aristos" (NC 181), her actions are marked both by assimilation to and subversion of the system.

Mary Russo argues that a woman who makes a spectacle of herself inevitably disturbs the dominant discourse.[21] Woman produces a parody of the very spectacle that she is supposed to embody in twentieth-century cultural production. Sally Robinson refers to the notion of masquerade and considers Fevvers' displaying herself as highly ironic and subversive: masquerade, a self-conscious repetition of stereotypical notions of femininity, implies the power to employ the mask according to strategic aims: "For a woman ... a flaunting of the feminine is a take-it-and-leave-it possibility. To put on femininity with a vengeance suggests the power of taking it off."[22] The concept of masquerade is reminiscent of Butler's theory of gender parody. Like masquerade and the postcolonial notion of mimicry, parody repeats with a difference: "almost the same, but not quite."[23] Deriving from Foucault's concept of power, masquerade, mimicry and parody represent de-naturalising strategies that subvert from the inside, through appropriating and mocking stock images of the feminine. Fevvers masquerades as spectacle, as body on display.

According to Robinson, *Nights at the Circus* employs masquerade as a strategic means of disrupting the culturally dominant conceptions of femininity. Indeed, the mask is connected to freedom in *Nights at the Circus*. As a clown Walser experiences "the freedom that lies behind the mask, within dissimulation, the freedom to juggle with being ..." (NC 103). The clowns experience "perfect freedom" (NC 122) when they construct themselves: "We can invent our own faces! We *make* ourselves" (NC 121). The apes practice mimicry in their parody of humanity:

> One who had made a profound study of those creatures as they went through their routines that mocked us, the cycle race, the tea party, the schoolroom, might have

---

[21] Russo 1986, 213 ff..

[22] Russo 1986, 224. Robinson 1991, 118. The term 'masquerade' has been adopted from Nietzsche and Freud. Nietzsche defines femininity as masquerade which masks non-identity. Freud and Lacan define female sexuality as masquerade which masks a lack. In feminist theory (Joan Rivière, Spivak, Mary Ann Doane, Russo, Robinson) the term designates a strategy which women consciously adopt to undermine patriarchal representations of the feminine. Irigaray uses the term 'mimicry' for this strategy; 'masquerade' carries negative connotations in Irigaray's writing, designating women's assimilation to masculine desire. Irigaray 1985b, 27,76,220.

[23] Bhabha 1994, 86. See also III.1.2.2 note 36.

concluded that the apes, in turn, were putting their own studious observation of ourselves to use in routines of parody, of irony, of satire. (NC 141,142)

The apes' performance in the circus is turned into a mockery of humanity. Masquerade and mimicry are strategies of subversion employed by the disempowered in the circus: the women, the animals and the clowns.

'To repeat with a difference' is also a principal comic device in the novel. Not only Fevvers' body 'repeats with a difference'. Among the primitive tribesmen the deranged Walser is transformed into a mock version of the colonel, who is himself a caricature of American pioneer spirit and capitalism. The narrative creates several parallels between the lost circus crew and the primitive tribe in Siberia: the bear and the Shaman's magic amulet bag represent mock versions of the Colonel's pig and Lizzie's handbag, respectively; the Shaman and the Colonel share the ability to fool the world while looking "preternaturally solemn" (NC 263). Carter claimed that she inserted the passage on the tribe as a critique of the idealisation of primitivism that was in vogue at the time.[24] At the same time, however, she presents a mocking view of the Colonel's colonial enterprise, of patriotism, chauvinism and capitalism. The Colonel's indefatigable belief in the pioneering spirit and conquest, his search for profit under the banner of liberty go along with a child-like naivety and a lack of self-criticism that mirrors the mental condition of the secluded tribesmen. 'To repeat with a difference' is a disruptive strategy employed by the characters as well as the major parodistic principle that structures the narrative.

3.2 The Faceless Clown: Masquerade and the Horror of the Void

However, masquerade and mimicry are not just comic and subversive devices in the novel. When Sally Robinson reads *Nights at the Circus* as a celebration of masquerade, she seems to ignore the negative connotations that masquerading carries in the novel. Robinson endorses a radical performative view of gender that negates female essence behind masquerade. Her celebratory, anti-essentialist view of masquerade suggests that the mask of femininity hides "nothing".[25] Yet it is exactly this "nothing", the desperate cry of the clowns, which represents the dark side of masquerade in the novel. Buffo loses his self beneath the mask:

---

[24] Carter in Haffenden 1985, 89.
[25] Robinson 1991, 121.

... my face eclipses me. I have become this face which is not mine, and yet I chose it freely .... Am I this Buffo whom I have created? Or did I ... create, ex nihilo, another self who is not me? And what am I without my Buffo's face? Why, nobody at all. (NC 122)

Horror of the void pervades *Nights at the Circus*. The narrative echoes *King Lear*: "Nothing will come of nothing" (NC 123). The text seems to allude to a theoretical concept in the figure of the faceless clown: the poststructuralist view of the subject that deconstructs essences and conceives subjectivity as a mere performance. The clowns enact the dissolution of identity beneath the mask. In fact, Buffo literally deconstructs himself in the performance of the clown's funeral:

At the climax of his turn ... he starts to deconstruct himself. His face ... contorted ... as if he were trying to ... shake out his teeth, shake off his nose, shake away his eyeballs, let all go flying off in convulsive self-dismemberment .... (NC 117)

Staging the death of the subject and the loss of agency, the clowns represent the fate of the postmodern subject that reduces itself to a disembodied "untenanted replica" (NC 116).[26] Masquerade is no longer a "self-conscious re-enactment", nor a free choice, but a substitute for the autonomous self. The clowns suffer the same fate as Tristessa: the simulacrum has eclipsed the body. Like the clowns, Fevvers is not always in control of spectacle and masquerading. The concept of masquerade implies the freedom to put the mask on and take it off, to choose the mask freely. Yet Fevvers has no other choice than of "making a spectacle of herself", as Lizzie expounds:

All you can do to earn a living is to make a show of yourself. You're doomed to that. You must give pleasure to the eye, or else you're good for nothing. For you, it's always a symbolic exchange in the market-place. (NC 185)

In fact, Fevvers' body shrinks when she does not have an audience anymore in the wilderness. In Rosencreutz' mansion and in the Duke's palace, she is in danger of being pinned down like the clowns, of being transformed into a symbol or a toy, an object that is defined by the gaze. When she encounters the mad Walser in Siberia, she suffers a crisis of identity:

She felt her outlines waver; she felt herself trapped forever in the reflection of Walser's eyes. For one moment ... she suffered the worst crisis of her life: Am I fact? Or am I fiction? Am I what I know I am? Or am I what he thinks I am? (NC 290)

Fevvers' confusion traces the blurring of the boundaries between fact and fiction, between the real and the constructed that dissolves the notion of the

---

[26] The clowns carry several different meanings in the multi-layered allegorical structure of the narrative: they embody the modern grotesque (Turner), the limits of carnival (cf. 2.2), nihilism (see Hanson, 1997, 65) and the paralysing effect of masquerade and deconstruction.

autonomous subject in postmodernity. Like Buffo ("Am I this Buffo whom I have created?" [NC 122]), Fevvers is in danger of losing her self in the role she plays. However, she finds a way back to herself through displaying her wings to the tribesmen. Fevvers' bodily difference saves her from the clowns' fate.

The horror of disembodiment is, moreover, expressed through another figure in the narrative. Toussaint reports that he found "nothing" inside Madame Schreck's clothes:

> It came to me that there was nothing left inside the clothes and, perhaps, there never had been anything inside her clothes but a set of dry bones agitated only by the power of an infernal will and a voice that had been no more than the artificial exhalation of air from a bladder or a sac, that she was, or had become, a sort of scarecrow of desire. (NC 84)

Madame Schreck, who began her career as a "living skeleton" in freak shows, embodies another threat that endangers Fevvers' integrity: Madame Schreck's greed for profit has literally swallowed her self. Financially exploiting a system that commodifies her, Fevvers is in danger of adapting herself to this system, which fetishises money. The text constructs several parallels between Fevvers and the gruesome Madame Schreck which highlight this potential threat. Both Fevvers and Madame Schreck represent spectacles: the bird woman and the living skeleton. Both are driven by their insatiable greed for money. Madame Schreck jumps into the safe to hug her riches and Fevvers dreams of bank accounts. It is greed which lures Fevvers into the Duke's arms and almost imprisons her as a bird in a gilded cage. Walser notes a ghostly artificiality in Fevvers' voice which resembles Madame Schreck's artificially produced voice: "Such a voice could almost have its source, not within her throat but in some ingenuous mechanism or other behind the canvas screen, voice of a fake medium at a seance ...."(NC 43). Madame Schreck is Fevvers' uncanny double. Both are avatars of the twentieth-century society of the spectacle, simulacra in the service of the profit motive.

Linda Hutcheon describes parody as a double-coded genre that both repeats and subverts that which it parodies.[27] The very ambivalence of parody can produce misreadings. Similarly, masquerade may reproduce what it intends to criticise. In fact, there is not much difference between repeating and *self-consciously* repeating gender stereotypes, between being and pretending to be a spectacle. The subversive potential of masquerade also relies on the reader's (and the audience's) ability to decipher the irony of the representation. Robert Clark argues that Carter often reinscribes patriarchal values for all but the feminist reader who can deconstruct the ideologies she

---

[27] Hutcheon 1989, 101.

presents.[28] While Carter's earlier novels may be vulnerable to this criticism, I doubt it if any reader will mistake Fevvers for the 'Angel in the House'. The narrative again and again stresses the way in which Fevvers capitalises on the illusion she creates and remains in control of her performance. In addition, *Nights at the Circus* incorporates the limits and dangers of masquerading in the narrative.[29] The text metafictionally points to the ambivalence of its own subversive strategy. While Fevvers demonstrates the subversive potential of the mask, the clowns and Madame Schreck represent the danger inherent in postmodern playfulness, in the juggling with identities which might reduce us to 'untenanted replicas'. Is resistance possible without a face behind the mask? Is resistance possible without a body behind appearance? As Winged Victory, Fevvers manages to retain her autonomy, the "vibrant potentiality" of her self beneath the mask:

> My face and top half of my body was spread with the wet white that clowns use in the circus .... The wet white would harden on my face and torso like a death mask .... Yet, inside this appearance of marble, nothing could have been more vibrant with potentiality than I! (NC 37,39)

Nights at the Circus does not eliminate the body behind the guise. It is, in fact, the body which rebels in the novel, as I wish to expound in the following section.

4. The Panopticon: Confinement and Liberation
4.1 The Body as the Object of the Gaze

One of the central images in *Nights at the Circus* is the panopticon – the women's prison in Siberia. Although the panopticon episode only touches the action on the margin (the escaped inmates discover Walser in the train wreck), it epitomises the central theme of the narrative: confinement and liberation. The panopticon is a prison in which each inmate is constantly visible to a controlling authority and remains isolated from fellow prisoners:

> It was a panopticon she forced them to build, a hollow circle of cells shaped like a doughnut, the inward-facing wall of which was composed of grids of steel and, in the middle of the roofed, central courtyard, there was a round room surrounded by windows. In that she'd sit all day and stare and stare and stare at her murderesses .... (NC 212)

---

[28] Clark 1987, 159.

[29] I disagree in this point with Palmer who claims that even in her late fiction Carter does not explore the problematic aspects of the concept of "gender as performance". See Palmer 1997, 32. See also my analysis of Carter's short story "In Pantoland" in Chapter IV.2.1.3.

As mentioned in Chapter Two, Foucault analyses the panopticon as part of a discursive formation that produces the disciplinary society in the eighteenth century. In the disciplinary society power no longer functions through interdiction but through surveillance and normalisation:[30]

> There is no need for arms, physical violence, material constraints. Just a gaze. An inspecting gaze, a gaze which each individual under its weight will end by interiorising to the point that he is his own overseer, each individual thus exercising this surveillance over, and against himself.[31]

The gaze of the Countess represents a symbol of this new formation of power that is engaged in the production of the normalised subject.[32] The motif of the gaze permeates the various intertwined stories in *Nights at the Circus*. Fevvers does her apprenticeship in "being looked at" in Ma Nelson's brothel, posing as Cupid and Winged Victory for the customers. In the museum of woman monsters the deformed bodies of the women are exposed to the lecherous gaze of the male visitors. "Look, don't touch!" reads the instruction with regard to Fevvers in the circus arena, the brothel and the museum of woman monsters. Mignon poses as the object of the gaze when she impersonates the dead for Herr M.. Like Mendoza in *The Infernal Desire Machines,* the figure of Herr M. is related to the technological changes at the end of the nineteenth century which culminated in the invention of the motion pictures.[33]

> ... as a hobby, he experimented with various optical toys and magic lanterns of the most sophisticated kind. Herr M. ... engaged in perfectly respectable research on systems of

---

[30] See II.3.1. for Foucault's analysis of the panopticon and the disciplinary society. The panopticon was invented by Jeremy Bentham (1748-1832) as a progressive penitentiary institution in the eighteenth century. The invention of the panopticon marks the point where the "codified power to punish" turns into "the disciplinary power to observe" (Foucault 1977, 224). Instead of chastising the body, as medieval torture did, the gaze controls the body from a distance and shapes the soul: constant surveillance produces the disciplined subject that internalises the gaze and controls its own behaviour. The panopticon thus transformed punishment into an operation of correction: "It was a machine designed to promote penitence ... a laboratory for the manufacture of souls" (NC 212).
[31] Foucault 1980, 155.
[32] In an interview with Carter, Helen Cagney Watts suggested that the figure of the countess was a reference to Mrs. Thatcher. Carter asserted that it were indeed Thatcher's eyes which came to her mind when she created the figure of the Countess. However, she stressed that the Countess is not a character but a proposition: she represents the law, a certain sort of authority. Carter in Watts 1987, 162.
[33] See III.2.2.2. See also Keenan who interprets Herr M. as exemplifying "both the blind faith in the miraculous power of technology to extend human capabilities, and the cynical exploitation of the vulnerable that often accompanies scientific progress." Keenan 1992, 103.

mechanical reproduction and, indeed, possessed many of the characteristics of a scientist manqué. (NC 135)

Nights at the Circus traces the beginning of the age of mechanical reproduction that will produce the society of the simulacrum and the spectacle in the twentieth century.[34] Mignon is in this sense Tristessa's forerunner. Not only do the two women share the angelic and morbid appearance with Justine, the "patroness of the screen heroine" (SW 60; cf. IV.1.2.1). Both are impersonators, creatures of the "persistence of vision" who sell illusions by profession: while Mignon impersonates the dead, Tristessa sells 'femininity incarnate'. Both are commodified and put into service for the production of dreams.

Linda Williams relates the new technology of the cinema to the emerging scientific discourse on sexuality at the turn of the century.[35] Referring to Foucault, Williams argues that both are part of the new discursive formation that fixes the gaze on the female body in modernity. The narrative alludes to the proliferation of scientific discourses on the female body when it refers to Fevvers' "friendship" with the scientists from the Royal College of Surgeons. After displaying herself in the brothel, in the museum of woman monsters and in the circus, Fevvers is again expected to pose for the male gaze in the Royal College of Surgeons:

> The young woman had entertained the curiosity of the entire Royal College of Surgeons without so much as unbuttoning her bodice for them, and discussed navigation in birds ... with so great a wealth of scientific terminology that not one single professor had dared be rude enough to question her on the extent of her personal experience. (NC 60)

In contrast to Mignon, Fevvers turns the tables on the male gaze: instead of posing as the silent object of scientific investigation, she usurps the language of expertise and eludes the scientific gaze that examines the female body and its sexuality. "Seeing is believing" is the slogan the narrative uses to parody the scientific-philosophical belief in the visible as source of truth.[36] This slogan recurs in Carter's fiction and rings with several different meanings. It refers to the empiricist and rational tradition of the Enlightenment, a tradition which questions myth and quasi-mythic religious concepts and to which Carter, as Day forcefully points out[37], is passionately indebted. "Seeing is

---

[34] Guy Debord describes the spectacle as the condition of late capitalism. See Debord 1996, 13,14.

[35] Williams 1990, 49. See also III.2.2.2.

[36] See also III.2.2.3.1 on the primacy of vision in Western philosophy. See also Comolli on the "ideology of the visible" and Debord on "seeing" and the spectacle (Comolli 1986, 126; Debord 1996, 20).

[37] Day 1998, 12.

believing", Little Red Riding Hood asserts in the short story "The Company of Wolves" when she inspects the hunter's compass, which is the very symbol of this tradition. However, the slogan is charged with a certain irony in *Nights at the Circus* which employs the confidence trick as one of its major motifs. Fevvers exploits the scopic economy which merges vision, knowledge, power and desire to her own advantage when she turns herself into a spectacle.[38] Her fantastic body is, in fact, a paradox in itself which mocks the belief in the visible as source of truth. Fevvers skilfully exploits the new formation of power that fixes the gaze on the female body in the nineteenth century.

Yet it is not only Fevvers and Mignon but all the performers in the circus ring who are subjected to the audience's gaze. In fact, the circus ring resembles the "doughnut form" of the panopticon.[39] Both are closed circular spaces which are structured around the gaze. The madhouse, the brothel, the prison and the circus are institutions which safeguard society from disruptive elements: the prison and the madhouse by shutting them in, the circus and the brothel by offering a legalised outlet for them. Put on display as 'jokes', the clowns are deprived of their subversive potential (cf. 2.2): "The clowns ... could terrify, enchant, vandalise, ravage, yet always stay on the safe side of being ... you can do anything you like, as long as nobody takes you seriously" (NC 151,152). The circus provides an outlet for the repressed in the rational civilised subject:

> But the aroma of horse dung and lion piss permeated every inch of the building's fabric, so that the titillating contradiction between the soft, white shoulders of the lovely ladies whom young army officers escorted here and the hairy pelts of the beasts in the ring resolved in the night-time intermingling of French perfume and the essence of steppe and jungle in which musk and civet revealed themselves as common elements. (NC 105)

Unmasking the animality of the audience, the circus both disrupts and stabilises the order that it temporarily suspends. At the same time, it reflects the violence in the social system beyond the circus ring. Like the museum of woman monsters, the circus commercialises and commodifies the eccentric.[40] Dominated by the Colonel's greed for profit, the circus might be considered a

---

[38] As I have argued in Chapter Three, the peep-show embodies this scopic economy in *The Infernal Desire Machines* (see III.2.2.3.1). In *The Infernal Desire Machines* the critique of this economy is not put into a specific social and economic context. *Nights at the Circus,* by contrast, links the gaze to a capitalist economy of commodification (see below). In contrast to Carter's earlier novel, *Nights at the Circus,* moreover, envisions the possibility of resistance: while the peep-show subjects woman, Fevvers manages to elude subjection and capitalises on the scopic economy and the gaze.

[39] See also Gass 1994, 74.

[40] Robinson and Peach point to the ambivalent meaning of circus in the narrative. See Robinson 1991, 127; Peach 1998, 141.

microcosm of the patriarchal capitalist system, which exploits and abuses the subjugated other: the Ape-Man beats Mignon "as though she were a carpet" (NC 115). The sound of the "rhythmic" beating and the rattling chains of the confined elephants form the violent backdrop of the carnivalesque circus world.

The brothel, the museum of woman monsters, the clinic and the circus function according to the same principle as the panopticon: they all employ the gaze as an instrument of power. The novel draws an impressive image of the disciplinary society in Foucault's sense: panopticism that has governed life since the eighteenth century is manifest in the rise of institutions like the prison, the hospital and the madhouse.[41] In *Nights at the Circus* this panoptic scenario is bound up with a capitalist economy of commodification. It is specifically the female body that is subjected to the gaze in the novel. Carter adds a materialist – Marxist and feminist – element to Foucault's notion of panopticism. The gaze and the spectacle are part of a complex network of male voyeurism, scientific knowledge, surveillance and commodification.

It should be noted, however, that it is a woman who imprisons the female inmates in the panopticon and in the museum of woman monsters. On the one hand, the narrative points to female complicity in the male gaze: the Countess is herself imprisoned by the gaze. Dealing with structural violence, the narrative does not draw a simple division along gender lines between oppressors and oppressed. On the other hand, as Keenan points out, Carter seems to focus on oppression as a function of class difference in the panopticon episode.[42]

> No reasonable female would hold it against their Countess P. that she poisoned her obese, oafish count, although the blend of boredom and avarice that prompted her to do so was in itself the product of privilege – she suffered sufficient leisure to be bored ....
> (NC 211)

The Countess's privilege blinds her to her own oppression. Gender and class interact in the panopticon episode to bring about an intricate system of domination in which oppressors are themselves voluntary prisoners.

The eye and the gaze are recurring motifs in Carter's work. The gaze constructs the female body in *The Passion of New Eve*. In Carter's short story "The Erl-King" the gaze is linked to the motif of the entrapped bird. The female protagonist both desires and fears the Erl-King, who wants to turn her into a "bird in a gilded cage":

---

[41] Foucault 1977, 195-228.
[42] Keenan 1992, 104.

169

Your green eye is a reducing chamber. If I look into it long enough, I will become as small as my own reflection, I will diminish to a point and vanish. I will be drawn into that black whirlpool and be consumed by you. I shall become so small you can keep me in one of your osier cages and mock my loss of liberty. (BB 191)

The paragraph merges the cannibalistic metaphor that occurs in *The Infernal Desire Machines*, the mirror metaphor that dominates *The Passion of New Eve* and the image of the entrapped bird in *Nights at the Circus*. The eye is a vortex that draws the other into the self and annihilates her: the gaze imprisons, diminishes and consumes the other. The Erl-King's eye turns into a "bloody chamber" that sacrifices the protagonist's autonomous self. What is at stake is, as Fludernik puts it, "sexual incorporation as a prelude ... to life imprisonment as a bird"[43]. The narrative draws attention to the self-destructive power of desire that is on the verge of turning the protagonist into a willing victim of subjection.[44] In *Nights at the Circus* Fevvers is also threatened to be confined in Walser's mad gaze. For a brief moment Fevvers' fears being "trapped forever in the reflection of Walser's eyes" (NC 290; cf. 3.2). The self that is imprisoned in the gaze is a powerful image of the loss of a self-determined identity. Displaying her feathers, Fevvers manages to reassert herself in the eyes of her beholders. Her identity, though, remains dependent on the look of the other. In fact, the absence of Walser's gaze diminishes Fevvers:

... she presented a squalid spectacle .... Day by day she felt herself diminishing .... She longed for him to tell her she was true. She longed to see herself reflected in all her remembered splendour in his grey eyes .... Her once-startling shape sagged as if sand were seeping out of the hour-glass .... (NC 200,273,276)

Fevvers' body crumbles when the eye turns away. In *Nights at the Circus* the gaze produces the self. Regarding her "pretty spotless self with utmost detestation" (NC 68), the Wiltshire Wonder has internalised the humiliating gaze of her sexual exploiters. Reminiscent of Walter de la Mare's Miss M., the mind of the miniature woman has been colonised to such a degree that she

---

[43] Fludernik 1998, 224.
[44] Makinen reads the Erl-King as the narrator's fantasy which displays the ambivalence of her desire: the female protagonist both fears and desires engulfment. Finally, however, she takes control and kills the fantasy that threatens to destroy her. See Makinen 2000, 30. According to Kramer Linkin, the story draws on several motifs in Romantic and Victorian poetry in a 'bloody re-visioning' of the Romantic aesthetic that confines and silences the female voice. The motif of the bird in a cage whose loss of liberty is mocked alludes to Blake's poem "How Sweet I Roam'd". Kramer Linkin reads the strangling of the Erl-King as an inversion of the male persona's murder of his lover in Browning's "Prophyria's Lover". Kramer Linkin 1998, 119,121. For another reading of Browning's poem see also Goetsch 2002, 128-129.

has literally been diminished.[45] The gaze defines, produces and subjects the body it controls. *Nights at the Circus* reiterates the theme of surveillance and control which is so vividly captured in the image of the panopticon.

4.2 Inverting the Gaze: the Body as Site of Subversion

Nights at the Circus, however, does not draw a deterministic image of panopticism that relentlessly subjects the body to the gaze. The other also turns the gaze back at the self in the novel. Walser is subjected to a veritable "bombardment" from Fevvers' eyes during the interview: "She subjected Walser to a blue bombardment from her eyes, challenge and attack at once ...." (NC 54); "She turned her immense eyes upon him ...." (NC 29); "She fixed Walser with a piercing regard ...." (NC 35). The mirror scene in which Leilah dresses under the male gaze in *The Passion of New Eve* is inverted in the novel: Fevvers undresses in front of the mirror, watching the intimidated Walser in the back of the dressing room. While the compelling, inward turning force of Fevvers' eyes is reminiscent of the Erl-King's eyes, this is not a source of horror but occasions the most pleasurable emotions in Walser:

> ... the pupils had grown so fat on darkness that the entire dressing-room and all those within it could have vanished without a trace inside those compelling voids. Walser felt the strangest sensation, as if these eyes of the aerialiste were a pair of sets of Chinese boxes, as if each one opened into a world, an infinite plurality of worlds, and these unguessable depths exercised the strongest possible attraction, so that he felt himself trembling as if he, too, stood on an unknown threshold. (NC 30)

In Carter's late fiction eyes acquire a depth that is characteristically absent in her earlier texts. In *The Infernal Desire Machines* and *The Passion of New Eve* eyes were mirrors, reflecting surfaces. In the love scenes in both novels the subject looks into the eyes of the other to find an image of the self. Fevvers as well looks for the confirmation of the self in the other. However, in *Nights at the Circus* eyes also open doors into a world of difference. Not only Fevvers' eyes lead Walser to an "unknown threshold". The apes perform a parody of the human search for the truth of the body when they undress Walser and turn the scientific gaze onto his body. Walser experiences a "meeting across the gulf of strangeness" (NC 108) in the Professor's eyes:

> The Professor's face ... was not six inches from Walser's own .... Their eyes met. Walser never forgot this first intimate exchange with this ... inhabitant of the magic circle of

---

[45] Carter has written a preface to Walter de la Mare's novel *Memoirs of a Midget*, in which the diminutive Miss M. suffers from her difference and isolation from the rest of society and joins the circus in the search for recognition.

difference, unreachable ... but not unknowable; this exchange with the speaking eyes of the dumb. It was like a clearing of a haze. (NC 108)

Walser experiences a similar, vertiginous feeling of strangeness when he dances with the tigress: "Looking into the tigress's depthless, jewelled eyes, he saw reflected there the entire alien essence of a world of fur, sinew and grace, in which he was the clumsy interloper ...." (NC 164). The glimpse into the abyss of difference marks the beginning of Walser's transformation. Walser does not appropriate difference, nor does he try to kill it off like Zero. *Nights at the Circus* cracks the shell that encapsulates the male self in Carter's earlier fiction and opens this self to an exchange with otherness.

The look into the other's eyes is a prominent motif in Emmanuel Levinas' philosophy. When I face the other, Levinas argues, there will always be something I will not be able to know and understand about this person. Pleading to respect this interiority and separateness of the other, Levinas devises an ethics of alterity that acknowledges otherness as an enigma which is beyond the self's comprehension. This acknowledgement marks the end of certainty and the beginning of trust in human relations. Levinas' ethics transfers the religious concept of infinity to the social relation to the other: it is the face of the other which expresses an infinite alterity.[46] Carter's late fiction suggests a secular ethics in Levinas' sense: an ethics in which infinity is not found in heaven but in the depth of the other's eyes. Looking into these eyes, Walser learns to 'believe without seeing'. In his essay on "Levinas and the face of the other", Waldenfels comments on the notion of alterity in Levinas' philosophy:

> The otherness or strangeness of the other manifests itself as the extraordinary par excellence: not as something given or intended, but as a certain disquietude, as a dérangement which puts us out of our common tracks.[47]

It is the depth of the other's eyes that induces this sense of disquietude, of *dérangement* in Carter's late fiction.

At the same time it is the female body which emerges as a site of alterity in Carter's work in the eighties. The image of infinite regress that draws Walser into Fevvers' eyes echoes Carter's short story "Peter and the Wolf". In the initiation story Peter undergoes a transformation after an encounter with his step-sister, the female wolf-child his parents capture in the forest. The view of the wolf-girl's sex confronts Peter with a radical experience of alterity. The sight of the sex and the lips of the howling wolf-girl offer him

---

[46] Levinas 1996, 65-78; Levinas 1987, 54 ff.. See also Critchley; Bernasconi 2002, 26.
[47] Waldenfels 2002, 63.

... a view of a set of Chineses boxes of whorled flesh that seemed to open one upon another into herself, drawing him into an inner, secret place in which destination perpetually receded before him, his first, devastating, vertiginous intimation of infinity. (BB 287)

The image of the lips recalls Irigaray's description of female sexuality that draws on the metaphor of the female genitalia: two lips touching each other. In "This Sex Which is Not One", Irigaray claims that a phallic male sexual economy, as it has been described by Freud and Lacan, privileges sight over touch ("seeing is believing") and reduces female sexuality to zero. While the phallus embodies the privileged signifier, the ONE, woman represents castration: NOT ONE, *"the horror of nothing to see"*.[48] Against Freud, Irigaray argues that female sexuality is multiple, diffuse, eluding the masculine dichotomy of the one and the other:

> Woman "touches herself" all the time, and moreover no one can forbid her so, for her genitals are formed of two lips in continuous contact. Thus, within herself, she is already two – but not divisible into one(s) – that caress each other.[49]

Continually touching herself, woman precludes the distinction between active subject and passive object and is thus neither one nor two: "'She' is indefinitely other in herself".[50] Alterity is inscribed into the female body. In Carter's story the image of the lips is ambiguously doubled, applying both to the mouth and the wolf-girl's sex. Betty Moss reads the wolf-girl in the story as an instance of the boundless and hybrid body of the female grotesque. The female grotesque celebrates the body which is open and excessive, undermining modern conceptions of female beauty that idealise the closed and contained body.[51] In fact, the mouth, the vagina and the eyes are apertures of the body that offer glimpses of otherness in Carter's late fiction. The female body is no longer a plastic and card-board construction; nor is it a screen, a mirror of the male imaginary. In Carter's late fiction the female body is a radical site of alterity.

This alterity is turned into an instrument of subversion in the panopticon episode. Instead of repenting their crimes, the women prisoners fall in love

---

[48] Irigaray 1985b, 26. Wyatt argues that the passage represents an answer to Freud's concept of woman as a castrated being, depicting female sexuality as a "set of Chinese boxes of whorled flesh". Wyatt 2000, 59.

[49] Irigaray 1985b, 24.

[50] Ibid., 28. Irigaray's notion of the irreducible difference of femininity has been influenced by Levinas' philosophy. For Irigaray's critique of the masculine bias in Levinas see Irigaray 1991b, 178-189; see also Sandford 2002, 144 ff..

[51] Moss 2001, 193. Moss refers to Russo's study of the female grotesque which points to Bakhtin's failure to take account of the category of gender in his concept of the grotesque body. Russo 1986, 221.

with each other and turn against the countess in a "united look of accusation" (NC 218). The prisoners and the wardresses break the isolation through an act of physical communication:

> One day, when the silent wardress served breakfast through the grille, Olga Alexandrovna slipped one lovely hand into the gap and clasped the hand in the leather glove that pushed in the tray from the other end. At the touch of Olga Alexandrovna's white fingers, the hand under the black glove quivered. Emboldened, Olga Alexandrovna clasped the leather glove more warmly. With a courage far beyond Olga Alexandrovna's imaginings, the woman in the hood raised her eyes to meet those eyes that Olga Alexandrovna now fixed on her. (NC 216)

Touch and a mutual, loving gaze undermine the controlling gaze of power and mark the end of isolation. Communicating through menstrual blood and excrement, the inmates and wardresses literally employ their bodies as a means of subversion. The narrative re-appropriates the abjected part of the female body and turns bodily fluids into agents of love and rebellion. Booker considers the writing in menstrual blood to be a literalisation of the concept of *écriture féminine*.[52] Whereas in *The Passion of New Eve* French feminist notions of woman's closeness to the body are satirised in the figure of Mother, Carter seems to re-approach these concepts in *Nights at the Circus*. Like the amazons in Beulah, the women prisoners are reminiscent of Wittig's *Le Corps Lesbien*, which creates a radical vision of an all-lesbian community. Whereas in *The Passion of New Eve* Wittig's vision is savagely satirised, *Nights at the Circus* retains a sense of female solidarity, even if the viability of an all-female utopia remains to be questioned (cf. V.I.2). The novel re-signifies the abjected female body and its stigmatised physical functions, providing it with a liberatory potential that the body in Carter's earlier fiction lacks.

5. Monstrous Bodies, Monstrous Texts

In *Nights at the Circus* difference is both a site of power and subjection. Their monstrosity confines and humiliates the women in the museum of woman monsters. Cobwebs neither smiles nor speaks so that her face has been covered by cobwebs. Cobweb's silence, the immobility of her face and her marginal position in the text seem to suggest her complete petrifaction into an object of the gaze. The Wiltshire Wonder has been psychologically diminished by the gaze. Inhabiting the undefinable space between life and death, Sleeping Beauty embodies the complete loss of agency. Toussaint, the

---

[52] Booker 1991, 234.

mouthless black servant, represents a literalised version of the silenced racial other. The monstrosity of these bodies embodies an exaggerated version of the difference that marks the female and the black body and distinguishes it from the white male norm. The novel depicts the subjugation and exploitation of otherness.

At the same time, *Nights at the Circus* imagines the liberation of the body marked by difference. Toussaint[53] is successfully operated on and becomes an eloquent speaker, fighting for the cause of the underprivileged. Lizzie points to the irony of the fact that "it was ... the white hand of the oppressor who carved open the aperture of speech in the very throat ... that it had in the first place rendered dumb ...." (NC 60). Similarly, it will be Walser, the male journalist, who will give a voice to women:

> Think of him ... as a scribe, as an amanuensis ... of all those whose tales we've yet to tell him, the histories of all those women who would otherwise go down nameless and forgotten, erased from history as if they had never been .... (NC 285)

Fevvers frees the monstrous women from the site of abjection in Madame Schreck's museum of horror. Fevvers relates the stories of humiliation these women have suffered. Toussaint, the Princess and Mignon find a voice to tell their own stories. *Nights at the Circus* gives a voice to the abject, the silenced and the marginalised. The boundaries of the closed spaces that contain the monstrous bodies break down in the wilderness of Siberia. The circus and the panopticon release their inmates into the open space and mark a new start, a transformation at the beginning of the twentieth century. In the wilderness the characters undergo a magical transformation: the strong man discovers his sensibility, the silent Princess learns to speak, Lizzie loses her "household magic" and Walser his scepticism. The wilderness dissolves the structures of domination and subordination that define life in the circus. This brave new world, however, has to be read with a twinkling in the eye. Referring to the romance tradition, the novel's final part ironically depicts an unreal world of the marvellous and the improbable.[54] The text draws attention to the fact that it is a *fantasy* of liberation and points to the violent future of authentic history waiting in the wings at the beginning of the twentieth century: "The old witch sees storms ahead, my girl. When I look to the future, I see through a glass, darkly" (NC 286), Lizzie forebodes. While it retains a sound sense of reality and scepticism, *Nights at the Circus* is nevertheless a visionary novel that

---

[53] Toussaint seems to owe his name to Toussaint L'Ouverture who led a slave revolt against plantation owners in Santo Domingo at the time of the French Revolution. Carter mentions Toussaint L'Ouverture in her short story *Black Venus* (BB 237).

[54] The magical transformations, the love plot, the supernatural and the setting in a distant place are elements which are borrowed from the romance tradition.

creates an experimental space to imagine an alternative world and a transformation of power relations.

Right at the beginning the novel enacts a reversal of power relations when Fevvers, the object of investigation, usurps the narrative and overwhelms the Walser, the journalist, with her excessive narration.

> He felt more and more like a kitten tangling up in a ball of wool it had never intended to unravel in the first place; or a sultan faced with not one but two Scheherezades, both intent on impacting a thousand stories into a single night. (NC 40)

Fevvers' and Lizzie's narration cannot be contained by Walser's notebook anymore (NC 57). The text spills over the frame of the notebook just as bodies transgress their boundaries in *Nights at the Circus*. The women's dialogic orality overpowers Walser, whose hand "no longer felt as if it belonged to him" (NC 78). Fevvers does not only tell Walser her own story. She also relates the biographies of the women working at the brothel and in the museum of woman monsters. For example, she gives an elaborate account of the childhood of the Wiltshire Wonder as well as of the latter's mother. Included in the narration is also a letter written by Toussaint in which he reports on his escape from Madame Schreck. Appearing as a set of "Chinese boxes" which open into an "infinite plurality of worlds" (NC 30), Fevvers' eyes mirror the narration which is ever opening new stories. The extensive digressions produce a decentered narrative structure that corresponds to the ex-centricity of the monstrous bodies in the novel.[55] In the second and third section of the novel, which describe Fevvers' picaresque journey to Petersburg and Siberia, the plot ramifies and introduces a whole set of new characters and their stories, which break into the main plot of Fevvers' and Walser's journey. Thus, a detailed account of Mignon's life, of Colonel Kearney's childhood, and of the Shaman's view of the world is included. The omniscient point of view, which dominates the first part of the novel, is disrupted and the narrative is related from different perspectives. The text traces the empowerment of the female subject when Fevvers repeatedly appropriates the narrative voice so that the omniscient narrator alternates with her first-person narration. In addition, the narrative contains gaps and fissures that hide even more stories that are not related but still present by virtue of the allusion to their absence. Among these stories are Lizzie's Communist struggle, the violent future of St. Petersburg (NC 97), and Baboushka's life, whose voice is stifled in the dreary routine of drudgery and poverty: "no

---

[55] The complex structure of embedding is reminiscent of another 'monstrous' narrative about a monster: Mary Shelley's *Frankenstein*.

Scheherezade, she" (NC 97). After the end of the novel there are still more stories to be told which await their "amanuensis" (NC 285).

As a result, the text itself becomes a metaphor for the monstrous body which proliferates beyond its customary boundaries. Mars-Jones considers the "compulsively elaborated histories" of *Nights at the Circus* a flaw which is "likely to baffle the reader" and "weaken the focus of the book".[56] He further criticises anachronistic intertextual allusions and an incoherent point of view in his review – a criticism which made Boehm accuse Mars-Jones of "androcentric reading strategies".[57] In fact, Mars-Jones seems to miss the point as anachrony is not a formal mistake but one of the central elements in the 'magic realism' of the novel. The novel disrupts the continuity of time when Walser grows a beard in a week and Fevvers escapes from the Duke to the train station within seconds. Like Lizzie, Angela Carter enjoys playing tricks on Father Time in *Nights at the Circus*. What was impossible for Beulah – the "feminisation of Father Time" – is on a smaller scale very well possible with the help of Lizzie's household magic. In the prisoners' revolt the clock, which symbolises the mechanical order that is imposed on the prison inmates, is shot. Father Time suffers the same fate when the lesbians disrespectfully throw him away: "Wherever we go, we'll need no more fathers" (NC 221). The lesbians' radical dismissal of Father Time is reminiscent of Beulah's attempt to feminise time and hence casts doubt on the success of their utopian project. In contrast, Lizzie takes to a small-scale, local strategy of resistance in Foucault's sense. Her method of disrupting instead of "abolishing" time corresponds to Carter's narrative technique and to Fevvers' masquerade: again, to undermine the system from within seems to be more fruitful than to overturn it from outside. On a formal level the subversion of time is reflected in "anachronistic" intertextual allusions to Mae West, Foucault and the late Yeats in the nineteenth-century setting. As for Mars-Jones' second criticism, to "weaken the focus" is exactly what the narrative seeks to accomplish. It is the margins, the blurred edges and the heterogeneous experience of the "ex-centric" that the novel foregrounds.[58] The fragmentation of form and the proliferation of stories in *Nights at the Circus* is essential for Carter as it is part of her project of "decolonizing language":

It is so enormously important for women to write fiction as women – it is part of the slow process of decolonizing our language and our basic habits of thought .... It is to do

---

[56] Mars-Jones 1984, 1083.
[57] Boehm 1995, 43.
[58] See also Hutcheon who argues that the novel centralises the ex-centric. Hutcheon 1988, 61.

with the creation of a means of expression for an infinitely greater variety of experience than has been possible, heretofore, to say things for which no language previously existed.[59]

Nights at the Circus produces an opening up of discourses, a heteroglossic orchestra of voices of the formerly silenced and "mouthless". In this sense the monstrous bodies in the novel have a double meaning. As victims of commodification and sexual abuse, they point to systems of patriarchal capitalist exploitation which appropriate the subversive and commodify difference. Producing excess and transgression, they parody traditional notions of woman as body and spectacle, and envisage the possibility of freedom, of breaking up the boundaries that are drawn around the female body.

6. The Emergence of Alterity in Carter's Late Fiction

In *Nights at the Circus* a radical sense of alterity disrupts the sameness that governs Carter's preceding texts. The mirror rules in *The Infernal Desire Machines. The Passion of New Eve* destroys the mirror, suggesting a new concept of identity to arise in the fissures of the cracked reflection. *Nights at the Circus* figures this new, powerful subjectivity. The emerging sense of difference creates space for the articulation of a self-determined female identity. The novel imagines an alternative to the heterosexual romance in the love between Mignon and the Princess. Alterity is pictured in Fevvers' extravagantly female body. Walser discerns it in the jewelled eyes of the tigress. The very shards of the mirror become a site in which alterity articulates itself: the Blakean tigers have gone into the broken mirrors, burning in the snowy desert of the Siberian wasteland. The emergence of difference in Carter's fiction might explain her turn to 'magic realism': the fantastic elements embody the radical sense of otherness that breaks into the realistic narrative in her late fiction.

This change in Carter's fiction takes shape in the short stories that Carter wrote in the late seventies and early eighties. "The Tiger's Bride", "The Company of Wolves", "Wolf-Alice" and "Peter and the Wolf" employ the wild animal as an image for the difference of femininity. Published in two short story collections – *The Bloody Chamber* and *Black Venus* – the tales rework the same themes in different variations.[60] Carter refers to Perrault's

---

[59] Carter 1983, 75.
[60] *The Bloody Chamber* and *Black Venus* are published in *Burning Your Boats* (Carter 1996a).

"Little Red Riding Hood" and Madame de Beaumont's "Beauty and the Beast" and engages in a critical dialogue with Bruno Bettelheim's psychoanalytic reading of these tales. In Perrault and Beaumont's tales carnivores typically signify male sexuality. In Carter, the tigers and wolves are externalisations of a female libido that has not found expression in her fiction preceding the eighties.[61]

Bettelheim reads Beaumont's "Beauty and the Beast" as an illustration of the successful maturation of a girl who overcomes the oedipal stage by transferring her attachment from the father to the lover. The Beast's transformation into a man at the end of the story symbolises the girl's successful completion of this transfer: male sexuality loses its threatening aspect.[62] Carter rewrites "Beauty and the Beast" in "The Courtship of Mr Lyons" and "The Tiger's Bride". "The Courtship of Mr Lyon" foregrounds the gender politics of Perrault's story, which turns Beauty into an exchange object that is passed from the father to the Beast and driven to marriage by moral blackmail.[63] After Beauty consents to marry Mr. Lyon, the Beast loses its fascinating difference and turns into an ugly, slightly pathetic man. "The Tiger's Bride" imagines an alternative version of the plot that grants Beauty autonomy and self-determination. Beauty freely decides to stay with the Beast that licks off her skin until she is furred like he is. Carter re-signifies the image of the wild animal and turns it into a powerful expression of female desire.

The movie "The Company of Wolves" figures a similar metamorphosis of the female protagonist. Directed by Neil Jordan, the film is based on Carter's short story "The Company of Wolves". The main plot of the movie is an alternative version of "Little Red Riding Hood" which is dreamt by the bourgeois adolescent Rosaleen in the frame narrative of the film. In Perrault's version of "Little Red Riding Hood" the wolf is explicitly related to an aggressive, male sexuality of which the girl is taught to be wary. In Rosaleen's dream, by contrast, Red Riding Hood is not devoured by the handsome, sexually attractive werewolf. Instead, she is herself transformed into a wolf, joins her mate's pack and storms the house of her sleeping alter

---

[61] See Carter in Haffenden 1985, 84. See also Makinen 2000, 30.

[62] Bettelheim 1995, 360-362. A collection of the tales has been edited by Bruno Bettelheim, *Les Contes de Perrault*, Paris, 1978.

[63] The Beast purports to be starving from unrequited love in the story. In an interview Carter calls the fairy tale an "advertisement for moral blackmail": "... when the Beast says that he is dying because of Beauty, the only morally correct thing for her to have said at that point would be, 'Die, then'." Carter in Haffenden 1985, 83. See also Day 1998, 135 ff..

ego.[64] The movie ends with an ambivalent image of liberation and terror: in a metaleptic 'strange loop' the wolf leaves the hypodiegetic level of the dream and enters the reality of the sleeping Rosaleen in the frame narrative.[65] The girl wakes up screaming in terror when her wolfish alter ego smashes the window and breaks into the room. In the unrestrained energy of the wild animal the movie creates a sublime image of difference.[66] Like *Nights at the Circus*, the film creates a complex narrative structure in which several stories are embedded within the main plot of the Red Riding Hood story. Images of difference also occur in these embedded tales. While the first of the tales are told by Granny and demonize male sexuality in Perrault's sense, Rosaleen finally makes up her own stories in which the wolves are no longer the incarnation of an aggressive male sexuality but of female alterity. As in *Nights at the Circus*, this change in narrative perspective reflects the empowerment of the female subject. For instance, Rosaleen tells the story of a mute, wild wolf-woman who grew up outside of the symbolic. The wolf-woman is injured and looks for shelter with a priest before she descends back into a well, returning to where she came from.[67] As mentioned above, a mute wolf-girl also occurs in the story "Peter and the Wolf", which depicts Peter's encounter with the radical otherness of female sexuality (cf. V.4.2).

The Blakean tigers in *Nights at the Circus* are reminiscent of these sublime images of wild animals in Carter's movie and in the stories. Carter herself commented on the symbolical meaning of Blake's tigers:

> He is talking about something blind, furious, instinctual, intuitive, savage and right. If Blakes's placid and didactic horses are delegates from the Fabian Society of the superego, his tiger is the representative of the unrepressed subconscious, even the id, possibly the mob storming the Bastille.[68]

---

[64] Neil Jordan and Carter intended to create a final image of "repression being liberated by libido" in the movie. See Carter in Haffenden 1985, 84. "The Company of Wolves" has also been turned into a radio play. The story and the radio play end with Little Red Riding Hood in bed with the wolf: "See! Sweet and sound she sleeps in granny's bed, between the paws of the tender wolf" (BB 219,220). "For to their own, the wolves are tender, are they not?", the fearless Rosaleen comments in the radio play (Carter 1985, 81). For a different ending see also the screen play in Carter 1996b, 244.

[65] See McHale for the notion of 'strange loops' that transgress the boundaries of different narrative levels in a 'Chinese box' narrative structure. McHale 1987, 120.

[66] I am referring to Burke's notion of the sublime. Associated with darkness and the infinite, the sublime is both awe-inspiring and terrifying. Burke 1958, 57 ff.,73 ff.,80 ff..

[67] Rosaleen's story is an abridged version of Carter's short story "Wolf-Alice". Carter has possibly been inspired by an old tale, "Fecunda Ratis", written by Egbert von Lüttich in 1023, which describes a girl dressed in red living in the company of wolves. For "Fecunda Ratis" see Bettelheim 1995, 193.

[68] Carter 1997, 306.

The tigers represent passion and unrestrained energy. Does Carter return to a Romantic idealisation of nature and the body in her work in the eighties? Carter rejects the Romantic vision of a return to an original unity. Yet at the same time she is heiress to a Blakean, politically committed Romanticism which turns against repression and celebrates energy and passion. Allusions to *Wuthering Heights* and Blake's poetry abound in the movie and in *Nights at the Circus*. Does Carter return to the liberatory paradigm she has rejected in her earlier fiction? *The Infernal Desire Machines* refutes the sixties' notion of the liberatory potential of sexuality and conceives desire as implicated in a system of power and subjection. The novel seems to formulate a poststructuralist position that erases essences and leaves a blank where the female body was. In the movie and in the late stories, by contrast, Carter depicts a powerful female sexuality that turns against the constraints that society tries to impose on it. Has Carter passed through the 'nihilistic' stages of a radical deconstruction to arrive at a liberatory position which gives the body its due? In *Nights at the Circus* Carter seems to distance herself from a poststructuralist position that negates the subversive potential of the body and the subject. The clowns enact the self-destructive nihilism of such a position. At the same time Carter turns from the exclusive "recycling" of written texts to the oral tradition of folklore and fairy tales in *The Bloody Chamber*. She connects this orality with the people, the lower class, and implicitly assumes a degeneration of the original tales in their bourgeois written appropriation.[69] Similarly, Carter's late fiction accords a subversive vitality to the world of the stage, in particular the vaudeville tradition, which is contrasted with the normalising and subjecting force of the cinema and the mass media. *Wise Children* represents a homage to this tradition. Does this move away from the poststructuralist focus on writing express an emerging nostalgia for unalienated presence, for the body and the voice, instead of the image and the letter? Carter, the scriptor, who was excessively concerned with re-presentation, with the writing of "books about books"[70], now seems to favours immediacy, presence and the word over re-production.

---

[69] In several interviews in the 1980s, Carter evinced interest in folklore as orally transmitted "culture of the poor". In an interview with Helen Cagney Watts, she said: "I'm Gramscian in relation to folk lore, in the sense that I also feel that the bourgeoisie have stolen the culture of the poor .... The tales in my volume *The Bloody Chamber* are part of the oral history of Europe, but what has happened is that these stories have gone into the bourgeois nursery and therefore lost their origins. It's important to remember that many folk tales were never written down, but passed from generation to generation by people who were mostly illiterate ....". Carter in Watts 1987, 170; see also Carter in Haffenden 1985, 85.
[70] Carter in Goldsworthy 1985, 5. See also III.2.4.

However, even if Carter modifies her exclusive focus on textuality and turns to a world beyond the text in the eighties, this does not imply an idealisation of nature and the body. While resistance is located in the body in *Nights at the Circus*, this body is not beyond representation. The ambivalent meaning of Fevvers' wings illustrates her implication in a patriarchal system of signification. In *Nights at the Circus* nature is, moreover, no *locus amoenus* but the wide, inhospitable space of Siberia which is terrifying to Fevvers in its vacuity. Nature is *per se* utterly meaningless, a blank space inscribed with meaning only by the human mind. This blank space is neither Fevvers' nor Carter's terrain. "As soon as I'm out of sight of the abodes of humanity, my heart gives way beneath me like rotten floorboards, my courage fails. ... I hate to be where the hand of Man has badly wrought ...." (NC 197), Fevvers laments in the face of the vast spaces of Siberia. Similarly, Carter focuses on the human, social relations and the material conditions of life in society. Her fiction passionately pursues the ideal of equality. The deconstructive analysis of the myth of femininity is employed in the service of this ideal. In this sense both Day and Müller stress that Carter is not a proponent of postmodern relativity: driven by a feminist impetus, her fiction is committed to rationality and social equality.[71] Carter's work oscillates between a deconstructive scepticism concerning myths on the one hand, and the utopian vision of equality and reciprocity on the other. The wild animals – the beast, the wolves and the untamed tigers – are embodiments of this vision. Carter's utopianism, however, is far from a naive belief in liberation and from an idealisation of the 'pure' body that precedes repression. It is based on a materialist view of history which takes account of the "long shadow of the past historic" to shape this body. It envisions a world which may be – to speak with Lizzie's words – not perfect but a "little better, or, not to raise too many false hopes, a little less bad" (NC 240).

7. Conclusion

Empowering the Marginalised

Nights at the Circus is a story of empowerment. The novel leaves the subject speechless and empowers the object with a verbosity that transgresses all limits. As a celebration of excess and transgression, the narrative produces monstrous grotesque bodies as well as a 'monstrous' uncontainable body of text. However, *Nights at the Circus* does not celebrate a utopia in which the marginalised have safely occupied the centre but points to the perpetual

---

[71] Müller 1997, 238,240; Day 1998, 12.

struggle that empowerment involves. The monstrous female bodies are continually in danger of being confined within systems of exploitation and commodification. The "giant comedy" (NC 295) is shaded by the violent history of the upcoming century. The novel oscillates between horror and laughter, the gothic and the comic: the clowns and Madame Schreck represent the terrors of the dark which crowd in from the margins of the text.

Most critics celebrate *Nights at the Circus* as Carter's most optimistic text up to the eighties. Palmer heralds the new focus on the utopian and the introduction of a woman-centered perspective in Carter's fiction.[72] Gasiorek describes the novel as an "exuberantly utopian text" that "rewrites history as utopia, envisaging the closing of the last century as the opening of a brave new feminist world".[73] Referring to the common belief that dreams of flying are dreams of sex, for Linda Ruth Williams the bird woman is a symbol of *jouissance*.[74] Day reads Fevvers' laughter as the "delight of the victor" anticipating the "notable victories" of the women's movement in the twentieth century.[75] Interestingly, Hanson takes the very opposite view, arguing that the novel underscores the "limited nature of the freedoms gained by the New Women of the 1880s and the 1890s":

> The sense of difficulty of effecting any real social change is reinforced for the contemporary feminist reader of Nights at the Circus, who will be only too well aware of the discrepancy between Fevvers' extravagant claims for the future and the actual extent of the changes in women's lives over the last hundred years.[76]

It is a matter of perspective if the changes in women's lives in the last hundred years are considered to be remarkable or disappointing. Hanson's reading of the novel, however, seems to me too pessimistic. Hanson focuses on Lizzie's materialist scepticism, which she equates with the early Foucault's deterministic concept of history and power. But Lizzie's participation in the socialist "struggle" would hardly make sense if she subscribed to a deterministic notion of history. Marxism postulates a utopian, progressive concept of history utterly at odds with Foucauldian 'determinism'. Lizzie is a realist, not a pessimist, and risks her life in the "struggle" for a world which is – in her own words – "a little better" or a "little less bad" (NC 240). Moreover, her position is just one of several views that are expressed in the narrative and should not be equated with the novel's

---

[72] Palmer 1987, 180. For a similar view see also Jordan 1990, 39; Makinen 2000, 21,22; Blodgett 1994, 54.
[73] Gasiorek 1995, 126,131.
[74] Williams 1995, 94.
[75] Day 1998, 194.
[76] Hanson 1997, 66,67.

meaning as a whole. Angela Carter's penultimate novel is, if not utopian, at least hopeful and optimistic. The clowns' nihilism is blown out of the narrative by the blizzard in Siberia. The novel ends on a liberatory note of carnivalesque laughter, in which Fevvers' voice mocks not only male gullibility but all the constraints, boundaries and myths which try to turn her into a "bird in a gilded cage".

The 'Woman Question': the Birth of the Female Subject

The action of *Nights at the Circus* and *The Passion of New Eve* is located in periods of gender change: the late nineteenth and the late twentieth century. In these periods the nature of femininity is under question ("Is she fact or is she fiction?") and discourses proliferate about 'The New Woman' and 'The Woman Question'. *Nights at the Circus* captures the enthusiasm of first-wave feminism. The novel relates the crisis in the representation of sexual difference at the *fin-de-siècle* to the twentieth-century debate about the nature of femininity at issue in *The Passion of New Eve*. Neither of the two novels, however, attempt to answer the question of the nature of femininity. After having been both man and woman, Eve concedes that she still does not know "what the nature of the masculine and the nature of the feminine might be" (PNE 150). *Nights at the Circus*, in fact, mocks this very question in the figure of Walser whose pursuit of Fevvers is a parody of the age-old male search to solve the enigma of femininity. While refraining from any fixed definition of femininity, the two novels still offer different answers to the 'Woman Question'. *The Passion of New Eve* explores the ideal of androgyny as it has been theorised in Anglo-American feminism in the seventies. The female body is revealed to be a construction which loses its distinctive difference in the image of the hermaphrodite. In *Nights at the Circus*, by contrast, Fevvers joyfully affirms her bodily difference: "My being, my me-ness, is unique and indivisible .... The essence of myself may not be given or taken, or what would there be left of me?" (NC 280, 281). The female body is turned into a site of power and pleasure. Her monstrosity enables Fevvers to transcend the restrictions that define a 'woman's place' at the end of the nineteenth century.

Carter's feminist politics are characterised by a certain ambivalence. Her work is influenced by a radical deconstructive and anti-essentialist position in Butler's vein. *The Infernal Desire Machines, The Passion of New Eve* and *Nights at the Circus* are major texts in Carter's "de-mythologising project" that deconstructs and de-naturalises stereotypes of the 'feminine' and the 'masculine'. However, in *Nights at the Circus* and *The Bloody Chamber* Carter seems to modify her former radical (de)constructivist position and re-approaches French feminism. *Nights at the Circus* literalises the concept of "writing the body" in the panopticon episode. In the movie "The Company of Wolves" and in her short stories Carter employs the image of the wild animal as a metaphor for the irreducible difference of femininity. Inhabiting a space beyond language and culture, the mute wolf-woman in "Peter and the Wolf" and "Wolf-Alice" grows up in the realm of the semiotic. Is Carter, one might wonder, re-articulating the very stereotypes she has been attacking in her earlier fiction? Is she re-inscribing a concept of femininity that locates woman in a pre-symbolic space beyond rationality and culture? The image of the carnivore as female libido undermines the stereotype of woman as a passive and asexual victim of a predatory male sexuality. Yet, as I have argued above, the notion of the libidinous female body is another stereotype which represents the repressed underside of this concept of the 'asexual angel' (cf. IV.1.2.2). Does Carter run the risk of reproducing the notion of the animalistic female body ('woman as whore'), thus legitimising male control of this 'animality'?

Carter circumvents this danger in two ways. First, she undermines the Platonic privileging of the mind over the body which is the very basis of the angel/whore binary. In the short stories the libidinous emerges as a sublime and empowering force. Human violence is revealed to be more terrifying than the wild animals are. In "Peter and the Wolf", for instance, the hunters cruelly shoot the wolf-girl's mother; in *Nights at the Circus* the apes are superior to their human keeper. Second, in "The Company of Wolves" and "The Tiger's Bride" woman and man share an equal sexual energy which turns them *both* into beasts: Red Riding Hood finds her match in the wolf, Beauty in the Beast. The stories trace the emergence of a reciprocal desire that is based on equality and exchange. Carter seems to be indebted to Bataille in her depiction of desire as a utopian force. In *L'érotisme* Bataille claims that eroticism opens up the closed, finite self in a momentary surrender to otherness.[77] Carter does not draw the image of a libidinous femininity that threatens male rationality but imagines a passionate relation of reciprocity in her fiction in the eighties.

Literalising Metaphor

Carter's fiction traces the violence of the process that turns woman into myth and transforms the real, material body into an icon of femininity. It focuses on the difficulty of rendering female experience visible in a 'phallogocentric' language. The glass coffin in *The Passion of New Eve* and

---

[77] Bataille 1965, 15-30.

the duke's ice sculpture in *Nights at the Circus* are powerful images that convey the violence that myth perpetrates on woman. The discrepancy between myth and life points to the problematic relation between materiality and representation in a wider sense. Language carries within it an abstracting force which distances bodily experience. In "White Mythology" Derrida describes the development of Western culture in terms of 'metaphorisation'.[78] Metaphorisation is a process in which the sensible, the proper dimension is effaced and replaced by a figurative meaning. In idealistic thought the metaphorisation of the literal has been described both as a loss (effacement of the literal, the physical) and as a gain (development of abstraction, internalisation and the metaphysical).[79] Whereas the figures of Albertina and Tristessa epitomise the death of woman in the trope, *Nights at the Circus* resuscitates woman through the 're-literalisation' of the trope. By literalising the notion of the 'Angel in the House', Carter ironically reverses the process of metaphorisation that turns the body into a symbol. The retrieval of the 'original figure' from beneath the metaphor has a comic and satirical effect, revealing the absurdity of the metaphors we live by. Feminist writers like Fay Weldon and Jeanette Winterson employ the literalisation of the metaphorical as a linguistic strategy which de-familiarises by making worn-out words new, thus questioning the preconceived habits and naturalised assumptions which regulate everyday life. This strategy represents a response to the 'masculine' philosophical tradition that privileges metaphor over the literal, the conceptual over lived experience. It is an attack on Cartesianism and Platonic idealism which aspire towards the transcendence of the body, constructing the latter as the "low other" that impedes abstraction (cf. II.1.). Whereas in Carter's earlier novels woman remains frozen in the symbol, *Nights at the Circus* brings the dead back to life and reverses the effacement of the female body in the language of "white mythology". The materiality of the body is recovered from the process of abstraction that lies at the heart of rationalist Western culture.

Re-signifying Abjection

Carter's novels trace the constitution of the subject by force of exclusion and abjection. Leilah, the prostitutes in the House of Anonymity and the women in the museum of woman monsters represent the abject against which the male subject defines himself. The transgressive bodies in the novels point

---

[78] Derrida 1982, 209 ff..
[79] While Rousseau conceives of this process as a loss, Hegelian philosophy considers it a gain. Cf. III.1.1.1, note 6.

to the violent mechanism that excludes the other, the ambiguous and produces the very meaning of 'intelligible identities' in a society. In *Bodies that Matter* Judith Butler calls for a "politicization of abjection in an effort to rewrite the history of the term, and to force it into a demanding resignification."[80] *Nights at the Circus* accomplishes this 'resignification' of abjection. In the museum of woman monsters Toussaint claims that "it is those fine gentlemen who paid down their sovereigns to poke and pry at us who were the unnatural ones, not we. For what is 'natural' and 'unnatural', sir?" (NC 61).[81] In the panopticon, abjected bodily fluids are turned into instruments of love and liberation. *Nights at the Circus* releases the monstrous women from the "abyss" of abjection. The novel invests the abject with the power to disrupt the system that has been based on its exclusion. In *The Passion of New Eve* and *Nights at the Circus* Walser and Evelyn descend into the repressed imaginary zone "that every culture has ... for what it excludes".[82] The confrontation with the repressed results in a magical transformation of the male subject.

Nights at the Circus renders bodily boundaries fluid. The novel undermines the borders that have been drawn between the subject and the abject. The reconceptualisation of bodily boundaries aligns Carter with several other feminist writers who re-imagine the female body and female subjectivity in the twentieth century: Monique Wittig, Fay Weldon, Margaret Atwood, Kathy Acker and Jeanette Winterson being notable examples of the writers who conceive new forms of bodies, sexuality and identities. Carter joins the feminist project of re-writing the body and envisages a breaking down of boundaries that assists in a "radical resignification of the symbolic domain ... to expand the very meaning of what counts as a valued and valuable body in the world"[83].

---

[80] Butler 1993, 21.

[81] Lidia Curti notes a proliferation of monsters in contemporary women's writing that question this boundary between the natural and the unnatural: between "foulness and loveliness, the human and the animal, you and me, male and female". Curti 1998, 107.

[82] Clement 1986, IX.

[83] Butler 1993, 22.

VI. The 'Lived Body': Age, Death and Maternity in *Wise Children*
Introduction

Wise Children opens with a powerful female voice and a carnivalesque image of vitality: "What a wind! Whooping and banging all along the street, the kind of wind that blows everything topsy-turvy .... The kind of wind that gets into the blood and drives you wild. Wild!" (WC 3). The novel continues where *Nights at the Circus* left off. In *Nights at the Circus* Fevvers' laughter dominates the novel's ending. *Wise Children* depicts the "giant comedy" (NC 295) unfolding beneath Fevvers' laughter. The comic novel celebrates duality and the body in excess, the body which is two, not one, which is "identical" though not "symmetrical" (WC 5). Yet *Wise Children* is also a profoundly sad, melancholic text. The exuberant tone of the narrative is undercut by a melancholic strain that runs beneath the novel's carnivalesque celebrations. Cracks and fissures open in the comic surface of the text to reveal the terror of death and mortality.

Wise Children features the ageing and the handicapped body, the body beset by the forces of time and mortality. The textualised, flat body, immune to pain and humiliation, finally takes its leave in Carter's last novel. In *Wise Children* bodies are 'real', three-dimensional and alive to a degree unprecedented in Carter's work. A new concept of the subjective experience of the 'lived body' emerges in the novel.

This chapter examines the return to the body in *Wise Children*. The emergence of the 'lived body' is bound up with the theme of ageing and the recovery of the mother in Carter's late work. In the first part I trace a development in Carter's fiction which reaches from the radical rejection of maternity in her early work to the recognition of a non-biological concept of mothering and care in *Wise Children*. I argue that the resurgence of the maternal indicates an abeyance of anxiety about embodiment in Carter's late fiction. The second part analyses the way in which the comic mode deals with the theme of death and ageing in the novel. After an analysis of the comic use of the figure of the double, I conclude by examining narrative structure that symbolically defers death in the novel.

Wise Children was Carter's last novel before she died at the age of 51 in 1992. The carnivalesque celebrations of the narrative bespeak a passionate love of life, which acquires its intensity against the dark foil of the novel's tragic subtext. *Wise Children* indicates a relief of anxiety and the acceptance of death as part of human corporeality. At the same time, the narrative transcends death through storytelling. Creating a dialogically constructed, open text on the model of the quilt, Dora's narrative weaves a bond of continuity with the reader that offers solace and protection in the face of mortality.

1. The Maternal Body in Carter's Fiction

Patriarchs are easily subverted in Carter's fiction. The patriarchal tyrant is revealed to be a pathetic creature whose power is either illusory or rests on an internal lack: Zero's sadism compensates for his impotence, Melchior suffers from an unresolved oedipal complex and Uncle Philip is turned into a cuckold by his family. The relation to the mother is, in contrast, much more ambivalent and complex. Jouve notes the absence of mothers in most of Carter's work.[1] Particularly in Carter's early fiction, mothers tend to be negative role-models and agents of patriarchy. After giving a brief overview of the critique of motherhood in feminist theory, this chapter traces the way in which Carter's late fiction reclaims the maternal within the context of an ethics of care. Through the recovery of the mother, the notion of a female genealogy emerges in *Wise Children*.

1.1 Feminism and Maternity in the 1970s

Matrophobia and Somatophobia in Seventies' Feminism

Carter's work reflects the sceptical attitude towards motherhood in the feminism of the 1970s. While 'mythopoeic' feminists refer to matriarchal myths and maternal goddesses as models of female power in the seventies,[2] most Anglo-American feminists radically reject motherhood as a patriarchal construction. Mothers are regarded as victims of patriarchy who try to fashion their daughters in their own image.[3] Contemporary feminism, then, is haunted by 'matrophobia', which Adrienne Rich describes as the fear of "becoming one's mother":

> Matrophobia can be seen as a womanly splitting of the self, in the desire to become purged once and for all of our mothers' bondage, to become individuated and free. The mother stands for the victim in ourselves, the unfree woman, the martyr.[4]

However, it is not only 'matrophobia', the fear of reproducing the fate of the mother in the patriarchal family, which accounts for the feminist

---

[1] Jouve 1994, 156.
[2] See IV.1.4.
[3] Rich 1977, 235,243. "Thousands of daughters see their mothers as having taught a compromise and self-hatred they are struggling to win free of, the one through whom the restrictions and degradations of a female existence were perforce transmitted .... Many daughters live in rage at their mothers for having accepted, too readily and passively, 'whatever comes.' A mother's victimization does not merely humiliate her, it mutilates the daughter who watches for clues as to what it means to be a woman."
[4] Ibid., 235,236.

condemnation of maternity. Maternity plays a prominent role in essentialising definitions of femininity which identify women with the body. Hirsch traces "somatophobia", a "discomfort with the body"[5] behind the feminist rejection of essentialism and motherhood. Not only is the mother economically dependent upon men in the process of child-rearing; in pregnancy and birth she is also subjected to a biological process that evades her control. Birth and death are liminal situations which drastically reveal the ineluctability of the body and leave us at the mercy of biology. Pregnancy implies the experience of being inhabited by otherness. Behind the somatophobic rejection of motherhood lies the fear of this uncanny, alien creature within the self, of the splitting of the subject and the loss of autonomy. Various psychoanalytic approaches draw attention to the association of the maternal body with death. The maternal body evokes the fear of engulfment (Melanie Klein) and the fear of castration (Freud). As the repressed site of the constitution of the subject, it is a reminder of death (Kristeva).[6] All these approaches, however, privilege the infant's perspective. They ignore the subjectivity of the mother and the female fear of splitting which likewise associates birth-giving with death and the uncanny.

Maternity in Object-Relations Theory

Feminist object-relations theorists examine the ambivalence of the mother-daughter relationship and formulate a critique of mothering in the 1970s. They deviate from traditional psychoanalysis in two ways. First, object-relationists criticise Freud's privileging of the son's perspective and adopt the daughter's point of view. Second, they reject the focus on the oedipal period and highlight the pre-oedipal mother-child relation as formative in the development of a gendered identity.

According to Nancy Chodorow, boys achieve a male identity by dissociating themselves from the mother. As mothers tend to identify more strongly with daughters, girls are less encouraged to separate from the same-sex parent. Boys subsequently develop a stronger sense of individuality, while girls tend to define themselves in relation to others:

> From the retention of preoedipal attachments to their mother, growing girls come to define and experience themselves as continuous with others; their experience of self contains more flexible and permeable ego boundaries. Boys come to define themselves as more separate and distinct, with a greater sense of rigid ego boundaries and

---

[5] Hirsch 1989, 166.
[6] For Klein and Freud see also III.1.3.1 and III.2.4. For Kristeva see II.6.

differentiation. The basic feminine sense of self is connected to the world, the basic masculine sense of self is separate.[7]

Referring to Chodorow, Jessica Benjamin contends that these different personality structures contribute to the creation of hierarchical relations between men and women. Striving for autonomy from the maternal body, masculinity is haunted by the fear of maternal engulfment. The objectification of women represents a reaction against this fear: the male subject fends off anxiety by asserting control over the other. While men strive for autonomy and mastery, women tend to downgrade their individuality and copy maternal altruism.

> The male posture ... prepares for the role of the master ....The female posture disposes the woman to accept objectification and control .... He asserts individual selfhood, while she relinquishes it.[8]

While the role of the master associates masculinity with sadism, female altruism predisposes woman to masochism. According to Benjamin, the early mother-child relation hence contributes to a culture of sado-masochism in which the relation between the sexes are based on inequality and violence.[9] In Dorothy Dinnerstein's theory, by contrast, it is not the altruistic, but the powerful mother who drives the daughter to submission in patriarchy. In her analysis of the psychological effects of exclusively female parenting, Dinnerstein explains woman's submission to patriarchy as a reaction against the omnipresence of maternal authority in infancy: we never completely rid ourselves of the infantile view of the omnipotent mother on whose goodwill we depend. To find relief from maternal omnipresence, the daughter turns to the father and willingly submits to patriarchal rule.[10]

Analysing the detrimental effects of exclusively female parenting on the sex-role division of society, Chodorow, Benjamin and Dinnerstein thus all arrive at the conclusion that mothering produces hierarchical relations between men and women. This explains why the celebration of sisterhood came to replace the mother-daughter bond in Anglo-American feminism of the 1970s.

The Mother in French Feminism

French feminist theory is more ambivalent in its evaluation of motherhood than Anglo-American feminism. In French feminism the maternal is both a

---

[7] Chodorow 1978, 169.
[8] Benjamin 1980, 167.
[9] Benjamin 1994, 74-84.
[10] Dinnerstein 1999, 163-197.

conservative and a disruptive force. On the one hand, the mother is believed to hamper the child's development. Kristeva advocates 'matricide' as a therapeutic strategy against melancholia, which she derives from the failure to separate from the mother.[11] On the other hand, Kristeva's notion of the semiotic assigns a disruptive force to the maternal (cf. IV.1.4). The experience of doubleness, of being self and other, predisposes the mother to a questioning of the stable, unified subject and turns her into a "permanent dissident".[12] As "dual and alien space", maternity undermines and threatens the symbolic.[13] In a similar way, Cixous' notion of *écriture feminine* conceives the maternal body as a subversive force that empowers woman's writing. The unity of the mother-child dyad turns the mother's body into a site of *jouissance*. As a specifically 'feminine' economy of pleasure and excess, *jouissance* permeates woman's writing. In Cixous' work the mother's milk represents a recurring image for a sensuality of writing that is located in the maternal body.[14]

Luce Irigaray's work moves from an initial rejection of the mother to the appreciation of the maternal as the foundation of our being. Her early essay "When Our Lips Speak Together" marks a turn away from the mother to the female lover: "I love you who are neither mother (forgive me, mother, I prefer a woman) nor sister."[15] In "And the One does not stir without the other" the closeness of the mother-daughter relation paralyses and suffocates the daughter, who searches to escape from the mother and turns to the father and the law. While the mother impedes movement, the father enables the child to walk in a robot-like, mechanical way. The metaphor of the robot conveys an image of the alienation of the female subject in patriarchy. Irigaray traces the same development that Dinnerstein describes in *The Mermaid and the Minotaur*: the daughter seeks refuge from a suffocating maternal presence in patriarchy. The end of the essay, however, suggests a change in the daughter's relation to the mother and envisions the possibility of communication between mother and daughter. Pleading for a breach of silence between mother and daughter, Irigaray imagines a concept of maternity that does not negate itself in nurturing: "... that in giving me life, you still remain alive."[16] The end of the essay anticipates Irigaray's late work, which pleads for an acknowledgement of the maternal as the nourishing ground of our existence.

---

[11] See also III.1.1.2.2 note 18.
[12] See also Gallop 1982, 123.
[13] Kristeva 1980, 237.
[14] Cixous 1976, 251 ff..
[15] Irigaray 1985b, 209.
[16] Irigaray 1981a, 67.

Considering matricide, the sacrifice of natural fertility, as the founding act of our society, "The Bodily Encounter with the Mother" strives to recover the mother from repression.[17] The essay calls for a voice to be given to the mother-daughter relationship in order to free woman from her "ingratitude toward her maternal genealogy":

> We must also find ... the words, the sentences that speak the most archaic and most contemporary relationship with the body of the mother, with our bodies, the sentences that translate the bond between her body, ours, and that of our daughters.[18]

Envisioning a language which articulates the relationship between mother and daughter, the essay develops the notion of a female genealogy that empowers women:

> It is also necessary ... for us to assert that there is a genealogy of women. There is a genealogy of women within our family: on our mothers' side we have mothers, grandmothers, and great-grandmothers, and daughters .... Let us try to situate ourselves within this female genealogy so as to conquer and keep our identity.[19]

The recognition of a maternal genealogy is essential in the creation of an ethical order among women that is not only characterised by a horizontal dimension (the axis of sisterhood), but also by a vertical dimension (the genealogical mother-daughter axis). In *An Ethics of Sexual Difference* Irigaray calls for an ethics which discards the humanist notion of the universal subject and takes account of sexual difference. The recognition of the maternal emerges as a central element in this ethics which strives to rediscover the 'debt' that man owes to the 'natural' and the 'nourishing'.[20] The sacrifice of the maternal is bound up with the failure to think the self embodied. Conceiving himself as master, and not as part of nature, man loses the "pleasure of his own body"[21].

Conclusion

Object-relations theorists reject the patriarchal construction of maternity and present a radical critique of mothering. Most of Carter's novels seem to be influenced by the rejection of maternity in Anglo-American feminism. As I

---

[17] Cf. III.1.2.2 note 29. Irigaray takes a very different view on melancholia than Kristeva. She argues that it is the non-symbolisation of woman's relation to the mother that leads to melancholia and psychosis. Irigaray 1985a, 71.

[18] Irigaray 1991a, 43.

[19] Irigaray 1991a, 44. See also Irigaray 1985b, 143.

[20] Irigaray 1984, 106,122.

[21] Irigaray 1985b, 143: "In this 'phallocratic' power, man loses something too: in particular, the pleasure of his own body." See also Irigaray 1984, 123: "... l'homme, toujours, négligerait de se penser incarné, ayant reçu son corps comme cette première maison ....".

have argued in Chapter Four, *The Passion of New Eve* attacks mythic conceptions of motherhood. Presenting ambivalent views on maternity, French feminism neither exclusively celebrates nor condemns the mother. In Irigaray's work the initial rejection of the mother gives way to a return to the maternal and the notion of a female genealogy. Carter's fiction traces a similar trajectory. Like Irigaray, Carter revises her earlier position on maternity in her late work. *Wise Children* re-establishes the maternal by devising an ethics of mothering and the concept of a female genealogy that empowers rather than cripples the daughter in her fiction.

1.2 "As I am, so you will be": Matrophobia in Carter's Early Fiction
1.2.1 Raging Against the Mother: Matricide and Maternal Violence

Carter's early work commits a symbolic matricide. The child's subjectivity is founded on the death of the mother. Matricide is the necessary condition for the development of an independent subjectivity. One of her very first stories, "A Very, Very Great Lady and Her Son at Home" (1965), depicts this matricide, which initiates Carter's writing. In the story the shy, silent son asserts himself against his egocentric mother. This self-assertion – the first words the son addresses to his mother – literally 'kills' the mother: "She crashed forward on to the carpet and lay there, a tree felled, motionless" (BB 15). The son comes to life and self-confidence through a symbolic murder that releases him into adulthood. "The boy went to the door and vanished, laughing, into the night" (BB 15). Leaving the mother behind, the child enters the symbolic.

The development of Carter's protagonists seems to depend on the absence of mothers.[22] In the majority of Carter's short stories the protagonists are either orphaned or motherless.[23] In *The Magic Toyshop* and *Heroes and Villain,* the mother of the female protagonist dies at the beginning of the narrative. Lee's mad mother is locked up in an asylum in *Love.* In *The Infernal Desire Machines* mothers lead a shadowy existence as decomposing corpses or ghosts. Yet even as ghost the mother has a debilitating effect on her daughter. In "Ashputtle *or* The Mother's Ghost", the mother's ghost

---

[22] Carter's novels share this feature with the nineteenth-century novel, in particular with the female *Entwicklungsroman.* See 1.3.1.

[23] Orphans occur in "Our Lady of the Massacre" and "The Cabinet of Edgar Allan Poe". Motherless protagonists feature in "Penetrating to the Heart of the Forest", "The Courtship of Mr Lyon", "The Tiger's Bride", "The Fall River Axe Murders", "Lizzie's Tiger" and "John Ford's *'Tis a Pity She's a Whore'*".

drives the daughter to marriage and self-mutilation: "'Step into my coffin.' ... 'I stepped into *my* mother's coffin when I was your age'" (BB 396). The story reveals maternal power to be dependent on the father, the "unmoved mover" (BB 392), who directs the mother/daughter script and the patriarchal marriage plot.

The maternal body is bound up with deep-running anxieties in Carter's work. Carter's early fiction tends to take the son's perspective of the maternal body as abject site that threatens individuation and subjectivity. Joseph is swallowed by Mrs. Boulder's engulfing body in *Several Perceptions*. Desiderio's incestual unity with "Mama" among the river people is a prelude to his literal, cannibalistic incorporation in the tribe. The maternal body represents an object of anxiety and a site of regression in the psychological topography of the male protagonists. In the seventies, though, Carter begins to treat this perspective in an increasingly ironic way: Mother represents a grotesque parody of the abject maternal body in *The Passion of New Eve*. As mentioned before, the maternal also plays a crucial role in the constitution of melancholia in Carter's early novels. The unacknowledged libidinal attachment to the mother haunts the melancholic male characters as a fear of female sexuality. The dead mother uncannily returns as a grunting animal in Desiderio's dreams and Morris' memories (cf. III.1.1.2.2). The maternal body is saturated with an animal sexuality that poses a threat to the son's identity. Perceived through the male focalisation of the novels, in Carter's early fiction maternal bodies thus tend to be uncanny (Desiderio's mother), grotesque (Mother in *The Passion of New Eve*), and engulfing (Mrs Boulder in *Several Perceptions*, Buzz' mother in *Love*).

The Magic Toyshop and *Heroes and Villains* adopt the daughter's point of view. The daughter's subjectivity is also founded on the death of the mother. In *The Magic Toyshop* the dead mother engenders a guilt complex in Melanie. As an "emphatically clothed woman" (MT 10), Melanie's prudish mother epitomises the maternal as the "denial of the idea of sexual pleasure"[24]:

> Her mother ... was an emphatically clothed woman, clothed all over, never without stockings whatever the weather .... A wide-brimmed brown velvet hat ... superimposed itself on Melanie's picture of her mother being made love to. Melanie remembered that, when she was a little girl and her mother cuddled her, the embraces were always thickly muffled in cloth – wool, cotton or linen .... Her mother must have been born dressed, perhaps in an elegant, well-fitting caul .... (MT 10)

Far from promising *jouissance*, the mother's embraces offer no real bodily

---

[24] Carter comments on the mother in Sade's work: "Mother is in herself a concrete denial of the idea of sexual pleasure since her sexuality has been placed at the service of reproductive function alone" (SW 123,124).

196

encounter. The mother's clothes symbolically act as a protection against bodily contact, thus diminishing the first sensual experience of the infant in the mother-child dyad. They indicate distance in the mother-daughter relation and the repression of the body that makes a taboo of the mother's sexuality. The maternal body remains unknown, forbidden space to the adolescent daughter, who is in the process of discovering her own sexuality. Melanie feels that she transgresses into a field "hedged by taboo" (SW 124) when she fantasises about her mother's sexuality and secretly puts on her mother's white wedding dress. Inadvertently, she spoils the dress with blood. The daughter destroys the image of the mother as a 'pure', asexual being and becomes the latter's sexual rival. Usurping the mother's place, the burgeoning sexuality of the daughter symbolically 'kills' the sexually repressed mother. When in the same night her parents die in a plane crash, Melanie feels responsible for her mother's death. Again, Carter's fiction stages an imaginary matricide: Melanie believes herself to be "the girl who killed her mother" (MT 24).

Distance also characterises Marianne's relation to her mother in *Heroes and Villains*. Marianne's mother prefers her son to her daughter, just as Mrs Green, Marianne's "surrogate mother" among the Barbarians, favours Jewel over Marianne. Like biological mothers, surrogate mothers are ambivalent figures in Carter's early fiction. Daughters receive no whole-hearted support from their foster mothers.[25] Mrs Green co-operates with the Barbarians and forces Marianne into marriage and submission in the patriarchal clan. While Aunt Margaret is more benevolent towards Melanie in *The Magic Toyshop*, she is too weak to function as a role model for her. Neither she nor Mrs Rundle are able to save Melanie from Uncle Philip's tyranny. Surrogate mothers in Carter's early novels are either disempowered or conservative agents of patriarchy.

Carter's fiction thus takes sides with the daughter who strives for independence from the mother's fate in a patriarchal society. *The Sadeian Woman* interprets Eugénie's violent abuse of her mother in Sade's *Philosophy in the Boudoir* as a symbolic destruction of the reproductive function that enslaves women:[26]

The daughter may achieve autonomy only through destroying the mother, who represents her own reproductive function, also, who is both her own mother and the potential mother within herself .... Mother seeks to ensure the continuance of her own repression, and her hypocritical solicitude for the younger woman's moral, that is, sexual

---

[25] See also Müller 1997, 85.
[26] In *Philosophy in the Boudoir* Eugénie rapes her mother and sews up her womb afterwards. See Carter 1979, 116 ff..

welfare masks a desire to reduce her daughter to the same state of contingent passivity she herself inhabits, a state honoured by custom and hedged by taboo. (SW 124)

Carter's analysis echoes Rich's description of matrophobia: "If the daughter is a mocking memory to the mother – 'As I am, so you once were' – then the mother is a horrid warning to her daughter. 'As I am, so you will be'" (SW 124).

Adopting the son's or the daughter's point of view, Carter's early fiction evades the representation of the mother's subjectivity. While the son equates the maternal body with a threatening, engulfing sexuality, the daughter de-sexualises her as the very "embodiment of the repression of sexual pleasure" (SW 123). Maternal bodies are either engulfing and abject (the son's perspective) or inaccessible: "thickly muffled in cloth" (the daughter's perspective). In *The Passion of New Eve,* Carter's critique of maternity culminates in the radical deconstruction of the maternal body: "... Mother is a figure of speech and has retired to a cave beyond consciousness" (PNE 184). Destroying the male fantasy of the maternal body as abject, *The Passion of New Eve* creates a *tabula rasa* as a new basis for the reconceptualisation of the maternal in Carter's late work.

1.2.2 Somatophobia and the Pregnant Body

While the subjectively experienced maternal body is absent in Carter's early fiction, pregnancy does occur in *Shadow Dance, Heroes and Villains* and *The Passion of New Eve*. Marianne is pregnant when Jewel dies at the end of the novel. Marianne perceives her unwanted pregnancy as a defeat that renders her dependent on the Barbarian clan. Motherhood puts her at the service of reproducing the patriarchal tribe. In *Shadow Dance* Emily is pregnant when she learns about Honey's murder of Ghislaine. While pregnancy represents a threat to Emily's and Marianne's independence, the women do not give in, but assert their autonomy in the face of this threat. Emily decides to love the baby as if "Honey by now had nothing to do with it" (SD 179). Marianne desperately keeps to the "passionately held conviction" of her autonomy (HV 132). Pregnancy simultaneously signifies defeat and hope, a new, uncertain beginning at the end of the narrative. In *The Passion of New Eve* pregnancy also occurs as the closing motif of the text: pregnant Eve embarks on the ocean and sails into an uncertain future. Eve's pregnancy primarily has a symbolic function: as a symbol of life, it counterbalances the dark imagery of death at the end of the narrative and creates an open, ambiguous ending. In fact, Eve experiences a strangely disembodied pregnancy. Leilah's botched abortion is similarly perceived in a distanced, detached way through Evelyn's indifferent and chauvinistic eyes. The pregnant 'lived body' is absent in the narrative. In *Heroes and Villains* and *Shadow Dance* the subjective experience of pregnancy manifests itself in a purely negative way, in Marianne's terror and in Emily's sickness: " 'I am terrified, she [Marianne] said. 'I've never been so terrified in my whole life'" (HV 120). Emily's sickness is part of her obsession with cleanliness and symbolically expels Honeybuzzard from her self. In *The Passion of New Eve* Leilah is also sick after a desperate attempt to abort the baby by eating broken glass: "She ground up glass and ate it but she vomited it all up helplessly ...." (PNE 32).

Psychoanalytic feminism relates sickness in pregnancy to a somatophobic anxiety about an alien presence within the self. Morning sickness has been derived from an unconscious desire to expel the baby from the body. In both Emily's and Leilah's sickness and in Marianne's anxiety somatophobia emerges as fear of the maternal body as "dual and alien space"[27], inhabited by an other, as fear of death and the loss of subjectivity. Childbirth is, in fact, a frequent cause of death in Carter's fiction. In "Penetrating to the Heart of the Forest", "The Courtship of Mr Lyon" and *Wise Children* mothers die in childbirth. Regarding pregnancy as a loss of autonomy, *The Sadeian Woman* describes the mother as the "violated passive principle" in Sade: "... her autonomy has been sufficiently eroded by the presence within her of the embryo she brought to term. Her unthinking ability to reproduce ... is beyond choice, not a specific virtue of her own" (SW 124). In Carter's early work the representation of pregnancy bespeaks a somatophobic anxiety about dependency. Pregnancy is a fearful, uncanny experience that endangers woman's autonomy and puts her at the mercy of patriarchy and biology.

'Somatophobia' may be likewise at the root of Carter's radical anti-essentialism, which turns the maternal body into a "figure of speech" (PNE 184) and evades the representation of the mother's 'lived' corporeality. Female bodies are again and again revealed to be cultural constructions in Carter's fiction. While this radical anti-essentialism contests patriarchal stereotypes of femininity (cf. IV.1), it also indicates a fear of being identified with the body, an anxiety about corporeality and mortality in a wider sense. It is only in Carter's late fiction, in *Wise Children* and her late short stories, that somatophobia is allayed and the concept of the 'lived' maternal body begins to emerge.

---

[27] Kristeva 1980, 237.

1.3 Maternity in *Wise Children*
1.3.1 Beyond the Oedipal Triangle: Bard House and Grandma's Invented Family

Biological mothers are absent in most of Carter's late novels. In *Nights at the Circus* Fevvers has been hatched by an egg. D/Nora's[28] mother – herself an orphan – died in childbirth: "... our maternal side founders in a wilderness of unknowability ...." (WC 12). Grandma Chance, who claims to have come "out of a bottle" (WC 223), adopts the girls. Again it is a non-biological surrogate mother who takes the mother's position. Yet the representation of surrogate mothers has changed compared to Carter's early work. Foster mothers in Carter's late novels are neither weak creatures nor agents of patriarchy, but positive role-models who imbue their foster-daughters with self-confidence and push them to autonomy. In *Nights at the Circus* Lizzie literally pushes Fevvers to fly. In *Wise Children* Grandma Chance – feminist, pacifist and a vegetarian nudist – exemplifies Rich's notion of "courageous mothering"[29], which gives a model of strength and autonomy. Like Fevvers, Grandma Chance represents the New Woman who invented herself at the beginning of the century:

> ... she'd arrived at 49 Bard Road on New Year's Day, 1900, with a banker's draft for the first year's rent and the air of a woman making a new start in a new place, a new century and, or so the evidence points, a new name.[30] (WC 26)

Grandma Chance embodies the self-confidence that women acquired in a time of radical gender change at the beginning of the twentieth century. In Grandma's house D/Nora receive unlimited love and an education that teaches them independence and the ability to survive: "She lullabyed us, she fed us. She was our air-raid shelter; she was our entertainment; she was our breast" (WC 29). The breast is no longer the Kleinian object of envy and aggression as in Carter's early novels (cf. III.1.3.1). In *Wise Children* the maternal body has become a shelter and a home.

---

[28] Considering Dora and Nora as complementary doubles (see 2.4.1), I will linguistically treat them as one person and use the abbreviation "D/Nora" in my interpretation.

[29] Rich 1977, 246.

[30] Grandma Chance might owe some of her features to Carter's grandmother, a "'South Yorkshire matriarch' with an innate conviction of the irreducible superiority of woman", who embarrassed Carter's adolescent mother by wearing a "Votes for Women" badge. See Sage 1977, 54. In "The Mother Lode" Carter describes her maternal grandmother as a woman of "such physical and spiritual heaviness she might have been born with a greater degree of gravity than most people": "She ... imparted a sense of my sex's ascendancy in the scheme of things, every word and gesture of hers displayed a natural dominance, a native savagery ....". See Carter 1982, 8.

Motherlessness has a long tradition in fiction and aligns Carter's work with the realist nineteenth-century novel in which protagonists are frequently orphaned. Marianne Hirsch defines motherlessness as a characteristic feature of nineteenth-century realist fiction by women.[31] The absence of the mother enables the heroine to create her own story and to avoid reproducing her mother's destiny. Adrienne Rich interprets motherlessness in *Jane Eyre* as a literary device that enhances the heroine's self-determination, offering her a variety of 'surrogate mothers' and female friends to choose from.[32] In a similar way, the absence of a biological mother enables D/Nora and Fevvers to invent themselves and to evade the maternal fate in the oedipal constellation of the patriarchal nuclear family. In fact, it is not just the biological mother, but the whole traditional family structure which is discarded in *Wise Children*. Fathers are dispensable in Grandma's invented family. Discarding marriage as a happy ending, *Wise Children* is even more radical in its rejection of the nuclear family than is *Nights at the Circus*, which ends with a 'woman-on-top marriage'. The novel creates an alternative feminist family romance[33], which eludes the oedipal triangle in the utopian space of Bard House:

> Grandma raised us, not out of duty, or due to history, but because of pure love, it was a genuine family romance .... Grandma invented this family. She put it together out of whatever came to hand – a stray pair of orphaned babes, a ragamuffin in a flat cap. She created it by sheer force of personality. (WC 12,35)

Carter's early novels – *Shadow Dance, Several Perceptions, Love* and *The Infernal Desire Machines* – tend to create 'all-male-spaces', in which femininity is a projection mediated through a male narrative consciousness. Female narrators in *The Magic Toyshop* and *Heroes and Villains* have to assert themselves in a hostile patriarchal environment. *The Passion of New Eve* is Carter's first text to imagine an exclusively female space, but this space is a feminist dystopia which reproduces patriarchal violence. In *Nights at the Circus* female solidarity is presented in a more positive light. Female bonding is a powerful weapon in the revolt against the Countess in the Siberian prison. Whereas the brothel in *The Infernal Desire Machines* objectifies women, Ma Nelson's "academy" creates a realm of female

---

[31] Hirsch 1989, 46 ff..
[32] Rich 1979, 91 ff..
[33] *Wise Children* alludes to the Freudian family romance in which the child negates its parents and imagines to be of aristocratic descent. The child believes itself the offspring of the mother's infidelity and creates the fiction of a noble father. The Freudian family romance implies the moral degradation of the unfaithful mother and the elevation of an imaginary father. Freud 1953b, 235-241. See below 1.3.4.

solidarity in which the prostitutes act as benevolent foster mothers to Fevvers: "I was reared by these kind women as if I was the common daughter of half-a-dozen mothers" (NC 21). *Nights at the Circus* is Carter's first text to suggest the ethics of mothering and care that will dominate the spirit of Bard House. *Wise Children* radicalises this concept of female alliances and transfers most of the action into the all-female space of D/Nora's home in Brixton. In the protective environment of Bard House, D/Nora are able to develop their individuality: their doubleness and their dancing talent, both of which will become means of empowerment in their later lives. The twins grow up in a world which defeats the law of the father, whose only representative – grandfather clock – has been castrated. The castration of grandfather clock creates the illusion of Bard House existing outside of time and history.[34] Yet history violently intrudes into this 'idyllic' space when Grandma Chance is killed in a German bomb attack. Again, Carter's fiction is sceptical about the ideal and the utopian. Sympathies lie with Grandma, but Carter is far from idealising her household. Grandma is, in fact, slightly 'nuts'. There is a certain irony in the presentation of Bard House as a prelapsarian nudist space in which not only the killing of animals but even the plucking of flowers is taboo. Hence, there is no sense of nostalgia when the daughter's adolescence leads to the Fall in the nudist's vegetarian 'paradise': with the girls' puberty, men, crocodile bags, the desire for the father and shame about the naked body intrude into the Grandma's pre-oedipal paradise. D/Nora fall in love with their absent father: "You could say, I suppose, that we *had a crush* on Melchior Hazard, like lots of girls" (WC 57). Grandma takes to wearing clothes after an humiliating encounter with her teenage daughter in the mirror:

> She came into the bathroom, once, ... she hadn't got a stitch on .... There we both were, captured in the mirror, me young and slim and trim and tender, she vast, sagging, wrinkled, quivering. I couldn't help but giggle. I shouldn't have .... 'That's all very well, Dora,' she said, 'but one fine day, you'll wake up and find you're old and ugly, just like me.' Then she cackled .... All the same, she went to get a dressing gown before she came

---

[34] The clock as symbol of the inexorability of time is associated with the law of the father and the reality principle in Carter's fiction. Considering "linear time" as "phallic projectory", Mother plans the "feminisation of Father Time" in *The Passion of New Eve* (PNE 53). Big Ben occurs as "Father Time" in *Nights at the Circus*. While some characters, like Lizzie and Grandma, are to a certain extent able to escape from the law of the father, utopian spaces outside of time are typically fragile spaces in Carter's fiction. See III.1.1.2.3. See also Müller on the theme of time in the novel. Müller 1997, 156-164.

back to have her wee and there was a coolness between us, after that, lasted for months. (sic) (WC 94)[35]

With puberty, conflict intrudes into the mother-daughter relationship. In fear of turning into Grandma, the fun-loving twins become passionate carnivores. Yet 'matrophobia' is a passing stage in the twins' development and does not destroy the spirit of Bard House, nor does it effect a radical break in the mother-daughter relationship. For a moment there may be something demonic about Grandma who, cackling and witch-like, forebodes Dora's death. The narrative echoes the notion of the mother as a "horrid warning" to the daughter in *The Sadeian Woman*. However, *Wise Children* introduces a change in perspective: in retrospect, the narrative assumes the point of view of the aged Dora, who now takes sides with Grandma. The daughter-as-autobiographer adopts the perspective of her mother. In criticising the mindlessness of the daughter's point of view, the narrative implicitly revises Carter's old position which exclusively perceived of the mother as a rival, seeking to ensure the "continuance of her own repression" (SW 124): "Sometimes we thought, in our youthful, heedless vanity, that the old bag was jealous of us. Stars on our door, stars in our eyes, stars exploding in the bits of our brains where the common sense should have been" (WC 91).

1.3.2 Towards a Female Genealogy: Mothering as Performative Ethics of Care

Redefining mother as a performative term – "mother is as mother does" (WC 223) – *Wise Children* celebrates mothering and yet evades the trap of essentialism. Mothering is severed from biology and displaced from the traditional nuclear family. Carter's late work manages to devise a maternal ethics of care and responsibility while it avoids idealising motherhood as the mainstay of the patriarchal family. Replacing rivalry by solidarity, the novel creates a female genealogy in which mothers and daughters are no longer antagonists but support each other. The change in Carter's conception of the mother/daughter relationship is indicated by a quote from Ellen Terry in the epigraph of the novel: "How many times Shakespeare draws fathers and daughters, never mothers and daughters." *Wise Children* ironically mocks the

---

[35] The narrative echoes Carter's description of a visit to her grandmother at the age of eighteen: "... I went to visit her rigged out in all the ... splendour of the underground high-style of the late fifties, black-mesh stockings, spike-heeled shoes, bum-hugging skirt .... She laughed so much she wet herself. 'You wait a few years and you'll be old and ugly, just like me,' she cackled." See Carter 1982, 11.

incestual implications of the father-daughter romance in Shakespeare (*King Lear*) and the oedipal anxiety of influence that structures the father-son relation. Gorgeous George's performance parodies this anxiety: due to the father's infidelity, the son is unable to find a wife who is not related to him.[36] The father has always been there before him, imposing the incestual law and restraining the son's freedom.[37] In a similar way, Melchior is overshadowed by his dead father's fame. Melchior's compulsive emulation of his father's success as a Shakespearian actor indicates an unresolved oedipal conflict. In *Wise Children* paternal absence produces father complexes in both sons and daughters, who are obsessed with the regaining of the absent father's love. As a result, female characters turn into Cordelias who make up for paternal absence by marrying Lears, while sons transform themselves into cardboard impersonations of their fathers and reproduce the latters' failures. At the same time, the narrative foregrounds what has been neglected in the Western literary tradition: the mother-daughter relation.[38] Nora draws attention to the missing mother in *King Lear*:

> 'If the child is father of the man ... then who is the mother of the woman? Speaking of which, has it ever occurred to you to spare a passing thought as to the character of the deceased Mrs Lear? Didn't it ever occur to you that Cordelia might have taken after her mother while the other girls ....'" (WC 224,225)

Wise Children projects a female ethics of care and responsibility that is not rooted in origins but in action, and connects different generations of women in a bond of solidarity. Within this ethics the younger woman may nurture the older woman just as the older woman may support her 'daughter'. Grandma Chance gives, in fact, only one example of maternal care in the novel. In her role as teacher, Mrs Worthington represents another 'foster mother' who rears the twins. The Hazard's "generic Old Nanny" has nurtured almost everybody

---

[36] This problem is, however, solved when the son is revealed to be himself the offspring of his mother's infidelity.

[37] The literary equivalent of the son's anxiety of belatedness is captured in Harold Bloom's concept of the 'anxiety of influence' that structures literary history and turns it into the scene of an oedipal struggle. Through creative acts of misreading, the 'son-poet' attempts to overcome the crippling influence of the preceding 'father-poet'. See Bloom 1973, 5 ff..

[38] In particular the absence of mothers in Shakespeare's plays has been noted by feminist criticism: "... where is the mother of Jessica? Desdemona? Ophelia? What woman carried in her womb Regan, Goneril, *and* Cordelia? What happened to the Duchess of Milan after Miranda was born? ... In plays where woman-as-daughter is so essential to the meaning of the drama, what does this absence of the mothers imply?" (Schotz 1980, 45). Chedgzoy argues that in her representation of pregnant Tiffany (Ophelia as mother) and Estella (the pregnant Hamlet) Carter "inscribes a maternal subjectivity which Shakespeare's text occludes". See Chedgzoy 1994, 265.

in the Lynde and Hazard clan. D/Nora carry on Grandma's tradition of inventing a family by taking care of Lady Atlanta, Tiffany and the new Hazard twins. The new Chance family represents a mirror image of the old Chance family. N/Dora have slipped into Grandma Chance's role: the daughter turning into her mother is no reason for matrophobia anymore: "... the older we grow, the more like her we become" (WC 28). Running a dancing Academy, the twins follow in Mrs Worthington's footsteps and pass on what they have been taught by her. The novel creates a female genealogy which is self-made, without biological origin and yet has a tradition to carry on. A powerful image of this female genealogy is drawn in the mirror scenes in Mrs Worthington's dancing academy:

> Once upon a time, there was an old woman ... pounding away at an upright piano ... and her daughter ... slapped at your ankles with a cane if you didn't pick up your feet high enough .... Grandma sat by the door ... squinting at us between the spots on her veil .... The mirror in Miss W.'s front room showed two times two Chance girls, us and our reflections, doing high kicks like trick photography in flesh and blood. Bang, crash, wallop went Miss Worthington's old mum on the piano, and smack! smack! smack! Miss W.'s cane on our legs .... (WC 53,60)

Mothers, daughters and sisters are mirror images of each other. The sisters, themselves 'doubles' as twins, are once more duplicated by the mirror. Old Mrs Worthington at the piano is the aged double of young Mrs Worthington, just as Grandma represents an image of D/Nora's future self: "Mother and daughter live as each one the other's image" (SW 125). The dizzying proliferation of mothers, daughters and sisters in the mirror creates an array of non-biological family resemblance. The scene draws the image of a female genealogy that empowers the twins and imparts a strong sense of identity to them. In fact, the mirror scene in the dancing room is itself mirrored by the dancing lessons the Chance Sisters later give at their own Academy. Now Tiffany is dancing in front of the "big mirror" (WC 35) and her mother Brenda "banging away" at the piano. N/Dora pass on the education of empowerment they have received from Grandma and Mrs Worthington. In *Wise Children* the repetitiveness of plot structure and imagery creates a formal analogue of continuity, of a female tradition of solidarity and care, which reproduces itself in the creation of a female genealogy.

Like Ma Nelson's academy in *Nights at the Circus*, Mrs Worthington's dancing academy is a production site of female independence. Dancing is not only a source of pleasure and self-fulfilment in *Wise Children*. Dancing will become the twins' capital and their means of survival on the "left-hand", illegitimate side of life. Just as Fevvers' power resides in her wings and in her ability to fly, so D/Nora make a living out of their similarity and dancing talent. In an inversion of Irigaray's image of the paralysing mother, surrogate mothers in *Nights at the Circus* and *Wise Children* do not impede movement, but literally set their daughters dancing and flying. The Lucky Chances contrast with paralysed Lady Atlanta, who epitomises the crippling effect of maternity. Lady Atlanta is turned into the victim of her biological daughters, who divest her of her fortune and mobility.[39] In contrast to Carter's earlier fiction, the narrative adopts the maternal perspective when it is the mother, not the daughter, who is debilitated by maternity. The Lynde seal – the Pelican pecking at its own breast – points to *King Lear* as intertext and undermines biological definitions of 'family' and 'origin'. While Lady Atlanta's biological children, Saskia and Imogen, reincarnate the cannibalistic "pelican daughters" Goneril and Regan[40], illegitimate D/Nora adopt Cordelia's part of the loving daughter. Again, the novel takes to a performative definition of family relations: "lovely is as lovely does" (WC 7).

D/Nora's power does not only depend on Grandma's caring and Miss Worthington's training, but also on their relation to each other: "By ourselves, neither of us was nothing much but put us together, people blinked" (WC 60). Deliberately creating their selves as same, the twins turn themselves into spectacles and capitalise on their baffling resemblance. The similarity of the characters has no uncanny quality but is an expression of the power that resides in connection and intersubjectivity. In the metaphor of the missing limb, the narrative conceives of Nora as part of Dora's body and thus describes the sisters as one flesh: "They say, if you get your leg cut off, you

---

[39] By creating a whole pattern of oppositions between the upper-class Lady and the lower-class sisters, the narrative points to debilitating and empowering conceptions of femininity and subjectivity. Clinging to Melchior's portrait after her divorce, Wheelchair lives in the past whereas D/Nora know that "Memory Lane is a dead end" (WC 190). While Lady Atlanta desperately tries to hide her ageing appearance behind a suffocating veil, N/Dora "debate invisibility hotly" at Melchior's party (WC 199). D/Nora's refusal to be victimised and their resolution to take control of their lives contrasts with Wheelchair's passive incapacitated state as "geriatric little girl" (WC 189).

[40] Shakespeare 1958, 118 (III,4,75). *King Lear* is only one of the numerous Shakespearian intertexts of the novel. Ironic references to the father-daughter relation and the romance theme of reunion and reconciliation link *Wise Children* to *Pericles, Cymbeline, The Winter's Tale, The Tempest* and *King Lear*. The novel's title echoes *The Merchant of Venice*. The bastard theme recalls *The Winter's Tale, King Lear* and *Much Ado about Nothing*. Reincarnations of Imogen (*Cymbeline*), Hamlet (in drag) and Ophelia (Tiffany) emerge in the narrative. The motif of twinship connects the novel to *Twelfth Night* and *The Comedy of Errors*. The Shakespearian 'All the world's a stage' theme, the play-within-a-play motif, is reminiscent of the *Midsummer Night's Dream*, which is itself reproduced in the novel, creating a complex *mis-en-abyme* structure of metafictional reflections. This is only a small selection of the countless Shakespearian allusions in the text. For the novel's intertextual complexity see also Webb 1994, 95 ff..

don't notice it, at first, until you try to put your weight on it. Then you fall down. It was like that with me and Nora" (WC 102,103). Female bonding between the twins recalls Chodorow's concept of women's identity as residing in connection. However, in *Wise Children* the strong sense of relationship does not lead to the relinquishing of individual selfhood as Chodorow and Benjamin assume it in their theories of female identity formation.[41] Sameness and interrelation do not restrict the freedom, nor do they endanger the individuality of each of the twins. Respecting each other's privacy, the twins claim to be "identical, well and good; Siamese, no" (WC 2). Reminiscent of Irigaray's notion of female identity as eluding the distinction between self and other, Dora and Nora are at the same time one flesh and different, same and other: "Neither one nor two".[42] *Wise Children* reinterprets intersubjectivity and connection as sources of female power and strength. Identity is grounded in relation and likeness, in plenitude and excess, not, as Freud and Lacan argue, in difference, separation and lack. In Freudian psychoanalysis the separation from the mother represents the primordial foundation of a healthy subjectivity. The severing of the bond to the mother is the necessary precondition for identity formation in the oedipal phase. Freudian accounts of individuation downgrade the role of the maternal, which exists only *ex negativo* as that which has to be left behind. According to Irigaray and Judith Butler, this repression of the maternal lies at the root of a patriarchal culture of melancholia.[43] D/Nora's vitality indeed contrasts with the melancholic constitution of the male characters who suffer from an unacknowledged loss in Carter's fiction. A sense of indifference, of detachment from his life and body, typically characterises the psyche of the male protagonist in Carter's work.[44] *Wise Children*, by contrast, acknowledges the maternal. The maternal figure is neither engulfing nor abject, but imbues the daughter with a strong sense of security and self-confidence: "She seemed to fill up all the space available, so there wasn't any room left in the whole of southern California for insecurity" (WC 160). D/Nora are not detached observers, but joyfully take part in life, feel identical with and proud of their ageing bodies. In *Wise Children* identification with a

---

[41] Müller argues that focusing on the "positive implications of the mother-child bond", which Chodorow ignores, *Wise Children* devises an intersubjective notion of identity as open, shifting and incomplete. See Müller 1997, 176.

[42] Irigaray 1985b, 207.

[43] Irigaray 1985a, 71; Butler 1997, 136 ff.; see above note 17. See also III.1.1.2.2.

[44] Desiderio, Evelyn, Walser and the British Officer in "The Lady of the House of Love" suffer from this sense of detachment. As I have pointed out above, Buzz, Desiderio and Morris are haunted by the absent mother. See III.1.1.2.2 and VI.1.2.1. Joseph in *Several Perceptions* is another melancholic character in Carter's fiction.

maternal figure is not regressive but the source of a powerful independent subjectivity.

1.3.3 "The Quilt Maker": Recovering a Female Tradition

Carter's changing perception of female bonding and motherhood is reflected in her short stories. In the early stories in *Fireworks* mothers hardly ever occur. In "The Snow Child" the relation between the Countess and the young girl, the incarnation of the Count's desire, is characterised by rivalry and hostility. Carter's later stories adopt a more sympathetic stance towards mothers and the elder woman generation. The first positive image of maternal power, inspired by Colette's mother Sido[45], occurs in "The Bloody Chamber" (1979): the "eagle-featured indomitable mother" (BB 111) rescues her daughter from the sadistic Marquis. "The Kitchen Child" (1979) presents another powerful mother, who turns the domestic art of cooking into an assertion of independence. "Impressions: The Wrightsman Magdalene" (1992) takes Georges de La Tour's painting of the repenting harlot Mary Magdalene as an occasion to reflect on maternity, virginity and the female body. It is Carter's first story to give a voice to the mother and her experience of giving birth. Trying to bear the pain in labour, the narrator concentrates on the candle flame in Georges de La Tour's painting until she is subsumed by the "blue absence at the heart of the flame" (BB 412). The woman's ordeal is conveyed through an image of beauty and stillness.

Another late short story, "The Quilt Maker", in many ways anticipates *Wise Children*. The story creates a female space of mirroring which prefigures the duplications and reflections in Carter's last novel. The narrator describes her eighty-year-old neighbour's accident, the woman's admission to hospital and her unexpected return to life and vitality. Letty, an "octogenarian redhead" (BB 456), represents the younger, henna'd narrator's double. In the image of the Russian doll, Letty is metaphorically conceived as 'mother' who contains the narrator's younger self within her bones: "... my big babushka who contains my forty, my thirty, my twenty, my ten years within her fragile basket of bones ...." (BB 456). While the older woman represents an image of the younger woman's future self, this does not arouse the 'daughter's' anger and aggression. "As I am now, so ye will be!" (BB 448) is not an expression of matrophobia but a *memento mori* that connects the two women through the

---

[45] Adele Eugenie Sidonie Landoy, known as Sido, is a powerful female character who features prominently in the autobiographical work of her daughter, the French writer Colette (1873-1954).

shared experience of ageing. The narrative highlights similarity, not difference and closes the intergenerational gap through a mirroring of self and other. Letty is, in fact, not a "horrid warning" (SW 124) to the narrator but a model of self-determination. In her willingness to survive in the face of adversity, Letty resembles Grandma Chance in *Wise Children*: "Hope for the best, expect the worst" (WC 33,61). Her resolute will to live, displayed in her freshly henna'd hair on her return from hospital, resurrects Letty from the dead. While Letty could be the narrator's mother, the narrator herself mothers Letty when she takes care of the increasingly helpless and aged woman. "The Quilt Maker" prefigures the ethics of care that emerges in Carter's late novels and conceives 'mothering' as independent of biology and age difference. The story draws an image of an all-female-neighbourhood in which women of different generations reflect each other: Letty and the narrator, Letty's niece and her great-great niece, the brown-haired woman from upstairs and the golden-haired woman on the market are organised in a pattern of similarity and difference. The ageing body appears as the common bond between these women. Men only occur in the narrator's memory of the past in the story.

"The Quilt Maker" opens with a meditation on the household art of patchwork. Carter draws on a female tradition when she employs the metaphor of the quilt as an image for the conscious creation of one's life. The story itself appears as a patchwork of memories: an apparently random collection of remembrances organised around certain leitmotifs – the cherry blossom, the ageing body, dyed hair – which yet forms a "harmonious overall design" (BB 444). As a patchwork of memories, "The Quilt Maker" mirrors Dora's narrative style in *Wise Children*. Dora creates a "crazy patchwork" which combines various heterogeneous narrative modes: a strong subjective orality (Dora as reader-teaser[46]), cinematographic modes (Dora as director who "freeze-frames" the narrative) and writing as digital communication. "Tapping away at ... [the] word processor" (WC 189), Dora is the scriptor who weaves a mottled quilt of intertextual allusions. The patchwork is an image for a specifically 'female' intertextuality. As feminist 'bricoleur', Dora employs the bits and pieces of a male literary tradition, which she gets to know through Irish, and ironically rewrites them in her 'patchwork-narrative'.[47] Although she "can't keep a story going in a straight line" (WC

---

[46] Webb 1994, 295: "Dora's a reader-teaser, endlessly drawing attention to herself by postponing the moment of revelation ('but I don't propose to tell you, not now ...') or prodding her reader into paying attention because 'Something unscripted is about to happen'."

[47] For Dora's feminist intertexuality see also Müller 1997, 206. Müller refers to Nancy Miller's notion of "arachnology" as a feminist form of intertextuality which "reads against

158), Dora still remains in control, plays with and undermines the reader's expectations. Discarding origins and deferring endings, she does not follow a linear narrative thread but – like the quilt maker – works from the middle. Quilting as part of a female tradition has been passed on to Dora by Grandma. Putting together her invented family "out of whatever came to hand" (WC 35), Grandma creates life as a "crazy patchwork" (BB 444). The female household art of quilt making, which tries to make the best of the "miscellany of experience", of the bits and pieces that "turn up in the ragbag" of life (BB 445,444), becomes a metaphor for a self-determined way of life. At the same time the quilt represents an image for a materialist anti-elitist conception of art as being part of life: art which is – like dancing – work, a way of earning your life, embedded in the economic context of a society. Carter comments on her materialist conception of art in an interview with Kerryn Goldsworthy: "I don't see art as distinct from work. ... Show me somebody who writes for art's sake and I'll show you a bad writer."[48]

To summarise, the image of the patchwork works on several levels: on a formal level, it reflects the combination of different narrative modes, the a-linear narrative structure and the feminist intertextuality of Dora's story; on a thematic level, it may be read as a symbol of a self-determined way of life and of a materialist conception of art. While in her early work Carter was at pains to deconstruct the difference between 'male' and 'female', in her late fiction she rediscovers the metaphorical power that lies in a peculiarly 'female' tradition and in the continuation of a female genealogy.

1.3.4 Family Romances: Maternity and Paternity as Social Fiction

The female tradition of care portrayed in *Wise Children* is reminiscent of Irigaray's notion of an ethics that appreciates the maternal as a life-giving, nourishing principle. *Wise Children*, however, makes sure to divest this ethics of any possible essentialising implications. Even Little Kitty's biological motherhood is in doubt at the end of the novel. If father is a "movable feast" (WC 216), this does not necessarily mean that mother is a "biological fact" (WC 216). In *Expletives Deleted* Carter notes that the "fact of maternity" has

---

the weave of indifferentiation to discover the embodiment in writing of a gendered subjectivity". See Miller 1988, 80.

[48] Goldsworthy 1985, 8-9. In another interview with Helen Cagney Watts, Carter complains that "many artists, far from being the unconscious mediators of their time, tend to be parasitic on those in productive labour. I'd rather do many things to do with productive labour in a way, than simply being a writer." Carter in Watts 1987, 164.

become increasingly problematic with the decline of the traditional nuclear family and the advent of artificial reproduction in the late twentieth century: "... am I the mother of the fertilised egg I carry when it does not originate in my own ovary?" She concludes that 'mother' is, just like father, "primarily a conceptual category"[49]. D/Nora finally recognise that it is indeed irrelevant if Grandma is their biological or their foster mother: "mother is as mother does" (WC 223).

In Carter's work the separation from the mother appears as a necessary stage in the daughter's identity formation. D/Nora finally clear out Grandma's room and turn it into a nursery. Fully grown up, the twins are ready to pass on what Grandma has taught them. Redefined in a non-biological way, the maternal heritage still plays a crucial role in the daughter's identity formation and in the transmission of human values. *Wise Children* inverts the "degradation of the mother" and the "elevation of the father" that the child imagines in the Freudian family romance.[50] In contrast to Freudian models of identity formation, it is the role of the (absent) father – not that of the mother – which is downgraded in the novel. At the end of the narrative, the twins rid themselves of the fictional hold their imaginary father has on their lives. While Melchior grows unreal, insubstantial in D/Nora's eyes, Grandma has left a lasting imprint on the Chance sisters: "... we owe her everything and the older we grow, the more like her we become ...." (WC 28). Desperately clinging to his alleged father, Melchior, in contrast, fails to reach maturity and remains a kid jumping after a cardboard crown. On the one hand, the narrative demonstrates the irrelevance of biological origins: "One little sperm out of millions swims up the cervix and it is so very, very easy to forget how it has happened" (WC 174). On the other hand, *Wise Children* reveals paternity to be a powerful fiction that controls the characters' lives. Melchior has turned into the very reincarnation of his father, even though the latter is not his biological father. In *Expletives Deleted* Carter reflects on the importance patriarchal culture assigns to the question of paternity:

That dreadful question – how do we know whose child we are? – has dogged patriarchy since its inception, yet it is a profoundly absurd question .... But the question has been so pressing it has even resolved itself in metaphysics, in the invention of an omnipotent but happily non-material father to whom everyone can lay claim as a last resort. 'Father' is always metaphysics: a social artefact, a learned mode.[51]

---

[49] Carter 1992, 203-4.
[50] Cf. 1.3.1 note 33.
[51] Ibid., 203. Carter echoes Stephen Dedalus' reflections on paternity as "legal fiction" in *Ulysses*. Stephen describes fatherhood as a "mystical estate", as a "void" and as "incertitude" upon which the church is founded. Joyce 1961, 207.

As "social artefact", the narrative of origins still has an obsessive hold on the psychic reality of the characters in the novel. N/Dora recognise this: "We can tell these little darlings here whatever we like about their mum and dad if Perry doesn't find them but whatever we tell them, they'll make up their own romance out of it" (WC 230). The allusion to the Freudian family romance foregrounds both the fictional character of the concept of origins and the central meaning we tend to assign to it. Constructed as it may be, the 'fiction of paternity' nevertheless creates social reality, as it (re)produces and legitimises class difference and separates the Lynde Villas from the Bard Houses. Low origin bars D/Nora from high society. Carter is too much of a materialist not to realise the effect that this "social artefact" has on the material conditions of life in a patrilinear class society. Liberating them from the oedipal grip of the 'fiction of paternity', D/Nora's bastardy may be their freedom; but this freedom is just a personal, relative freedom which has its limits and does not necessarily give them access to the Hazard Villas.

1.4 The Return to the Maternal in Carter's Late Fiction

Carter's work reflects different stages in the daughter's development. The early identification with patriarchy and the devaluation of the mother manifest themselves in the adoption of a male perspective and the perception of the maternal body as abject. Carter's fiction treats the male perspective in an increasingly ironic way and adopts the daughter's point of view. The daughter's search for autonomy produces absent, distant and failing mothers in Carter's early fiction. *The Passion of New Eve* attacks mythic notions of maternity as they prevail in 'mythopoeic' and French feminism. Carter's late work revises this radical critique of motherhood. *Wise Children* resurrects the maternal that has been buried in *The Passion of New Eve*. Daughters turn into mothers in Carter's late work. Lynn Z. Bloom traces the process by which the "daughter-as-autobiographer" becomes her own mother in women's autobiographies: "... in recreating and interpreting her childhood and maturing self, [she] assumes a number of functions that her own mother fulfilled in the actual family history".[52] The autobiographic, retrospective form of Dora's narrative highlights this change in perspective in Carter's work.

In *The Lost Tradition: Mothers and Daughters in Literature,* Davidson and Broner trace a development in literary history that parallels the trajectory of Carter's fiction. While the mother-daughter relation appears as the "lost

---

[52] Bloom 1980, 292.

tradition" in modern literature from the medieval period onwards, a new "matrilineage" emerges at the end of the twentieth century:

> At last we have a new generation of mother-writers. In autobiographies, short stories, novels, plays, poems, movies, personal statements, writers are acknowledging their mothers, looking back to their mothers' mothers and the mothers before them that extend back through time. The rebellious daughter has reclaimed her mother.[53]

Notably, the literature of minority women that has roots in a strong oral tradition recovers the maternal.[54] Carter's turning to folk tales and the oral tradition might be considered important in this context: with the emergence of the maternal, writing gives way to voice, the text to the body. In particular *The Bloody Chamber* draws on this "oral history of Europe" that was dominated by women.[55] However, Carter does not become a "body writer" in Cixous' sense. *Wise Children* is no *écriture féminine*. Even in Carter's late work, the body does not eclipse the text. Dora is both tale-teller *and* scriptor: "tapping away" at the word-processor (WC 189), she still claims to "tell you a tale". The narrative cuts across the genres of novel and comedy, of the written and the spoken word. Oral immediacy exists alongside a dense web of intertextuality[56] and a strong sense of irony and reflexivity. As Carter's last, most 'mature' novel, *Wise Children* finds a balance between mind and body, between reflexivity and corporeality.

It may have been Carter's own experience of maternity which introduced the change in perspective in her late work. It may have been the experience of ageing that made her become sympathetic toward the mother generation. Carter's late work indicates a growing concern with the subjective experience of corporeality. "The Quilt Maker" deals with the ageing body. "Impressions" conveys a powerful image of the mother's pain in childbirth. Turning D/Nora into 'mothers' of a pair of twins at the end of the narrative, *Wise Children* is

---

[53] Davidson, Broner 1980, 256.

[54] Nan Bauer Maglin traces the emergence of the maternal in minority writers like Alice Walker, Margaret Walker, Gayle Jones, Nikki Giovanni, Lucille Clifton and Carolyn Rodgers. Hirsch makes a similar argument with regard to the formation of a maternal discourse in Walker and Morrison. Maglin 1980, 257 ff.; Hirsch 1989, 176 ff..

[55] See Carter in Watts 1987, 170; Haffenden 1985, 85. Cf. V.6, note 69.

[56] Apart from allusions to Shakespeare and Joyce (see note 40, 51, 95), *Wise Children* refers to numerous literary and non-literary intertexts, such as Milton ("Lo, how the mighty have fallen" [WC 10]), Dylan Thomas ("Nobody could say the Chance girls were going gently into that good night" [WC 6]) and various Hollywood productions (see Sage 1994, 295 ff.). In contrast to Carter's early work, *Wise Children* quotes extensively from high *and* low culture (the pantomime tradition, the vaudeville music halls etc.), from written and oral traditions, which is in line with the deconstructive thrust of the novel that celebrates the decline of the 'great divide' (see 2.5.2).

Carter's first novel to adopt the maternal point of view. However, D/Nora become mothers without giving birth. The text avoids the representation of the uncanny experience of pregnancy and birth. The novel confuses gender roles when it is Perry who gives birth to the twins. Flying in the face of biology, the narrative creates a child-bearing father and two septuagenarian mothers. On the one hand, this might be seen as somatophobia not quite vanquished in Carter's late work, which still evades the representation of pain. In Carter's late fiction somatophobic anxiety is allayed, but not conquered. On the other hand, the severing of mothering and fathering from the biological process of reproduction is bound up with the utopian aspect of Carter's work. "To emphasise the biological aspect of parenthood is to deny culture in a way that makes us less human", Carter argues in *Expletives Deleted*.[57] Against biological determinism, Carter's late fiction puts freedom of choice and the determination of the characters to forge their lives and destinies. We do not love by biological necessity, the novel seems to suggest, but by free choice. In "The Quilt Maker" the narrator rejects the "blind-action painter metaphor" that "we make our destinies like blind men chucking paint at a wall" and prefers the image of the patchwork which is put together in an intentional way, involving hard work, thrift and patience: "... for I do believe we all have the right to choose" (BB 444). It is this utopianism which explains Carter's choosing art over nature: Fevvers and D/Nora freely fashion their bodies and reconstruct their selves. The dyeing of hair and the use of make-up are images of self-invention that recur in Carter's late fiction. N/Dora re-create themselves as 'The Lucky Chances' by dyeing their hair black. Like Fevvers, Grandma is a peroxide blonde whose eccentric use of make-up is part of her reinvention as a 'New Woman'. In "The Quilt Maker" Letty's henna'd hair epitomises her unshakeable belief in autonomy and her defiance of old age and dependency.

The deconstruction of biological origins does not only enhance the daughter's freedom to invent herself. Envisaging alternatives to biological mothering, it may also free the mother to exert her right to choose. In the age of artificial reproduction this is not an unrealistic – if highly controversial – vision.[58] The belief in self-determination might be read as an expression of Enlightenment optimism in Carter's fiction. However, in *Wise Children* this vision is constantly haunted by that what it excludes: the inexorability of death.

---

[57] Carter 1992, 203.
[58] Carter's view of the liberating potential of reproductive technologies has met with critical response (see Jouve 1994, 166).

2. Laughter in the Face of Death: the Ageing Body in *Wise Children*
Introduction

Death is a perpetual presence in *Wise Children*. Tiffany's presumed death looms over Dora's narrative. The exuberant tone and the carnivalesque subversions of the novel are undermined by Dora's repeated allusions to the evanescence of time, fame and the body: "Lo, how the mighty have fallen" (WC 10,16,75,196). In *Wise Children* the ageing body is a perpetual reminder of death and mortality:

> Piles of scrapbooks, the cuttings turned by time to the colour of the freckles on the back of an old lady's hand. Her hand. My hand, as it is now. When you touch the old newsprint, it turns into brown dust, like the dust of bones. (WC 78)

Yet the celebratory nature of the novel transforms the *memento mori* into a *carpe diem*. D/Nora regard impending death as an imperative to make the most of time and enjoy the day: "Everything slightly soiled, I'm sorry to say. Can't be doing with wash, wash, wash, polish, polish, polish, these days, when time is so precious ...." (WC 2). The twins' vitality defies old-age depression: "Nobody could say the Chance girls were going gently into that good night" (WC 6).

Wise Children creates a protective space that bars death and tragedy from the narrative. The novel employs the comic mode which defies death through the force of laughter. Celebrating the ability of storytelling to hold destruction at bay, the text nevertheless foregrounds the continuing presence of the dark forces of life beyond the carnivalesque frame of the narrative. Death remains perpetually present at the margins of the text.

The following chapter analyses the strategies the novel employs to approach the painful experience of ageing and mortality. I particularly focus on the comic mode and its relation to the body and death in the novel. After giving a brief overview of theories of the comic, I explore different functions of comedy in the narrative: the comic emerges as carnivalesque conquest of death (2.2), as mask of pain (2.3) and as a deconstructive force in the narrative (2.4.2). Relating the theme of death to an analysis of narrative structure, I argue that *Wise Children* creates an open, dialogic text that symbolically postpones endings in order to defer the death of narrative.

2.1 Laughter, Death and Resurrection: Theories of the Comic
2.1.1 Comedy and the Return of the Body

Several theories of laughter associate the comic with a return of the body. As uncontrollable bodily eruption, laughter disrupts the discourse of rationality. Impulsive vitality undermines the order of signification and stages the subversive return of the "other of reason":

> Laughter is a corporeal reaction, in which the body affirms itself against the predominance of the mind, against rationalisation and abstraction ... In laughing, the body (not the self) expresses itself and resists its instrumentalisation by the subject ....[59]

In what follows, I will briefly comment on notions of the comic as a liberation of the body and contrast them with conceptions that highlight the social and cultural dimension of the comic.

In his *Philosophische Anthropologie* Helmuth Plessner argues that human beings' 'eccentric' position in the world is conditioned by the fact that they both *have* and *are* a body. While we are at the mercy of the 'body-we-are', the 'lived body' with which we identify ourselves, we control the objectified 'body-we-have' and use it as an instrument. Laughter is defined as a reaction in which the body-we-have overrules the body-we-are. The self loses control and the body takes over command.[60] From a historical perspective, the comic has been conceived as a reminder of the corporeal part of our existence that has been increasingly repressed in the "process of civilisation".[61] Renate Jurzik transfers this historical argument to an ontogenetic level. Her psychoanalytic approach derives the comic from the early stages of infantile development: the comic and the obscene represent a return to infantile, anal pleasures.[62] These 'anal pleasures' also figure prominently in Bakhtin's concept of the carnivalesque that celebrates the corporeal dimension of the comic.[63] Bernhard Greiner considers Bakhtin's notion of carnival as an instance of the grotesque bodily form of the comic, the 'humour of elevation',

---

[59] Kamper/Wulf, 1986, 7. "Das Lachen ist eine Reaktion des Körpers, in der dieser sich gegen Vergeistigung, Rationalisierung und Abstraktion behauptet. Der Lachende überläßt seinen Körper sich selbst; er verzichtet auf Kontrolle .... Im Lachen bringt er, der Körper (nicht das Ich), sich nachdrücklich zum Ausdruck. Er widerstrebt der Instrumentalisierung durch das Subjekt ...." (my translation).

[60] Plessner 1970, 41ff., 162.

[61] Elias 1969, 312 ff..

[62] Jurzik 1985, 32.

[63] As mentioned in IV.2.2.1, Bakhtin describes laughter as triumph of the body over the "high", "spiritual", "ideal", and "abstract". Dragging the serious and the abstract into the material, bodily lower stratum, laughter "degrades" and "materialises". Bakhtin 1984, 19,20.

which he distinguishes from the 'humour of disparagement'.[64] While the humour of disparagement deflates a heroic ideal, the grotesque form of the comic expresses an affirmation of the instinctual, untamed body. Elevating the material aspect of life, the comic grotesque celebrates the body which transgresses the law.[65]

Theories that conceive laughter as a triumph of the body tend to assign a subversive force to the comic. In Bahktin, carnival is an expression of an oppositional culture of the people which subverts hierarchies and dethrones authorities. Kamper/Wulf view laughter as bodily eruption that poses a threat to the rational subject and the social order. In the corporeal immediacy of laughter we experience a utopian regaining of a 'lost unity'.[66] Many feminist critics view comedy and female humour as a subversive force. In her cross-class analysis of women's humour in Victorian literature, Regenia Gagnier, for instance, perceives an anarchic, democratising quality in female wit. Female humour in the Victorian period particularly attacks class differences and social codes that constrain women. Gagnier concludes that "women's humour tends toward anarchy rather than the status quo, to prolonged disruption rather than, in Freudian theory, momentary release."[67] In Kristeva and Cixous' psychoanalytic approaches, laughter disrupts the symbolic. Medusa's laughter emerges from the unconscious, transgresses boundaries and opposes the law.[68] Relating humour to the "abyss of chaos", the "primordial darkness" in myth, Anton Zijderveld may seem close to Kristeva and Cixous' concept of laughter as unconscious, subversive force. However, Zijderveld also assigns a reflexive function to humour: holding up a mirror to reality, the jester reveals the truth about human nature. Defining humour as playing with traditional meanings, Zijderveld accords a utopian dimension to the humorous. Demonstrating that reality as we know it "could well be otherwise", humour offers alternatives to our existence and turns people into

---

[64] Greiner 1992, 98. Greiner adopts the distinction between the humour of disparagement and the humour of elevation from Jauss (Jauss 1976, 104). He counts Hobbes, Kant, Bergson and Hegel among the 'disparagement theorists', Baudelaire, Nietzsche and Bakhtin among the 'elevation theorists'. See Greiner 1992, 97 ff..

[65] The strict division between the grotesque humour of elevation and the humour of disparagement seems problematic, however, as in many cases the deflation of the heroic ideal implies the elevation of the body. The reversal of hierarchies in Bakhtin's notion of carnival, for instance, stages both a degradation of the high and an elevation of the lower material stratum.

[66] Kamper/Wulf, 1986, 7ff..

[67] Gagnier 1988, 145.

[68] Kristeva 1984, 223 ff.; Cixous 1976, 258.

"Luftmenschen": "freely floating, fantastic, utopian, irresponsible, crazy, yet very human."[69]

A focus on the social and cultural context of the comic tends to produce a more pessimistic view of the regenerative power of laughter. As mentioned before, carnival has been considered a safety-valve in the service of the dominant culture, offering only temporary release from an oppressive social reality.[70] Carter herself takes this view in her short story "In Pantoland":

> The essence of the carnival, the festival, the Feast of Fools, is transience. It is here today and gone tomorrow, a release of tension not a reconstitution of order, a refreshment ... after which everything can go on again exactly as if nothing had happened. (BB 389)

Instead, Carter aligns herself with Marcuse's concept of repressive desublimation (cf. III.2.1.1), which counters Bakhtinian optimism:

> It's interesting that Bakhtin became very fashionable in the 1980s, during the demise of the particular kind of theory that would have put all kinds of question marks around the whole idea of the carnivalesque. I'm thinking of Marcuse and repressive desublimation, which tells you exactly what carnivals are for. The carnival has to stop. The whole point about the feast of fools is that things went on as they did before, after it stopped.[71]

In fact, the comic is not a pre-cultural, corporeal phenomenon that is *per se* subversive. Comedy derives its comic force from its reference to the rules and norms of a society. Henri Bergson foregrounds the social and intellectual character of the comic: laughter is not the "other of reason", but an intellectual activity that presupposes emotional distance and takes place within a social context. As a "social corrective", laughter punishes "mechanical" behaviour which fails to adapt to the changing requirements of the environment. A means of social control, the comic does not liberate, but disciplines the body.[72] Criticising Bergson's ahistorical focus on

---

[69] Zijderveld 1983, 36, 58. Each author makes different terminological distinctions between 'laughter', 'humour', the 'comic' and 'wit'. Zijderveld employs humour as a general term for concepts like 'wit', 'mirth' and the 'comic' (Zijderveld 1983, 2). Freud, in contrast, makes a conceptual distinction between the 'comic', 'wit' and 'humour'. According to Freud, the primary difference between the three terms concerns the number of participants which are involved: 'wit' typically involves three people (target of the joke, teller of the joke, listener), the 'comic' two (the comic object and the perceiving subject) and 'humour' contents itself with one person (Freud 1993, 288, 372). As these terminological distinctions seem rather vague and arbitrary, I employ a broad definition of the comic which does not strictly distinguish between 'wit', the 'comic', and 'humour'.

[70] See IV.2.1.3; V.2.2. See also Kröll 1994, 11 ff.; Moser 1990, 89-111; Stallybrass; White 1987, 13 ff.; Purdie 1993, 126.

[71] Carter in Sage 1992, 188.

[72] Bergson 1972, 12-15; 128-132. Theories that view laughter as an instrument of social control are derived from the 'disparagement theory of laughter', which dates back to Plato and Hobbes: "The passion of laughter is nothing else but the *sudden glory* arising from

mechanisation, Plessner likewise foregrounds the social nature of the comic when he derives the comic effect from a collision of norms. Laughter as eruption of the body-we-have is conditioned by a specific social context. The comic is neither an exclusively corporeal nor a social phenomenon, but results from the way in which human beings belong to different orders of existence – nature and culture, the individual and the social – which collide with each other.[73] In a similar way, Stefanie Köhler defines laughter as located on a semiotic borderline: the comic effect marks the boundary between nature and culture, the body and society. On the one hand, laughter is the 'other' of a society and disrupts the production of meaning (Kristeva, Kamper/Wulf). On the other hand, it is a sign that has a certain function within a system of signification. As punishment of deviant members of a group, it points to the very rules that constitute this group (Bergson).[74] In this sense Purdie's analysis of jokes highlights the way in which pleasure in joking is complicit with the ruling power structure: through the marked trangression of a law, this very law is reinstated. Jokers constitute themselves as "masters of discourse", as "proper speakers" who demonstrate their knowledge of the law by breaching and reinstating it. Constructing the target of the joke as "inept speaker", they have the power to denigrate the other and deny him/her the status of a "proper subject" in the group.[75]

Freud's famous essay *Wit and Its Relation to the Unconscious* has been particularly influential in the formation of the safety-valve theory of the comic. According to Freud, jokes express the unconscious in a socially acceptable manner. In wit the repressed is articulated in a disguised form, which allows for a relief from repression. Saving the expenditure of psychic energy needed for repression, wit produces pleasure.[76] The comic thus deals with taboo subjects of a society: sexuality, the body and death. Considering repression as a necessary condition of civilisation, Freud is far from an idealistic concept of the liberatory power of laughter as it has been formulated by Bakhtin. Wit only temporarily lifts repression in a way that neither endangers the psychic stability of the individual nor the power structure of a society.

Between these 'optimistic' and 'pessimistic' positions on the subversive potential of the comic, Joachim Ritter seems to take the middle ground. For

---

some ... *conception* of ... *eminency* in ourselves, by comparison with the *infirmity* of others". See Hobbes 1971, 46.
[73] Plessner 1970, 96.
[74] Köhler 1997, 5.
[75] Purdie 1993, 130 ff..
[76] Freud 1993, 180 ff..

Ritter the body does not triumph over society and its regulations; comedy is not a radically revolutionary force. Yet neither is the comic an ephemeral phenomenon, a safety-valve in the service of the dominant culture. Like Freud, Ritter claims that the comic makes the repressed visible. Norms and customs exclude various forms of human behaviour which continue to exist in an unacknowledged way on the margins of the social order. However, the comic does not only point to the excluded part of reality but makes this marginalised realm visible as a part of the dominant, serious order of life.[77] Ritter goes further than Freud when he argues that humour implies a critique of reason that is based on an exclusion of otherness. The comic does not just produce a temporary release of energy, but has a critical function which reveals the 'reasonable' to be a limited and one-dimensional concept.[78] Köhler extensively refers to Ritter's approach. Conceding that laughter is a heterogeneous phenomenon with several different functions and meanings, Köhler yet uncovers a common denominator in various theories of the comic: the comic makes the other, the excluded and the marginalised visible. The comic effect is not just an elusive phenomenon but has a lasting impact. By making the unconscious conscious and the invisible visible, laughter works against taboos and toward a revision of norms that marginalise difference.[79]

The different conceptions of the comic discussed above can be located on a scale. At its most pessimistic, the comic represents an instrument of social control which produces the disciplined body. Laughter demonstrates the inferiority of the object of derision (Hobbes) and punishes the members of a social group which fail to adapt to the group's norms and regulations (Bergson). Joking may be harmful as it constructs its targets – which are in many cases minorities – as 'non-subjects' while it constitutes the joker as 'master of discourse' (Purdie). A little further down the scale, the safety-valve theory perceives the comic as a licensed release in the service of the dominant culture (Marcuse). The safety-valve theory is derived from Freud's concept of wit that produces a relief from repression and a saving of psychic energy. Like Freud, Ritter associates the comic with a relief from repression, yet also assigns a critical function to it beyond the mere release of tension. Zijderveld also stresses the critical, reflexive dimension of the comic: holding a mirror up to society, the fool speaks the truth. The jester is at the same time part of the dominant culture as he represents its critical counterpoint. At its most

---

[77] Ritter 1974, 75.
[78] Ibid., 86: "... die Vernunft selbst erscheint hier eben darin, daß sie mit der Setzung ihres Seinsinnes Unendliches ausgrenzt, auch als unendlich begrenzt ....".
[79] Köhler 1997, 45 ff..

optimistic, at the other end of the scale, the comic points to a utopian liberation of the body (Kamper/Wulf) and the oppressed (Bakhtin) and imagines alternative modes of being to reality (Zijderveld).

2.1.2 The Comic and Death

Some theories of the comic celebrate the ability of comedy to transcend death and resurrect the body. Death loses its terror in the Bakhinian carnival as it does not concern the 'body of the people' that perpetually grows and reproduces itself.[80] Northope Frye associates comedy with the myth of spring and the ritual death-resurrection pattern. Growing out of fertility rites and the worship of Dionysus, comedy stages rebirth and regeneration.[81]

The intricate connection between the comic and death has drawn attention from many philosophers, psychologists and literary critics. Ritter notes that the situations that elicit laughter are often identical with the causes of pain, sadness and scepticism.[82] The comic deals with the repressed anxieties of a society. As the body and mortality are primary taboo subjects in Western societies, death and sexuality feature prominently in comedy and wit. Jurzik considers the comic as an indicator of the taboos of a society as well as of "specific catastrophes" that have occurred in the life of an individual.[83] The comic mode creates a safe distance which allows us to deal with these anxiety-ridden subjects. Freud traces this process of distancing in his late essay on humour. According to Freud, the super-ego employs humour to ward off pain and negate the reality principle. As an example for humour, he quotes the ironic remark of the prisoner to be executed on Monday: "Well, the week's beginning nicely." Adopting a distanced attitude to the ego's predicament, the super-ego refuses to give in to the reality principle and asserts the superiority of the self in the face of death. Humour asserts the triumph of the pleasure principle which joins forces with the super-ego to fend off pain.[84]

The 'catastrophic' nature of laughter has been noted in several other conceptions of the comic. Steffen Dietzsch analyses laughter as a reaction to paradoxical and catastrophic situations: the body is able to deal with problems

---

[80] Bakhtin 1984, 354 ff..
[81] Frye 1957, 163 ff..
[82] Ritter 1993, 92.
[83] Jurzik 1985, 34 ff.. Jurzik refers to the theory of catastrophic laughter that has been developed by Klaus Heinrich. See Heinrich 1980, 12-31, qtd. in Jurzik 1985, 34,35.
[84] Freud 1953m, 159-166.

the mind cannot cope with anymore.[85] Plessner counts embarrassment and despair among the situations that evoke laughter. We take recourse to laughter in crises when we do not know how to react. Laughter signals capitulation: the body-we-have takes the lead and we break up as body-mind unity. However, Plessner rather vaguely claims, while capitulating as body-mind unity, the self still asserts itself as a "person" in laughing.[86] Whereas Freudian humour is defiant and affirmative[87], Plessner highlights the ambivalent nature of catastrophic laughter which may either express affirmation or resignation. Catastrophic laughter balances between self-assertion and capitulation, triumph and defeat.[88]

Different readings of *Wise Children* depend upon contrasting views of the nature of comedy in the novel. While most critics celebrate *Wise Children* as Carter's most optimistic, life-affirming novel,[89] Warner views Carter's late "clowning" as an indicator of a defeat of her political aspirations.[90] Is laughter in the novel affirmative or fatalistic? Carnivalesque or catastrophic? Defiant or defeatist? In what follows, I will try to answer these questions, focusing in particular on the theme of death and ageing in the novel.

2.2 Transcending Death and Resurrecting the Body: Carnivalesque laughter in *Wise Children*

Wise Children resounds with laughter. Dora and Nora again and again burst out laughing, Perry guffaws, Grandma Chance cackles. Carnivalesque laughter governs the narrative. The wind that makes the world dance on the twins' birthday anticipates the motto that will govern their life: "What a joy it is to dance and sing" (WC 5, 232). In *Wise Children* it is, first of all, Dora's voice which is carnivalesque. Dora's narrative profanes the holy and deflates the 'high', 'ideal' and 'abstract'. Translating Lady Atlanta's high-flown rhetoric into colloquial English, Dora's down-to-earth common sense logic unveils the class pretensions beneath the "high tone" of her speech: "... always, the high tone .... The nub of what she was saying now was, she'd had a tumble with her brother-in-law ... and, as a result, there were two more girls in the world ...." (WC 215). Dora foregrounds the terminological problems

---

[85] Dietzsch 1993, 234.
[86] Plessner 1970, 118-121, 153, 165 ff..
[87] "Humour is not resigned; it is rebellious." Freud 1953m, 163.
[88] See also Jurzik 1985, 35.
[89] See, for instance, Day 1998, 215; Müller 1997, 147; Deleyto 1995, 180.
[90] Warner 1994, 253.

that the language of the body, sexuality and procreation poses for the Lady A. and thus reveals the inhibitions, on which her rhetoric is based:

> ... I'd been wondering how the Lady A. would verbalise the technical aspect of her adultery, given the refinement of her vocabulary. Having made the distinction between 'blood' and the actual procreative juice, what would she call the latter? 'Jism'? 'Come'? ... I was glad she'd settled on the tasteful compromise of 'seed', although it occurred to me ... that a serious language problem existed between the two branches of the Hazard family .... (WC 215)

The literalisation of the metaphorical represents another strategy that Dora employs to mock the pretentious. Taking Melchior's nationalistic rhetoric at face value, Dora's narrative returns to the body and deflates pathos. "The tongue that Shakespeare spoke" is literally presented on a "red satin cushion, under glass" (WC 135). As a living parody of the British Empire, Gorgeous George's tattooed body literalises the chauvinistic muscle-flexing that lies at the heart of the mission that Randulph and Melchior subscribe to. The narrative produces a comic effect by yoking the literal and the metaphorical together: "... now all the dirty secrets hidden in the cupboards had come out at last, had come to fuck in his bed ...." (WC 219). Dora transfers the "high ceremonial gesture" in Bakhtin's sense to the material sphere of the body. The body running out of control undermines style and dignity: Dora discovers evidence of incontinence in the side-room next to Melchior's distinguished master bedroom. The awe that Melchior inspires makes her lose control of her bladder. The cat's excrement profanes Melchior's holy earth, mocking the nationalistic discourse that employs this earth as a symbol of British superiority.

Yet in *Wise Children* it is above all Perry who appears as the very embodiment of carnival.[91] Perry incarnates vitality, fertility and an inexhaustible sexuality. The centenarian lover, who produces twins from his pockets, seems to be the father of almost all the characters in the novel. Perry embodies the "death-defying somersault of love" (ID 124), the force of desire that annihilates time in the narrative. 75-year-old Dora experiences *jouissance* while making love to Perry. "While we were doing it, everything seemed possible, I must say. But that is the illusion of the act" (WC 222). Desire, the site of subjection in Carter's early fiction, is a utopian force in the novel which has the power to create "alternatives to the stultifying sameness of conventional reality".[92] In the magic circle of desire Perry does not see a

---

[91] See also Peach 1998, 143; Day 1998, 201; Webb 1994, 302.
[92] In an interview with Scott Bradfield, Carter described *Wise Children* as being about "the power of the imagination to create alternatives to the stultifying *sameness* of conventional reality". See Carter in Bradfield 1994, 91.

difference between the young teenage D/Nora and the aged twins' "crow's feet, the grey hairs and turkey wobblers" (WC 208):

> ... he saw the girls we always would be under the scrawny, wizened carapace that time had forced on us for ... where he loved, he never altered, nor saw any alteration. And then I wondered, was I built the same way, too? Did I see the soul of the one I loved when I saw Perry, not his body? And was his fleshly envelope, perhaps, in reality in much the same sorry shape as those of his nieces outside the magic circle of my desire? (WC 208)

The fantastic power of the narrative brings time to a standstill and turns the ageing body into a site of *jouissance*.[93] Perry represents the fantastic in the narrative, which is mostly populated by 'real' bodies and realistic characters: growing larger and larger, his body never ages and never dies. As a comic version of the puppetmaster[94], Perry likes to "pull the strings" (WC 92). Not only does he write the script of Melchior's TV production; he also directs D/Nora's life and the plot of the narrative. It is Perry who carries the carnivalesque joy of life into the twins' life: his music sets the twins dancing and his money pays their dancing lessons. Taking them to see Gorgeous George's bawdy performance on Brighton Pier, he pushes the girls to adolescence and sexual initiation. But not only does Perry control the script of the narrative; as 'everybody's father' (WC 222), he also brings most of the scripts' characters into being and revives them when they are believed to be dead. In a comedic rewriting of the tragic Ophelia-plot, Perry resurrects Tiffany and, parodying *Finnegans Wake*, reanimates Irish by scattering liquor on him.[95]

In the carnivalesque mode, death is conquered by the human species that regenerates itself beyond the life of the individual. *Wise Children* likewise transcends death through continuity, through the succession of generations and the creation of a female genealogy. Grandma's heritage survives in N/Dora, who will pass on the Chance tradition to their foster children. The Hazard Clan and the Chance family perpetually reproduce themselves and survive through the interconnectedness of generations. But this continuity is not, as Carter again and again stresses, grounded in origins: neither is it rooted in the (British or American) soil, nor in blood relations. The future of the Hazard and the Chance family lies in impurity, hybridity and

---

[93] See also Boehm 1994, 86. Boehm argues that the magic of carnival symbolically defeats time and death in the novel.

[94] On "masculinist gameplayers" in Carter's fiction see Day 1998, 204.

[95] *Finnegans Wake* is a major intertext of the novel. *Wise Children* alludes to the death-resurrection theme, the motif of the world as stage, the theme of the antipodal brothers etc.. Like *Finnegans Wake*, *Wise Children* is about complementary opposites and polarity: the life-death, male-female, and age-youth contrast.

displacement: in a "criss-crossing" (WC 19) of the great divide between the right and the left-hand side of the river, in that "between-two-worlds, neither Brit nor Yank" (WC 16), in Tiffany, the first black in the family, and in the gender-mix of the new Hazard/Chance twins. It is only after she has been displaced to London, having crossed the great divide, that Daisy's American cat turns into a "breeding machine" and becomes the founder of the cat chance dynasty. In *Wise Children* hybridity promises regeneration and fertility.[96] In the carnivalesque tradition, the ending of the novel thus asserts a victory over death: "... the barren heath was bloomed, the fire that was almost out sprung back to life and Nora a mother at last at seventy-five years old and all laughter, forgiveness, generosity, reconciliation" (WC 227).

2.3 Laughter as Mask of Pain: Catastrophic Laughter in *Wise Children*

Wise Children is a double-voiced narrative. The comic and the tragic mask, "one mouth turned up at the ends, the other down", are the insignia of the novel (WC 58). Carnivalesque laughter covers up deep-running anxieties in the narrative. Beneath the comic surface of the text lies the fear of loneliness, dependency, old age and mortality. Age is the "fourth guest" at the table in Bard Road (WC 189). Nora complains about loneliness, being "shut up in the basement with old age" (WC 189). After Grandma's death, Bard House is "nothing but spare rooms": "... old clothes, dust, newspapers stacked in piles tied up with strings, cuttings, old photographs. The rest is silence" (WC 36). Handicap and age have dehumanised Lady Atlanta and turned the "most beautiful woman of her time" into "Wheelchair" (WC 7). Lady Atlanta's dehumanised existence may be considered to be an example of the mechanical that imposes itself on the living in Bergson's sense. Like a record player that got stuck, Wheelchair mechanically repeats the traumata of her past:

> Sometimes she goes on a bit, on and on, on and on and bloody on, in fact, worrying away at how Melchior took away the best years of her life ... and on and on and on until you want to throw a blanket over her, like you do to shut up a parrot. (WC 7)

Like a mechanical device, D/Nora "plug" Wheelchair into the TV (WC 8). However, the comic effect is derived less from Lady Atlanta's behaviour than from Dora's narrative voice that radically breaks with the euphemisation of

---

[96] For the celebration of hybridity in carnival see Bakhtin 1984, 317 ff.. Uniting the old and the new, the Bakhtinian hybrid body represents an image of renewal which transcends death. On Bakhtin's notion of 'hybridization' as a mixture of two social languages see also Bakhtin 1981, 385.

death. Metonymically reducing the Lady on the mechanical appliance of her handicap ("Wheelchair"), Dora's narrative depicts the process of ageing in a shockingly direct manner. "Wheelchair" is alternately described in terms of an object ("we've been storing Wheelchair in the basement ..." [WC 7]), a pet animal ("we've got quite attached to her ... take her out ... give her some fresh air" [WC 7]) or a baby ("our geriatric little girl" [WC 189]). The ethics of care advocated by the novel is counteracted by the blunt narrative voice that keeps the narrative from turning sentimental. Dora's black humour represents a paradigmatic case of catastrophic laughter in Freud's sense: lifting repression on the taboo of death, it asserts superiority through the adoption of a distanced attitude. At Melchior's birthday party D/Nora laugh at the grotesque vision of their ageing bodies in the mirror:

> ... I suffered the customary nasty shock when I spotted us both in the big gilt mirror at the top – two funny old girls, paint an inch thick, clothes sixty years too young, stars on their stockings and little wee skirts skimming their buttocks. Parodies ... 'Oooer, Dor',' she [Nora] said. ' We've gone and overdone it.' We couldn't help it, we had to laugh at the spectacle we'd made of ourselves and, fortified by sisterly affection, strutted our stuff boldly into the ballroom. (WC 197,198)

D/Nora's laughter is highly ambivalent in this scene. On the one hand, it indicates defeat in the face of the ineluctability of ageing. The sisters' attempt to recover the past and restore their younger selves fails in a grotesque way. On the other hand, catastrophic laughter signals ironic distance and the twins' mastery of the situation. In fact, D/Nora even manage to transform defeat into a situation of power. Far from being embarrassed, the twins relish the situation they have inadvertently produced and turn themselves into spectacles. Catastrophic laughter turns into a carnivalesque triumph: Melchior's repressed past returns to haunt him in its most obnoxious form. Dressed like "harlots" (WC 192), the twins transgress social norms of etiquette in old age. D/Nora are painted clowns who intrude into the world of class and deflate Melchior's display of dignity. The twins' laughter is both catastrophic and carnivalesque, fatalistic and triumphant.

Carter's early novels adopt a similar distancing strategy of coping with sexual violence. In Carter's early fiction rape victims try to escape humiliation by dissociating themselves from their bodies. In the staged rape scene in *The Magic Toyshop,* Melanie "felt herself not herself, wrenched from her own personality, watching this whole fantasy from another place ...." (MT 166). In *The Passion of New Eve,* Eve feels a "sense of grateful detachment from this degradation" when she is violently raped by Zero: "I registered in my mind only the poignant fact of my second rape in two hours. 'Poor Eve! She's being screwed again!'" (PNE 91). Critics have been shocked by the distanced narrative voice, the "bloodlessness"[97] of violence, and the way in which the body is turned into an object in Carter's early fiction. However, dissociation in the face of sexual violence expresses the characters' refusal to accept the victim position. Reminiscent of the psychological defence mechanism of 'isolation'[98], the self splits off the emotional experience of pain, rationalises it and turns it into an object that is exclusively viewed by the intellect. Intellectually asserting mastery, the subject negates pain and the lived experience of the body.

In *Wise Children* catastrophic laughter also creates distance. Nevertheless, the comic mode does not negate suffering and death as subjective experiences of the body in the novel: as the ageing body, the 'body-we-are' is constantly present in the text. Death is a blank in the narrative that is paradoxically foregrounded by Dora's repeated allusions to its absence. Emphatically proclaiming her refusal "to play in tragedy" (WC 154), Dora again and again draws attention to the tragic omissions of her tale: "Let other pens dwell on guilt and misery .... I do not wish to talk about the war. Suffice to say it was no carnival, not the hostilities. No carnival" (WC 163), she echoes Jane Austen. Gareth's fate is excluded in the text as it does "not belong to the world of comedy" (WC 227). While Dora rejects the tragic mask, the 'white melancholic clown' remains present in the narrative and speaks through its silences: the empty spare rooms, the yellowed photographs, the tragic blanks of the novel. In *Wise Children* the comic represents a bridge over the abyss of death and tragedy.

2.4 Comedy, Death and the Return of the Repressed: the Double in *Wise Children*

The figure of the double is intricately connected with the theme of death. The double originally embodied a defence against death. In his psychoanalytic study on doubles, Otto Rank derives the emergence of the double from the ego's narcissistic negation of death.[99] Death is conquered through the reproduction of the self. Following Rank, Freud describes the immortal soul as the "first double of the body":

> ... the 'double' was originally an insurance against the destruction of the ego, an 'energetic denial of the power of death', as Rank says; and probably the 'immortal' soul was the first 'double' of the body.[100]

---

[97] Jouve 1994, 142.
[98] Beutel 1988, 11 ff., 21.
[99] Rank 1969, 162.
[100] Freud 1953h, 235.

Yet the threat of death returns in the very figure which has been used to fend it off: in a metonymic shift, the double turns into the uncanny "harbinger of death" in folk belief.[101]

According to Christoph Wulf, the 'myth of rebirth' and the 'myth of the double' both express a yearning for immortality. The myth of rebirth celebrates the biological cycle in which the individual may die while the human species renews itself. In the myth of the double, death is transcended through multiplication and reproduction.[102] Both these 'myths' are major elements of the comic mode. The myth of rebirth finds its prototypical expression in the celebration of marriage and regeneration in a comedy's ending. Twins are stock figures in comedy due to their ability to produce comic confusion. The ubiquity of doubles, however, is more than just a plot device in comedy. From a psychoanalytic perspective the comic genre is closely aligned with the figure of the double as both are associated with a return of the repressed. Freud defines the double as a projection of negated parts of the self.[103] In the gothic mode the return of the repressed is a violent and uncanny force: the encounter with the double forebodes the death of the subject. In comedy, by contrast, doubles are a source of pleasure: through a licensed release, the repressed is deprived of its uncontrollable, destructive power (cf. 2.1.1).[104] The encounter with the double has a cathartic effect and may even lead to self-knowledge and the acceptance of hidden parts of the

---

[101] Freud 1953h, 235; Rank 1969, 163,164. According to Freud, changing conceptions of the double reflect different stages in ontogenetic development. First, the double embodies the child's narcissistic belief in its immortality. At the end of the narcissistic stage, the double changes its meaning and comes to signify death as the uncanny return of the repressed. After the formation of the super-ego, it symbolises the split self in psychic development. See Freud 1953h, 235 ff..

[102] Wulf 1982, 261. Wulf refers in this context to the genetic and cultural process of reproduction: the biological process of cellular reproduction and the cultural transmission of experience from one generation to another.

[103] While some critics define doubles in a wide sense (two persons that look alike and/or represent different aspects of one personality), others employ a narrow, psychoanalytic definition of the term in Freud's sense. Twins are not necessarily doubles in the psychoanalytic sense. Keppler, for instance, stresses that in *The Comedy of Errors* and *Twelfth Night* "twins ... have nothing whatever to do with the figure of the second self" (Keppler 1972, 7). Herdman and Hildenbrock also refer to doubles as complementary characters. (Herdman 1990, 2; Hildenbrock 1986, 20). I will both refer to the notion of doubles as complementary characters (see 2.4.1) and to Freud's definition of the double as the return of the repressed (see 2.4.2).

[104] Similarly, repetition may produce an uncanny or a comic effect. Freud discusses the double and compulsive repetition in his essay "The Uncanny". Like the double, compulsive repetition indicates a return of the repressed past and manifests the power of the unconscious to govern the ego's behaviour. See Freud 1953h, 237 ff..

self. Moreover, comedy revives the old belief in the double as a protection against death. The double is not the emissary of death as it is in folk belief, but ensures the ego's survival. In a similar way, 'comic' repetition loses its uncanny associations and fends off death through the creation of continuity. Repetition and the duplication of identities both transcend death through reproduction.

In what follows, I will look at the comic use of the figure of the double and its relation to the theme of death in *Wise Children*. Doubles have different functions in the narrative: they embody the polarity of life (2.4.1), regeneration (2.4.1) and the return of the repressed (2.4.2). Finally, I will examine 'two-dimensional doubles' as they appear in the mirror and in the world of mechanical reproduction in Hollywood (2.4.3).

2.4.1 Family Resemblance: Duality and Continuity in *Wise Children*

Doubles emerge in several forms in *Wise Children*. First, Carter resumes the old comedy motif of twinship. Physically similar with contrasting personalities, twins are doubles in the novel:[105]

> Nora is fluxy; me, constipated. She was always free with her money, squandered it on the fellers, poor thing, whereas I tried to put a bit by. Her menstrual flow was copious to a fault; mine, meagre. She said: 'Yes!' to life and I said, 'Maybe ...'. (WC 5)

Melchior's 'gift of gravitas' (WC 21) contrasts with Perry's celebration of chaos and fun: whereas Melchior is "all for art", Perry is "out for fun" (WC 22). This difference in temperament is reproduced in Melchior's children, Tristram and Gareth. While the priest Gareth dedicates his life to god, hedonist Tristram worships sex. Embodying the duality of life – the serious and the joyful, the ascetic and the sensual – the twins represent "differing aspects of a sundered whole"[106]. The narrative foregrounds the way in which these "differing aspects" are interconnected and dependent on each other: defining themselves in contradistinction to each other, D/Nora are sameness in difference.[107] The image of twinship functions as a central metaphor in the text which points to the interdependence of the dark and light sides of life, of the tragic and the comic and thus implicitly conceives death as a necessary part of life.

---

[105] I am referring to a wider definition of doubles as complementary characters. See note 103.

[106] Herdman 1990, 2.

[107] See also Müller 1997, 148. According to Müller, the motif of the twins celebrates duality as the essence of life and pushes against a monolithic notion of identity in *Wise Children*.

Second, to complicate things further, twins are themselves duplicated by their biological and non-biological children. Tristram and Gareth are "duplicates" (WC 183) of Perry and Melchior. Melchior turns himself into Randulph's double: "... he'd chosen to become his own father, hadn't he, as if the child had not been the father of the man, in his case, but, during his whole long life, the man had waited to become the father of himself" (WC 224). Spreading the Word around the globe, Gareth imitates his grandfather's missionary zeal. D/Nora grow more and more like Grandma the older they get. Intra- and intergenerational family resemblance turns the characters into mirror images of each other in the novel. There is something uncanny in this proliferation of doubles. Yet what may seem as a deterministic and uncanny recurrence of the same asserts the vitality of the incestual family clan. Far from dying out, the degenerating Hazard clan is "bursting out in every direction" (WC 227) at the end of the novel. Carrying on the family tradition, the child as the double of its parent ensures the continuation and regeneration of the family line.

2.4.2 The Double, Death and Deconstruction

Brothers and sisters, fathers and sons, mothers and daughters are doubles in *Wise Children*. Yet not only is there family resemblance within each of the two families. The structure of doubling reaches across the family lines and undermines the strict division between the two clans: embodying the Hazards' unacknowledged past, the Chance family itself emerges as a repressed double of the Hazard Clan. It is this third structure of duplication that lies at the heart of the novel and points to the text's central message: working-class low culture, the song-and-dance girls, represent the unacknowledged other of high culture and British upper-class identity.[108] Several parallels are drawn between the Chance and the Hazard families which deconstruct the distinction between the high and the low. Just like the Hazard brothers, D/Nora are engaged in show-business. Notwithstanding its Romance origins and its formal character, the name "Hazard" has the same meaning as its Anglo-Saxon counterpart "Chance".[109] As the tragic main plot (the Hazard dynasty) and the comic subplot (the Chance sisters) are both derived from Shakespeare, the high and the low can equally claim their descent from the "Bard", with whom the illegitimate Chance sisters and Melchior share their

---

[108] See also Webb 1994, 280.
[109] See also Day 1998, 204; Müller 1997, 213.

birthdays. In an interview with Scott Bradfield, Carter comments on the "two sides" of British culture.

> You've got this one class in Britain which pretends to be so proper and respectable, but all the time they're completely repressed. This other culture they're trying so hard to distance themselves from – the live sex shows, the louts, the hooligans – is their culture, too. They just don't know it yet. ... What I find fascinating is not that there are two sides to British culture – but that the English pretend that such an absolute division exists between them, between the bawdy and the remote.[110]

In *Wise Children* the comic mode makes the "bawdy" visible at the heart of the "remote". The structure of duplication points to the repressed other being part of the self and recalls Ritter's definition of the comic: the comic displays the way in which the marginalised is entangled with the dominant order of life. It makes the 'trivial' and 'indecent' visible as the repressed underside of the serious and the decent.[111] In *Wise Children* the comic mode undermines the 'great divide' between high and low culture and reveals how the low has always been enmeshed with the high.

The comic mode thus emerges as a deconstructive force in the novel. In fact, Ritter's definition of the comic seems to anticipate the logic of deconstruction. Like deconstruction, the comic is engaged in the dismantling of binary structures. It exposes the mechanism of exclusion that marginalises the other in order to assert the self. Making otherness visible at the heart of the self, the comic acknowledges death as part of life. Deconstruction likewise aims to open the self towards death. Derrida describes death as "movement of differance".[112] As 'difference' and 'deferral', *différance* denotes absence and undermines the concept of an original plenitude as 'full presence'. The deconstructive method follows the movement of *différance*. Disrupting the notion of a stable, self-same identity, deconstruction makes otherness invade the self. The subject's experience of ruptures and fissures within the self pre-empts death. In "Circonfession" Derrida employs the image of the 'wound' and 'bleeding' to describe these metaphorical ruptures and fissures within the self, which make us experience a 'little', 'slow' death in a lifetime.[113] In this sense Byung-Chul Han conceives of deconstruction as 'euthanasia' which deprives death of its horror and prepares the subject for

---

[110] Carter in Bradfield 1994, 91,93.

[111] Ritter 1974, 76. "Was mit dem Lachen ausgespielt und ergriffen wird, ist diese geheime Zugehörigkeit des Nichtigen zum Dasein; sie wird ergriffen ... nicht in der Weise des ausgrenzenden Ernstes, der es nur als das Nichtige von sich weghalten kann, sondern so, daß es in der es ausgrenzenden Ordnung selbst gleichsam als zu ihr gehörig sichtbar ... wird."

[112] Derrida 1974, 143.

[113] Derrida 1991,79,89,97 ff..

mortality. Deconstruction is, as he puts it, a reading with the 'melancholic gaze' which perceives a 'landscape of cracks and fissures' in the deep structure of the text – a reading which makes the 'skeleton' of the text visible.[114] Both the comic mode and deconstruction destabilise the boundary between self and other, life and death.

2.4.3 Deconstructing Boundaries: the Pharmakos, the Clown and the Bastard

The destabilisation of boundaries is the theme which opens the narrative in *Wise Children*. The border between the left and the right-hand side of the river, between the bastard and the legitimate side of the city, has been undermined by a "diaspora of the affluent", who "dispersed throughout the city" (WC 1). In the ensuing narrative, D/Nora are comic intruders who destabilise boundaries through transgression. Undermining the power of the Hazard dynasty, D/Nora contribute to the demolition of high culture and the decline of the 'great divide'. Melchior's parties – self-representations of the Hazard clan – end up in disaster due to the twins' influence. Distracting Ghengis and the waiter, D/Nora unwittingly cause the fire that destroys Lynde Court. At Melchior's birthday celebration, it is again Dora who wreaks havoc at the party. Like Desiderio in *The Infernal Desire Machines*, the Chance sisters are ambivalent bastard figures that intrude into 'alien' domain. The twins appear as comic versions of the *pharmakos* who escapes punishment.[115] In fact, like tragedy, comedy is related to the structure of scapegoating. The clown is the *pharmakos*, the transgressor, who is punished by laughter. Laughter symbolically substitutes the sacrifice of the scapegoat, re-establishes the normative order and reintegrates the transgressive 'bastard' into this order. The subversive potential of comedy, however, lies in the uncontainable nature of laughter, in its capacity to turn the normative order itself into the

---

[114] See Han 1998, 229, 230: "Die Dekonstruktion ist ein Lesen mit dem traurig-melancholischen und zugleich tödlichen Blick .... Die Melancholie des dekonstruktiven Lesers versenkt dessen Blick in die Tiefenschicht des Textes, erblickt eine Landschaft des Todes. Der melancholische Blick sieht hinter den vom Begehren errichteten heilen Fassaden eine Landschaft aus Rissen und Brüchen. Die Dekonstruktion ... ist eine Lektüre des Todes, ein Akt, im Text sein Skelett sichtbar zu machen ... die ruinöse Unsicherheit ... aufzudecken.'"

[115] As in III.1.2.2, I am referring to Derrida's definition of the *pharmakos* in his reading of Plato's *Phaedrus*. The *pharmakos* is ambivalent and transgressive, the bastard that comes from "afar" and threatens the "purity of the inside". Derrida 1981, 104,128. See also III.1.2.2. note 30.

butt of the joke. Comedy in its subversive form aligns itself with the bastard. *Wise Children* celebrates bastards: "Go off and drink a health to bastards!" (WC 197), Dora advises Gorgeous George on Shakespeare's birthday. Finally acknowledged by the humiliated Melchior, the 'bastard' sisters emerge victorious and end up laughing "fit to bust a gut" at Melchior's party (WC 213). Instead of turning into sacrificial scapegoats, the twins parasitically "worm" their way into "the heart of the family" (WC 226) and successfully undermine the alleged "purity of the inside"[116] of the Hazard clan.

However, even if D/Nora break up the Hazard parties, they do not, as Dora puts it, "bring the house down" (WC 220). Like the deconstructionist, the clown is not a revolutionary.[117] Nor does the return of the repressed bring about the shattering of the old order in comedy. The novel does not expound a naive belief in comic liberation that "wipe[s] the slate clean" (WC 221,222). Dora reminds Perry that there are "limits to the power of laughter" (WC 220): "... wars are facts we cannot fuck away, Perry; nor laugh away, either" (WC 221). While the twins' vitality seems to defy a pessimistic defeatism, the novel also refutes a romantic escapism and a naive liberationist belief in the subversive power of the carnivalesque.

Is comedy in the novel rather conciliatory in the Shakespearean tradition, reintegrating the bastard and transgressor into a transformed family clan? Integration and reunion are the dominant motifs in the image of the "house we all had in common ... even though we'd lived in different rooms" (WC 226). *Wise Children* reiterates the Shakespearean romance motif of love lost and regained: "... that which had been lost was found ...." (WC 218). N/Dora finally receive what they longed for when Melchior acknowledges his illegitimate offspring. *Wise Children* presents an exemplary New Comedy ending in Frye's sense:

> A new society is created on the stage in the last moments of a typical New Comedy, and is often expanded by a recognition scene and a restoring of a birth-right. In the common device of the foundling plot, the recognition is connected with the secret of somebody's birth.[118]

The final recognition scene reveals Saskia and Imogen's illegitimacy, restores D/Nora's birth-right and celebrates the birth of the new Hazard twins. Integrating the marginalised, the ending reconciles the 'blind' father and his

---

[116] Derrida 1981, 128.

[117] According to Zijderveld, the jester is deeply sceptical of ideologies and typically rejects a revolutionary position. See Zijderveld 1983, 10 ff., 42,43. Working from the 'inside', he is vulnerable to the same critique as the deconstructionist: both are considered to lack political efficacy.

[118] Frye 1978, 11.

'loving' daughter in a comedic rewriting of the tragic ending in *King Lear*: "... all laughter, forgiveness, generosity, reconciliation" (WC 227). But, as Dora immediately admits, this is "hard to swallow" (WC 227). Conceding that her ageing memory fails her, Dora foregrounds the unreliability of her narrative. In fact, the truce between the Chance girls and the Hazard sisters is only a temporary truce and the happy ending just a "glorious pause" (WC 227) in the continuing narrative of life. The narrative is reminiscent of the Shakespearean late romances that celebrate reunion and reconciliation while they acknowledge the continuing presence of darkness on the edges of the happy ending. Does this presence work to reinforce the happiness of the moment? Or does it point to a more pessimistic, fatalistic reading of the novel which accepts the bastard into the family but leaves the binary structure of power unchanged? "Not that anything had changed. But we'd had a bit of love" (WC 201). *Wise Children* leaves these questions open and passes them on to the reader to decide: "... if you choose to stop the story there ... you can call it a happy ending .... I am not sure if this is a happy ending" (WC 227,228). The choice of a subversive, conciliatory or fatalistic reading of the novel hinges on the reader's interpretation of the comic mode and his/her evaluation of the subversive power of deconstruction.

2.4.4 Versions of the Self: Photography and Mirror Images in *Wise Children*
2.4.4.1 The Double in the Mirror

Mirror images and photographs display two-dimensional doubles of the self. In *Wise Children* mirror images reflect the evanescence of time and the ageing process. An uncanny encounter with the past awaits D/Nora in the mirror of Grandma's wardrobe:

> As we opened up the wardrobe, we saw ourselves swimming in the mirrored door as if in a pool of dust and, for a split second, in soft focus, we truly looked like girls, again. (WC 187)

The double in the mirror embodies D/Nora's desire to turn back time and regain their younger selves. The scene drastically contrasts with the mirror scene to follow at Melchior's party. D/Nora are here confronted with the reality of their ageing bodies and the impossibility to return to the past (cf. 2.3). The third mirror scene in the novel, the bathroom scene, depicts Grandma's reflection as Dora's aged double: "... one fine day, you'll wake up and find you're old and ugly, just like me" (WC 94; cf. 1.3.1). The theme of the maternal is bound up with the theme of death and the figure of the double.

The ageing mother as image of the daughter's future self forebodes death. Like Grandma in *Wise Children*, Letty functions as the narrator's aged double in "The Quilt Maker". Yet, as I have argued above, these doubles are not terrifying, but represent role models for their younger selves. Letty refuses to be a plaything of destiny and consciously creates her life as a patchwork of experiences. The narrator follows Letty's example and turns her face "vigorously against the rocks and trees of the patient wilderness waiting round us" (BB 457). The oxymoron of the patient wilderness suggests that nature and death are terrifying and tender, an alien space and a home. Letty and Grandma help their younger doubles to come to terms with ageing and mortality. In Carter's late work the maternal double as a future version of the self engenders a relief from anxiety and gives a model for the acceptance of age and mortality.

2.4.4.2 The Double and the World of the Simulacrum

Paul Coates relates the double in *fin-de-siècle* literature to the uncanny effect of the new art of photography in the nineteenth century. Typically appearing at dusk, the double resembles the photograph which freezes a moment of life in a monochrome.[119] Photography confronts us with younger versions of the self and preserves the memory of the dead. Dora is deeply moved and bewildered by the experience of listening to Randulph's recorded voice, sounding "alien" and "strange", "a voice from before the Flood, from another kind of life" a hundred years ago (WC 15,16). The twins live surrounded by photographs. Dora begins her family history by describing pictures to the reader which lend authenticity to her narrative. The camera, the VCR and the movies are of central significance in the life and memory of the aged inhabitants of Bard House: "Nostalgia, the vice of the aged. We watch so many old movies our memories come in monochrome" (WC 10). Lady Atlanta worships Melchior's portrait; the twins' youth is preserved in Grandma's scrapbooks. Dora meets her younger self in the movies, sitting in the "fleapits" in her "used body watching it when it was new" (WC 110): "... if you've put your past on celluloid, it keeps. You've stored it away, like jam, for winter .... I could have wished we'd done more pictures" (WC 125). As in *The Infernal Desire Machines*, the mechanical means of reproduction transcend time and conserve the memory of the past (cf. III.2.3).

---

[119] See Coates 1988, 4.

Dora meets her double in the world of mechanical reproduction. In Hollywood Ghengis' ex-wife transforms herself into a copy of Dora. Müller notes the uncanny quality of the encounter between the 'real' and the 'fake' Dora, which introduces a dark, schizophrenic moment into the comic narrative.[120] Yet the uncanny instantaneously gives way to the tragicomic when Dora discerns the realistic explanation of the grotesque apparition: Genghis' wife has literally remodelled her body to fit her husband's desire. She is, in fact, not an exact replica but only a failed imitation, a "blurred photocopy" (WC 155) of Dora. The transition from the uncanny recognition of the double to the realisation of its pathetic reality is exemplary for Dora's Hollywood experience in the novel: in Ghengis' movie production, Shakespeare falls from the sublime to the ridiculous. Dora experiences the pathetic reality of *kitsch*, cash and exploitation behind the glamorous facade of Hollywood. It is no accident that Dora meets her double in Hollywood of all places. A fake Dora seems to be the only thing missing under the paper moon and cardboard stars in the artificial Arden forest. Hollywood is the world of the simulacrum which engages in an infinite production of doubles. Melchior's attempt to save the aura of the genius in this world of endless duplications appears as a hopelessly anachronistic enterprise. Hollywood does away with high-culture notions of originality, individuality and the 'genius-creator'. Walter Benjamin traces the way in which the mechanical means of reproduction have changed the concept of art in modernity.[121] In film and photography, the work of art is no longer unique but reproducible and thus loses its 'aura', the distance that was created by its uniqueness. The ritual value of the work of art is replaced by its value as a commodity and exhibitional object for the masses. According to Benjamin, the movies represent the modern non-auratic art form *par excellence*. Benjamin's essay anticipates the postmodern notion of the society of the simulacrum: as any copy of a photograph is equally authentic, the distinction between 'real' and 'fake' vanishes. Melchior's nationalistic 'blood and soil'-rhetoric that draws on metaphors of 'origin' and puts Shakespeare into the service of the British colonial mission is hopelessly outdated in the society of the simulacrum: the 'British native soil' from which Shakespeare's genius grew is in reality a displaced copy drawn from the Arden forest after the original has been profaned by the excrement of an American cat. Even Melchior's crown, the very symbol of British sovereignty, is just an *ersatz*, a cardboard imitation.

---

[120] Müller 1997, 135. "The sudden realisation of a somebody beside herself who looks the same and yet is materially a totally different person, makes Dora – momentarily – verge on a near-schizophrenic state."

[121] Benjamin 1981, 7-44.

Benjamin stresses the democratic potential of the loss of the 'aura' in the age of mechanical reproduction: with the advent of mass-production, art becomes accessible to the masses. In contrast, Horkheimer and Adorno have a much more pessimistic view of the 'culture industry'. Generating variations of the "ever-same", mass production creates aesthetic monotony and political conformity. Art in the service of mere amusement has lost its critical potential.[122] In *Wise Children* Hollywood represents a conformist version of the circus in *Nights at the Circus*: the spectacle in its ultimate state of commodification. Adorno and Horkheimer share their critical attitude with Brecht, who also spent his exile years in Los Angeles.[123] As several critics have noted, Brecht can be identified with the "German" in the novel who reveals the "love of Mammon", the "cash nexus" (WC 142) to lie behind the Hollywood machinery.[124] Alienation and reification characterise the working process in Hollywood:

> ... we ourselves weren't so much part of the process as pieces of the product. They laid us back in chrome recliners and sprayed us with paint, as if we were a motor chassis. We watched the mirror as if the faces it reflected were those of two other women. (WC 140)

The self turning into an other in the mirror is a powerful image of alienation. *Wise Children* presents an economic, Marxist critique of commodification and exploitation in the production process of *The Midsummer Night's Dream*. At the same time, the novel echoes Adorno and Horkheimer's aesthetic critique of a world of *kitsch* and conformity which is "too literal" and leaves "nothing to the imagination" (WC 125). In fact, the mass-produced proliferation of doubles in Hollywood profanes the figure of the double itself. Coates argues that due to the inflation of doubles in the twentieth century the double ceases to signify death or self-knowledge, but "pops up fleetingly and irritatingly wherever one walks": "The appearance of one's own image becomes a banal and casual punctuation of everyday life."[125] The Arden forest is a "deathtrap" (WC 143) in which life itself turns into its one-dimensional double. In Hollywood, the double represents an image of an alienated, inauthentic death-in-life existence. Reality is eclipsed by its representation and turns into a "blurred photocopy" of life.

---

[122] Horkheimer; Adorno 1984, 141 ff., 156. To escape from fascism in Germany, Horkheimer and Adorno emigrated to the United States, where they formulated their critique of Hollywood mass culture.

[123] For Brecht's dislike of American culture see Brecht 1973, 313 ff., 402 ff..

[124] See, for instance, Webb 1994, 296; Müller 1997, 102. Müller argues that the novel's feminism is complemented by a critique of capitalist production methods.

[125] Coates 1988, 35.

But Carter does not wholly condemn Hollywood in *Wise Children*. Hollywood successfully resists Melchior's belated attempt at colonisation in the novel. It is America that takes over Shakespeare, not Shakespeare that takes back America for the British, as Melchior had planned it. In Benjamin's sense the novel points to the democratic potential of mass culture, in which the so-called 'British colony' as an enclave of British class-culture is nothing but a comic anachronism. The old insignia of power – the crown, the native soil – are revealed to be cardboard imitations which lose their validity in the postcolonial world of the simulacrum.

2.5 The Sense of an Ending and the Death of Narrative
2.5.1 Transcending Death through Storytelling

Dora's narrative revolves around birth and death, origins and endings. "... the urge has come upon me ... to seek out an answer to the question ...: whence came we? Whither goeth we?" (WC 11). As I have argued above, *Wise Children* answers the first question with a deconstruction of origins (cf. 1.3.4). It is, however, not only the origin but also the ending, the point of closure which Western culture conceives as a prominent site of meaning. Western hermeneutic constructs the end as a privileged signifier that confers meaning to the beginning and the middle. Barthes claims that the hermeneutic narrative is modelled on the image of the sentence in which a subject is followed by a predicate: "... truth ... is what is *at the end* of expectation ... truth is what completes, what closes."[126] Birth and death, origins and endings play a central role in the creation of meaning in human life and fiction. Walter Benjamin suggests that life first assumes a transmissable form at the moment of death. Storytelling, which attempts to capture the meaning of life, originates in death: "Death is the sanction of everything the storyteller can tell. He has borrowed his authority from death."[127] In a similar vein, Frank Kermode argues that meaning is created retrospectively. "We project ourselves ... past the End, so as to see the structure whole, a thing we cannot do from our spot of time in the middle."[128] Human beings, who are "born and dead in the middest"[129], try to make sense of the world by creating fictions whose ends are in harmony with beginnings. The way in which meaning is constructed from the end is particularly evident in the retrospective mode of

---

[126] Barthes 1974, 76.
[127] Benjamin 1969, 94.
[128] Kermode 1966, 8.
[129] Ibid., 31.

autobiographical narration. In a paradoxical way autobiography pre-empts the death of the narrator who looks back at his/her younger self from a point of view which transcends and frames the embedded life of the latter. Describing his narrative as a "coffin", Desiderio's last words herald death in *The Infernal Desire Machines*.[130] The end of the narrative coincides with the death of the narrating subject. In contrast, Dora's autobiographical narration does not form a closed frame. Dora frequently leaves the hypodiegetic level of her family history and jumps into the narrative instant of the presence to relate, for instance, Brenda's despair about Tiffany's disappearance or the twins' visit to the movies. Far from being an obituary, Dora's autobiography remains open-ended. Against all expectations, the life of the 75-year old narrator continues for "at least" another twenty years: "Which only goes to show, you never know in the morning what the night will bring ...." (WC 230,231).

In *Reading for the Plot* Peter Brooks analyses the role of beginnings and endings in plot construction. Brooks projects a psychoanalytic model on narrative structures and defines plot as a form of desire. Employing the metaphor of male sexuality, he describes the beginning of the plot as an arousal of desire that "creates the narratable as a condition of tumescence, appetency, ambition, quest, and gives narrative a forward-looking intention".[131] The end, the discharge of tension and the death of narrative, must be reached through a detour: the dilatory space of the plot. The Aristotelian middle of the narrative is a space of retard, postponement and repetition in which the fulfilment of desire must be perpetually deferred. Brooks' psychoanalytic theory creates a parallel between narrative and oedipal family structures: in the same way in which desire has to be displaced to an erotic object beyond the oedipal triangle, narrative requires a detour to prevent desire from reaching its aim prematurely, to evade the "danger ... of achieving the im-proper death."[132] This "improper death" of narrative is in most cases implied by the choice of the "mistaken erotic object": the incestual love of the same. The plot continually has to ward off desire from the regressive "temptation to over-sameness", the most potent image of which is incest.[133]

---

[130] Desiderio echoes Sartre's comment in his autobiographical narration *Les Mots*: "I became my own obituary." Sartre 1968, 171.

[131] Brooks 1984, 103.

[132] Ibid., 104.

[133] Ibid., 109. Brooks particularly refers to the incest theme in Romantic literature. Incestuous love, which recurs in various Romantic texts in a more or less explicit way (Southey's *Thalaba*, Byron's *Bride of Abydos, Manfred, Parisina, Laon and Cythna*, Shelley's *Rosalind and Helen*), is typically shattered by death.

Carter's fiction both inscribes and subverts Brooks' model of the oedipal structure of narrative. In *The Infernal Desire Machines* Desiderio's desire for Albertina represents the driving force of the picaresque text. Desiderio's journey is structured as a space of delay which repeatedly postpones satisfaction in the chase of the elusive object of desire. In the incestual regression among the river people, Desiderio almost chooses the "mistaken erotic object": his quest, his old identity and Albertina sink into oblivion. The incestual is presented in Brooks' sense as the death of the subject in regression and implies the premature end of the plot. *Wise Children,* in contrast, inverts this image. Incest recurs in the Chance and Hazard family and keeps the narrative going, instead of breaking it off. Dora's intercourse with her centenarian foster father Perry is not desire gone wrong but an expression of her vitality and dedication to life.[134] Turning Freudian notions of identity on its head, the narrative extols the love of the same which is potently captured in the image of the twins who are fond of each other: "To tell the truth, I love her best and always have" (WC 102). Like the theme of the double, incest undergoes a comic reinterpretation in the novel which transforms it from an image of death into one of vitality.

On a stylistic level the danger of the premature discharge of tension is reflected in the narrators' tendency of running ahead of themselves in Carter's novels. Desiderio repeatedly pre-empts the events to come and thus spoils the climax: "But there I go again – running ahead of myself! See, I have ruined all the suspense. I have spoiled my climax" (ID 208).[135] Dora, by contrast, manages to remain in control of her narrative: "No. Wait. I'll tell you all about it in my own good time" (WC 13). Dora successfully creates a narrative space of postponement, delay and rising suspense. However, in contrast to Brooks' model, the narrative's ending does not conclude but extends this space and evades closure. Delaying the end for "at least another twenty years", the novel's ending suggests the beginning of several new stories, which are left to the reader's imagination: the twins' life as wise children, Gareth's fate in South America, Tristram's and Perry's journey to South America etc.. *Wise Children* eludes the plot's ending as "quiescence", "death" and "final discharge of tension".[136] The leading questions of the text concerning birth and death are undermined on a thematic *and* stylistic level.

---

[134] The narrative ironically alludes to Freud's analysis of the hysteric patient Dora. Freud perceived an unconscious oedipal desire for the older Herr K. in Dora's hysteria. Webb comments: "Unlike Freud's Dora, Dora suffers very little psychic damage from lusting after her father/uncle". Webb 1994, 293.

[135] See also III.2.2.1 note 79.

[136] Brooks 1984, 107-109.

Deconstructing origins and postponing endings, the narrative creates an open text as a quilt, which the reader may continue to weave if s/he chooses to. The notion of the text as "quilt", as a work in progress, perpetually unfinished and resisting closure, is reminiscent of Barthes' concept of the text as woven:

> Text means Tissue; but whereas hitherto we have always taken this tissue as a product, a ready-made veil, behind which lies, more or less hidden, meaning (truth), we are now emphasizing, in the tissue, the generative idea that the text is made, is worked out in a perpetual interweaving ....[137]

The crucial difference between Carter and Barthes' notion of the text lies in the role the subject plays in the weaving of the quilt. While the Bartheian subject is dissolved in the texture it creates, Dora remains in control of the dense web of intertextuality she creates and utilises her 'weaving skills' to assert, not to dissolve, her subjectivity. The narrative opens with the powerful assertion of her identity: "Let me introduce myself. My name is Dora Chance" (WC 1). At the same time the reader is invited to join Dora in the construction of stories.[138] Quilting as female housework is, in fact, a communal activity. The process of reading is turned into a construction of the text in Iser's sense: by creating gaps and withholding information, Carter's fiction actively engages the reader who has to supply missing information in the production of textual meaning.[139] Dora holds back information on the twins' mother and on Gareth's whereabouts: "Perry told us, of course, ... but I don't propose to tell *you* ...." (WC 227). While Desiderio self-aggrandisingly believes in his ability to "remember everything perfectly" (ID 11), Dora concedes the partial unreliability of her recollections: "At my age, memory becomes exquisitely selective" (WC 195). It remains up to the reader to decide if she has slept with Perry in her youth or not.[140] In addition, a strong sense of reader presence is created by the oral quality of Dora's narrative. Dora repeatedly addresses the reader as listener: "Hard to swallow, huh? Well, you might have known what you were about to let yourself in for when

---

[137] Barthes 1976, 64.

[138] See also Müller on the reader's involvement in the text 1997, 209.

[139] As one of the major proponents of reader-response criticism, Wolfgang Iser has developed the concept of textual gaps that demand reader participation in the construction of meaning. The reader fills out these gaps and eliminates indeterminacy in the process of 'concretization'. 'Concretization', a term Iser borrows from Roman Ingarden, denotes the production of textual meaning in the reading process through the interaction between text and reader. See Iser 1994, 257-355.

[140] "I couldn't for the life of me remember sleeping with him before and I shocked myself, to have forgotten that – if I *had* forgotten, that is, and if he wasn't making a general rather than a particular enquiry ... and then I thought, perhaps he can't remember, either ...." (WC 219).

you let Dora Chance ... tell you a tale" (WC 227). Extolling duality and twinship on a thematic level, *Wise Children* also creates a dialogic narrative perspective.

Replete with gaps, ambiguities and open endings, Carter's texts enhance the active participation of the reader.[141] In an interview with John Haffenden, Carter suggests that Fevvers' exclamation "I fooled you then" at the end of *Nights at the Circus* makes the reader "start inventing other fictions, things that might have happened": "It's inviting the reader to write lots of other novels for themselves .... It is not like saying that you should put away the puppets and close the box." [142] In *Wise Children* the happy ending is likewise not final, but one of these "pauses" in the "narratives of our lives" (WC 227), at which the reader may either stop or continue with the invention of further stories. In *Expletives Deleted* Carter comments on the power of narrative to put off finality and death: "... the end of all stories ... is death, which is where our time stops short. Sheherezade knew this, which is why she kept on spinning another story out of bowels of the last one ....".[143] Carter refers to a Balinese burial ritual which employs the power of narrative to protect the deceased from demons.[144] She devotes *Expletives Deleted* to storytelling and the "strategies writers have devised to cheat the inevitability of closure, to chase away the demons, to keep them away for good".[145] Coded in the temporal medium of language, narrative is subjected to time: the syntagmatic chain of language visualises the flow of time. Yet at the same time narrative has the power to subvert time, to speed it up, slow it down and bring it to a standstill:

---

[141] In *Heroes and Villains, The Magic Toyshop*, and *The Passion of New Eve* the reader may choose his/her own way of reading the highly ambivalent, open endings which conflate images of birth and death, hope and despair. Carter's texts may be considered to carry features of the 'writerly' text as Barthes has defined it. The writerly text is a plural, open text which is ambiguous to such an extent that the reader is "no longer a consumer, but a producer of the text". Barthes 1974, 4.

[142] Haffenden 1985, 90-91. As Carter reports, Paul Bailey was particularly intrigued by the suggestiveness of her fiction, by the way in which an "entire novel" may be contained in certain 'throwaway lines' in *Nights at the Circus*. Bailey refers to the novel's aside on Walser having gone through a "a sharp dose of buggery in a bedouin tent beside the Damascus road" (NC 10). See Carter in Haffenden 1985, 89.

[143] Carter 1992, 2.

[144] Ibid., 3. The Balinese read stories aloud for several days after they have prepared a corpse for burial. Containing tales within tales, these stories are believed to form a Chinese box, at the core of which the corpse is protected from the demons.

[145] Ibid..

> All writers are inventing a kind of imitation time when they invent the time in which a story unfolds, and they are playing a complicated game with our time, the reader's time, the time it takes to read a story. A good writer can make you believe time stands still.[146]

Freeze-framing and rewinding her narrative, Dora – like Perry and Lizzie (cf. V.5) – plays tricks on time. Jumping between past and presence, the text weaves one episode after another and thus demonstrates that origins (beginnings) are random and endings not final. Like the Hazard Clan which "wasn't at its last gasp" but turns out to be "bursting out in every direction" (WC 227), the narrative seems to proliferate at the very point when it is expected to fade out. Leaving the narrative thread to the reader, the text reaches beyond the novel's ending. The text as quilt, open, unfinished, a communal work in progress, creates a bond of continuity with the reader that symbolically transcends isolation and death.

2.5.2 Change and Repetition: Ending on a New Beginning

Wise Children has provoked diverse, diametrically opposed critical readings. Pointing to the tone of optimistic exuberance in Carter's late work, critics like Day, Müller and Deleyto read the novel in a celebratory way.[147] In contrast, Warner, Hanson and Britzolakis perceive a pessimistic defeatism as the major message beneath the comic surface of the text. In a fatalistic reading of the comic, Warner claims that "Carter clowned more and more ... because she saw ... that in her struggle for change she was losing ground ....".[148] These different readings of the text depend on diverging views of the novel's ending. Britzolakis suggests that *Wise Children* attempts to deflate British high culture and the Shakespeare myth, but finally ends up reinforcing this very myth in the reconciliation scene, which licenses a "reconstitution of the family under the sign of Shakespeare" at the end of the novel. *Wise Children*, she argues, may be read as the disillusioned attempt to make the best of the "failed ... hopes of the 1960s".[149] In a similar way, Hanson turns against a celebratory reading of Carter's novel, which in her view expresses a

---

[146] Carter 1992, 2.

[147] Deleyto celebrates the carnivalesque power of the narrative's ending in which Dora seems to be "laughing the whole of history and patriarchy away" (Deleyto 1995, 180). According to Day, *Wise Children* provides a utopian vision of a remodelled British society that dismantles old divisions of class, gender and race (Day 1998, 209). Müller points to the "optimistic philosophy of the novel" that embraces duality in a life-affirming way (Müller 1997, 145,147,227).

[148] Warner 1994, 253.

[149] Britzolakis 1997, 55.

disappointed will-to-change and emphasises the persistence of power: "It is a novel in which the principles of legitimacy and legitimation may be questioned, but in which the structures of both remain intact." Dora ends up as "little more than a pub bore".[150] The artists on the left side of the tracks are unable to leave their imprint on culture.

In fact, a pessimistic reading of the novel is suggested by the way in which the narrative's ending repeats the beginning. In contrast to *The Passion of New Eve* and *Nights at the Circus,* there is no reformation of masculinity in *Wise Children.* At the end of the novel, the wheel runs full circle: again, paternal failure produces illegitimate children, who will be raised in the absence of fathers. Suggesting a static, deterministic concept of history, the recurrence of the same may be read as an expression of a "sceptical Nietzschean pessimism"[151] that runs beneath the celebratory tone of the comedic ending.

However, as I have argued above, repetition also creates continuity and produces a female tradition of responsibility and care in the novel. Moreover, a closer look at the text reveals that the novel's ending does suggest a change in the power structure in the new generation: in the end, the future of the Hazard dynasty lies in D/Nora's and Tiffany's hands, who will raise the Hazard's offspring. In a way the twins triumph over the legitimate Hazard Clan that will be submerged in the illegitimate branch of the family. Gareth's children will become part of the invented 'patchwork family' in the Chance tradition. The repressed heritage of British colonial history and class culture returns in a position of power at the end of the narrative: the black Tiffany metamorphoses from a tragic Ophelian figure into a self-confident, autonomous woman, who turns her back on Tristram. Turning things upside down, spilling "all the dirt on everybody" (WC 3), Dora's narrative itself represents the return of the repressed side of British upper-class identity. This return, however, is not a destructive, but a regenerative force in *Wise Children.* Invigorating the degenerating Hazard line, D/Nora's vitality will produce wise children. Against a fatalistic reading of the text, I would suggest that the novel celebrates a 'gentle', non-violent form of comic subversion that engages in the slow process of eroding boundaries through transgression. Even though *Wise Children* is sceptical about the liberatory power of the carnivalesque, it does not project a radical pessimism about the subversive potential of comedy. The novel's subversive strategy is reminiscent of Ritter's concept of the comic as modifying norms and challenging taboos and boundaries. Suggesting a gradual erasure of the border between the high and

---

[150] Hanson 1997, 70.
[151] Hanson 1997, 71.

the low, the utopian dimension of the text lies in its vision of a British identity that does not depend on the repression of its other. The end of the narrative does not only witness the decline of the degenerating Hazard Clan, but also suggests the creation of something new: the birth of a hybrid British culture which merges the legitimate and the illegitimate, the high and the low, black and white. Hence, the postmodern feature of the novel does not consist in a "sceptical Nietzschean pessimism" but in the joyful celebration of the decline of the 'great divide'.[152] Far from being pessimistic, the novel may be read as ending on a new beginning.

3. Conclusion

Ageing, Death and Beauty in Carter's Late Fiction

The subjective experience of the body resists representation. Elaine Scarry examines the difficulty of rendering pain visible in language. Pain has no object in contrast to other emotions like love and hatred.[153] While pain lacks referential content, death disrupts the very principle of representability. Peter Neumann conceives of death as a major challenge to modern aesthetics: how to depict an experience which denotes the very end of experience?[154] Carter employs two strategies to represent the liminal experiences of death and pain. On the one hand, the concrete bodily process of ageing is naturalistically depicted in its abject and humiliating implications. In *Wise Children* "Wheelchair" drastically demonstrates the helplessness and humiliations of old age. "The Quilt Maker" refers to Letty's incontinence, the smell of old age and the vomit of the dying cat. The middle-aged narrator notes the signs of mortality on her body: "... my skin fits less well than it did, my gums recede apace, I crumple like chiffon in the thigh" (BB 446). On the other hand, Carter works with contrast and approaches pain and death through images of life and beauty. In *Wise Children* comedy creates a protective space that enables the self to face painful experiences like ageing and mortality. Death and destruction are conveyed in the image of flowers popping up on bomb-sites: "... as if to say, life goes on, even if you don't" (WC 163). In "The Quilt maker" the evanescence of time is pictured in the cherry blossom in Letty's garden. Death is present in the wildness and beauty of nature.

---

[152] On the decline of the 'great divide' between high and low culture in postmodernism see also Andreas Huyssen, *After the Great Divide: Modernism, Mass Culture, Postmodernism*, Bloomington, 1986.
[153] Scarry 1985, 1-23.
[154] Neumann 1980, 1071-1080.

London is a "thin layer on top of a wilderness that pokes through the paving stones ... in tufts of grass and ragwort" (BB 446). The colourful, harmonious design of the 'patchwork story' itself offers solace and protection in the face of old age and death: "... this product of thrift and imagination, with which I hope to cover myself in my old age to keep my brittle bones warm" (BB 457). In "Impressions" the candle flame represents an objective correlative for the pain the narrator suffers in labour. Relating the woman's ordeal to Mary Magdalene's penitence, the story deals with liminal experiences of the body: birth and death, suffering, martyrdom and ecstasy. The blue, still space of the flame represents a space beyond language: the body overwhelming the self. Carter's fiction conveys the abstract, the unrepresentable and the terrifying through the sensuous and the beautiful, through blanks and absences in language. Offering solace and protection from death, images of beauty and stillness enable the self to contemplate its mortality. They create a double-voiced narrative and function as a bridge over the abyss of death.

"Nothing like real blood and flesh": the Lived Body in 'Wise Children'

Wise Children is Carter's first novel to depict a female body which is real, unfetishised and unreflected by a mirror, a body which is not meat but flesh:

> It was a shock to see her breasts under the cruel lights – long, heavy breasts, with big dark nipples, real breasts, not like the ones she'd shown off like borrowed finery to the glamour lenses. This was flesh, you could see that it would bleed, you could see how it fed babies. (WC 46)

The maternal body is neither grotesque nor engulfing but vulnerable: "flesh that would bleed". 'Real' blood occurs in the narrative when Nora loses her baby: "Nothing like real blood in the middle of a the song-and-dance act" (WC 81). The materiality of the body is conveyed in the image of the dancing body. In the process of dancing the self is identical with the 'body-we-are', which is turned into a source of pleasure. At the same time, dancing involves the disciplining of the 'body-we-have'. Like flying in *Nights at the Circus*, D/Nora's dancing skills are acquired through rigorous training and exercise. Dancing is hard work which pays the twins' living in the novel:

> ...we came home on the night tram, every bone in our body aching in concert and our feet burning, we girls half asleep, half awake, propping against one another, rain slashing the window, soaking our coats as we ran from the stop for home. ... we jumped away with low fevers and septic throats and influenza and the curse, jump, jump, jump, carrying on smiling, smilin' thru', show those teeth, kick those legs, tote that barge, lift that bale. (WC 75,76)

Dancing combines work and fun, pleasure, play and discipline. *Wise Children* conveys the experience of corporeality in its various, multi-faceted forms.

The body is experienced as the site of *jouissance*, exhaustion and pain. D/Nora's bodies are three-dimensional and brimming with life: "We can still lift a leg higher than your average dog ...." (WC 2). The twins enjoy their ageing bodies and display their "antique but not quite catastrophic legs with wild abandon" (WC 197). Grandma's maternal body, smelling of gin and cabbage, is likewise of an incontestable materiality that extends to fill the "whole of southern California" (WC 160). In contrast, Melchior dwindles and turns unreal at the end of the novel: "... like one of those ... papier-maché heads they have in the Notting Hill parade ...." (WC 230). It is no longer the female body but the patriarch who is revealed to be a cardboard construction in Carter's final novel. Woman has finally become an embodied self. The female subject emerges victorious from the long road of de- and reconstruction it has taken in Carter's fiction.

VII. Conclusion

Angela Carter rejected the Romantic notion of the writer as a vessel of the imagination and 'unconscious mediator' of her time.[1] For Carter writing is work – "endless endless rewrites" –, a product of patience and a means to make a living.[2] Carter's notion of the artist is reflected in the self-conscious, constructed nature of her fiction. As a student, she specialised in medieval literature, which foregrounds the character of art as *made* and creates an elaborate allegorical structure from a multiplicity of rhetorical figures.[3] The medieval writer is no *poeta vates*, no prophet or genius-creator, but a craftsman. The highly literate, intertextual eclecticism of Carter's work in the seventies makes her appear as the *poeta doctus*, the postmodern scriptor and the bricoleur, who ironically constructs the text from a variety of intertexts. The image of the picture-puzzle – the reconstructed Hollywood figures in *The Passion of New Eve* – seems to capture what Carter is doing in these works: her radical deconstructivism takes the Western literary tradition apart and reassembles it in fragmentary parodistic ways. Carter herself commented on the strong metafictional character of her work in the seventies: "I thought that writing, all fiction, really was about other fiction. ... And I would have regarded my own writing as a kind of elaborate form of literary criticism, and in some respects I still do."[4]

In the eighties, however, the *poeta doctus* metamorphoses into the quilt maker. Still highly literate, the quilt maker weaves high *and* low culture, written *and* oral discourses into a "crazy patchwork" (BB 444) of both intertextual and 'lived' experience. This change in Carter's fiction corresponds to her desire for a way of writing that approximates "more closely to the actual real circumstances of our lives".[5] As female household art, the patchwork is part of the lived experience of women. While the *poeta doctus* is indebted to a male, elitist tradition, quilt-making carries working-class connotations of thrift and hard work.[6] Put together in an intentional way,

---

[1] See Carter in Watts 1987, 164.

[2] In an interview with Kerryn Goldworthy, Carter commented on the writing process: "Endless rewrites. Endless endless endless. Longhand and typewriter – but, basically, endless endless rewrites, reworkings." Carter in Goldsworthy 1985, 7-9. On Carter's materialist concept of art see also VI.1.3.3.

[3] See Carter in Goldsworthy 1985, 12.

[4] Ibid., 5.

[5] Ibid.; cf. III.2.4.

[6] The narrator in "The Quilt Maker", who chooses the patchwork as a metaphor for life, appreciates these connotations: "Born and bred as I was in the Protestant north working-class tradition, I am pleased with the metaphor's overtones of thrift and hard work.

quilting still stands for a constructed and self-conscious form of fiction which starkly contrasts with conceptions of art as unconscious creation and 'spontaneous overflow of feeling'. Carter's notion of the female artist is radically different from both the 'masculine' Romantic aesthetic of art as vision and the feminist concept of *écriture féminine* that writes the body and the unconscious: it is unmistakably the brain, not the body that has written Carter's fiction.

Reflexivity, irony and intertextuality remain characteristic features of Carter's late work. In Carter's post-seventies fiction, however, a space of alterity emerges which is beyond irony and parody. This space of alterity is pictured in the white candle flame which subsumes the narrator in pain in "Impressions". It is present in the double-voiced style in *Wise Children* that continually seems to suggests more than has been articulated in the comic surface of the text. It is suggested by the burning tigers in *Nights at the Circus* and the utopia of desire that Carter inherits from Bataille (cf. V.7). A sense of Romantic vision creeps into the "crazy patchwork" of Carter's late writing.

It is this late work that concentrates on the lived experience of the female body. Carter's fiction in the seventies is written in the mode of alienation. Bodies are constructions designed by the combined forces of patriarchy and media technology. The novels preceding *Wise Children* employ the body as a metaphor. In *The Infernal Desire Machines* female bodies are elusive, shape-shifting apparitions, clockwork-driven machines or 'meat'. Disembodiment points to the absence of the female subject in patriarchal culture. Dissociating sex and gender, *The Passion of New Eve* decomposes the gendered body into its basic constituents and rearranges these constituents in arbitrary ways. The transsexual and transvestite bodies reveal the contingent nature of gender in the novel. *Nights at the Circus* is Carter's first text to depict the female body as a site of empowerment. Imparting a strong sense of physicality, Fevvers' monstrous body nevertheless remains a metaphor whose reality status is questionable: "Is she fact or is she fiction?" (NC 7). As a metaphor and a symbolic representation, the body is perceived from a distance. The allegorical mode eliminates the subjective experience of corporeality. In particular *The Infernal Desire Machines* and *The Passion of New Eve* elude the 'body-we-are' and deal exclusively with the 'body-we-have'. *Nights at the Circus* marks a change, introducing a powerful female subject into the narrative. In *Wise Children*, finally, a new concept of the 'lived body' emerges. It is no longer the constructed body, but the 'real' subjective experience of the ageing body which is the centre of attention. The female

---

Patchwork. Good." (BB 445). In America, by contrast, quilting has been practised by women of all classes and races. See Freedman 2002, 317 on quilting as female art form.

body has an irrefutable materiality which is the site of the narrating subject's identity.

While Carter rejects the Romantic notion of the artist, her work takes an ambivalent attitude to Romantic vision. Carter's fiction displays a tension between a Foucauldian scepticism and a utopian vision of liberation. This tension is reflected in her body politics. On the one hand, Carter's work dismantles essentialist conceptions of femininity to the point of obliterating the female body. It attacks an idealistic philosophy which is at the very root of Romanticism and reveals it to be a 'cannibalistic' philosophy that transmutes otherness into itself (cf. III.1.1). On the other hand, Carter's work is driven by a liberatory project that is indebted to Romanticism and aims at liberating woman's sexuality. It attacks the repression of the body and shares a deep-running sympathy with marginal groups, wild beasts and nature. While the 'visionary moment' grows stronger in the course of Carter's writing career, ambivalence is still present in the 'crazy patchwork' of Carter's late novels that combine the hopeful and the sceptical, the marvellous and the rational, the comic and the melancholic.

Carter's novels move from the reiteration of the same, from a claustrophobic confinement of women in narratives of male desire to the articulation of a female corporeality as radical difference. The changing meaning of the motif of the mirror may serve to illustrate this development. *The Infernal Desire Machines* and *The Passion of New Eve* reveal the female body in the mirror to be a figment of the male imagination. The novels focus on the silencing of women in patriarchal narratives. In Irigaray's sense the mirror represents an image for the masculine economy of sameness that negates a self-determined female corporeality. In Baudry's and Mulvey's sense the mirror refers to the cinematic screen which functions as a projection space for the male spectator's regressive desire. *The Passion of New Eve* traces the interpellation of the female subject through the cinematic apparatus. Several different discourses in Carter's work thus intersect in the mirror theme: her critique of male narcissism, of a phallogocentric signifying economy, of the cinema and other media, of panopticism and the Foucauldian gaze. Like the screen, the amber and the cage, the mirror epitomises containment. In *The Infernal Desire Machines* there is no outside of this containment. The narrative itself represents a mirror of Desiderio's mind, a reflecting surface which claustrophobically stifles the articulation of a female corporeality. *The Passion of New Eve*, by contrast, highlights the cracks and fissures within patriarchal representation. The novel steps through the looking glass and reveals the conditions of the production of the myth of woman. At the end of the text the mirror is cracked and loses its reflective power. The ending of the novel prepares for *Nights at the Circus* which stages the grotesque body that spills over the frame of the mirror and the voice that will not be confined within patriarchal narratives: "... she stretched herself suddenly and hugely, extending every muscle as a cat does, until it seemed she intended to fill up all the mirror, all the room with her bulk ...." (NC 52). Fevvers stages corporeality and narration in excess. The monstrous body epitomises the radical sense of alterity that emerges in Carter's fiction in the eighties. The mirror itself turns into a screen of alterity, merging with the burning Blakean tigers in the snowy wilderness of Siberia. The flat, reflecting surface of Carter's early novels is replaced by a sense of depth that transforms bodies from textual ciphers into three-dimensional entities. Eyes are no longer mere reflection screens but open an abyss of difference.

After the 'monstrous' female subject has been born in Carter's fiction in the eighties, the motif of the mirror undergoes a radical change of meaning in her final novel. In *Wise Children* woman appropriates the mirror. Repetition, sameness and reflection construct a powerful female identity. The mirror is no longer the symbol of a narcissistic economy of male desire in Irigaray's sense: the reflections of daughters, mothers and sisters create the image of a female tradition of solidarity and care which reproduces itself in the making of a female genealogy. This change in the meaning of the mirror is bound up with the adoption of the comic mode in Carter's late novels. The uncanny recurrence of the same – the proliferation of doubles and the repetitiveness of plot structure – is turned into a source of pleasure in *Wise Children*. Multiplying possibilities, duplications and reflections reinforce an autonomous identity and create a self-determined female subject. The mirror no longer imprisons the body, nor does it jeopardise the integrity of the self. In Carter's late fiction the body has outgrown the mirror. Having stepped out of the frame of the mirror, woman has become an embodied self.

I think it is befitting to end a study on Carter's fiction of speculation – "the fiction of asking 'what if'"[7] – not with an ending but with a speculation: what if Carter had not died in 1992? Eve's child lives on as Fevvers in *Nights at the Circus*. In fact – but this is pure speculation – may be Fevvers lives on in *Wise Children* as Grandma Chance: the New Woman at the beginning of the twentieth century, self-made, not born, "making a new start in a new

---

[7] See Carter in Katsavos 1994, 14: "Speculative fiction really means that, the fiction of speculation, the fiction of asking 'what if?' It's a system of continuing inquiry ." See also Chapter I, note 3.

place, a new century and ... a new name" (WC 26).[8] After her divorce from Walser, of course, and after she has shed her wings (which were, it goes without saying, a fake). Hence, it would be only consistent if the twins' life would feature in some form or another in Carter's fiction in the nineties. Perhaps just in a minor role. The twins are – and Dora stresses that this is new in the family – mixed. After woman is recreated as subject in Carter's late fiction, it might not be necessary anymore to send the male subject through various hoops of degradation. The male focalisation has moved to a female point of view in Carter's work in the eighties. Perhaps man and woman would both adopt a voice in Carter's fiction in the nineties. What would have happened to the body in Carter's fiction in the 21st century? The body grew more and more prominent in the course of Carter's writing. Carter's work moves from text to voice, from the image to the body. In *Wise Children* Dora's powerful voice merges the novelistic form with the oral immediacy of drama. Perhaps Carter would have turned away from the novel to a genre which lends itself to performance and reader/audience involvement in the nineties. Or, she might have kept to the novelistic form, turning to the writerly text in Barthes' sense, a radical indeterminate fiction that turns the reader not into a consumer but into a producer of a text.[9]

But probably she would have done something completely different. I would like to leave this question to the reader to continue weaving the thread Carter's final novel has left us with – to spin "another story out of the bowels of the last one"[10] and evade the death of narrative. Because, as Carter put it, "... the end of all stories ... is death, which is where our time stops short. .... we travel along the thread of narrative like high-wire artistes. That is our life."[11] In this sense I would like to pass the narrative thread to the reader and end this study with a new beginning.

---

[8] "She [Grandma Chance] liked to keep her secrets. I asked her once, where she came from herself and she said, "Out of a bottle, like a bloody genie, dearie" (WC 223).
[9] See Barthes 1974, 4. See also VI.2.5.1 note 141.
[10] Carter 1992, 2.
[11] Ibid.

Bibliography

I. Works by Angela Carter

Carter, Angela, *Shadow Dance*, London, 1966.

Carter, Angela, *The Magic Toyshop*, London, 1967.

Carter, Angela, *Heroes and Villains*, London, 1969.

Carter, Angela, *Love*, London, 1971; revised edition: London, 1987.

Carter, Angela, *The Infernal Desire Machines of Doctor Hoffman*, London, 1972.

Carter, Angela, *The Passion of New Eve*, London, 1977.

Carter, Angela, *The Sadeian Woman: an Essay in Cultural History*, London, 1979.

Carter, Angela, *Nothing Sacred: Selected Writings*, London, 1982.

Carter, Angela, "Notes from the Front Line", in: *On Gender and Writing*, ed. by Michelene Wandor, London, 1983, 69-77.

Carter, Angela, *Nights at the Circus*, London, 1984.

Carter, Angela, *Come Unto These Yellow Sands: Four Radio Plays*, Newcastle upon Tyne, 1985.

Carter, Angela, *Wise Children*, London, 1991.

Carter, Angela, *Expletives Deleted*, London, 1992.

Carter, Angela, *Burning Your Boats. Collected Short Stories*, London, 1996a.

Carter, Angela, *The Curious Room: Collected Dramatic Works*, London, 1996b.

Carter, Angela, *Shaking a Leg: Journalism and Writings*, London, 1997.

II. Other Works

Appleton Aguiar, Darah, *The Bitch is Back: Wicked Women in Literature*, Carbondale, 2001.

Ariès, Philippe, *L'homme devant la mort*, Paris, 1977.

Aristotle, *The Complete Works of Aristotle*, ed. by Jonathan Barnes, Princeton, 1984.

Ashenden, Samantha; Owen, David (eds.), *Foucault contra Habermas: Recasting the Dialogue between Genealogy and Critical Theory*, London, 1999.

Bakhtin, Mikhail, *The Dialogic Imagination*, trans. by Caryl Emerson and Michael Holquist, London, 1981.

Bakhtin, Mikhail, *Rabelais and His World*, trans. by Hélène Iswolsky, Bloomington, 1984.

Bannock, Sarah, "Auto/biographical Souvenirs in 'Nights at the Circus'", in: *The Infernal Desires of Angela Carter: Fiction, Femininity, Feminism*, ed. by Joseph Bristow and Trev Lynn Broughton, London, 1997, 198-215.

Barnes, Djuna, *Nightwood*, New York, 1961.

Barreca, Regina (ed.), *Last Laughs: Perspectives on Women and Comedy*, New York, 1988.

Barthes, Roland, *S/Z: An Essay*, trans. by Richard Miller, New York, 1974.

Barthes, Roland, *The Pleasure of the Text*, trans. by Richard Miller, London, 1976.

Barthes, Roland, *A Barthes Reader*, ed. by Susan Sontag, New York, 1982.

Barthes, Roland, *Mythologies*, trans. by Annette Lavers, New York, 1984.

Batailles, Georges, *L'érotisme*, Paris, 1965.

Baudrillard, Jean, *L'échange symbolique et la mort*, Paris, 1976.

Baudrillard, Jean, *America*, trans. by Chris Turner, London and New York, 1988.

Baudry, Jean-Louis, "Ideological Effects of the Basic Cinematographic Apparatus", in: *Narrative, Apparatus, Ideology: A Film Theory Reader*, ed. by Philip Rosen, New York, 1986, 286-298.

Bedford, William, "Interview", *New Yorkshire Writing 3*, Winter 1978, 1-2.

Benjamin, Jessica, "The Bonds of Love: Rational Violence and Erotic Domination", *Feminist Studies 6*, no. 1, Spring 1980, 144-74.

Benjamin, Jessica, *Die Fesseln der Liebe: Psychoanalyse, Feminismus und das Problem der Macht*, Frankfurt/Main, 1994.

Benjamin, Walter, "The Storyteller", in: *Illuminations*, trans. by Harry Zahn, New York, 1969.

Benjamin, Walter, *Das Kunstwerk im Zeitalter seiner technischen Reproduzierbarkeit*, Frankfurt/Main, 1981.

Bennett, Jane, "'How Is It, Then, That We Still Remain Barbarians?': Foucault, Schiller and the Aesthetization of Ethics", in: *Critical Essays on Foucault*, ed. by Karlis Racevskis, New York, 1999, 171-190.

Bergson, Henri, *Das Lachen: Ein Essay über die Bedeutung des Komischen*, Zürich, 1972.

Berry, Philippa, "The Burning Glass: Paradoxes of Feminist Revelation in 'Speculum'", in: *Engaging with Irigaray: Feminist Philosophy and Modern European Thought*, ed. by Carolyn L. Burke, Naomi Schor and Margaret Whitford, New York, 1994, 229-246.

Bettelheim, Bruno, *Kinder brauchen Märchen*, München, 1995.

Bettelheim, Bruno, *Les Contes de Perrault*, Paris, 1978.

Beutel, Manfred, *Bewältigungsprozesse bei chronischen Erkrankungen*, Weinheim, 1988.

Bhabha, Homi K., *The Location of Culture*, London, 1994.

Blake, William, *The Complete Writings*, ed. by Geoffrey Keynes, Oxford, 1966.

Blodgett, Harriet, "Fresh Iconography: Subversive Fantasy by Angela Carter", *The Review of Contemporary Fiction*, Fall 1994, 49-55.

Bloom, Harold, *The Anxiety of Influence*, New York, 1973.

Bloom, Lynn Z., "Heritages: Dimensions of Mother-Daughter Relationships in Women's Autobiographies", in: *The Lost Tradition: Mothers and Daughters in Literature*', ed. by Cathy N. Davidson, E. M. Broner, New York, 1980, 291-303.

Boehm, Beth A., "'Wise Children': Angela Carter's Swan Song", *The Review of Contemporary Fiction*, Fall 1994, 84-89.

Boehm, Beth A., "Feminist Metafiction and Androcentric Reading Strategies: Angela Carter's Reconstructed Reader in 'Nights at the Circus'", *Critique: Studies in Contemporary Fiction*, 37:1, Fall 1995, 35-49.

Bogue, Ronald, *Deleuze and Guattari*, London, 1989.

Bonca, Cornel, "In Despair of the Old Adams: Angela Carter's 'Infernal Desire Machines of Dr. Hoffman'", *The Review of Contemporary Fiction*, Fall 1994, 56-62.

Booker, M. Keith, *Techniques of Subversion in Modern Literature*, Florida, 1991.

Bordo, Susan, *The Flight to Objectivity*, New York, 1982.

Bordo, Susan, "The Body and the Reproduction of Femininity: A Feminist Appropriation of Foucault", in: *Gender/Body/Knowledge*, ed. by Alison M. Jaggar and Susan R. Bordo, New Brunswick and London, 1989, 13-29.

Bordo, Susan, *Unbearable Weight: Feminism, Western Culture and the Body*, Berkeley, Los Angeles and London, 1993.

Bradfield, Scott, "Remembering Angela Carter", *The Review of Contemporary Fiction*, Fall 1994, 90-95.

Brecht, Bertolt, *Arbeitsjournal*, Frankfurt/Main, 1973.

Bristow, Joseph; Broughton, Trev Lynn (eds.), *The Infernal Desires of Angela Carter: Fiction, Femininity, Feminism*, London, 1997.

Britzolakis, Christina, "Angela Carter's fetishism", in: *The Infernal Desires of Angela Carter: Fiction, Femininity, Feminism*, ed. by Joseph Bristow and Trev Lynn Broughton, London, 1997, 43-59.

Bronfen, Elisabeth, *Over Her Dead Body: Death, Femininity and the Aesthetic*, Manchester, 1992.

Brooks, Peter, *Reading for the Plot: Design and Intention in Narrative*, Oxford, 1984.

Brooks, Peter, *Body Work: Objects of Desire in Modern Narrative*, Havard, Cambridge and London, 1993.

Brown, Norman O., *Life Against Death: The Psychoanalytical Meaning of History*, Middletown, Connecticut, 1959.

Burke, Edmund, *A Philosophical Enquiry into the Origin of our Ideas of the Sublime and Beautiful*, London, 1958.

Butler, Judith, *Subjects of Desire: Hegelian Reflections in Twentieth-Century France*, New York, 1987.

Butler, Judith, *Gender Trouble: Feminism and the Subversion of Identity*, New York, 1990.

Butler, Judith, *Bodies that Matter: On the Discursive Limits of 'Sex'*, New York, 1993.

Butler, Judith, *The Psychic Life of Power: Theories in Subjection*, Stanford, 1997.

Chedgzoy, Kate, "The (Pregnant) Prince and the Showgirl: Cultural Legitimacy and the Reproduction of Hamlet", in: *New Essays on Hamlet*, ed. by Mark Thornton Burnett and John Manning, New York, 1994, 249-269.

Chodorow, Nancy, *The Reproduction of Mothering: Psychoanalysis and the Sociology of Gender*, Berkeley, 1978.

Cixous, Hélène, "The Laugh of the Medusa", 1976, trans. by Keith Cohen and Paula Cohen, reprinted in: *New French Feminisms: An Anthology*, ed. by Elaine Marks and Isabelle de Courtivron, Massachusetts, 1981, 245-264.

Cixous, Hélène, "Sorties: Out and Out: Attacks/Ways Out/Forays", in: *The Newly Born Woman*, ed. by Catherine Clement and Hélène Cixous, Minneapolis, 1986, 63-132.

Clark, Robert, "Angela Carter's Desire Machine", *Women's Studies: An Interdisciplinary Journal*, 14:2, 1987, 147-161.

Clement, Catherine, "The Guilty One", in: *The Newly Born Woman*, ed. by Catherine Clement and Hélène Cixous, Minneapolis, 1986, 1-59.

Cleland, John, *Fanny Hill or Memoirs of a Woman of Pleasure*, ed. by Geoffrey Sauer, Pittsburgh, 1996.

Coates, Paul, *The Double and the Other: Identity as Ideology in Post-Romantic Fiction*, Basingstoke, 1988.

Comolli, Jean-Louis, "Machines of the Visible", in: *The Cinematic Apparatus*, ed. by Teresa de Lauretis and Stephen Heath, New York, 1980, 121-143.

Connor, Steven, *The English Novel in History 1950-1955*, London and New York, 1996.

Conway, Daniel W., "Pas de deux: Habermas and Foucault in Genealogical Communication", in: *Foucault contra Habermas: Recasting the Dialogue between Genealogy and Critical Theory*, ed. by Samantha and David Owen, London, 1999, 60-89.

Copjec, Joan, *Read My Desire: Lacan against the Historicists*, Cambridge, Mass. and London, 1994.

Corea, Gena, *Mother Machines: Reproductive Technologies from Artificial Insemination to Artificial Wombs*, London, 1985.

Critchley, Simon; Bernasconi, Robert (eds.), *The Cambridge Companion to Levinas*, Cambridge and New York, 2002.

Crunelle-Vanrigh, Anny, "The Logic of the Same and Différance: 'The Courtship of Mr Lyon'", in: *Angela Carter and the Fairy Tale*, ed. by Danielle M. Roemer and Cristina Bacchilega, Detroit, 2001, 128-145.

Curti, Lidia, *Female Stories, Female Bodies. Narrative, Identity and Representation*, Basingstoke, 1998.

Dallery, A. B., "The Politics of Writing (the) Body: Écriture Feminine", in: *Gender/Body/Knowledge*, ed. by Alison M. Jaggar and Susan R. Bordo, New Brunswick and London, 1989, 52-67.

Daly, Mary, *Beyond God the Father: Toward a Philosophy of Women's Liberation*, Boston, 1973.

Davidson, Cathy N.; Broner, E. M. (eds.), *The Lost Tradition: Mothers and Daughters in Literature*, New York, 1980, 257-267.

Day, Aidan, *Angela Carter. The Rational Glass*, Manchester and New York, 1998.

Debord, Guy, *Die Gesellschaft des Spektakels*, Berlin, 1996.

De Lauretis, Teresa, *Alice Doesn't: Feminism, Semiotics, Cinema*, London, 1984.

Deleuze, Gilles, *Nietzsche and Philosophy*, New York, 1983.

Deleuze, Gilles; Guattari, Félix, *Anti-Oedipus: Capitalism and Schizophrenia*, trans. by Robert Hurley, Mark Seem and Helen R. Lane, London, 1983.

Deleuze, Gilles, *Foucault*, Frankfurt/Main, 1992.

Deleyto, Celestino, "'We Are No Angels': Woman versus History in Angela Carter's 'Wise Children'", in: *Telling Histories*, ed. by Susanna Onega, Amsterdam, 1995, 163-180.

Derrida, Jacques, *Of Grammatology*, trans. by Gayatri Chakravorty Spivak, Baltimore and London, 1974.

Derrida, Jacques, "The Purveyor of Truth", *Yale French Studies*, 52, 1975, 31-113.

Derrida, Jacques, *Writing and Difference*, trans. by Alan Bass, Chicago, 1978.

Derrida, Jacques, *Dissemination*, trans. by Barbara Johnson, Chicago, 1981.

Derrida, Jacques, *Margins of Philosophy*, trans. by Alan Bass, Chicago, 1982.

Derrida, Jacques, *Positionen*, ed. by Peter Engelmann, Wien, 1986.

Derrida, Jacques, "Circonfession", in: *Jacques Derrida*, ed. by Geoffrey Bennington and Jacques Derrida, Paris, 1991, 7-291.

Descartes, René, *A Discourse on Method*, London, 1975.

Desmond, William, *Desire, Dialectic, and Otherness: An Essay on Origins*, New Haven and London, 1987.

Desnos, Robert, *La liberté ou l'amour*, Paris, 1968.

Dietzsch, Steffen (ed.), *Luzifer lacht: Philosophische Betrachtungen von Nietzsche bis Tabori*, Leipzig, 1993.

Dinnerstein, Dorothy, *The Mermaid and the Minotaur: Sexual Arrangements and Human Malaise*, New York, 1999.

Doane, Mary Ann, *Femme Fatales: Feminism, Film Theory, Psychoanalysis*, New York, 1991.

Douglas, Mary, *Purity and Danger: An Analysis of Concepts of Pollution and Taboo*, London, 1966.

Dreyfus, Rabinow, *Jenseits von Strukturalismus und Hermeneutik*, Frankfurt/Main, 1987.

Duden, Barbara, "Die Frau ohne Unterleib: Zu Judith Butlers Entkörperung. Ein Zeitdokument", *Feministische Studien*, 2, 1993, 24-34.

Duden, Barbara, *Der Frauenleib als öffentlicher Ort: Vom Mißbrauch des Begriffs Leben*, Hamburg, 1991.

Duncker, Patricia, "Re-imagining the Fairy Tales: Angela Carter's 'The Bloody Chamber'", *Literature and History*, 10.1, Spring 1984, 3-14.

Dworkin, Andrea, *Pornography: Men Possessing Women*, London, 1981.

Eagleton, Terry, *The Ideology of the Aesthetic*, Oxford, 1990.

Easton, Alison (ed.), *Angela Carter: Contemporary Critical Essays*, Basingstoke, 2000.

Elias, Norbert, *Über den Prozeß der Zivilisation. Soziogenetische und psychogenetische Untersuchungen*, Bern, 1969.

Eliot, T. S., "The Waste Land", in: *T. S. Eliot. Collected Poems 1909-1962*, London, 1963, 61-87.

Engelmann, P., (ed.), *Philosophien: Gespräche mit M. Foucault, Jacques Derrida u. a.*, Wien, 1985.

Epstein, Julia; Straub, Kristina, *Body Guards: The Cultural Politics of Gender Ambiguity*, New York, 1991, 1-29.

Featherstone, Mike, "The Body in Consumer Culture", *Theory, Culture and Society*, 1982:1, 18-33.

Firestone, Shulamith, *The Dialectic of Sex*, London, 1970.

Fludernik, Monika, "Angela Carter's Pronominal Acrobatics: Language in 'The Erl King' and 'The Company of Wolves'", *European Journal of English Studies*, Vol. 2, No. 2, 1998, 215-237.

Foucault, Michel, *Madness and Civilization: A History of Insanity in the Age of Reason*, trans. by Richard Howard, New York, 1965.

Foucault, Michel, *Discipline and Punish: The Birth of the Prison*, trans. by Alan Sheridan, London, 1977.

Foucault, Michel, *Power/Knowledge: Selected Interviews and Other Writings 1972-1977*, New York, 1980.

Foucault, Michel, "Nietzsche, Genealogy, History", in: *The Foucault Reader*, ed. by Paul Rabinow, London, 1984, 76-100.

Foucault, Michel, *The Use of Pleasure: The History of Sexuality, Vol. 2*, trans. by Robert Hurley, London, 1985.

Foucault, Michel, "The Minimalist Self", in: *Michel Foucault: Politics, Philosophy, Culture*, ed. by L. Kritzman, New York and London, 1988a, 3-16.

Foucault, Michel, "An Aesthetics of Existence", in: *Michel Foucault: Politics, Philosophy, Culture*, ed. by L. Kritzman, New York and London, 1988b, 47-53.

Foucault, Michel, "The Return of Morality", in: *Michel Foucault: Politics, Philosophy, Culture*, ed. by L. Kritzman, New York and London, 1988c, 242-254.

Foucault, Michel, "The Concern for Truth", in: *Michel Foucault: Politics, Philosophy, Culture*, ed. by L. Kritzman, New York and London, 1988d, 255-267.

Foucault, Michel, *The History of Sexuality, Vol. 1: An Introduction*, trans. by Robert Hurley, New York, 1990.

Frank, Manfred, *Was ist Neostrukturalismus?*, Frankfurt/Main, 1984.

Fraser, Nancy, *Unruly Practices: Power, Discourse and Gender in Contemporary Social Theory*, Cambridge, 1989.

Freedman, Estelle B., *No Turning Back: the History of Feminism and the Future of Women*, London, 2002.

Freud, Sigmund, "Three Essays on the Theory of Sexuality", in: *The Standard Edition of the Complete Psychological Works*, Vol. 7, ed. and trans. by James Strachey, London, 1953a, 123-245.

Freud, Sigmund, "Family Romances", in: *The Standard Edition of the Complete Psychological Works*, Vol. 9, ed. and trans. by James Strachey, London, 1953b, 235-241.

Freud, Sigmund, "Totem and Taboo", in: *The Standard Edition of the Complete Psychological Works*, Vol. 13, ed. and trans. by James Strachey, London, 1953c, 1-162.

Freud, Sigmund, "On Narcissism: An Introduction", in: *The Standard Edition of the Complete Psychological Works*, Vol. 14, ed. and trans. by James Strachey, London, 1953d, 73-104.

Freud, Sigmund, "Instincts and their Vicissitudes", in: *The Standard Edition of the Complete Psychological Works*, Vol. 14, ed. and trans. by James Strachey, London, 1953e, 109-140.

Freud, Sigmund, "Mourning and Melancholia" in: *The Standard Edition of the Complete Psychological Works*, Vol. 14, ed. and trans. by James Strachey, London, 1953f, 243-258.

Freud, Sigmund, "Thoughts for the Times on War and Death", in: *The Standard Edition of the Complete Psychological Works*, Vol. 14, ed. and trans. by James Strachey, London, 1953g, 275-302.

Freud, Sigmund, "The Uncanny", in: *The Standard Edition of the Complete Psychological Works*, Vol. 17, ed. and trans. by James Strachey, London, 1953h, 219-252.

Freud, Sigmund, "Beyond the Pleasure Principle", in: *The Standard Edition of the Complete Psychological Works*, Vol. 18, ed. and trans. by James Strachey, London, 1953i, 7-64.

Freud, Sigmund, "The Ego and the Id", in: *The Standard Edition of the Complete Psychological Works*, Vol. 19, ed. and trans. by James Strachey, London, 1953j, 3-63.

Freud, Sigmund, "Civilization and its Discontents", in: *The Standard Edition of the Complete Psychological Works*, Vol. 21, ed. and trans. by James Strachey, London, 1953k, 59-151.

Freud, Sigmund, "Humour" in: *The Standard Edition of the Complete Psychological Works*, Vol. 21, ed. and trans. by James Strachey, London, 1953m, 159-166.

Freud, Sigmund, "Negation", in: *General Psychoanalytical Theory*, ed. by Philip Rieff, New York, 1963.

Freud, Sigmund, *Wit and its Relation to the Unconscious*, trans. by A. A. Brill, New York, 1993.

Frye, Northope, *Anatomy of Criticism: Four Essays*, Princeton, 1957.

Frye, Northope, "Romance as Masque", in: *Shakespeare's Romances Reconsidered*, ed. by Carol McGinnis Kay and Henry E. Jacobs, Lincoln, 1978, 11-40.

Fussell, Paul, *Abroad: British Literary Traveling Between the Wars*, New York, Oxford, 1980.

Gagnier, Regenia, "Between Women: a Cross-Class Analysis of Status and Anarchic Humour", in: *Last Laughs: Perspectives on Women and Comedy*, ed. by Regina Barreca, New York, 135-148.

Gallop, Jane, *The Daughter's Seduction: Feminism and Psychoanalysis*, Ithaca, New York, 1982.

Gallop, Jane, *Thinking Through The Body*, New York, 1988.

Gamble, Sarah, *Angela Carter: Writing from the Front Line*, Edinburgh, 1997.

Garber, Marjorie, *Vested Interests: Cross-Dressing & Cultural Anxiety*, New York & London, 1992.

Garfinkel, Harold, *Studies in Ethnomethodology*, Princeton, 1967.

Gasiorek, Andrzej, *Post-war British Fiction: Realism and After*, London and New York, 1995.

Gass, Joanne M., "Panopticism in 'Nights at the Circus'", *The Review of Contemporary Fiction*, Fall 1994, 71-76.

Giddens, Anthony, *Modernity and Self-Identity*, Cambridge, 1991.

Gilbert, Sandra; Gubar, Susan, *The Madwoman in the Attic*, New Haven, 1984.

Gilbert, Sandra, "Costumes of the Mind: Transvestism as Metaphor in Modern Literature", in: *Gender Studies*, ed. by Judith Spector, Athens, Ohio, 1986.

Girard, René, *La violence et le sacré*, Paris, 1972.

Goetsch, Paul, *Monsters in English Literature: From the Romantic Age to the First World War*, Frankfurt/Main, 2002.

Goffman, Erving, *Behavior in Public Places*, New York, 1963.

Goldsworthy, Kerryn, "Angela Carter. An Interview", *Meanjin*, March 1985, 4-13.

Goodchild, Philip, *Deleuze and Guattari: an Introduction to the Politics of Desire*, London, 1996.

Goodheart, Eugene, *Desire and its Discontents*, New York, 1991.

Greiner, Bernhard, *Die Komödie*, Tübingen, 1992.

Grosz, Elizabeth, *Volatile Bodies: Toward a Corporeal Feminism*, Bloomington and Indianapolis, 1994.

Habermas, Jürgen, *Der philosophische Diskurs der Moderne*, Frankfurt/Main, 1985.

Habermas, Jürgen, "The New Obscurity: The Crisis of the Welfare State and the Exhaustion of Utopian Energies", in: *The New Conservatism: Cultural Criticism and the Historians' Debate*, ed. by Sherry Weber Nicholson, Cambridge, 1991, 48-70.

Habermas, Jürgen, "Modernity: An Unfinished Project", in: *Habermas and the Unfinished Project of Modernity*, ed. by Maurizio Passerin d'Entrèves and Seyla Benhabib, Cambridge, 1996, 38-55.

Habermeier, Steffi, *Science, Gender, Text*, Essen 1996, 161-193.

Haffenden, John, *Novelists in Interview*, London, 1985, 76-96.

Han, Byung-Chul, *Todesarten: Philosophische Untersuchungen zum Tod*, München, 1998.

Hanson, Clare, "'The Red Dawn Breaking over Clapham': Carter and the Limits of Artifice", in: *The Infernal Desires of Angela Carter: Fiction, Femininity, Feminism*, ed. by Joseph Bristow and Trev Lynn Broughton, London, 1997, 59-73.

Haraway, Donna, *Simians, Cyborgs, and Women: The Reinvention of Nature*, New York, 1991.

Hardin, Michael, "The Other Other: Self-Definition Outside Patriarchal Institutions in Angela Carter's 'Wise Children'", *The Review of Contemporary Fiction*, Fall 1994, 77-83.

Hark, Sabine, "Queer Interventionen", *Feministische Studien*, 2, 1993, 103-109.

Harpham, Geoffrey Galt, *On the Grotesque*, Princeton, 1982.

Hartsock, Nancy, "Foucault on Power: A Theory for Women?" in: *Feminism/Postmodernism*, ed. by Linda Nicholson, New York, 1990, 157-175.

Hegel, G. W. F., *The Philosophy of History*, trans. by J. Sibree, New York, 1956.

Hegel, G. W., F., *Phänomenologie des Geistes*, Hamburg, 1988.

Heidegger, Martin, *An Introduction to Metaphysics*, trans. by Ralph Manheim, New Haven, 1959.

Heidegger, Martin, *Being and Time*, trans. by John Macquarrie and Edward Robinson, New York, 1962.

Heidegger, Martin, "Wissenschaft und Besinnung", in: ders., *Vorträge und Aufsätze*, Pfullingen, 1978, 41-66.

Heilbrun, Carolyn G., *Toward a Recognition of Androgyny*, Toronto, 1973.

Heinrich, Klaus, "Theorie des Lachens", in: *Karikaturen*, ed. by K. Herding, G. Otto, Gießen, 1980, 12-31.

Herdman, John, *The Double in Nineteenth-Century Fiction*, London, 1990.

Heywood, Leslie, *Dedication to Hunger: the Anorexic Aesthetic in Modern Culture*, Berkeley, 1996.

Hildenbrock, Aglaja, *Das andere Ich: künstlicher Mensch und Doppelgänger in der deutsch- und englischsprachigen Literatur*, Tübingen, 1986.

Hirsch, Marianne, *The Mother/Daughter Plot: Narrative, Psychoanalysis, Feminism*, Bloomington and Indianapolis, 1989.

Hirschauer, Stefan, "Dekonstruktion und Rekonstruktion", in: *Feministische Studien*, 2, 1993a, 55-67.

Hirschauer, Stefan, *Die soziale Konstruktion der Transsexualität*, Frankfurt/Main, 1993b.

Hobbes, Thomas, *The English Works of Thomas Hobbes*, Vol. IV, London, 1840.

Hodge, Joanna, "Irigaray Reading Heidegger", in: *Engaging with Irigaray: Feminist Philosophy and Modern European Thought*, ed. by Carolyn L. Burke, Naomi Schor, and Margaret Whitford, New York, 1994, 191-211.

hooks, bell, *Yearning: Race, Gender, and Cultural Politics*, Boston, 1990.

Horkheimer, Max; Adorno, Theodor W., *Dialectic of Enlightenment*, trans. by John Cumming, London and New York, 1997.

Husserl, Edmund, *Ideas Pertaining to a Pure Phenomenology and to a Phenomenological Philosophy*, trans. by R. Rojcewicz and A. Schuwer, Dordrecht, 1989.

Hutcheon, Linda, *A Poetics of Postmodernism*, London, 1988.

Hutcheon, Linda, *A Politics of Postmodernism*, London, 1989.

Huyssen, Andreas, *After the Great Divide: Modernism, Mass Culture, Postmodernism*, Bloomington, 1986.

Irigaray, Luce, "And the One Doesn't Stir without the Other", trans. by Hélène Vivienne Wenzel, *Signs*, Autumn 1981a, 60-67.

Irigaray, Luce, *Le corps-à-corps avec la mère*, Ottawa, 1981b.

Irigaray, Luce, *Éthique de la Différence Sexuelle*, Paris, 1984.

Irigaray, Luce, *Speculum of the Other Woman*, trans. by Gillan C. Gill, Ithaca, New York, 1985a.

Irigaray, Luce, *This Sex Which is Not One*, trans. by Catherine Porter with Carolyn Burke, New York, 1985b.

Irigaray, Luce, *Genealogie der Geschlechter*, Freiburg, 1989.

Irigaray, Luce, "The Bodily Encounter with the Mother", in: *The Irigaray Reader*, ed. by M. Whitford, Oxford, 1991a, 34-47.

Irigaray, Luce, "Questions to Emmanuel Levinas", in: *The Irigaray Reader*, ed. by M. Whitford, Oxford, 1991b, 178-189.

Iser, Wolfgang, *Der Akt des Lesens: Theorie ästhetischer Wirkung*, München, 1994, 257-355.

Jameson, Frederic, *Postmodernism, or, the Cultural Logic of Late Capitalism*, Durham, 1991.

Jauss, Hans Robert, "Über den Grund des Vergnügens am komischen Helden", in: *Das Komische*, ed. by W. Preisendanz; R. Warning, München, 1976, 103-133.

Johnson, D. H., "The Body: Which one? Whose?", *Whole Earth Review*, Summer 1989.

Johnson, Heather, "Textualizing the Double-Gendered Body: Forms of the Grotesque in 'The Passion of New Eve'", *The Review of Contemporary Fiction*, Fall 1994, 43-48.

Johnson, Heather, "Unexpected Geometries: Transgressive Symbolism and the Transsexual Subject in Angela Carter's 'The Passion of New Eve'", in: *The Infernal Desires of Angela Carter. Fiction, Femininity, Feminism*, ed. by Joseph Bristow and Trev Lynn Broughton, London, 1997, 166-183.

Jordan, Elaine, "Enthralment: Angela Carter's Speculative Fiction", in: *Plotting Change: Contemporary Women's Fiction*, ed. by Linda Anderson, London, 1990, 19-40.

Jordan, Elaine, "The dangers of Angela Carter", in: *New Feminist Discourse: Critical Essays on Theories and Texts*, ed. by Isobel Armstrong, London, 1992.

Jordan, Neil (dir.), *The Company of Wolves*, ITC Entertainment/Palace Production, 1984.

Jouve, Nicole Ward, "Mother is a Figure of Speech", in: *Flesh and the Mirror. Essays on the Art of Angela Carter*, ed. by Lorna Sage, London, 1994, 136-170.

Joyce, James, *Ulysses*, New York, 1961.

Judovitz, Dalia, *The Culture of the Body: Genealogies of Modernity*, Ann Arbor, 2001.

Jurzik, Renate, *Der Stoff des Lachens: Studien über Komik*, Frankfurt/Main, 1985.

Kamper, Dietmar; Wulf, Christoph (eds.), *Lachen-Gelächter-Lächeln: Reflexionen in drei Spiegeln*, Frankfurt/Main, 1986.

Kamper, Dietmar; Wulf, Christoph (eds.), *Die Wiederkehr des Körpers*, Frankfurt/Main, 1982.

Kappeler, Susanne, *The Pornography of Representation*, Cambridge, 1986.

Katsavos, Anna, "An Interview with Angela Carter", *The Review of Contemporary Fiction*, Fall 1994, 11-17.

Kaveney, Roz, "New New World Dreams: Angela Carter and Science Fiction", in: *Flesh and the Mirror: Essays on the Art of Angela Carter*, ed. by Lorna Sage, London, 1994, 171-189.

Keenan, Sally, *From Myth to Memory: The Revisionary Writing of Angela Carter, Maxine Hong Kingston & Toni Morrison*, Essex U, 1992, 1-122.

Keenan, Sally, "Angela Carter's 'The Sadeian Woman': Feminism as Treason", in: *The Infernal Desires of Angela Carter. Fiction, Femininity, Feminism*, ed. by Joseph Bristow and Trev Lynn Broughton, London, 1997, 132-149.

Keppler, C. F., *The Literature of the Second Self*, Tucson, 1972.

Kermode, Frank, *The Sense of an Ending: Studies in the Theory of Fiction*, London, 1966.

Kessler, S. J.; McKenna, W., *Gender: An Ethnomethodological Approach*, New York, 1978.

Kilgour, Maggie, *From Communion to Cannibalism: An Anatomy of Metaphors of Incorporation*, Princeton, 1990.

Klein, Melanie, *The Selected Melanie Klein*, ed. by Juliet Mitchell, Harmondsworth, 1986.

Klein, Naomi, *No Logo*, London, 2000.

Koch, Gertrud, "Netzhautsex - Sehen als Akt", in: *Die nackte Wahrheit: Zur Pornographie und zur Rolle des Obszönen in der Gegenwart*, ed. by Barbara Vinken, München, 1997, 114-129.

Köhler, Stefanie, *Differentes Lachen: Funktion, Präsentation und Genderspezifik der Ridicula im zeitgenössischen englischen Roman*, Tübingen, 1997.

Koenen, Anne, *Visions of Doom, Plots of Power: the Fantastic in Anglo-American Women's Literature*, Frankfurt/Main, 1999.

Konitzer, Martin, *Wilhelm Reich zur Einführung*, Hamburg, 1987.

Korte, Barbara, *Body Language in Literature*, Toronto, Buffalo, 1997.

Koschorke, Albrecht, "Die zwei Körper der Frau", in: *Die nackte Wahrheit: Zur Pornographie und zur Rolle des Obszönen in der Gegenwart*, ed. by Barbara Vinken, München, 1997, 66-92.

Kramer Linkin, Harriet, "'Isn't It Romantic?' Angela Carter's Bloody Revision of the Romantic Aesthetic in ' The Erl-King'", in: *Critical Essays on Angela Carter*, ed. by Lindsey Tucker, New York, 1998, 119-134.

Krapp, Peter, "Auf die Zunge beißen: Zur Kannibalischen Kommunikation", in: *Verschlungene Grenzen: Anthropophagie in Literatur und Kulturwissenschaften*, Tübingen, 1999, 345-359.

Kristeva, Julia, *Desire in Language. A Semiotic Approach to Literature and Art*, ed. by Leon Roudiez, trans. by Thomas Gora, Alice Jardine and Leon Roudiez, New York, 1980.

Kristeva, Julia, *Powers of Horror: An Essay on Abjection*, trans. by Leon Roudiez, New York, 1982.

Kristeva, Julia, *Revolution in Poetic Language*, trans. by Margaret Waller, New York, 1984.

Kristeva, Julia, *Black Sun: Depression and Melancholia*, trans. by Leon Roudiez, New York, 1989.

Kröll, Katrin, "Die Komik des grotesken Körpers in der christlichen Bildkunst des Mittelalters: Eine Einführung", in: *Mein ganzer Körper ist Gesicht. Groteske Darstellungen in der europäischen Kunst und Literatur des Mittelalters*, ed. by K. Kröll and H. Steger, Freiburg, 1994, 11-94.

Kutschman, Werner, *Der Naturwissenschaftler und sein Körper*, Frankfurt/Main, 1986.

Lacan, Jacques, "Les Quatre Concepts Fondamentaux de la Psychanalyse", in: *Le Séminaire de Jacques Lacan*, Livre XI, ed. by Jacques-Alain Miller, Paris, 1973.

Lacan, Jacques, *Écrits: A Selection*, trans. by Alan Sheridan, New York, London, 1977.

Laqueur, Thomas, *Making Sex: Body and Gender from the Greeks to Freud*, Cambridge, Mass. and London, 1990.

Lasch, Christopher, *The Culture of Narcissism*, New York, 1978.

Lee, Alison, "Angela Carter's New Eve(lyn): De/En-Gendering Narrative", in: *Ambiguous Discourse: Feminist Narratology and British Women Writers*, ed. by Kathy Mezei, Chapel Hill & London, 1996, 238-249.

Levin, David Michael, *The Opening of Vision: Nihilism and the Postmodern Situation*, New York and London, 1988.

Levinas, Emmanuel, *Collected Philosophical Papers*, trans. by Alphonso Lingis, The Hague, 1987.

Levinas, Emmanuel, *Emmanuel Levinas: Basic Philosophical Writings*, ed. by A. Peperzak, S. Critchley and R. Bernasconi, Bloomington, 1996.

Lévi-Strauss, Claude, *The Savage Mind*, trans. by Weidenfeld and Nicolson, London, 1966.

Levy, Barbara, *Ladies Laughing: Wit as Control in Contemporary American Women Writers*, Amsterdam, 1997.

Lewallen, Avis, "'Wayward Girls but Wicked Women?' Female Sexuality in Angela Carter's 'The Bloody Chamber'", in: *Perspectives on Pornography: Sexuality in Film and Literature*, ed. by Gary Day and Clive Bloom, Basingstoke and London, 1988, 144-58.

Lindemann, Gesa, "Wider die Verdrängung des Leibes aus der Geschlechtskonstruktion", *Feministische Studien*, Heft 2, 1993, 44-55.

Lorey, Isabell, "Der Körper als Text und das aktuelle Selbst: Butler und Foucault", *Feministische Studien*, Heft 2, 1993, 10-24.

Lukács, Georg, *Die Theorie des Romans: Ein geschichtsphilosophischer Versuch über die Formen der großen Epik*, München, 1994.

MacDonald, Susan Peck, "Jane Austen and the Tradition of the Absent Mother", in: *The Lost Tradition: Mothers and Daughters in Literature*, ed. by Cathy N. Davidson and E. M. Broner, New York, 1980, 58-70.

Maglin, Nan Bauer, "'Don't never forget the bridge that you crossed over on': the Literature of Matrilineage", in: *The Lost Tradition: Mothers and Daughters in Literature*, ed. by Cathy N. Davidson and E. M. Broner, New York, 1980, 257-267.

Makinen, Merja, "Sexual and Textual Aggression in 'The Sadeian Woman' and 'The Passion of New Eve'", in: *The Infernal Desires of Angela Carter. Fiction, Femininity, Feminism*, ed. by Joseph Bristow and Trev Lynn Broughton, London, 1997, 149-165.

Makinen, Merja, "The Decolonisation of Feminine Sexuality", in: *Angela Carter: Contemporary Critical Essays*, ed. by Alison Easton, Basingstoke, 2000, 20-37.

Manlove, Colin, "'In the Demythologising Business': Angela Carter's 'The Infernal Desire Machines of Dr Hoffman'", in: *Twentieth-Century Fantasies*, ed. by Kath Filmer, Basingstoke, 1992, 148-160.

Marcuse, Herbert, *Eros and Civilization*, New York, 1955.

Marcuse, Herbert, *Triebstruktur und Gesellschaft: Ein philosophischer Beitrag zu Sigmund Freud*, Frankfurt/Main, 1984.

Marcuse, Herbert, *One-Dimensional Man: Studies in the Ideology of Advanced Industrial Society*, Boston, 1991.

Mare, Walter de la, *Memoirs of a Midget*, Oxford, 1982.

Mars-Jones, Adam, "From Wonders to Prodigies", *Times Literary Supplement*, Sept. 28, 1984, 1083.

Marx, Karl, *Writings of the Young Marx on Philosophy and Society*, New York, 1967.

McHale, Brian, *Postmodernist Fiction*, New York, 1987.

Meaney, Gerardine, *(Un)like Subjects: Women, Theory, Fiction*, London and New York, 1993.

Megill, Alan, *Prophets of Extremity: Nietzsche, Heidegger, Foucault, Derrida*, Berkeley, 1985, 247.

Merchant, Carolyn, *The Death of Nature: Women, Ecology and the Scientific Revolution*, New York, 1980.

Merleau-Ponty, Maurice, *Phénoménologie de la perception*, Paris, 1945.

Metz, Christian, "The Imaginary Signifier", in: *Narrative, Apparatus, Ideology: A Film Theory Reader*, ed. by Philip Rosen, New York, 1986, 244-278.

Michael, Magali Cornier, "Angela Carter's 'Nights at the Circus': An Engaged Feminism via Subversive Postmodern Strategies", *Contemporary Literature*, Vol. 35, no. 3, 1994, 492-521.

Mikkonen, Kai, *The Writer's Metamorphosis: Tropes of Literary Reflection and Revision*, Tampere, Finland, 1997.

Miller, Nancy K., "Arachnologies: the Woman, the Text, and the Critic." in: *Subject to Change*, ed. by Nancy K. Miller, New York, 1988, 77-101.

Minson, Jeff, "Strategies for Socialists? Foucault's Conception of Power", in: *Towards a Critique of Foucault*, ed. by Mike Gane, London, 1986.

Mortensen, Ellen, "Woman's Untruth and *le féminin*: Reading Luce Irigaray with Nietzsche and Heidegger", in: *Engaging with Irigaray: Feminist Philosophy and Modern European Thought*, ed. by Carolyn L. Burke, Naomi Schor and Margaret Whitford, New York, 1994, 211-229.

Morris, David B., *The Culture of Pain*, Berkeley, Los Angeles, London, 1991.

Moser, Dietz-Rüdiger, "Lachkultur des Mittelalters? Michail Bachtin und die Folgen seiner Theorie", *Euphorion* 84, 1990, 89-111.

Moss, Betty, "Desire and the Female Grotesque in Angela Carter's 'Peter and the Wolf'", in: Danielle M. Roemer and Cristina Bacchilega, *Angela Carter and the Fairy Tale*, Detroit, 2001, 187-204.

Müller, Anja, *Identity Constructed/Deconstructed*, Heidelberg, 1997.

Mulvey, Laura, "Visual Pleasure and Narrative Cinema", 1975, in: *Contemporary Literary Criticism: Literary and Cultural Studies*, ed. by Robert Con Davis and Ronald Schleifer, 1994, New York, 421-431.

Neumann, Peter Horst, "Die Sinngebung des Todes als Gründungsproblem der Ästhetik", *Merkur 11*, 1980, 1071-1080.

Nietzsche, Friedrich, *On the Genealogy of Morals and Ecce Homo*, trans. by Walter Kaufmann, New York, 1967.

Nietzsche, Friedrich, *Jenseits von Gut und Böse*, München, 1990.

Norris, Christopher, *Spinoza and the Origins of Modern Critical Theory*, Oxford, 1991.

Nussbaum, Martha, "The Professor of Parody", *The New Republic: a Journal of Politics and the Arts*, Febr. 1999, 1-22.

O'Day, Marc, "'Mutability is Having a Field Day': the Sixties Aura of Angela Carter's Bristol Trilogy", in: *Flesh and the Mirror: Essays on the Art of Angela Carter*, ed. by Lorna Sage, London, 1994, 24-60.

Olson, Greta, *Reading Eating Disorders: Literary Accounts of Anorexia and Bulimia within the Context of American Culture*, Frankfurt/Main, 2003.

Ortner, Sherry, "Is Female to Nature as Male is to Culture?" in: *Woman, Culture and Society*, ed. by Michelle Zibalist Rosaldo and Loise Lamphère, Stanford, 1974, 67-87.

Osborne, Thomas, "Critical Spirituality: On Ethics and Politics in the Later Foucault", in: *Foucault contra Habermas*, ed. by Samantha Ashenden & David Owen, London, 1999, 45-60.

Overall, Christine, *Ethics and Human Reproduction: A Feminist Analysis*, Boston, 1987.

Palmer, Paulina, "From Coded Mannequin to Bird Woman: Angela Carter's Magic Flight", in: *Women Reading Women's Writing*, ed. by Sue Roe, Brighton, 1987, 179-205.

Palmer, Paulina, "Gender as Performance in the Fiction of Angela Carter and Margaret Atwood", in: *The Infernal Desires of Angela Carter. Fiction, Femininity, Feminism*, ed. by Joseph Bristow and Trev Lynn Broughton, London, 1997, 24-42.

Peach, Linden, *Angela Carter*, London, 1998.

Pearson, Roberta, "Early Cinema", in: *The Oxford History of World Cinema*, ed. by Geoffrey Nowell-Smith, Oxford, 1996, 13-23.

Pitchford, Nicola, *Redefining Postmodernism: Contemporary Feminist Fiction and Persistent Myths of Modernism*, U of Wisconsin-Madison, 1994.

Pitchford, Nicola, *Tactical Readings: Feminist Postmodernism in the Novels of Kathy Acker and Angela Carter*, Lewisburg, London, 2002.

Plato, *Plato's Erotic Dialogues: the Symposium and the Phaedrus*, trans. by William S. Cobb, Albany, 1993a.

Plato, *Republic*, trans. by Robin Waterfield, Oxford, New York, 1993b.

Plessner, Helmuth, *Philosophische Anthropologie*, Frankfurt/Main, 1970.

Poe, Edgar Allan, "The Philosophy of Composition", in: *Essays and Reviews*, New York, 1984.

Preschl, Claudia, "Geschlechterverhältnisse im Blickfeld von Liebe und Begehren. Ein Beitrag zum Kino", in: *The Body of Gender: Körper. Geschlechter. Identitäten*, ed. by Marie-Luise Angerer, Wien, 1995, 131-151.

Proust, Marcel, *A la recherche du temps perdu*, Paris, 1993.

Punter, David, "Angela Carter: Supersessions of the Masculine", *Critique: Studies in Modern Fiction*, Summer, 25, 4, 1984, 209-222.

Purdie, Susan, *Comedy: The Mastery of Discourse*, New York, 1993.

Raditsa, L., *Wilhelm Reich: Eine philosophisch-kritische Betrachtung*, Frankfurt/Main, 1987.

Rank, Otto, "Der Doppelgänger", in: *Imago*, Band III, 1914, reprint 1969, 97-164.

Reich, Wilhelm, *Die sexuelle Revolution*, Frankfurt/Main, 1971.

Reich, Wilhelm, *Der Einbruch der sexuellen Zwangsmoral: Zur Geschichte der sexuellen Ökonomie*, Köln, 1972.

Rhode, Eric, *A History of the Cinema from its Origins to 1970*, New York, 1976.

Rich, Adrienne, *Of Woman Born: Motherhood as Experience and Institution*, London, 1977.

Rich, Adrienne, *On Lies, Secrets, and Silence: Selected Prose 1966-1978*, New York, 1979.

Ritter, Joachim, *Subjektivität*, Frankfurt/Main, 1974.

Robinson, Sally, *Engendering the Subject: Gender and Self-Representation in Contemporary Women's Fiction*, New York, 1991.

Roe, Sue, "The Disorders of Love: Angela Carter's Surrealist Collage", in: *Flesh and the Mirror: Essays on the Art of Angela Carter*, ed. by Lorna Sage, London, 1994, 60-98.

Roemer, Danielle M.; Bacchilega, Cristina, *Angela Carter and the Fairy Tale*, Detroit, 2001.

Rosenberg, Ingrid v., "Angela Carter: Mistress of Voices", in: *(Sub)Versions of Realism - Recent Women's Fiction in Britain*, ed. by Irmgard Maassen and Anna Maria Stuby, Heidelberg, 1997.

Rousseau, Jean-Jacques, *Émile ou de l'éducation*, Paris, 1992.

Rowland, Robyn, *Living Laboratories: Women & Reproductive Technologies*, Bloomington and Indianapolis, 1992.

Rubenstein, Roberta, "Intersexions: Gender Metamorphosis in Angela Carter's 'The Passion of New Eve' and Lois Gould's 'A Sea-Change'", *Tulsa-Studies-in-Women's-Literature*, 12:1, Spring 1993, 103-118.

Russo, Mary, "Female Grotesques: Carnival and Theory", in: *Feminist Studies/Critical Studies*, ed. by Teresa de Lauretis, Wisconsin, 1986, 213-229.

Russo, Mary, *The Female Grotesque*, New York, 1994.

Sadoul, Georges, *Louis Lumière*, Paris, 1966.

Sage, Lorna, "The Savage Sideshow: a Profile of Angela Carter by Lorna Sage", *The New Review*, June/July 1977, 51-57.

Sage, Lorna, "Angela Carter Interviewed by Lorna Sage", in: *New Writing*, ed. by Malcolm Bradbury and Judith Cooke, London, 1992, 185-93.

Sage, Lorna, *Flesh and the Mirror. Essays on the Art of Angela Carter*, London, 1994.

Sandford, Stella, "Levinas, feminism and the feminine", in: *The Cambridge Companion to Levinas*, ed. by Simon Critchley and Robert Bernasconi, Cambridge, New York, 2002, 139-161.

Sartre, Jean-Paul, *Les Mots*, Paris, 1968.

Sawicki, Jana, *Disciplining Foucault: Feminism, Power, and the Body*, New York, 1991.

Scarry, Elaine, *The Body in Pain*, New York, 1985.

Sceats, Sarah, "The Infernal Appetites of Angela Carter", in: *The Infernal Desires of Angela Carter. Fiction, Femininity, Feminism*, ed. by Joseph Bristow and Trev Lynn Broughton, London, 1997, 100-116.

Sceats, Sarah, *Food, Consumption and the Body in Contemporary Women's Fiction*, Cambridge, 2000.

Schiebinger, Londa, *Nature's Body: Gender in the Making of Modern Science*, Boston, 1983.

Schiesari, Juliana, *The Gendering of Melancholia: Feminism, Psychoanalysis and the Symbolics of Loss in Renaissance Literature*, Ithaca and London, 1992.

Schmid, Susanne, *Jungfrau und Monster. Frauenmythen im englischen Roman der Gegenwart*, Berlin, 1996.

Schmid, Susanne, "Angela Carter: 'Mythomania and Demythologising'", in: *Myth and its Legacy in European Literature*, ed. by Neil Thomas and Françoise le Saux, Durham, 1996, 145-159.

Schmidt, Ricarda, "The Journey of the Subject in Angela Carter's Fiction", *Textual Practice*, 3:1, Spring 1989, 56-75.

Schotz, Myra Glazer, "The Great Unwritten Story: Mothers and Daughters in Shakespeare", in: *The Lost Tradition: Mothers and Daughters in Literature*, ed. by Cathy N. Davidson and E. M. Broner, New York, 1980, 44-54.

Sexton, Anne, *Transformations*, Boston, 1971.

Shakespeare, William, *King Lear. The Arden Edition of the Works of William Shakespeare*, ed. by Kenneth Muir, London, 1963.

Sharaf, Myron, *Fury on Earth: A Biography of Wilhelm Reich*, London, 1983.

Shilling, Chris, *The Body and Social Theory*, London, 1993.

Sobchack, Vivian, "Phenomenology and the Film Experience", in: *Viewing Positions: Ways of Seeing Film*, ed. by Linda Williams, New Brunswick, 1995, 36-58.

Spinoza, "Ethics", in: *The Collected Works of Spinoza*, ed. and trans. by Edwin Curley, Princeton, 1985, 408-617.

Spivak, Gayatri Chakravorty, *The Spivak Reader*, ed. by Donna Landry and Gerald MacLean, New York and London, 1996.

Stallybrass, Peter; White, Allon, *The Politics and Poetics of Transgression*, London, 1986.

Stott, Rebecca, *The Fabrication of the Late-Victorian 'Femme Fatale': The Kiss of Death*, Basingstoke, 1992.

Suleiman, Susan Rubin (ed.), *The Female Body in Western Culture*, Cambridge, Mass. and London, 1986.

Suleiman, Susan Rubin, *Subversive Intent: Gender, Politics and the Avant-Garde*, Harvard, 1990.

Suleiman, Susan Rubin, "The Fate of the Surrealist Imagination in the Society of the Spectacle", in: *Flesh and the Mirror. Essays on the Art of Angela Carter*, ed. by Lorna Sage, London, 1994, 136-170.

Swift, Jonathan, *Gulliver's Travels*, Harmondsworth, 1982.

Theweleit, Klaus, *Männerphantasien*, Basel, 1986.

Treusch-Dieter, Gerburg, "Barbie und Inzest: Das letzte Stadium der Körpermodellierung/Jeder ist der Antikörper des Anderen", *Aesthetik und Kommunikation: Körper - Antikörper*, 23, Okt. 1994, 22-27.

Tucker, Lindsey (ed.), *Critical Essays on Angela Carter*, New York, 1998.

Turner, Bryan S., *The Body and Society*, Oxford, 1984.

Turner, Bryan S., *Regulating Bodies: Essays in Medical Sociology*, London, 1992.

Turner, Rory P. B., "Subjects and Symbols: Transformations of Identity in 'Nights at the Circus'", *Folklore Forum*, 1987, 20:1-2, 39-60.

Tyler, Carole-Anne, "Boys Will Be Girls: The Politics of Gay Drag", in: *inside/out: Lesbian Theories, Gay Theories*, ed. by Diana Fuss, New York and London, 1991, 32-71.

Van Ghent, Dorothy, *The English Novel: Form and Function*, New York, 1953.

Vinken, Barbara, *Unentrinnbare Neugierde: Die Weltverfallenheit des Romans*, Freiburg, 1991.

Vinken, Barbara (ed.), *Die nackte Wahrheit: Zur Pornographie und zur Rolle des Obszönen in der Gegenwart*, München, 1997.

Waldenfels, Bernhard, *In den Netzen der Lebenswelt*, Frankfurt/Main, 1985.

Waldenfels, Bernhard, *Das leibliche Selbst: Vorlesungen zur Phänomenologie des Leibes*, ed. by Regula Giuliani, Frankfurt/Main, 2000.

Waldenfels, Bernhard, "Levinas and the Face of the Other", in: *The Cambridge Companion to Levinas*, ed. by Simon Critchley and Robert Bernasconi, Cambridge, New York, 2002, 63-82.

Wandor, Michelene (ed.), *On Gender and Writing*, London, 1983.

Warner, Marina, "Angela Carter: Bottle Blonde, Double Drag", in: *Flesh and the Mirror. Essays on the Art of Angela Carter*, ed. by Lorna Sage, London, 1994, 243-256.

Watney, Simon, *Policing Desire: Pornography, Aids and the Media*, London, 1987.

Watts, Helen Cagney, "Carter, Angela: An Interview with Helen Cagney Watts", *Bête Noire*, August 1987, 161-175.

Webb, Kate, "Seriously Funny: 'Wise Children'", in: *Flesh and the Mirror. Essays on the Art of Angela Carter*, ed. by Lorna Sage, London, 1994, 279-307.

West, Candance; Zimmermann, Don H., "Doing Gender", *Gender and Society*, Vol. I no. 2, 1987, 125-151.

White, Stephen, *The Cambridge Companion to Habermas*, Cambridge, 1995.

Williams, Linda, *Hard Core: Power, Pleasure & 'The Frenzy of the Visible'*, London, 1990.

Williams, Linda, *Critical Desire: Psychoanalysis and the Literary Subject*, New York, 1995.

Williamson, Judith, *Consuming Passions: The Dynamics of Popular Culture*, London, 1986.

Wilson, Robert Rawdon, "Slip Page: Angela Carter, In/Out/In the Postmodern Nexus", *A Review of International English Literature*, 20/4, October 1989, 96-114.

Wittig, Monique, *Le corps lesbien*, Paris, 1973.

Wittig, Monique, "The Straight Mind", *Feminist Issues,* Summer 1980, 103-111.

Woolf, Virginia, *Orlando*, New York, 1928.

Wulf, Christoph, "Körper und Tod", in: *Die Wiederkehr des Körpers*, ed. by Dieter Kamper and Christoph Wulf, Frankfurt/Main, 1982, 259-274.

Wyatt, Jean, "The Violence of Gendering: Castration Images in Angela Carter's 'The Magic Toyshop', 'The Passion of New Eve', and 'Peter and the Wolf'", in: *Angela Carter: Contemporary Critical Essays*, ed. by Alison Easton, Basingstoke, 2000, 58-84.

Zijderveld, Anton, "The Sociology of Humour and Laughter", *Current Sociology*, Vol. 31, Number 3, Winter 1983, 1-100.

Zylinska, Joanna (ed.), *The Cyborg Experiments: the Extensions of the Body in the Media Age*, London, New York, 2002.

NEUE STUDIEN ZUR ANGLISTIK UND AMERIKANISTIK

Band 1 Ingeborg Weber-Brandies: Virginia Woolfs "The Waves": Emanzipation als Möglichkeit des Bewußtseinsromans. 1974.

Band 2 Meinhard Winkgens: Das Zeitproblem in Samuel Becketts Dramen. 1975.

Band 3 Klaus Simonsen: Erzähltechnik und Weltanschauung in Samuel Butlers literarischen Werken "Erewhon Revisited" und "The Way of All Flesh". 1974.

Band 4 Renate Mann: Jane Austen: Die Rhetorik der Moral. 1975.

Band 5 Bernhard Reitz: Das Problem des historischen Romans bei George Eliot. 1975.

Band 6 Wolfgang Sänger: John Millington Synge: "The Aran Islands". Material und Mythos. 1976.

Band 7 Norbert Schmuhl: Erfahrungen des Aufbruchs: Zur Perspektivität und Aperspektivität in James Joyces "Ulysses". 1976.

Band 8 Reinhard Mischke: Launcelots allegorische Reise: Sir Thomas Malorys "Le Morte Darthur" und die englische Literatur des fünfzehnten Jahrhunderts. 1976.

Band 9 Kurt Müller: Konventionen und Tendenzen der Gesellschaftskritik im expressionistischen amerikanischen Drama der zwanziger Jahre. 1977.

Band 10 Ursula Schaefer: Höfisch-ritterliche Dichtung und sozialhistorische Realität: Literatursoziologische Studien zum Verhältnis von Adelsstruktur, Ritterideal und Dichtung bei Geoffrey Chaucer. 1977.

Band 11 Ewald Mengel: Harold Pinters Dramen im Spiegel der soziologischen Rollentheorie. 1978.

Band 12 Norbert Bolz: Eine statistische, computerunterstützte Echtheitsprüfung von "The Repentance of Robert Greene": Ein methodischer und systematischer Ansatz. 1978.

Band 13 Klaus Peter Jochum: Discrepant Awareness: Studies in English Renaissance Drama. 1979.

Band 14 Rudi Camerer: Die Schuldproblematik im Spätwerk von Charles Dickens. 1978.

Band 15 Peter Stapelberg: Sean O'Casey und das deutschsprachige Theater (1948-1974): Empirische Untersuchungen zu den Mechanismen der Rezeption eines angloirischen Dramatikers. 1979.

Band 16 Hans Ulrich Seeber: Moderne Pastoraldichtung in England: Studien zur Theorie und Praxis der pastoralen Versdichtung in England nach 1800 mit besonderer Berücksichtigung von Edward Thomas (1878-1917). 1979.

Band 17 Klaus Martens: Negation, Negativität und Utopie im Werk von Wallace Stevens. 1980.

Band 18 Angela Lorent: Funktionen der Massenszene im viktorianischen Roman. 1980.

Band 19 Rotraut Spiegel: Doris Lessing: The Problem of Alienation and the Form of the Novel. 1981.

Band 20 Edda Kerschgens: Das gespaltene Ich: 100 Jahre afroamerikanischer Autobiographie. Strukturuntersuchungen zu den Autobiographien von Frederick Douglas, Booker T. Washington und W.E.B. Du Bois. 1980.

Band 21 Josef Oswald: "The Discordant, Broken, Faithless Rhythm of Our Time": Eine Analyse der späten Dramen Eugene O'Neills. 1981.

Band 22 Dietrich Strauß: Die erotische Dichtung von Robert Burns: Bedingungen, Textüberlieferung, Interpretation, Wertungen. 1981.

Band 23 Jill Bonheim: Paul Scott: Humanismus und Individualismus in seinem Werk. 1982.

Band 24 Claudia Stehle: Individualität und Romanform: Theoretische Überlegungen mit Beispielen aus dem 19. Jahrhundert. 1982.

Band 25 Helga Stelzer: Narzißmus-Problematik und Spiegel-Technik in Joseph Conrads Romanen. 1983.

Band 50   Michael Meyer: Struktur, Funktion und Vermittlung der Wahrnehmung in Charles Tomlinsons Lyrik. 1990.

Band 51   Heinz Eikmeyer: Angst und Furcht in den Dramen Harold Pinters. 1990.

Band 52   Gerd Hurm: Fragmented Urban Images: The American City in Modern Fiction from Stephen Crane to Thomas Pynchon. 1991.

Band 53   Alexander Folta: Donald Barthelme als postmoderner Erzähler: Poetologie, Literatur und Gesellschaft. 1991.

Band 54   Reinhard Schweizer: Ideologie und Propaganda in den Marvel-Superheldencomics: Vom Kalten Krieg zur Entspannungspolitik. 1992.

Band 55   Susanne Bach: Grenzsituationen in den Dramen Peter Shaffers. 1992.

Band 56   Ulla-Carina Reitz: Dialekt bei D.H. Lawrence. 1992.

Band 57   Helga Eßmann: Übersetzungsanthologien: Eine Typologie und eine Untersuchung am Beispiel der amerikanischen Versdichtung in deutschsprachigen Anthologien, 1920-1960. 1992.

Band 58   Bärbel Czennia: Figurenrede als Übersetzungsproblem: Untersucht am Romanwerk von Charles Dickens und ausgewählten deutschen Übersetzungen. 1992.

Band 59   Bert Schwarzer: Hamlet liest "Hamlet": Produktive Rezeption eines weltliterarischen Schlüsseltextes in der Moderne. 1992.

Band 60   Birgit Bödeker: Amerikanische Zeitschriften in deutscher Sprache, 1945-1952: Ein Beitrag zur Literatur und Publizistik im Nachkriegsdeutschland. 1993.

Band 61   Beatrix Dudensing: Die Symbolik von Mündlichkeit und Schriftlichkeit in James Fenimore Coopers "Leatherstocking Tales". 1993.

Band 62   Uta Reinicke: "The Vital Soul". Naturerleben als kreative Weltbegegnung bei William Wordsworth. 1994.

Band 63   Regina Twiste: Die Evolutionsthematik in Doris Lessings "Space Fiction". 1994.

Band 64   Kyung-Ae Kim: Quest for Salvation in Saul Bellow's Novels. 1994.

Band 65   Monika Steinert: Mythos in den Gedichten Sylvia Plaths. 1995.

Band 66   Alexander Stützer: Darstellung und Deutung der Moderne bei D.H. Lawrence. 1995.

Band 67   Petra Krimphove: Mutter-Tochter-Beziehungen in der US-amerikanischen Literatur. Eine interkulturelle Untersuchung. 1995.

Band 68   Michael Maintz: Die Rosales-Romane Franciso Sionil Joses. Die Suche nach nationaler Identität in der philippinischen Literatur. 1996.

Band 69   Manfred Menzel: Klatsch, Gerücht und Wirklichkeit bei Nathaniel Hawthorne. 1996.

Band 70   Katharina Hagena: Developing Waterways: Das Meer als sprachbildendes Element im *Ulysses* von James Joyce. 1996.

Band 71   Beate Hermes: Felix Paul Greve als Übersetzer von Gide und Wilde. Eine Untersuchung zum Übersetzerstil. 1997.

Band 72   Dagmar Priebe: Kommunikation und Massenmedien in englischen und amerikanischen Utopien des 20. Jahrhunderts. Interpretationen aus systemtheoretischer Sicht. 1998.

Band 73   Isabel Kobus: Dialog in Roman und Film. Untersuchungen zu Joseph Loseys Literaturverfilmungen *The Go-Between* und *Accident*. 1998.

Band 74   Hannelore Zimmermann: Erscheinungsformen der Macht in den Romanen Margaret Atwoods. 1998.